A Question of Truth

Christianity and Homosexuality

GARETH MOORE OP

To MARCUS
who will probably disagree with most of what I have written

Continuum
The Tower Building,
11 York Road,
London, SE1 7NX

15 East 26th Street,
New York,
NY 10010

www.continuumbooks.com

© Gareth Moore 2003

First Published 2003
Reprinted 2003

British Library Cataloguing-in-Publication Data
A catalogue record for this book is available from The British Library

Library of Congress Cataloging-in-Publication Data
Moore, Gareth.
    A question of truth: Christianity and homosexuality/by Gareth Moore.
        p. cm.
    Includes bibliographical references and index.
    ISBN 0–8264–5949–8 (pbk.)
    1. Homosexuality – Religious aspects – Catholic Church. 2. Catholic Church – Doctrines.
    I. Title.

BX1795.H66M66 2003
241′.66 – dc21

2003043765

ISBN 0–8264–5949–8

Typeset by YHT Ltd, London
Printed and bound by CPI Bath

'If ever it comes to a choice between Jesus and truth,
we must always choose truth, because disloyalty to
truth will always prove in the long run to have
been disloyalty to Jesus.'

Simone Weil

Contents

Contents

Foreword

Until he began the long struggle against cancer, and despite his profound understanding of the world in which he lived, Fr Gareth Moore OP, who died on 6 December, aged 54, remained somewhat mistaken in two important aspects: how much he was loved, and by how many people. During his last few months, however, he was finally persuaded by the existence of a great crowd of friends, and their deep love of him both as a priest and a person.

From a very early age, Gareth Moore was set apart by his outstanding intellectual abilities. The first pupil from his London grammar school to gain a scholarship to Oxford, he seemed destined for a long career as an academic, and was clearly groomed for this by his college, Corpus Christi. On completion of his postgraduate degree of B. Litt., however, he felt the irresistible call of the cloister and joined St Mary's Abbey, Quarr. The shift from university to Benedictine life was perhaps too abrupt for him at this stage, so he wisely left the monastery to spend two years teaching mathematics in Zambia.

On his return to England, Moore once again felt the call of religious life. This time he turned to the Order of Preachers, the Dominicans, joining the novitiate in 1977. Though he never turned his back on the Benedictine way of life (and indeed always maintained the superiority of their monastic chant over the perhaps simpler Dominican plainsong), there was never any doubt that in joining the Blackfriars he had at last found his true home.

It was clear from the start of his life in religion that his temperament and virtues were in total accord with the aims and, indeed, the motto of the Order of St Dominic – *Veritas* (truth). Gareth Moore demonstrated above all one particularly important aspect of truth, that of honesty. Indeed, not only did he strongly disapprove of falsehood of any sort, even if it were assumed to be for someone's benefit, but he was also frankly quite incapable of it. And as he had a tendency to be brutally honest with others, so he was with himself. He was always the first to point out any perceived weakness in his own character and personality, sometimes to the embarrassment of his closest friends, but this self-knowledge, coupled with a deep humility, gave him an enormous capacity for sympathy and understanding. During the many years he spent in Blackfriars, Oxford, he always had a stream of visitors seeking his counsel and pastoral care.

His thirst for truth was at its strongest in his intellectual and academic endeavours. He never once shied away from serious controversy and debate. His writings, lectures and sermons, which covered a wide range, from theology and philosophy to music and photography, may have sometimes worried his ecclesiastical superiors but never failed to stimulate his audience into careful consideration as he invited them to join him in the search for the truth – however painful and risky it might turn out to be. His extensive work on the difficult and currently dangerous subject of human sexuality was typical of the brave approach he brought to his work. His many publications include the two well-received books *Believing in God* (Edinburgh, 1988) and *The Body in Context* (London, 1992).

It would never have occurred to Moore to seek out public recognition or office, and so, when he was elected prior of the Belgian Dominican Couvent de l'Epiphanie, Rixensart, in 1995, nobody was more surprised than he. During his two terms as prior he radically reformed the nature of the institution.

He decided to return to university life and to his beloved Blackfriars in Oxford in 2001. Less than a year after his return, he was diagnosed as having kidney cancer. He was for the last time honest and true in facing death. He often expressed his fear of dying, but through his personal integrity, he found the strength both to endure his distressing illness, and, in the end, to find a clear path through the difficulties of dying.

As death approached, he was greatly surprised by the sheer fortitude and endurance of his own personal faith. His characteristic honesty often misled people into thinking that he might be at odds with the Church, and sometimes, indeed, he even beguiled himself. Yet he died as he had wished, at peace, surrounded by dear friends, fully fortified by the rites of the Church, a true and faithful son of his Order.

Marcus Hodges

Obituary published in *The Tablet*, 14 December 2002. Reprinted by kind permission.

Preface

The Christian debate about homosexuality has been short, energetic and sometimes violent. It has already given rise to too many books. Not all of these have been illuminating or have justified the use (or waste) of resources that have gone into their production. This, even though the authors of all of them sincerely thought that their particular book was necessary and justified. I think the same of mine. Whether it is in fact worth adding to the pile only the reader can judge. While I go over much – perhaps too much – familiar ground, my hope is that even those widely read in this area may find something new and worth pondering.

When I first began to write, my aim was to do a critical survey of the arguments about homosexuality most often deployed in the mainstream Christian churches in their debates on the subject. It soon became evident not only that the task would be way beyond my patience but that the result would be indigestible and of doubtful value. While argument remains a central concern for me, I have almost exclusively limited myself to such arguments as are current in the Roman Catholic Church.[1] I have paid particular attention to the document *Homosexualitatis Problema* issued by the Congregation for the Doctrine of the Faith (CDF) in 1986. I have done this not because I think it a particularly fine document, but because it looks like becoming the basis of the Catholic Church's approach to the subject. The restriction to Catholic arguments not only cuts down the size of the task, but is also natural in more than one way. First, as a Catholic myself my interest is naturally drawn above all to the debates within my own church. Second, the debate (sometimes row) is often louder and more heated than in other churches. Third, the arguments deployed cover broadly two great areas: the Bible and natural law. There can be few churches which do not, in general, consider at least one of these areas to be vital for an understanding of theological and moral questions. My hope is that in concentrating on the Catholic Church I shall at the same time be saying something of interest to members of other churches.

A further important restriction is that the great majority of my remarks concern specifically male homosexuality. This is a serious limitation and needs at least some justification. This book is reactive. That is, I deal for the most part with arguments others have put forward; and it is a fact that many of those arguments are framed in terms of male homosexuality, and cannot be reframed in terms of female homosexuality or in a way which will embrace both. This tendency is encouraged by the language of the Bible which, where it seems to furnish ammunition for anti-homosexual arguments, is concerned almost always with male behaviour. In addition, as a man I have a greater intuitive understanding of male than of female sexuality, and of the questions that arise in connection with it. This makes it is easier for me to talk in male terms. It would be presumptuous of me to talk, beyond a certain point, about female sexuality. This is a task which is better left to women, to those who really understand. Nevertheless, if my language remains excessively male, I believe that many of the points I have to make are applicable to both men and women. I apologize if my language seems to exclude women; if any women readers feel obliged mentally to alter what I say to make it more directly relevant to women, then I apologize also for the tedium that this involves.

The general thesis of the book, towards which the various subsidiary arguments are supposed to tend, can be stated briefly. It is that there are no good arguments, from either Scripture or natural law, against what have come to be known as homosexual relationships. The arguments put forward to show that such relationships are immoral are bad. Either their premises are false or the argument by means of which the conclusion is drawn from them itself contains errors. It is of this that I hope to persuade the reader. It is also why the book is in a sense an invitation to be critical: critical both of my arguments and, more importantly and less easily, of the words of important leaders of the churches. If most of the Christian anti-homosexual arguments are bad, this is not only because their authors make factual or logical errors; it is also partly because they do not concern themselves with the social context of sexual relationships. As a result, they fail to ask pertinent and important questions. Indeed, many Christian authors seem unaware that such questions are there to be asked. I have tried to make a small contribution to remedying this in my previous book *The Body in Context* (London, Continuum, 2001). But the important point is that Christian moralists cannot go on writing as if a great deal of work had not already been done outside Christian circles on the social and other aspects of sexuality. Few theologians, for instance, show awareness even of the existence of such important works as, to name but a few, Michel Foucault's *The History of Sexuality*, David F. Greenberg's *The Construction of Homosexuality*, and Jeffrey Weeks's *Sexuality and its Discontents*. While this remains the case, too many theologians and church authorities who attempt to pronounce on the subject of homosexuality simply lack credibility; they have not done their homework. While I do not have space to rehearse the theories of Foucault and others, I hope it will be clear to those familiar with their work that their influence lies behind much of my argumentation; I hope too that the reader will agree that such influence leads to a much more adequate theoretical appreciation of sexuality in general and homosexuality in particular.

I devote much space to the Bible. The biblical translations are basically my own, but it would be disingenuous not to acknowledge that they are influenced by a long familiarity with and appreciation of the excellent Revised Standard Version. It may well be that a translation I believe to be my own is drawn unconsciously from this source, or accidentally identical with the RSV text. Sometimes I have also transliterated biblical words. The transliterations are unscientific, dispensing with diacritical markings that are intelligible only to the experts to whom they are also unnecessary.

My opportunity and ability to write have been severely limited. Thus, should it ever appear in print, I cannot confidently claim responsibility for all the errors it contains. I ask the reader for a certain indulgence towards those that are mere slips and that can be rectified without detriment to the central arguments I am pursuing. But if any of those central arguments themselves are faulty, they should be rejected; for my concern here is, in the end, as I shall explain in Chapter 1, with truth, and the importance of good argument as a guide to it. Bad arguments, however well intentioned, are to be rejected, including my own.

One final word is necessary here. I am a Dominican, and rejoice to be a member of an Order whose motto is *Veritas*. But, while I am sure that, writing as I do in pursuit of the truth, my efforts here are fully in conformity with my Dominican vocation, I must make it clear that the Order has at no stage been involved in the project and bears no responsibility either for the content of the text or for the fact of its publication.

ACKNOWLEDGEMENTS
I am grateful to Robin Baird-Smith, Jack Cameron, Ros Hunt and Kevin Reilly.

Introduction

This book is intended as a contribution to the theological debate on homosexuality within the Roman Catholic Church. That debate has had a short life. Before the publication of John McNeill's book *The Church and the Homosexual* in 1977 little had appeared other than more or less cursory statements treating homosexuals as deviants, and homosexuality as a perversion or a quasi-criminal kind of activity. Sexuality was treated as more or less synonymous with heterosexuality, and homosexuality was seen as a marginal aberration. In O'Neill's book, for the first time in mainstream Catholic theology, an attempt was made to consider both homosexual people and homosexual activity in a more understanding and positive light. The history of that book's publication and of subsequent Vatican documents exhibits currents of thinking which run strongly in the opposite direction. This is particularly clear in two documents issuing from the Congregation for the Doctrine of the Faith (CDF): 1975 Declaration on Certain Questions Concerning Sexual Ethics (*Persona Humana*); 1986 Letter ... on the Pastoral Care of Homosexual Persons (*HP*); and 1997 Note on discrimination.

There has been little public theological debate of the positions adopted in these documents. To many, these interventions represent a timely defence and elaboration of traditional Catholic views on homosexuality and a much-needed reassertion of traditional Christian teaching on the nature and purpose of sex in human life at a time when other churches are abandoning the heritage to which they should be faithful and when there is pressure towards infidelity even inside the Catholic Church. On the one hand there has thus been an enthusiastic reception on the part of many who seem to have felt little need to criticize and refine the CDF's statements. On the other hand, these interventions have occasioned much negative reaction. Criticism from sources outside the church was to be expected, especially from those who see the church as a reactionary force inimical to true human freedom. But there have also been protests from within the church, from gay Catholic groups as well as lay people, not homosexual themselves, who are sympathetic to

1

what they see as gay people's fight for justice and understanding in the church. Many of these feel that the CDF has not thought seriously about the subject but has merely sought to justify a position that is the product of prejudice of bygone ages; a prejudice that is, in at least some countries, thankfully beginning to break down. The CDF is accused of refusing to listen to voices at variance with its own, and in particular of failing to take seriously the voice and experience of gay Catholics who find that the old teaching simply does not reflect the reality of their lives; its documents speak with the harsh voice of a remote and homophobic bureaucracy isolated from and ignorant of the lives of ordinary men and women.

There are three aspects of this negative reaction that call for particular attention. First, it has on the whole not taken the form of a theological discussion and appraisal, albeit negative, of the CDF's position. Those dissatisfied with it have rather developed alternative ways of understanding sexuality in general and homosexuality in particular. There has been no serious attempt at dialogue with what at the moment seems to have become the 'official' position. Second, whatever its justification, this criticism does show that a number of Catholics are alienated from the official teaching institutions of the church, believing that their voice is not heard and that they are confronted with an arrogant and intransigent bureaucracy which claims the right to speak and be obeyed without carrying out its prior and humbler duty to listen. Third, this criticism is in general voiced publicly by those remote from the standard arenas of theological debate in the church. There are many books and articles by active lay Catholics, but those who make their living as Catholic theologians, teaching and writing in universities and seminaries, have started no debate nor responded to lay initiative. This is not because all Catholic theologians are in complete agreement with the CDF's position. But criticism tends to be voiced in private and in muted tones. It is difficult to avoid the impression that a certain fear reigns among theologians when it comes to discussing homosexuality.

The net result of these positive and negative reactions, and of the ways they have been expressed, is that there has been little serious critical discussion of the interventions of the CDF and the views they express. This is a pity, for several reasons. First, the CDF is, for the present, an important voice in the church. The failure to discuss its views, resulting either from too enthusiastic an acceptance or from too categorical a rejection, is a failure to take its views seriously. All serious theological positions take time and debate in order to be properly assessed and elaborated. The current polarized reactions do not enable this debate to take place. Second, those who are developing their own views are doing so in an atmosphere where these views too cannot be properly debated. The church at large cannot profit from the new insights they claim to offer, and they cannot benefit from a reasoned criticism emanating from other currents in church thinking. While the church remains divided into camps, while each side sees the other as at best mouthing slogans and at worst betraying its Christian vocation, there will be no debate, only a dialogue of the deaf. Third, the church was not founded to be a place of polarization, of mutual hostility and suspicion or of fear. It was founded to be a place where the truth is spoken in love. St Paul asks us all to be of one mind. We are not all to pretend to be of one mind when we are not. Among human beings, unanimity is difficult to achieve. If it is possible at all, it can only be by a long process which demands charity of us all: the humility to listen carefully to others and always to seek the best in what they say, to speak without aggression, respecting the intelligence and integrity of those from whom we differ. What follows is written in the conviction that all members of the church who speak on this subject, as well as those who keep silent, from Cardinal Ratzinger to the most radical of his opponents, are brothers and sisters in Christ, called to live in peace and love with one another. If unanimity fails, that is a pity. If charity fails, if we no longer listen and speak in love, that is a disaster; we deny our fundamental identity as members of the one Body and as children of the one God.

No approach to this subject (or to any other) that simply ignores what the official teaching organs of the church say will have trouble making itself out to be Catholic. In the following pages I do not attempt to break new ground in the theological study of homosexuality. Rather, I go over old ground, in the belief that what is old may still have something to teach us. I am attempting to take seriously, but far from uncritically, what the church has said on this subject in recent years. This will mean looking yet again at, among other things, what the Bible says and what, if anything, the natural law tradition has to teach us. My hope is that by accurate thinking and by careful attention to texts we can discover something sufficiently new and interesting as to make this book worth reading. My commitment to taking seriously what the church has said in recent years means that my approach to what may be familiar questions will often have a particular slant: I shall often be asking, for example, not simply what a given passage of Scripture might mean, but whether it means what in recent church teaching it has been taken to mean, or whether it supports the specific position the church has taken it to support. In this way I hope to be not merely repeating old arguments but encouraging a critical engagement. Much of what I have to say will be critical of the CDF and those who think similarly. It should not, however, be construed as an attack. We are all engaged in a humble search for truth. If I criticize my fellow members of Christ it is in order to help the church towards the truth. I sincerely hope that what I write may be the object of similar criticism, so that I may discover my mistakes in order that neither I nor the rest of the church may be led astray by them. What is at stake here is not the authority of this or that part of the body of Christ, but the movement of the whole towards the truth, a movement that must be inspired by mutual fraternal concern that does its best to speak the truth in love. The church does not impose a discipline. In any case the church is today incapable of imposing its position either on Christians or on those outside the church. The church must seek to convince homosexuals that her position on homosexual acts is true, that homosexuality is contrary to what God wills for human beings. This is what the modern church in fact does. This means that certain principles have to be followed:

1.   Bad arguments need to be avoided. These do not convince, and give the impression that there are no good arguments. This undermines the church's position rather than strengthening it.

1.1 We sometimes have a tendency not to examine too closely arguments that support our own position. We have to be on our guard against this if we are in dialogue with others who do not share our views.

1.2 In fact we need to do this even if we are not in dialogue with people who disagree with us. Bad arguments do not help reveal the truth to ourselves. Bad arguments can be used to make us more comfortable in pre-conceived positions which may be false; they can serve only to reinforce our prejudices. But we are not here to be made to feel more comfortable or to have our prejudices reinforced. We are here for the truth.

1.3 In order to be on the lookout for bad arguments, we need to be aware that we may be prone to accept them. We must be on guard against ourselves, conscious that we want to be more comfortable, to have our positions reinforced.

1.4 To safeguard against error, we need to accept that our own position is open to scrutiny, both from those sympathetic to us and from those opposed to us. We often learn most from our opponents.

1.5 So we need to accept that we may be wrong. Cromwell wrote: 'I beseech you, in the bowels of Christ, think it possible you may be mistaken' (Letter to the General Assembly of the Church of Scotland, 3 August 1650, in Thomas Carlyle, *Oliver Cromwell's Letters and Speeches* (1845)).

1.6 Not to go on about infallibility. This does not impress people who disagree on a particular question. This does not put infallibility or the authority of the church in question; but the appeal to infallibility is simply not useful.

1.7 Being aware that one can make mistakes is not incompatible with a belief in the infallibility of the church, either. An a priori assurance that one is right is one of the surest ways to argue badly and to make mistakes, because one does not examine sufficiently closely what one says. One of the best ways to be right is to be vigilant against the possibility of error.

2. The only way to be listened to is to show that one is ready to listen.

3. *Omne quod recipitur secundum modum recipientis recipitur.*

4. Argue with the best of homosexual practice, not with the worst. The church wants to show that homosexual practices are *as such* contrary to the will of God, and so contrary to human well-being, not simply that the worst excesses of homosexuality are contrary to human well-being.

Closeted queers in the Vatican

Do not impute disreputable motives or characteristics to opponents as a way of discrediting them. Opponents of official church teaching not uncommonly ascribe to its proponents, particularly to the originators of official documents, a variety of uncomplimentary motives and qualities. They are only interested in power, suggest some, and react to squash anything that may be seen as a threat to that power. They are homophobes governed by prejudice rather than by reason. They are careerists, time-servers intent on supporting the establishment through whose ranks they are climbing, ready to deny the truth for the sake of preferment. They are closet queers, taking refuge from their own sexuality by devoting themselves to a power structure, frightened of the personal challenge posed by their more honest and liberated brothers and sisters. And so on. Stories circulate about this or that cardinal, this or that secretary. Of course some of this may be true. It would be surprising if there were no careerists and time-servers in the Vatican and in bishop's offices, as there are in any human institution. Given the distribution of homosexuals in the general population and in the clergy, it would be surprising if there were no homosexuals in the Vatican and its congregations. Given the pressures on homosexuals to keep quiet in church circles, it would be surprising if some of these were not very scared indeed of making themselves known. It is not beyond the bounds of possibility that some of this influences the way Vatican documents are produced. But to say this kind of thing in the context of an argument about the rights and wrongs of homosexuality is precisely a failure to argue. This kind of personal abuse directed against opponents in debate serves only as an excuse not to hear their arguments and take them seriously. It risks giving the impression, to an unbiased onlooker, that those arguments are not being answered because they *cannot* be answered. More importantly, the strength of an argument does not depend on the character of those who propose it, or on their motives for proposing it. An argument against homosexuality is no stronger and no weaker for being proposed by a sincere heterosexual or by a fearful, closeted homosexual. It is no better for being proposed for the highest motives, no worse for being proposed for base motives.

Such a reaction to church teaching and to arguments produced in its support is, then, a refusal to take part in rational debate, and it is as such also a failure to treat those who propound such arguments as rational human beings, worthy of respect and so worthy to be listened to. It is a failure of charity. This is a serious failing in any debate; in a Christian context it is a failure of our vocation. We need to replace a 'hermeneutic of suspicion' with a 'hermeneutic of charity'. We are after all brothers and sisters engaged together in the following of Christ and the service of God. We all finally have a common purpose and a common destiny, and are to be bound together by love. This does not mean that we have to be unaware of the weaknesses of those with whom we disagree, but it does mean that we should do our best to refrain from attacks upon them and upon their motives. Though they may say and do things from base motives, we should do our best to assume that this is not so. We should assume that they too, and not only ourselves, are engaged in an honest search for truth and a sincere presentation of the truth as they see it. Attacks on people should not replace an attempt to listen to them and engage with what they say, however much we may disagree with it.

Suppose for the sake of argument that it is true that the people who produce these documents are indeed all time-serving, power-seeking, closeted, homophobic homosexuals. What then? This assumption might amount to no more than a reminder that people at all levels of the church are dissemblers, that they say one thing and think another; or that they are hypocrites, that they say one thing and do another; or that they are morally weak, that they say what they believe but sometimes, perhaps regularly, do things they think they ought not to do. Such a reminder would be important. But our assumption is surely theologically interesting for our purposes only if we also assume that, if these people's circumstances were different, they would not take a negative view of same-sex relations. We have to assume that fundamentally they think same-sex relations are a good thing, and would say so were it not for the web of silence they find themselves caught up in. And behind that must be the further assumption that it is pretty evident that same-sex relations *are* a good thing, and that it is only being caught up in this web that prevents the people concerned from seeing it or saying it.

Behind the accusations of dishonesty, hypocrisy and weakness lie convictions about the moral acceptability of same-sex relations. The important question is whether those convictions are right. Church functionaries can be as dishonest, hypocritical and weak as you like. If they are, and we know it, then we will not be persuaded by their advocacy; but the doctrine they promulgate might still be true. And it is moral truth that has to be our main concern in this area. Are same-sex relations potentially a good thing or not? To that question assumptions about the personal *mores* of officials in Rome or Canterbury are finally irrelevant.

Materialism of pro-gays

If suppositions about the lives of church functionaries do not show same-sex relations to be morally good, generalizations about the mentality of those who openly approve of same-sex relations do not show them to be morally evil, either. The traffic in personal accusations is not all one way. For example, the 1986 Letter (*HP*)[1] argues in the following fashion:

> increasing numbers of people today, even within the Church, are bringing enormous pressure to bear on the Church to accept the homosexual condition as though it were not disordered and to condone homosexual activity. Those within the Church who argue in this fashion often have close ties with those with similar views outside it. These latter groups are guided by a vision opposed to the truth about the human person, which is fully disclosed in the mystery of Christ. They reflect, even if not entirely consciously, a materialistic ideology which denies the transcendent nature of the human person as well as the supernatural vocation of every individual.
>
> The Church's ministers must ensure that homosexual persons in their care will not be misled by this point of view, so profoundly opposed to the teaching of the Church. But the risk is great and there are many who seek to create confusion regarding the Church's position, and then to use that confusion to their own advantage. (§8)

Pro-gay ministers, writers and activists within the church are often, it is alleged, linked to groups outside the church which are materialistic and opposed to true spiritual values. They constitute, even if unwittingly, a kind of fifth column. There is much unclarity here. When it is said that 'they reflect, even if not consciously, a materialistic ideology', who are 'they'? Are they the groups outside the church, or those inside the church who argue for the acceptability of same-sex relations? If those outside the church are meant, then pro-gay Christians inside the church are simply being convicted of guilt by association; they have links with materialists, so they are not to be listened to. If this is what is meant, it looks very much like an unworthy attempt to smear pro-gay Christians. If the sentence refers rather to those inside the church, they are accused of being fundamentally unchristian. They may not know it themselves, of course; we may charitably suppose that they have not reflected deeply enough to see the materialistic implications of their own position. But no justification is offered for this grave accusation. No evidence is offered that pro-gay Christians are fundamentally unchristian, or that they have not reflected on the spiritual implications of their position. What seems to lie behind this section of

HP is the implicit assumption that all this *must* be true, because nobody who acknowledges the transcendent nature of the human person and the supernatural vocation of every individual could regard same-sex relationships favourably. But this is not true. While some who call themselves Christian are perhaps materialists at heart, there are certainly many Christians, largely homosexual themselves, who are very conscious of the importance of spiritual values and of the spiritual truths expressed in Christianity and who nevertheless find a positive place for homosexual relationships within the Christian way of life.

That is, in a way, precisely the problem. The reason why there are still such people within the church, despite the regular official attacks on them from within, and at a time when many others are leaving the church, is that they recognize the truths contained in the gospel and are profoundly attached to spiritual values. As well as being homosexual, and perhaps living in a same-sex relationship, they insist on being Christian and on being members of Christ's church. Nor is it true that pro-gay Christians have not reflected deeply on the implications of their own position. There is ample evidence that they have. For example, nobody who reads Eugene Rogers's *Sexuality and the Christian Body* with any attention can fail to be impressed by his deep seriousness and reflectiveness, even if they do not in the end agree with him. This is in any case only what we should expect. Any reasonably thoughtful homosexual worshipping in a church which is largely and volubly anti-homosexual is almost bound to question himself and his sexuality, to reflect on the relationship between his faith and his sexual behaviour, to meditate on what God wants of him, and to wonder about his place in the Christian community. People who are not homosexual are sometimes confronted with similar questions; for a thoughtful homosexual such questioning can be constant. On the whole we can expect homosexual Christians to have reflected longer, more deeply and more urgently on the subject than their heterosexual brothers and sisters. It is those who want to change prevailing attitudes and challenge prevailing certainties, rather than those who are content with them, who probe them more deeply. It is those struggling for a voice where they have had none, trying to formulate and articulate a position in the face of an audience that does not want to hear, who need to think deeply, not those who already have the right to be heard. This was true of feminists not so long ago; it is true of gay Christians now.

Ministers are to 'ensure that homosexual persons in their care will not be misled by this point of view' – the materialism, conscious or unconscious, which *must* be at the root of any favourable assessment of homosexual relations. But many of these homosexual persons will have thought and prayed longer and harder about these questions than their minister – unless he too is homosexual. They will also quite simply know more about homosexuality. In what way are they in danger of being misled? *HP* claims, again without offering evidence, that there are many who wish to sow confusion concerning the church's position, and then to use that confusion to their own advantage, whatever that might be. This gives the impression that what the Christian homosexual has to be protected from is confusion about what the church teaches. This would be in line with what is said earlier in the same document:

> special concern and pastoral attention should be directed toward those who have this [*sc.* homosexual] condition, lest they be led to believe that the living out of this orientation in homosexual activity is a morally acceptable option. It is not.
> An essential dimension of authentic pastoral care is the identification of causes of confusion regarding the Church's teaching. (§§3,4)

Here we see a view, prevalent throughout the document, of the homosexual as a more or less passive recipient of influences. He or she is one to be cared for, and is in danger of being misled by materialist opinions.

CHAPTER ONE

A Question of Truth

The fortune and misfortune of gay Christians

Gay Christians are very fortunate people. Their life is not vain; they do not go from dust to dust. They are created by the God whose love is the source of all things, and are sustained by that same sure and unalterable love. And God has made them for himself. Their destiny is to return to their origin, to be forever united in bliss with God, gazing on him in ecstasy and wonder, giving love for love. Not only are gay Christians surrounded by this love, not only are they destined for this happiness, they also have the happiness of knowing it. While all human beings are created through the love of God and all are made for God, there are many who do not know it, and who believe, wrongly, that they and their lives are of little present and no final worth, that their story is merely one of emergence from dust and return to dust. Not so gay Christians. Through the grace of God and through the communities to which they belong – their family, friends, school, church – they have been given and have received the message that they are precious in God's eyes. They know that Christ lived, died and rose again for them, and that nothing can separate them from the love of God. As St Paul says: 'I am convinced that neither death, nor life, nor angels, nor principalities, neither things present nor to come, nor powers, nor height, nor depth, nor any other created thing, will be able to separate us from the love of God in Christ Jesus our Lord' (Rom 8:38–39).

This is good fortune and a source of happiness. It is not, of course, a fortune and a happiness confined to gay Christians; it is shared by anybody who has accepted the love of God as revealed in Jesus, by all Christians, gay or straight. Gay and straight Christians can rejoice together on account of the love with which God loves them, on account of their common origin and destiny, and because through God's grace they have all come to know God's love and have been made members of one people by baptism. Despite this common joy, there are many homosexual Christians who account themselves less happy than their heterosexual brothers and sisters.

11

This is in part because of the way they are often regarded and treated in the wider society beyond the church; while gay men and lesbians can now readily find acceptance in parts of large towns in western Europe, North America and elsewhere, in many societies ridicule, rejection, discrimination, physical violence, harassment and even official persecution are still the lot of many homosexuals. But some of those who treat homosexuals in these ways are themselves members of the church, the brothers and sisters of those whom they mistreat, and they claim – often, no doubt, sincerely – that by their violent malice they are defending and affirming Christian teaching and values. While at an official level most churches condemn such behaviour,[1] there is still, at that level, often a very negative evaluation of homosexual relationships. Gay Christians find their Christian communities telling them that their desires for intimate sexual relationships are aberrant, contrary to the will of God as expressed in Scripture and tradition, to be struggled against, a source of danger rather than a potential element of that genuine human happiness which heterosexual Christians may find in marriage.

This sense of being specially disadvantaged, of being less happy than heterosexual Christians, is justified, and it is worth pausing a while to see why. It is sometimes argued that, though homosexual Christians do face difficulties, these are similar to and no more serious than those faced by many heterosexuals who seek to live a genuine Christian life. For example, the New Testament scholar Richard B. Hays finds that New Testament texts and a proper hermeneutical response to those texts imply that the church should neither sanction nor bless homosexual unions. He then poses the question: 'Does this mean that persons of homosexual orientation are subject to a blanket imposition of celibacy in a way qualitatively different from persons of heterosexual orientation?' and offers this answer:

> While Paul regarded celibacy as a charisma, he did not therefore suppose that those lacking the charisma were free to indulge their sexual desires outside marriage. Heterosexual persons are also called to abstinence from sex unless they marry (1 Cor. 7:8–9). The only difference – admittedly a salient one – in the case of homosexually oriented persons is that they do not have the option of homosexual 'marriage'. So where does that leave them? It leaves them in precisely the same situation as the heterosexual who would like to marry but cannot find an appropriate partner (and there are many such): summoned to a difficult, costly

obedience, while 'groaning' for the 'redemption of our bodies' (Rom. 8:23). Anyone who does not recognize this as a description of authentic Christian existence has never struggled seriously with the imperatives of the gospel, which challenge and frustrate our 'natural' impulses in countless ways.[2]

The position of gay people is, for Hays, essentially no different from that of would-be married heterosexuals, as they both have to hold their natural sexual impulses in check. But this analysis is hardly plausible, for it glosses over too many important distinctions. It is like saying that a person who dies serenely after a long and happy life, a teenager sadistically and senselessly tortured to death, a mother who dies in childbirth, and her baby who dies as it draws its first breath, are all in the same position in that they are all dead. It cannot be denied that they are all dead, but the reasons why they died, the time of their death and the manner of their death are important to us, and the similarity of their state should not be used to blind us to the diversity of their fate. So it is with homosexuals and unmarried heterosexuals. Take two Christians, the unmarried homosexual Christopher and the unmarried heterosexual Paul. Of course, as far as the habitual Christian position on homosexuality is concerned, Christopher and Paul are in the same position in the sense that neither of them can legitimately enter into a sexual relationship, even if they should both wish to. But there are important differences between them that this comparison glosses over. Christopher is not in the same position as Paul in that Paul can hope to find a partner in marriage. In the habitual Christian understanding of sexuality, Paul has a place in the sexual scheme of things, only he is not at the moment in that place; marriage is made for people like him and, if he desires to live in an intimate personal relationship with another, he can hope to marry one day. Paul's sexual instincts, which make him look forward to and perhaps actively seek marriage with a woman, are a good thing; they are a spur to forming a loving relationship which will have a sexual aspect and which will be an image both of that love with which Christ loves the church[3] and of that love with which the human soul naturally loves its creator.[4] If and when he finds the woman whom he loves and who loves him, and with whom he is willing to make an irrevocable, lifelong commitment, he will enjoy the blessing of the church, and his love, his relationship and his sexual activity with his wife will hold an honoured place within the Christian community.

Paul's hope of marriage may of course not be realized. We are all sometimes the victims of circumstance; bad things do happen to people which mean they cannot have what they want. But he can have hope; his hope is, in the eyes of the Christian community, not only a natural hope but a legitimate and a good one. Christopher, if he is to be a good Christian, cannot have this hope; while his hope may be in some sense natural to him, it is neither legitimate nor good. There is, then, an important asymmetry between the two cases. The real homosexual Christian parallel to Paul would be the gay man who is without love, who seeks it and may or may not find it; but that position, according to many Christians, is one which no truly Christian homosexual can be in. If Christopher does not find a partner, he can be described as an unfortunate victim of circumstance. But Christopher is not the victim of a circumstance that prevents him from enjoying the good he seeks. While Paul can hope to occupy his place in the sexual scheme of things, Christopher cannot hope to find his place, for he has none. If he does hope to find a partner whom he loves and who loves him, and with whom he is prepared to make an irrevocable, lifelong commitment, this amounts to a betrayal of his Christian calling. If he already has such a partner, the fact is not to be celebrated as would be Paul's marriage. It is shameful; the domestic intimacy he shares with his partner is not a source of innocent joy but an occasion of sin. Whatever his actual way of life, his sexual instincts are not to be spoken of in the same way as Paul's, as a spur to and an expression of love. They are a perversion, or a malady. He cannot fulfil them, but only indulge them, and any such indulgence is unchristian.

Homosexuality is sometimes spoken of as a symptom of the fallenness of humanity.[5] In reality what is meant is that it is a sign of the fallenness of homosexuals. Christopher's sexual instincts are a sign of his fallenness as Paul's are not a sign of his fallenness. It would hardly be intelligible to point to Christopher's homosexuality as an indication that Paul is fallen. Paul's sexuality may express itself in disordered ways: he may, for instance, seek and have sex with a woman outside marriage. But, in the right context, and approached in the right way, it becomes an aspect and an expression of that love which redeems us from the Fall. Christopher's sexuality, on the other hand, does not express itself in disordered ways; it is intrinsically disordered.[6] It is in itself an aspect of that Fall from which we need redeeming. In short, Paul's sexuality is a good thing, and that is how he is to regard it; only, he must seek out the right circumstances in which to have a sexual relationship. If

14

he feels sexually attracted to a woman he may hope that this is the beginning of a love that will blossom in marriage. Christopher's sexuality on the other hand is a bad thing, and that is how he is to regard it; for him, there are no right circumstances, no hope. If he feels sexually attracted to a man, he is to see this as a danger. While Paul may constantly look out for love, Christopher must constantly watch against himself. Paul's sexuality is his friend, Christopher's is his enemy.

If Paul can hope to find somebody whom he loves erotically, he can also hope that his love will be returned. He can hope that another will seek him out, delight to be near him, look upon him with pleasure, embrace him with joy. He can hope to be wanted by another, united to another, intimate with another. He can hope to know, not merely that others wish him well in a disinterested sort of way, but that another is attracted to him, and that he is an important part of that other person's happiness. All that joy and that intimacy is part of erotic love; to want it is a standard human desire, and its fulfilment is a standard component of human happiness. It is the joy that Adam expresses on seeing Eve, the intimacy he knows when he cleaves to her. Christopher is not to have this. He is never to have that natural human erotic joy of delighting in another and knowing himself wanted. And he is never to hope for it, either. For in his case that hope is perverted. Any relationship he could hope to form is a sinful one, and to desire it is to desire an evil. Any erotic delight he might feel in another man is a trap, any intimacy an occasion of sin.[7] Nobody is to be erotically interested in him, and he is to be erotically interested in nobody else; the only human relationship he can hope for is 'disinterested friendship'.[8] While Paul's natural erotic desire may spur him to find happiness in another, Christopher must renounce his own erotic desire, which is as deep in him as Paul's is in him. He must resist it, fight against it; and because this desire is no passing whim, no idle caprice, but is profound, insistent and lasting, he must in effect fight against himself. If he wins, his victory is solitude; he finds himself, in Andrew Sullivan's words 'alone again, naturally'.[9] If Christopher is to see the erotic side of his nature as a menace, if his most intimate experience of the erotic is negative, then this will have consequences for his life of faith too. All the erotic imagery of the Bible will be closed to him as a vehicle of faith. All the language of marriage between God and people, of Israel as the beloved of God, of God seducing his people, and the allegorical expression to be found in the Song of Songs of the loving intimacy between God and the soul

– all of this will be foreign to him. It is not simply a matter of this imagery being, as we would say, heterosexual; he can always transpose the imagery into homosexual terms. The real problem is that as soon as he understands and feels the erotic force of this imagery it will become repugnant, if he takes seriously the idea of his own sexuality as a threat. He will of course be able to see that for others this central theme of the Bible speaks positively, but it can never be positive for him.

Truth

So things can indeed be hard for gay Christians, if they take their faith seriously, in a way that they are not for their heterosexual brothers and sisters. This should not be minimized; the suffering of gay Christians can be real and terrible. But it should not be exaggerated, either. Whatever their hardships on earth, Christians look for a happiness which is not of this world, and many have been prepared to undergo terrible hardships for the sake of fidelity to Christ. Fidelity to Christ can demand, and has demanded, of Christians that they consecrate their lives to the service of others in difficult circumstances, or that they die bloodily for witnessing to Christ. People who are made to suffer like this, though they really do suffer, can be happy and victorious in their suffering, because they know they suffer for Christ, and they have a hope of a happiness to come. Their suffering is a result of their Christian living, and shows that they live well as disciples of Christ. Many of these people have suffered much more than the general run of Christian homosexuals. If fidelity can demand that some people give up their lives, it can demand of homosexuals not only that they live lives of complete sexual continence, but also that they be at odds with themselves, even deeply so, because of their sexuality. People like Christopher may have to suffer, but they can understand their suffering as a part of what Christ demands of them in the particular circumstances in which they live. They may even understand their own suffering as a share in the suffering of Christ himself. In this way that suffering becomes part of their Christian witness, and they can be genuinely happy in their suffering.

This is just how the Catholic Church at present teaches that homosexuals who try to remain faithful to Christ should see any suffering they may endure as a result. The first Vatican document dedicated to the subject of homosexuality, *Homosexualitatis Problema* (henceforth *HP*), puts it thus:

> What, then, are homosexual persons to do who seek to follow the Lord? Fundamentally, they are called to enact the will of God in their life by joining whatever sufferings and difficulties they experience in virtue of their condition to the sacrifice of the Lord's Cross. That Cross, for the believer, is a fruitful sacrifice since from that death come life and redemption. While any call to carry the cross or to understand a Christian's suffering in this way will predictably be met with bitter ridicule by some, it should be remembered that this is the way to eternal life for all who follow Christ.[10]

This is how the Catholic Church teaches that Christian homosexuals should live, and the spirituality to which it appeals – joining one's suffering to the cross of Christ – has long held an important and honourable place in Christian thought and life. It is no objection to the church's teaching on homosexuality that it entails suffering. If it is true that fidelity to Christ demands of homosexuals their particular kind of suffering, then, tough though it may be, homosexuals must suffer, and should be prepared to suffer. And this brings us to the real questions: Is it actually true that fidelity to Christ demands this of homosexuals? Is it true that the will of God is that they should abstain from the kind of intimate relationship for which it seems most people are made? Is it true that they are suffering from some kind of moral malady, that they should recognize this and struggle against their condition?

Now it is a plain fact that many Christians, among them many Catholics, do not believe this at all. They do not believe for a moment that fidelity to Christ and to the will of God demands of homosexuals either that they abstain completely from all sexual relationships or that they struggle against their own sexual nature. This is evident not only from what many individual gay Christians, including Catholics, say and do, but also from the existence of Christian groups, such as the Lesbian and Gay Christian Movement in Britain and Dignity in the United States, part of the programme of each being to uphold the goodness of homosexual desire and relationships and to assert that being gay and enjoying a sexual relationship is fully compatible with being a faithful disciple of Christ. These are groups which are either specifically designed for Catholics or which have a sizeable Catholic membership. Whether they belong to any such formal grouping or not, many Catholics, homosexual and heterosexual, lay people and clergy, do not believe what the church currently teaches in this area. How has this come about? *HP* puts much of this down to ignorance. Referring to the then recent discussions of homosexuality in Catholic circles, it complains that some people have given an 'overly benign' interpretation of what it calls, in common with other Catholic documents, the 'homosexual condition'; such interpretations do not recognize that this condition is an objective disorder. Therefore,

> special concern and pastoral attention should be directed toward those who have this condition, lest they be led to believe that the living out of this orientation in homosexual activity is a morally acceptable option. It is not.[11]

It is part of the purpose of *HP*, addressed as it is to the bishops who have responsibility for the pastoral care of the Catholics in their dioceses, to make sure that Catholic homosexuals get this attention, that they be not led astray into thinking either that it is morally acceptable to enter into sexual relationships or, more particularly, that the church thinks it is.

Now it is plainly a reasonable concern that Catholics should know, at least in outline, what their church teaches, and so it is reasonable also that Catholic homosexuals should know, at least in outline, what their church teaches about homosexuality. But it is very likely that the Congregation for the Doctrine of the Faith (henceforth referred to as CDF), in taking this approach, does not put its finger on the true problem. While there are no doubt some Catholic homosexuals who are completely ignorant about what their church teaches about homosexual relationships, there surely cannot be many who think their church does not disapprove of them, let alone actually approves of them. Even if there were some when the document was issued in 1986, despite the appearance of *Persona Humana* some years earlier, and despite public attitudes in the church being in recent centuries universally hostile to same-sex sexual relationships, few could have been in any doubt after the publication of *HP*, and yet there still remain many sincere practising Catholics who do not believe that fidelity to Christ and to the will of God demands total abstinence from homosexual relationships. The real problem confronting the Catholic Church is that many Catholics do indeed know, at least in outline, what their church teaches about homosexuality, and they simply do not believe it. Some, indeed, have studied the Catholic Church's position in considerable depth, as is only to be expected given that the teaching concerns them intimately, and from the depth of their knowledge they still do not agree with it; indeed, their study will probably have led them to articulate one or several quite precise points on which they believe their church has simply got it wrong,[12] such errors, in their view, either weakening or completely vitiating the church's position. That this is happening is clear from *HP* itself.

There are Catholics who believe that the church has got it wrong in this area because of a faulty understanding of biblical texts. For example, *HP* claims of the story of Sodom and Gomorrah in Genesis 19 that '[t]here can be no doubt of the moral judgement made there against homosexual relations' (§6). But not a few scholars have come to the conclusion that there is a great deal of doubt about whether this text expresses, or even can express, such a judgement. And similar questions have been raised about other biblical texts sometimes adduced in support of the church's teaching on homosexuality. These questions have been raised by those who have actually studied the Bible; it is not simply ignorance of Catholic teaching that has led them to raise them. Indeed, *HP* itself recognizes this, and one of the reasons the document was written was to repudiate such doubts. It complains about

> a new exegesis of Sacred Scripture which claims variously that Scripture has nothing to say on the subject of homosexuality, or that it somehow tacitly approves of it, or that all of its moral injunctions are so culture-bound that they are no longer applicable to contemporary life. (§4)

Again, there are Catholics who believe the church has got it wrong in thinking that what *HP* calls 'the homosexual condition' is disordered, and this is not through ignorance of what the church teaches, as again the document recognizes:

> [I]ncreasing numbers of people today, even within the Church, are bringing enormous pressure to bear on the Church to accept the homosexual condition as though it were not disordered and to condone homosexual activity. Those within the Church who argue in this fashion often have close ties with those with similar views outside it. These latter groups are guided by a vision opposed to the truth about the human person, which is fully disclosed in the mystery of Christ. They reflect, even if not

19

entirely consciously, a materialistic ideology which denies the transcendent nature of the human person as well as the supernatural vocation of every individual. (§8)

Whether the accusation that *HP* brings against these people – that they are influenced by a materialism opposed to the truth about the human person – is justified is another matter, but it is clear that even *HP* does not think that the real problem is ignorance of church teaching. There are also Catholic homosexuals who think the church has got it wrong because what the church says on the subject of homosexuality simply does not seem to them to tally with what they know of homosexual practice and the life of homosexuals. For example, *HP* asserts that 'homosexual activity prevents one's own fulfilment and happiness by acting contrary to the creative wisdom of God' (§7). No Christian believes that their final fulfilment and happiness is to be found on this earth, and homosexuals surely have difficulties in their intimate relationships as much as heterosexuals; but to anybody who has found any substantial fulfilment and happiness in a homosexual relationship – and one only needs to look around one in the right places to see that this is so – this assertion can hardly but appear to reveal a deep ignorance on the Vatican's part of the subject on which it pretends to pronounce with authority.[13]

The fundamental problem for these critics is not that the teaching is hard to follow, that it is old or outmoded, or even that it is unjust, but that it is untrue. They are not ignorant of what the church says; they have considered it and found it wanting. This position of informed disagreement involves a certain personal difficulty. Anybody who is led by study and personal experience to think that what the church says is false is liable to feel an amount of discomfort as a member of the church; a church which regularly denigrates them and their sexuality. Some have found this discomfort so acute that they have had to leave the Catholic Church and live as members of another Christian communion. Apart from this kind of difficulty, there is a certain more theoretical tension inherent in such a critical position. Most Christians who take this more positive view of homosexual desire and relationships received their faith through the very community with which they now find themselves in disagreement. They heard the gospel and came to faith in Christ through the words of others; they took their word for it that Christ was the saviour of all humankind. But now, when that same community tells them that following Christ entails a rejection of same-sex relationships and a struggle against same-sex desire, they will not take their word for it. They received the gift of faith by taking the word of the Christian community as authoritative, and now, while claiming still to be Christian, and while still accepting that word as authoritative in other areas of faith and morals, they refuse the same authority when it comes to homosexuality. While this is an uncomfortable situation, it is clearly not incoherent. We all, as children, begin by simply accepting that things are as our elders – parents, teachers and others – tell us, and we do so just because they tell us; we believe things on the authority of others whom we trust implicitly to be right, to know. Equally, we all come to learn that those whom we have trusted to tell us what is right sometimes get things wrong. But the fact that we find that our parents and teachers can get things wrong does not mean that we can never again believe them, or that we can never again believe anything to be so on their authority, just because they say so. We may still think that they can generally be trusted to get things right, even though they may make mistakes occasionally, or we may learn to sort out the areas in which they can be trusted from those in which they are liable to get thing wrong. As adults too, when we are new to a discipline – say, if we are beginning to study history or French literature – we begin by simply believing what our teachers, or the authors of the books we read, tell us. We treat them as authorities; if we did not do so we could hardly learn anything.[14] Yet once we have reached a certain level of competence we can and do begin to call into question some of the things our teachers told us and tell us, and this does not involve us in any claim that they are in general incompetent. Similarly, there is no contradiction involved if a Christian who has received his faith through a believing community differs from that community over a particular question, say that of homosexuality, while continuing in general to accept what he has been taught by that community.

What puts such a Christian – let it be Christopher again – in this position of disagreement with his church on the question of homosexuality is that he thinks his church's teaching on the subject is untrue. His reasons for thinking this may turn out on examination to be good, or they may be revealed as fundamentally faulty. He may in the first place have misunderstood or not fully appreciated why his church says what it does on this subject. He may have made mistakes in biblical exegesis, and he may also have committed logical errors in the way he reasoned. Anybody, gay or straight, can make this kind of mistake. Since Christopher is gay he may also be unduly influenced by a natural desire to see his own sexual desires as good, or an equally natural reluctance to spend time and energy in fighting against them, or fighting against himself; he may be so impressed by the positive aspects of any homosexual relationships he has experienced that he is blinded to their possible defects; he may be concerned to justify his sexual conduct in his own and others' eyes; and so on. But whether his grounds for questioning his church's teaching are ultimately convincing or not, and whether his motives are pure, he does have grounds for what he says, and the question he raises is one of truth. If Christopher does not believe that church teaching on homosexuality is true, an important logical point follows. Christopher may, despite his rejection of church teaching, actually live in a certain sense as the church says homosexuals should. He may abstain from all sexual activity, and he may even struggle against his own homosexual tendencies. But he can only do this out of fidelity to Christ if he *believes* that this is what fidelity of Christ demands of him. For it is only if he believes this that it can be the motive for his undertaking the way of life that he does. Since he does not in fact believe this, then he cannot undertake any self-imposed sexual abstinence or any struggle against his own sexuality as a necessary part of his Christian living. He may undertake it for all sorts of other reasons – perhaps because he fears discovery as homosexual, or because he has internalized and appropriated the contempt in which those around him hold homosexuals – but he cannot do it as an authentic expression of his Christian faith, and his abstinence and struggle can be no true witness to Christ, even if others mistakenly think it is.

It is part of the job of church authorities to teach, to pass on Christian doctrine to those for whom they have some pastoral responsibility, and to convince them that that doctrine is true. For, of course, to teach a doctrine in the sense in which the church teaches is to teach it as true. The church does not teach doctrines simply as ideas which have attracted certain people, or as things that some people have believed or do believe, as if it were engaged in giving an academic lecture on Christianity as part of a course on comparative religion. It does not teach doctrines as objects of academic curiosity, regardless of their truth or falsity. It teaches these doctrines as true, not merely to be studied but to be believed. And that they are true is the only justification for the church's teaching these doctrines at all. If the church did not hold them to be true, it would not teach them; and if they are not true the church should not teach them. Similarly, to accept the church's teaching is not simply to accept that the doctrines concerned were or are believed by certain people; it is to accept that these doctrines are actually true, and so to believe them. And, therefore, that they are true is the only possible justification for believing them. If Sally did not believe them to be true she would not believe them, she would not accept the teaching of the church; and if they are not true she should not believe them. In short, church teaching is of interest to anybody only if it is true. And this is fundamental to the approach of *HP*, as the document itself implies when it asserts:

> Scripture bids us speak the truth in love (cf. Eph. 4:15). The God who is at once truth and love calls the Church to minister to every man, woman and child with the pastoral solicitude of our compassionate Lord. It is in this spirit that we have addressed this Letter to the Bishops of the Church, with the hope that it will be of some help as they care for those whose suffering can only be intensified by error and lightened by truth. (§18)

And again:

> [W]e wish to make it clear that departure from the Church's teaching, or silence about it, in an effort to provide pastoral care is neither caring nor pastoral. Only what is true can ultimately be pastoral. (§15)

Underlying particularly the second of these extracts is the conviction, not only of the importance of the truth but of the truth of the church's teaching, that is, of the teaching of *HP* itself. And that is a conviction which Christopher does not share. Christopher will no doubt agree that only what is true can be pastoral, but asserts that the document's teaching is not true, with the implication that it is not pastoral either. Part of the point of the church teaching what it does is that it enables Christopher and others like him not only to abstain from certain kinds of behaviour of which the church officially disapproves but to do this as an authentic form of Christian living and witness. But, as noted earlier, it is only possible for Christopher to do this if he believes that such abstinence really is necessary if he is to be a faithful disciple of Christ; and he does not believe this. What are the church's teachers to say to Christopher and to all the others who, while remaining Christians, reject this aspect of current Christian teaching? Their exercise of their teaching

23

office can only be successful if they actually bring Christopher and the others to believe that the current teaching is true, and so enable them to live a truly Christian life. But how are they to do this?

It is immediately clear that certain approaches are inappropriate. To begin with, since what is at stake here is a question of truth, it would be a mistake to represent the problem as one of law, discipline or obedience. Not only is this a distortion of the nature of the problem, but it mislocates the proper place of Christopher's fidelity, the proper object of his obedience. It will not do to tell him that he *ought* to believe what church authorities tell him, as an act of obedience to duly constituted authority; for his due fidelity is, as *HP* implies, to the truth, and it is only if he sees the teaching as true that he can believe it. At a psychological level, such a disciplinary approach is almost bound to end in failure. This is well explained by Germain Grisez, who brings out once more the inevitable centrality of truth:

> A legalistic attitude makes it virtually impossible to live chastely. Anything felt to be an imposed restraint on one's deeply rooted appetites provokes anger and rebelliousness; and if sexual self-indulgence is regarded as a very desirable but unfortunately forbidden fruit, one is likely to look for some way of reconciling its enjoyment with Christian faith and life, for example, by a repeated round of sinning, 'repenting', confessing, and sinning again. Consequently, it is very important to understand, reflect on, and regularly call to mind what really is at stake and how much one stands to lose if one commits sexual sins.[15]

Again, to somebody like Christopher, who questions or denies the truth of a church teaching, it is simply irrelevant for church authorities to repeat that this is in fact the church teaching. If they try to teach Christopher in this way, they teach him badly, for this is not what he needs to know. He knows already that what he objects to is church teaching; only he believes that teaching to be untrue. While fully aware that it is church teaching, he believes that, because it is untrue, it ought not to be church teaching. It is equally beside the point to try to show him that the current teaching on the subject is traditional, that it has been taught by the churches for centuries. Regardless of whatever difficulties there may be in establishing that the teaching really is traditional, what is being questioned is not whether the teaching is old, but whether it is true. But this is too brief; a word more must be said on these topics.

Truth and tradition

First, tradition. One of the assertions made in recent church teaching on homosexuality is that church tradition has been constant in its condemnation of homosexual acts; *HP* claims that 'the Church's teaching today is in organic continuity with the Scriptural perspective and with her own constant Tradition'. This is certainly not unquestionable, and it has been questioned and denied.[16] It is an important claim, and so is the debate which surrounds it. But it lies beyond the scope of this book. The question I wish to pursue here is: even if it is true that the church does have a traditional stance on homosexuality, and even if that tradition is constantly negative in its attitude to homosexual acts, is the tradition itself correct? Is what it says true? It is this question, rather than any historical question about what the church taught in such and such a century, that is the fundamental one; it is the question that Christopher raises, and we are in any case fundamentally called to live not according to any tradition but according to the truth. The church of course sees its tradition as a source of truth. Indeed, it is only through tradition, through the patient handing on of the gospel from person to person and from generation to generation, that we today have access to the message which Jesus proclaimed many centuries ago and which we hold to be the revelation of God. Human beings live by tradition, even in matters divine. But that means that religious tradition is itself something human. And where humanity enters in, so too does the possibility of error. Christians believe that the church is helped in its transmission of the gospel message by the Holy Spirit. But the help of the Holy Spirit is just that: a help. It is a help to us in using our natural human faculties; it does not obviate the necessity to use those faculties, including our critical faculties, to guard against the introduction of error into our tradition. So we must not be afraid to ask whether our tradition is actually true. We have nothing to fear from this questioning. It may lead to deeper understanding of the tradition, to a more profound realization that what has long been taught actually is true, and to a more adequate comprehension of its sense. In that case critical questioning will serve only to clarify the tradition and let its truth appear more clearly. On the other hand, if we have through our human failings allowed mistakes to enter into our tradition, we should be eager to root them out, for error has no place in the handing on of the gospel. We are all aware that traditions, including religious traditions, and the traditions of those zealous for the truth, can be false. Jesus himself was not slow to point out that some of the Jewish traditions embodied false perceptions.[17] There are some elements of some Protestant traditions which Catholics believe to be false. And of course Protestants believe some elements of the Catholic tradition to be false, and that belief has itself become part of Protestant tradition. While Protestants and Catholics may both be wrong, they cannot both be right. Since they contradict each other, one of the traditions must be false. While we believe, Catholics and Protestants, that our tradition is a source of truth, truth cannot be identified with tradition. To say, even truly, that we have always believed such and such a doctrine does not show that doctrine to be true. To identify truth with tradition is not only a mistake, it also opens the way to relativism; it gives the false appearance that traditions as such, even mutually contradictory traditions, are immune to criticism. The name 'tradition' is often given not to a doctrine which has been fully examined, debated and accepted by the universal church, but to what Christians have been in the habit of saying, what it has been customary to say. What is said out of custom may well turn out to be true, but it is not the custom that makes it true. A tradition which is embodied in such a custom has no value in itself unless it is *true* tradition, a tradition which expresses true belief. For custom without truth, as Cyprian says, is merely error grown old.[18] Traditions must always be subject to the question of truth.

The question of truth is rarely if ever posed in a vacuum. Inquiry almost always takes place within the context of a tradition. A scientist or a historian, when seeking the truth, always works within the context of a received body of established belief which is counted as knowledge, and he makes use largely of received methods of enquiry; he situates himself within a tradition. He cannot challenge or doubt everything at once, for if he tries to do so he deprives himself of the tools he needs to ask his questions and pose his challenge. It is only by accepting the context of a tradition that he can pose any question or make any challenge at all. So it is with the church; any Christian theological enquiry must take place within the context of a tradition, and it is only that tradition which allows the enquiry to take place at all. The tradition supplies the background against which the enquiry can be understood, and it supplies the concepts in terms of which the question of truth can be put. Nevertheless, the question 'What is true?' is not equivalent to the question 'What does the tradition say?' This is so in science, it is so in history, and it is so in theology. The tradition precisely creates the context for the question of truth; it does not replace it or render it superfluous. This is why, in whatever field of knowledge, we can base ourselves on some elements of tradition in order to subject others to examination. In the church, taking some parts of our tradition as true, we can ask whether other parts are true. In particular, we can on the basis of parts of the tradition that are central, question parts which are less central. In many cases our questioning will reveal a coherence and an organic unity in the tradition. Less central parts of the tradition will be shown to be organically related to and consistent with more central elements. But we cannot close ourselves to the possibility that such an enquiry will reveal tensions, even contradictions. We may certainly hope that we will not find contradictions, but we should not be afraid of undertaking such an enquiry. Indeed, in the world of today it is almost necessary for us to examine our tradition in this way, for if we do not, others who are less sympathetic to the church will not be slow to do so.

Truth and authority

Tradition is transmitted by the whole church, but it is transmitted particularly by those who have the duty to speak publicly for the church: bishops, pastors of various kinds, theologians and teachers. So the question of tradition inevitably raises the question of authority; and authority, like tradition, has always had an important place in Christian thought. To question tradition implies questioning the authorities that hand tradition on. If Christopher questions the tradition of his church on homosexuality in quest of the truth on the subject, that can be less positively represented as lack of obedience to duly constituted, or even divinely ordained, authority. It may be said that he just *ought* to believe what he is told, to assent to the teaching that authoritative teachers hand down to him. This approach is wrongheaded, because it represents believing (or assenting) as a human act, and therefore as something that might be done out of obedience; but it is not. To see this more clearly, it is important to sketch a distinction between three different kinds of authority.

First, church authorities tell people in the church to engage – or, more often, not to engage – in certain kinds of activity; among other things, they tell people to engage in some kinds of sexual practice and to abstain from others. This is plainly an exercise of authority within the church. One may speak of an authority – which may be an individual or group of individuals – telling subordinates what to do, and of subordinates acting in obedience to that authority. This applies to any human institution in which there is an authority structure, and it applies also in the church. Popes, bishops, pastors, religious superiors, councils, committees, etc., sometimes exercise authority by telling subordinates to do certain things or to refrain from doing certain things. I will call this kind of authority *command* authority.[19] A person or body which has this authority is a command authority, and when it exercises its authority by commanding, I will call that an exercise in command authority.

Secondly, certain members of institutions, either as individuals or as groups, can have a peculiarly authoritative word. They have the authority, by their word, to determine what is the policy of the institution. In Britain, parliament effectively (here I simplify) has this kind of authority to determine what are the laws of the nation. If I say we have such and such a law, I may or may not be right. If parliament says we have such a law, then we do, just because parliament says so. There is no question of parliament getting it right or wrong, for it is the word of parliament that determines what the law is. I can only report the law, correctly or incorrectly; parliament does not report the law, but makes it. In certain countries, government policy on any question whatsoever is what the president says it is. He does not report, correctly or incorrectly, what the policy is, as a newspaper reporter or government spokesperson might; his word *decides* what it is. So also in the various parts of the church that we call 'churches': in almost every one, depending on its structure, there are people who, as individuals or as groups, have the authority to speak for the whole, whose word does not report but decides that church's policy on a particular matter. Such people effectively have authority to decide also what is their church's doctrine; they can draw up authoritative lists of that church's teachings. In none of the mainstream churches will such people present themselves as free to decide what they will in the area of doctrine; they will make their decisions as far as they can in fidelity to Christ, to the content of Scripture, and to the tradition of their church. But it is they who will decide authoritatively, speaking for their church, what such fidelity requires in the way of doctrine. So in the Catholic Church the pope has the authority to enunciate doctrine (I simplify again); the teaching of the church is what he says it is, because he says so. If I say what current Catholic teaching is, I merely report, correctly or not, what the church teaches; if the pope says what current Catholic teaching is, his voice decides what it is. His word is authoritative in a way that mine is not; such an authority as the pope I will call a *decisional* authority, and when a decisional authority exercises its authority by speaking decisively, I will call that an exercise in decisional authority.

But, thirdly, church authorities do not only tell people what to do, and they do not only decide what current church teaching is; they also tell people what is true and what is false, what is right and what is wrong. They teach, just as do mothers, university professors and writers of geography textbooks. We apply the word 'authority' to teachers, as we apply it to parliaments and military commanders, but when we do so we use it in a different way. We say that a teacher *is* an authority *on* a particular subject, say the Crimean War; and by that we do not mean that she is *in* authority in a particular institution and so can tell other members of that institution what to do; nor do we mean that she has any authority to decide policy or doctrine. We mean that she knows a lot about the Crimean War, that she is an expert on it, that she can be trusted to answer factual questions about it correctly, that she has thought deeply about it and come to reliable conclusions, and so on. A person or body that has this kind of authority I will call a *teaching* authority, and when the person or body exercises its authority by teaching, I will call that an exercise in teaching authority. These three kinds of authority are often linked in practice. Teachers, who are authorities on certain subjects, are often also in authority over those they teach. Somebody who has the power to decide what government policy is in a particular area can also be treated, by those who wish to learn, as an authority on that policy. Those who have the authority to decide often also have the authority to implement their decisions by commanding others to act in certain ways. Nevertheless, the three kinds are essentially distinct. Particularly important for our purposes is the distinction between command authority and teaching authority. A central difference between command authority and teaching authority is that the one tells people to *do* things (or not to do them), while the other gets people to *believe* things.[20] Among other things, church authorities tell people to refrain from all same-sex sexual activity. But they do not just tell people to refrain from same-sex sexual activity; they tell people that such activity is wrong, and it is this moral judgement that is the basis of their command[21] not to engage in it. Church authorities do not only command, they also teach. As elsewhere, these two activities are often intimately linked, and the teaching serves to justify the command. Abstention from same-sex activity is not proposed by church authorities merely as a kind of helpful discipline, like abstention from meat on Fridays or attendance at church services on Sundays. It is because the church teaches that homosexual activities are always wrong that it also tells people not to engage in them, and it is at least in part by convincing people to believe in the wrongness of the activities that they hope to get them to refrain from performing them.

Command authority is essentially concerned with action. So it is possible to obey and to disobey such an authority; we obey by performing the action the authority commands, and we disobey by failing or refusing to perform it. Teaching authority, on the other hand, is concerned with instilling belief, with bringing it about that people come to believe certain things, to be convinced that they are true. If we want somebody to believe something he does not at present believe, we cannot coherently command him to believe it. The reason for this is that we can only be commanded to perform an act, and believing is not an act of a person. Take the two sentences 'I switch on this engine' and 'I believe this proposition'. Both contain verbs, and in both 'I' is the subject. This superficial resemblance may make it look as if, in the second sentence as in the first, I am said to perform an act; only whereas in the first sentence the act is an act of starting an engine, in the second it is an act of believing a proposition. If this were true, I could perhaps be commanded to perform the activity of believing a proposition just as I can be commanded to perform the activity of starting an engine; and I could obey or disobey in the one case as in the other. But the resemblance between the two sentences is only superficial. This can be shown very easily. I can be commanded in rapid succession: 'Switch on the engine ... Now turn it off ... Now turn it on again ... Now turn it off again.' There is no difficulty in principle about my obeying such a series of commands. If I am willing to obey, I can do it. Indeed, somebody might give me such a series of commands precisely to test my willingness to obey, to see whether I will be obedient. Now, imagine the following series of would-be commands: 'Believe that the moon is made of green cheese ... Now believe that it isn't ... Now believe again that it is ... Now believe that it isn't.' There is no way that I could act in obedience to this series, or indeed to any member of it. This is not because it is a very difficult series of commands to obey, but because it is not a series of commands at all. There are no acts I could perform that might constitute obedience or disobedience.[22] If I do not believe that the moon is made of green cheese, then I cannot out of obedience believe that it is. And this does not indicate that my abilities are somehow limited; it indicates that there is no task of believing to perform. In order to believe, I need rather to be *convinced* that the moon is made of green cheese. Because there is no question of believing out of obedience, it would be a mistake to speak of my non-belief in terms of disobedience. If I do not believe, I do not disobey, I remain unconvinced.

The reason why there cannot be a command to believe is that, while there is an act of switching on an engine and an act of switching off an engine, there is no act of believing, or of coming to believe. Believing is not an act. Roughly speaking, to say that I come to believe any proposition whatever is not to say that I perform some mental act that might be called 'believing' or 'assenting'; it is equivalent to saying that the proposition appears (or comes to appear) to me to be true.[23] In general, if we take *A* to refer to a person and *p* to stand for any proposition whatsoever, the sentence '*A* believes that *p* is true' can be translated into the sentence '*p* appears to *A* to be true'. But if a proposition *p* appears to *A* to be true, this is not an action of *A*'s; *A* does not do anything. It is just that *p* strikes *A* in a certain way, as true; *A*'s role is passive, he is not an agent. But if, when *A* believes that *p*, *A* does not do anything, then *A* cannot be commanded to believe that *p*. Command does not enter into the picture here, because there is nothing to command anybody to do.[24] For the same reason, it is a mistake to say that *A* *ought* to believe that *p*, or has an obligation to believe that *p*, for one can only have an obligation to do something, to perform an act.[25] An authority can of course command me to *say* that I believe a particular proposition, or not to say that I do not believe it; an authority can command me to say that I do not believe a proposition, or not to say that I do believe it. This is possible because saying that one believes or does not believe something, as opposed to simply believing or not believing it, is a human act, and so is refraining from saying that one believes or does not believe. Problematically, I can be ordered to say that I believe a proposition that I do not in fact believe, or to refrain from saying that I do not believe it. The order to say that I believe a proposition that I do not believe is effectively, if it is clear to the one issuing the order that I do not believe it, the order to lie; the order not to say that I believe something that I do believe, often, depending on circumstances, amounts to the order to behave deceitfully or hypocritically. But none of this affects the essential point, that nobody can be ordered to believe or not to believe a proposition, and nobody can believe or not believe as an act of obedience.

The position we have arrived at is that if an authoritative body wants me to believe that *p*, it cannot command me to do so. That is to say, there is no such exercise of command authority. This applies to the church as it applies to any secular authority. One of the problems when it comes to teaching in the church is that those in authority are inclined not to make the distinction between command authority and teaching authority, effectively believing that it is all a question of command authority. It is not. On the contrary, it never is. This result does not imply any particular limitation on church authority; it is simply a matter of logic. Believing is just not the sort of thing that can be ordered, because it is not a human act. But that does not mean that there is no place for authority when it comes to questions of belief; there plainly is. Such authority is, however, not command authority but teaching authority. People can and do teach with authority. At the end of the Sermon on the Mount, Matthew remarks: 'And when Jesus finished these sayings, the crowds were astonished at his teaching, for he taught them as one having authority, and not like their scribes' (7:28f.). What Matthew means here is not that the crowds were astonished because Jesus commanded them to believe things, nor because he was authorized to teach them, nor because he was in authority over them; they were astonished because Jesus's teaching carried conviction, because it struck them with a force that convinced them, so that they treated him as an authority. Jesus is not here exercising command authority, but being recognized as a teaching authority. In general, what a teaching authority does is convince people of things; it brings it about in various ways that certain propositions appear to certain people to be true. This is what the church does, or tries to do, when it teaches.

When a teaching authority wants to teach us that *p*, it must present *p* to us in such a way that we believe that *p*. It has, roughly, to convince us that *p* is true, or make *p* appear to us to be true. In many cases there is no difficulty about this. Very often, it suffices for somebody we regard as authoritative simply to tell us that something is the case for us to believe it. We believe most of the things we believe because we have been told them by people we regard as authorities in the matter, whom we trust to give us the right answer, or because we have read them in books we regard as authoritative. Our parents, our teachers, the authors of our school and university textbooks, the television and radio newsreaders – all of these function or have functioned for us as teaching authorities. These people, we generally believe (rightly or wrongly) are in a position to know the truth of the matters on which they speak, and on which we perhaps consult them. When we ask a person what her name is, we do so in part because we expect her to know the truth about her name, what it actually is; we regard her as an authority on this question. A teaching authority does not, as such, exercise authority over certain people; he or she is an authority on certain subjects. Treating somebody as a teaching authority is treating him or her as somebody who can be relied upon to say what is true, what is right. For Christians, Jesus is such an authority, and a supremely important one, for he tells us things which we believe essential to our very salvation. For Christians, the Bible, the church and tradition also sometimes function as important teaching authorities, and we accept without problem what they urge us to believe, just because this belief is proposed to us by the church, its book and its tradition.

Overcoming scepticism

If it sometimes, even very often, suffices that an authority tells us that some proposition *p* is true for *p* to appear to us to be true, this is not always the case. Sometimes, the authority has to overcome scepticism or resistance. This is the case particularly when people have reason, or think they have reason, to believe that *p* is not the case. To overcome this resistance, authorities in the church as elsewhere often use rhetorical devices in order to make appear more probable those things that they propose for our belief. They may, for example, say effectively: 'Trust me, I know about these things better than you do'; or even: 'You must believe this.' Superficially, these sentences have the appearance of being commands to believe. But, as we have seen, there are no such commands. In reality, they function quite differently, as devices to induce conviction in the hearer. As well as using such devices, authorities also, and more importantly, often appeal to reason. If they want to teach us that a proposition *p* (say, a theological or moral doctrine) is true, they build up a case in support of *p* which, they hope, will be convincing and so in turn make *p* appear to us to be true. Evidence is presented, arguments deployed.

What devices and what arguments an authority has to employ in order to induce a conviction in a person must depend in some degree on the importance to that person of the point involved. Suppose that Christopher has hitherto believed firmly that Beethoven died in

1828; it has appeared to him certain that Beethoven died in that year. He may have had no very profound reason for this belief; he may simply have been misremembering what he read many years ago, or be confusing Beethoven with Schubert. If he now reads a book on Beethoven which he accepts as authoritative, and which tells him he died in 1827, then that is very likely what he will believe. He will not believe it because he is in some way committed to obeying the book or its author, but because the book convinces him of it. This will probably not be very difficult to do, for he may well imagine that anybody who goes to the lengths of writing a book about Beethoven is liable to know when he died, and so Christopher will readily accept the author as an authority on the subject; on reflection it may occur to him that he has no very strong reason for rejecting what the book tells him, and he will be able to explain his previous error as due to forgetfulness or confusion. But now suppose that Sophie has previously been an atheist and has believed that Jesus is definitely not her saviour. If she is to be convinced that Jesus is her saviour she will very probably require more than just a book telling her so. This not a thing about which one is easily convinced, for it may lead to a revolutionary change in the whole of one's outlook and way of living. For Sophie it will also require a re-interpretation of all her experience and of all the facts which have hitherto seemed to her to imply that there is no God and that Jesus cannot help her. Most people can easily accept that Beethoven died in 1827 rather than 1828, because, for most people, nothing very much hangs on it. They don't have to change their job, their way of life or their understanding of the meaning of the universe. The date of Beethoven's death is a detail for them, perhaps interesting, but without great importance. But the question whether Jesus is one's saviour is not a detail. To change her mind about this, Sophie might need a whole series of books, and of conversations with people whose views she respects; above all, she will probably need a certain experience of life, and perhaps of certain events which strike her with great force. Indeed, given the importance of the question at stake and the reasons she previously had for denying the existence of God, we would probably consider it irrational of her to change her mind lightly, and irrational of her to believe that Jesus is her saviour just because somebody told her so.

So it is likely to be with those Christians who do not share the customary negative Christian evaluation of same-sex relationships. If Christopher does not believe that these are always immoral, this may conceivably be for him a question like the date of Beethoven's death. It may be enough that people whom he takes as authorities on the matter – and these may be the church authorities to whom he normally looks for guidance on moral questions – tell him that these relationships are always immoral. If this is so, and he believes it because he is told so, this once again cannot be properly described as his performing an act of belief out of obedience to those people, for there is no such act and no such obedience. Rather, the fact that these particular people tell him that homosexual acts are always immoral convinces him that it is so, makes it appear to him that it is so. But the question is much more likely not to be such a light one for him, but to be closer in importance to the question whether Jesus is his saviour. This is particularly likely to be true if he himself is a homosexual with some experience of life. If he believes that homosexual acts are not always immoral, this is likely to be a strong belief; his own experience of life, the love that he has experienced in a same-sex partnership, and his knowledge of his gay and lesbian friends and their relationships may all have convinced him that homosexual relationships sometimes, perhaps often, bring happiness and well-being, and so are good. If his view is not that of his church and he is a sincere Christian, he may have studied what the Bible and the tradition of his church have to say on the matter, and his study and thinking may have led him to the conclusion that his church's position is mistaken. The question is an important one for him, because human happiness is a weighty matter, and because what he believes implies a judgement on a relationship that has been very important to him and on the relationships of his friends; and his experience and thoughtfulness mean he has serious grounds for his conviction. If all that is so, then to be convinced that he is wrong he will need more than just voices, even voices he respects greatly and normally treats as authoritative, telling him so. He will need more than rhetoric, he will need strong reasons to believe that his study of the Bible and of tradition was deeply flawed, that all the positive experience which seemed to him evidence of the potential goodness of same-sex relationships does not in fact constitute such evidence; he will need in addition compelling proofs that same-sex relationships are always immoral. Unless he can be shown all this not only will he be unlikely to change his mind on the question, but it would also be irrational of him to do so.

Church authorities who have pastoral care for Christopher and want him to change his mind have their work cut out. Their responsibility is to teach him, to bring it about that it appears to him true that same-sex relationships are always immoral. He raises the question of the truth of church teaching on this issue, and any adequate pastoral approach must set out to answer that question. As we have seen, it is not an appropriate response to his disagreement with church authorities to treat him as disobedient to authority, for no obedience or disobedience can be involved in matters of belief. He is not disobedient to a command authority but unconvinced by a teaching authority.[26] It is the responsibility of that authority to convince him, to present him with arguments cogent enough and considerations weighty enough, in view of his previous background, to make it reasonable for him to change his mind, and so to make it appear to him that church teaching in this matter is indeed true. Christopher has his responsibilities here, too. If he really is concerned to know the truth, he must be ready to listen to others, for listening is one of the major ways human beings learn. That means he must be willing to listen to, among others, Christian voices, particularly to authoritative voices in his own church, and to listen to them as sympathetically as he can. Church authorities are not devoid of responsibility in this area. If Christopher should be open to listening to them, they should in turn facilitate this for him. If they refuse to listen to him and take seriously what he says, they make it more difficult for him to listen to them. If in their teaching they make no attempt to reply seriously to objections he makes against church teaching, he will naturally conclude that they have no reply and be confirmed in his view that church teaching is wrong. If they argue in such a way as to give the impression that they are simply unaware of all the scholarly work that has been done in this area in recent years, they encourage him not to take them seriously as teachers. If they vilify him and others who put such objections, he will lose respect and sympathy for them and cease to listen. Once it has earned Christopher's attention, the church must present him with weighty and convincing arguments that will make the church's teaching on homosexuality appear to him to be true. Only so will it be rational for him to cease to think it good to be gay and to adopt the church's position. The rest of this book is devoted to an attempt to answer the simple questions: Does the church have such weighty and convincing arguments at its disposal? If Christopher has reasons, from his experience and from his study, to believe in the goodness of some same-sex relationships, does the church have arguments which should make him change his mind? What is it rational for Christopher to believe about the moral status of homosexual relationships? Answering these questions means looking at what the church actually says and at the arguments adduced in its support, in both official and unofficial documents. This will carry us over some familiar ground; principally, we shall have to reflect on relevant passages of the Bible, and on natural-law arguments. The terrain will be familiar to many, but here the perspective will be perhaps more restricted than in other visits to the same territory, for the question in view always will be whether such and such a text or argument actually supports the church's position, as the church claims it does.

CHAPTER TWO

'Homosexuality'

Like the word 'authority', we use the word 'homosexual' in a number of ways, and before proceeding to our central task we must explore some of these, so that, though we continue using the word, we do not use it unthinkingly. Centrally, we speak of homosexual desire, but also of homosexual women and men; of homosexual acts, but also of homosexual relationships, homosexual tendencies and homosexual orientations. We also use the word as a substantive, speaking of some people as homosexuals. And of course we also have the cognate term 'homosexuality'. Before we can argue sensibly about homosexuality, and about the various things we label homosexual, it is important to get clear some of the relations between those things, and to realize some of the consequences of our terminology. I will not go systematically through the list I have just given (which is in any case defective), but simply make some remarks about what seem to me the most important questions.

'Homosexuality', physical and psychological

The word 'homosexuality' is used in at least two different but linked ways. In this it is similar to the word 'sexuality'. People talk about their sexuality as a shorthand for talking about their sexual feelings and desires, the person or kind of people they are sexually attracted to, and the kinds of sexual activity they engage in or want to engage in. We might say that 'sexuality' is a term that comprehends both the psychological and the physical. It refers on the one hand to a person's mental or psychological life in so far as it relates to the person's thoughts, feelings, emotions and desires, and to the physical aspect of a person's life in so far as it relates to what the person actually does sexually with his or her body, the sexual activities in which he or she engages. For example, suppose that Anne is sexually attracted to Brian. Saying that she is sexually attracted to him is a shorthand way of referring to possible combinations of attitudes, feelings, desires and activities. She may find him beautiful;

she will take pleasure in seeing and looking at him; she may search him out in crowds, and flush with excitement when she sees him. She may rush to be near him, or be careful to stay at a distance from him. She may talk to him eagerly, or blush with embarrassment every time he speaks to her. She will probably dwell often and with pleasure on thoughts of him. She may want to be with him, to live with him, to touch him and be touched by him, to caress him and be caressed by him, to kiss him, to make love to him and have him make love to her. And so on. All this concerns what might be called her interior psychological life, her emotions and desires. But note that the interior is very often closely related to and manifested in the exterior, in Anne's body. I mean not just that her cheeks go red when she is embarrassed, but that her psychology is revealed in her activity. If Anne is attracted to Brian, she will look around for him, and she will glance surreptitiously at him in certain circumstances. She will seek him out or avoid him. That is, she will behave in a range of ways that others will be able to recognize as expressive of sexual desire or attraction. Her psychological state will naturally express itself in her activity. Unless she wants for some reason to conceal her attraction to him, and is successful in doing so, she will do a number of bodily, physical things that reveal it. Other people, if they are observant enough, will be able to tell, on the basis of how she acts, that she is attracted to Brian. Even if she is successful in hiding her attraction, there is a case for saying that she *must*, if she is attracted to Brian, behave in ways in which she would not otherwise behave, doing things she would not otherwise do. Does it make sense, for example, to suppose that she could be attracted to Brian and not look at him, even surreptitiously, when she has the opportunity, on occasions and in ways she would not if she were not attracted to him? Whether this is in theory possible, it is clear that in general the psychological or mental is not locked away inside us, but expresses itself in bodily behaviour, and we often ascribe mental states to people on the basis of how they act. But though Anne may and probably will act in certain ways because of her sexual attraction towards Brian, and her sexual desire for him, we would not normally call actions of the kind I have been describing sexual acts. By a sexual act we usually mean roughly an act performed with sexual intent involving at least one genital organ. There are questions to be answered if this is to be put forward seriously as a definition, principally: How do we distinguish sexual intent from other kinds of intent? What is meant by saying that an act *involves* a genital organ? And might we not sometimes want to call an act sexual even though it involves no genital organs at all? I will not go into those questions here, because I do not wish to formulate a definition of a sexual act.[1] It is enough for my purposes that we do make a distinction between acts which are sexual and acts which are not, even if there might be borderline cases where we are unsure what to say.

The relationship between the mental and physical aspects of sexuality is not straightforward. Though they are often found together, they can be separated. Anne can be sexually attracted to Brian without ever performing a sexual act with him. On the other hand, it is possible to want to perform, and in fact to perform, a sexual act with somebody without experiencing any of the other elements of sexual attraction. Brian may want to have sex with Anne, and may actually have sex with Anne, without wanting to spend a lot of time with her, caress her, look into her eyes, etc. He may not even like her. His only interest in her may be as a partner in sexual activity. One aspect of the difficulty can be expressed by saying that the scope of sexual desire and attraction is much wider than that of sexual activity. Take holding hands. When in some contexts we see two people holding hands, we recognize sexuality at work. This will be so, for example, when there is other deliberate bodily contact between them, or when there is prolonged eye contact accompanied by affectionate facial expressions, and when the two appear sexually mature. Desiring to hold hands like this comes within the scope of sexual desire, and forms part of the behaviour associated with what I am calling the psychological aspect of sexuality. But we would probably not want to say that holding hands was an instance of sexual activity. The same goes for any number of activities, such as gazing into another's eyes, stroking another's hair, resting one's hand on another's thigh, and so on: we recognize the presence of sexuality in these activities; they are acts that tell of mutual sexual attraction and may imply or form part of a sexual relationship, that is of a relationship in which there is also sexual activity. But we would probably not call these activities themselves sexual activities. (We would not say that somebody gazing into another's eyes was 'having sex' with him or her.) As I have noted, we tend to reserve the term 'sexual activity' to a much narrower range of activities, on the whole involving what we call the sexual organs. A proper analysis of sexual desire and attraction would need to go much further, but even from these limited remarks an important conclusion follows: sexual desire cannot be construed simply as the desire to engage in sexual acts. It may, to be sure, include the desire to engage in sexual acts, but it is much broader in its scope, embracing activities, and the desire to perform activities, which may go far beyond sexual activity. If Anne is sexually attracted to Brian, she will, unless she is very exceptional, want to do many more things with him than have sex. Any attempt to construe a standard case of sexual desire simply as the desire to engage in sexual acts would be reductionist and false. The fictional example I have used here – Anne being sexually attracted to Brian – is what today we would call an example of heterosexual attraction, since Brian, whom we may call the object of Anne's sexual attraction, is of a different sex from Anne herself, the one attracted.[2] So the explicatory remarks above may serve equally as an explication of heterosexual desire. Conceived as such, the difference of gender between Anne and Brian becomes not contingent but necessary, since it belongs to the definition of heterosexual attraction. Given that limitation, the same remarks apply to heterosexuality as to sexuality in general. It is important to note in particular that, just as what we call sexual attraction is wider in its scope than what we call sexual activity, so heterosexual attraction is wider in its scope than heterosexual activity. A heterosexual person has, in virtue of being heterosexual, normally a much richer and more complicated attitude to a member or members of the opposite sex than simply wanting to engage in sexual activity with that person or those persons. Heterosexual desire cannot without falsification be reduced to wanting to engage in sexual activity with a member of the opposite sex. Any attempt to do so reveals a misunderstanding of sexual desire.

When the label 'homosexual' is applied to somebody, it is generally meant that that person's sexual desire is directed to people of the same sex, or that he or she is sexually attracted to a person or people of the same sex: a homosexual man's sexuality is directed towards men, a homosexual woman's towards women. Just as heterosexuality is a specific form of sexuality, so is homosexuality. That is, the above remarks about the use of the word 'sexuality' apply to homosexuality also, just as they apply to heterosexuality, but with the added specification that the person who is what one might call the object of sexuality is of the same sex as the person whose sexuality is in question. There is a mental and a physical side to homosexuality. If Christopher is homosexual, he may be sexually attracted to David. Then he may feel about him just as Anne feels about Brian. He may find him beautiful; he may flush with excitement when he sees him; he may dwell often and with pleasure on

41

thoughts of him. He may want to be with him, to live with him, to touch him and be touched by him, to caress him and be caressed by him, to kiss him, to make love to him.[3] He may do all this without ever actually having sex with him, or with anybody. If David is also attracted to Christopher, they will want to do and may actually end up doing many things together, things which express that mutual sexual attraction. They may hold hands, embrace, smile radiantly into each other's eyes, caress each other, and so on. All this will express their sexual desire for each other. Unless they are exceptional people, their mutual sexual desire does not mean that all they want to do together is to have sex. It is, in short, a mistake to characterize normal homosexual desire as the desire to have sex with another of the same sex.

The inadequacy of the CDF's definition of homosexuality

I have pointed out that our concept of sexuality is complicated in that it has both what I have called psychological aspects and what I have called physical aspects; it covers both people's sexual feelings and desires on the one hand, and the various kinds of activity that express them, including their sexual activity, on the other. The pertinence of this distinction between the physical and the psychological is in part that it corresponds in some measure to a distinction made, in recent theological discussion of homosexuality, between homosexual acts and what has been called 'the homosexual condition'. This is a term current particularly in Catholic documents on homosexuality. It appears to have been introduced at official level in 1986 in *HP*, which uses the phrase several times. Thus it describes the 1975 document *Persona Humana* as stressing 'the duty of trying to understand the homosexual condition' (§3).[4] *HP* asserts further that

> At the same time the Congregation [for the Doctrine of the Faith, in *Persona Humana*] took note of the distinction commonly drawn between the homosexual condition or tendency and individual homosexual actions. These were described as deprived of their essential and indispensable finality, as being 'intrinsically disordered', and able in no case to be approved of (cf. n. 8, §4). (§3)

The distinction here referred to might be put more straightforwardly as that between being homosexual and engaging in homosexual acts. What it is to 'have the homosexual condition' is just to be a homosexual person. *HP* further states, in response to subsequent discussion of this homosexual condition:

> Although the particular inclination of the homosexual person is not a sin, it is a more or less strong tendency ordered toward an intrinsic moral evil; and thus the inclination itself must be seen as an objective disorder. (ibid.)

From this it appears that what is meant by 'the homosexual condition' is 'the particular inclination of the homosexual person'. This inclination is described as 'a more or less strong tendency ordered toward an intrinsic moral evil'. In context, the intrinsic moral evil referred to can only be 'individual homosexual actions'. But having the homosexual condition is just what it is to be a homosexual person. So *HP*'s position is effectively that to be a homosexual person is to have a more or less strong tendency to engage in homosexual acts. If I have correctly understood *HP*'s position, it is seriously mistaken, because reductionist. As we saw earlier, a person's sexuality is not correctly understood as a tendency to engage in sexual acts, but goes much wider. A homosexual's homosexuality is not reducible to a desire to engage in same-sex sexual activities. It is a tendency to have a whole range of desires, and will normally include the tendency take delight in, if anybody at all, another of the same sex, to want to be with them, to be at ease with them, to look at them, to share things with them, even to share life with them; to touch them and embrace them, to be touched and embraced by them, to want to make them happy and share happiness with them. No doubt the sexual desire will often include the desire to have sex with the other person, but it is certainly not reducible to it. Indeed, in the typical case, the desire to perform a sexual act with the other is only intelligible in the light of the other desires and activities that form an essential part of people's sexuality. That is to say, what I have been calling the physical aspect of sexuality is intelligible only in the light of the psychological aspect. This needs further explanation.

If we ask why a homosexual should be inclined to specifically homosexual acts, rather than simply sexual acts with another person regardless of the sex of the partner to the act, it seems the answer has to be that the homosexual is sexually attracted to *people* of the same sex. A homosexual man does not just want occasionally to perform sexual acts; he wants to perform them with another man, and perhaps with one particular man. A lesbian wants not only to engage in sexual acts but to do so with another woman, and perhaps with one particular woman. There are some common sexual acts which are the same or substantially similar whether they are performed by homosexual or heterosexual couples: e.g., fellatio, cunnilingus, anal intercourse. If Christopher is a homosexual man and wants to be fellated, there seems to be no reason, in terms of the physicality of the act itself, why he should prefer this act to be performed for him by a man rather than by a woman. His preference for fellatio as a homosexual rather than a heterosexual act must then depend on a prior inclination to share sexual activity with another man rather than with a woman. Even at this level, it appears that the fundamental aspect of homosexuality is therefore primarily not an inclination to homosexual acts but a sexual attraction to people of the same sex. The typical homosexual is such not because he or she is attracted to acts of a certain kind but because he or she is attracted to people. Christopher, like most homosexuals, is a homosexual because there are one or more men who attract him sexually and who, as part but only part of that sexual attractiveness, arouse him to seek sexual activity with them. This last point needs a little qualification. It is possible that a man be homosexual simply because he delights in certain kinds of sexual activity, and these activities are ones which he can only perform with other males. As Liam likes mowing the lawn, so he may also like fellating; and this, not because he is in any way otherwise attracted to men, enjoys their company, wants to please them, or share his life with them, but simply because he likes performing this particular activity. This is an activity which he needs the co-operation of another man to perform. But the man himself may be significant to him only as the owner of a penis. As Cathy likes knitting, so she may also like performing cunnilingus; and this has to be done on a woman, who may be otherwise unimportant to her. It is possible to be keen on activities in this way, even activities concerning people's organs, without paying any particular attention to the bearer of the organs. This would mean that Liam and Cathy perform these activities without being sexually attracted and aroused by another person. It would be reasonable, on the basis of their sexual activity, to describe both of them as homosexual. But though such cases are possible, they are marginal and of little interest. For most people, sexual activity with another person is dependent on sexual attraction to and arousal by that other person.

While the cases of Liam and Cathy must be recognized as representing a kind of homosexuality, most homosexuals are of another kind. Mostly, homosexual attraction is fundamental to homosexual activity. A homosexual man is interested in sexual acts with another man because he is sexually interested in that man; he finds him attractive, and sometimes, or often, finds encounters with him erotic, generating sexual arousal. Indeed, it is only on some such assumption that we can explain at all why he seeks sexual contact with this man rather than some other. CDF's way of putting the matter, apart from its other faults, makes the one gay man's sexual interest in another look completely arbitrary, as if what he wants is just sexual activity, so that, though he proposes sexual activity with this man, he might equally have chosen any other. For the great majority of gay men – for the normal gay man – this is simply false. The same is true, *mutatis mutandis*, for a homosexual woman: in general, a lesbian does not just want sex with another – any other – woman, but has reasons to prefer one woman to another, reasons which explain her choice and give a context to her desire for sexual contact with her in particular. Once again, CDF's account of what it is to be homosexual is revealed as seriously defective.

Homosexual relationships, homosexual acts

CDF's defective definition is of a piece with its determination to treat homosexuality in terms of homosexual acts. *HP* speaks always and only of 'homosexual actions' or 'homosexual activity' – crudely, what people do with their sexual organs. And this *is* crude, because it cuts out entirely the human dimension of sexual activity. 'Homosexual activity' is never contextualized as an element of a human relationship. It is never acknowledged, for example, that a homosexual act might be performed as an element of a permanent, intimate and loving relationship. This falsifying thinness is present throughout the document. A striking example of it is the following sentence:

> [The church] is ... aware that the view that homosexual activity is equivalent to, or as acceptable as, the sexual expression of conjugal love has a direct impact on society's understanding of the nature and rights of the family and puts them in jeopardy.(§9)

I am not concerned with the truth or falsity of the claim made here,[5] but with the language in which it is expressed. 'Homosexual activity' is juxtaposed to 'the sexual expression of conjugal love', with the implication that they are not to be compared. Note first the rich and proper contextualization of sexual activity between married people. It takes place within a *conjugal* relationship, the permanent and faithful joining of two lives. The two lives are joined not by force of circumstance or by mere habit, but by *love*. The sexual activity is accorded immense significance as the *expression* of this love. All this is right and proper; it is simply a reminder of the immense value attached to, and the central values embodied in, marriage in the Christian tradition. But now note by contrast the complete and improper decontextualization of sex between homosexual partners. It is reduced to what people do with their sexual organs. There is a complete refusal to see the activity in the context of a human relationship, a relationship which might well in many respects be similar to that of a married couple. There is of course a genuine and necessary difference between the sexual activity of a married couple and that of any homosexual couple: a homosexual couple cannot, by their sexual activity together, produce a child. But this obvious difference should not lead us to deny possible similarities. Two people of the same sex may, just like a married couple, live together in a faithful and permanent union, a union of love, and in such a context it would be natural to see their 'homosexual activity' as the sexual expression of that love, and one would need very good reason indeed not to view it and speak of it in that way. CDF does not even attempt to give such a reason. If homosexual activity cannot, as *HP* implies, be compared to the sexual expression of conjugal love, it is because like is not being compared with like. The disparity is built into the description. The poverty and thinness one is meant to see in all homosexual activity is a character of the description rather than of the reality. Anybody who has lived in a half-decent homosexual relationship, or who knows of one – and, as a matter of fact, there are such people – knows that 'homosexual activity' can in fact be love-making, a reality far richer than the sentence quoted above, or the rest of the document from which it is taken, allows. This is one reason – only one, but an important one – why for such people the CDF position on 'homosexual activity' is not authoritative, why it fails to convince. They simply know that it is false.[6]

Homosexual person

Homosexuality a real quality?

A recent book was entitled *One Hundred Years of Homosexuality*.[7] The point of this title was partly to signal that the word 'homosexual' and its cognates are of very recent origin. More deeply, it suggested that the *concept* of homosexuality was a recent one, unknown in bygone ages. The claim is not that people did not in past ages feel and behave in ways that we would call homosexual. There is plenty of evidence that they did; one has only to look at a few works of classical Greek and Roman literature to see that sentiment and behaviour which we would label homosexual have a long history in Europe. What is being claimed is rather that it is only in recent times that our system of classification of sexual sentiment and behaviour, a system in which the concept of homosexuality has an important, some would say central, place, is of recent origin. Fundamental to this system of classification is the idea that a person's sexual preferences tell us something deep and important about that person. In particular, the sex of the people a person is sexually attracted to, *in relation to the sex of the person attracted*, is seen as an important constituent of the nature of the person attracted, or revelatory of the nature of that person. If all we know of somebody is that their name is Evelyn and that they are in general sexually attracted to women, then we know so far very little about Evelyn. But if we also learn that Evelyn is a woman, then we know something about her: that her sexual desire is homosexual. And this is an important thing to know, so much so that she can now be seen as a particular kind of person, as a homosexual person. On the other hand, if we learn that Evelyn is a man, we learn that he is another kind of person, a heterosexual person. And this is, according to some, including some Christians, the normal kind of person. A homosexual person is supposed, by contrast, to be an abnormal or deviant person. The existence of the word 'homosexual' is evidence that we make certain distinctions, and that these distinctions are important to us for purposes of classification. Thus sexual preferences are more important to us, as far as concerns our classification of people and what they do, than culinary preferences. There are people who adore mushrooms. Suppose that Henry is one of these. When there is a choice, whatever else is on offer, even if there are piles of courgettes, aubergines, tomatoes, kidney beans, eggs, pork sausages, and roast beef, he only has eyes for the mushrooms; he will gleefully make straight for them. Others may remark this preference, or it may go completely unnoticed. If they do notice it, they may find it amusing, or a little irritating. If they remark on it to Henry, he may be amused, perhaps slightly embarrassed. What neither Henry nor anybody else is likely to do is, except for fun, to invent a word for people with culinary preferences, for nobody in our society can credibly say that his strong preference for mushrooms reveals something deep about his personality, or that it marks him out as a particular kind of person.

But it is one thing to use the word 'homosexual' to mark a distinction which is important to us, and another to suppose that those to whom we may apply the word share certain real qualities, or have a condition in common. In particular, we call a lesbian homosexual, and we also call a gay man homosexual; do they actually have anything in common? To speak of homosexual people is to speak of a phenomenon with male and female instantiations; men who have sex with men and women who have sex with women are instances of the *same* kind of person. It is not evident that this is a helpful way to characterize these sexual phenomena. On the face of it, men having sex with men seems to have little to do with women having sex with women, beyond the fact that we classify certain activities between men as sexual and certain activities between women as sexual. But they also have that in common with certain activities that men do with women; so that does not serve to link them together as precisely homosexual. We can raise the same kind of question about sexual desire and attraction, and about people. What does the sexual desire of a man for a man have in common with the sexual desire of a woman for a woman, that we should find it interesting, important or illuminating to attach the same label to them both? What does a man who is sexually attracted to men have in common with a woman who is sexually attracted to women, that we might want to call both of them homosexual people? There is an obvious answer to these questions. What characterizes sexual activity between men is that it goes on between people of the same sex; that's why we call it homosexual. Sex between women has exactly the same characteristic; it too goes on between people of the same sex, is homosexual. So sexual activity between men and sexual activity between women are both forms of homosexual sex. A woman's sexual desire for a woman is a sexual desire for a person of the same sex, just as is a man's sexual desire for a man; they have this in common, and that is why we call them both homosexual. A man attracted to men is a person attracted to persons of the same sex; a woman attracted to women is likewise a person attracted to persons of the same sex. They therefore have a common characteristic, that of being homosexual.

So much is obvious, but it does not answer the question why it should be considered at all interesting or illuminating to classify people, their desires and their acts in this way. There are those who believe that in speaking of people as homosexual and heterosexual they are being true to nature, and thus speaking in the only really true way possible. But this is not true; it is possible to look at things quite differently. Suppose that Christopher is sexually attracted to David, and Anne to Brian. Then Christopher and Anne have it in common that they are sexually attracted to a man. They might have it in common that they are attracted to men in general. Here is surely a real common quality. We might call them both andro-philes; equally, a man attracted to women and a woman attracted to women we might call gynaecophiles. We could, if we chose, and with equal or greater justification, divide people in general into androphiles and gynaecophiles rather than homosexuals and het-erosexuals. As a matter of fact we do not, but that is our choice, a social, linguistic fact, not our fidelity to some objective reality. It is a mistake to speak as if we can simply read off the phenomena of homosexuality from nature. In one way, we can: there surely are phenomena around which we label as homosexual. But we do so because we in our society read them as homosexual, one system of sexual classification rather than another, or rather than none at all. The relevance of all this to our subject is in part that not all societies classify things in the same way. In particular, we cannot assume without further ado that the societies that produced the Bible classified people or their actions in the same way as we do. Unfortunately, some moralists and exegetes assume that we can, therefore much time will be devoted in the following chapters on the Bible to argue that this is not so.

Homosexual desire and intensionality

Before talking about homosexual desire, it is necessary to say a few words about intensionality. Intensionality is a concept which will throw light on a number of questions raised in the course of this book, so it is important to get clear about it now. While 'inten-sionality' is a rare word, little used outside philosophical circles, it concerns matters which are very common and familiar. I will explain it with a fictional example. Suppose Lady Rotherhithe has been murdered, and suppose that the butler did it. Then the butler is the murderer; the person who is the murderer is the very same person who is the butler. This means that in a large number of sentences the expressions 'the murderer' and 'the butler' are interchangeable. For example, if it is true that the butler is six feet two inches tall, then it is true that the murderer is six feet two inches tall; if the murderer used arsenic to kill Lady Rotherhithe, then the butler used arsenic to kill Lady Rotherhithe; if the butler likes cocoa, then the murderer likes cocoa; and so on. This means that in certain sentences the two expressions 'the butler' and 'the murderer' can be substituted for each other. For example, if 'The butler likes cocoa' is true, we can substitute 'the murderer' for 'the butler' to obtain the sentence 'The murderer likes cocoa', and this sentence will be true also, in virtue of the truth of the first sentence; similarly, if 'The butler likes cocoa' is false, then 'The murderer likes cocoa' will also be false. Where expressions are substitutable in this way, with the truth-value of the first sentence preserved in the second sentence, we have extensionality. But there are also many sentences where 'the butler' and 'the murderer' are not mutually substitutable. Suppose that Inspector Sleuth comes to investigate the death of his old friend Lady Rotherhithe. He knows the household well, including the butler. Now Sleuth does not yet know that the butler did it. It is certainly true that Sleuth wants to discover the identity of the murderer; but it is not true that Sleuth wants to discover the identity of the butler. That is to say, in the sentence 'Sleuth wants to discover the identity of the murderer' the term 'the butler' is not substitutable for 'the murderer' *salva veritate*; while 'Sleuth wants to discover the identity of the murderer' is true, 'Sleuth wants to discover the identity of the butler' is false. Sleuth may also hope that the murderer will be punished severely; but he does not thereby hope that the butler will be punished severely; it does not follow from the truth of 'Sleuth hopes that the murderer will be punished severely' that 'Sleuth may also hope that the butler will be punished severely' is also true. Sleuth remembers that, during his last visit, the butler had a heavy cold; but he does not remember that the murderer had a heavy cold; while 'Sleuth remembers that the butler had a heavy cold' is true, 'Sleuth remembers that the murderer had a heavy cold' is certainly false. In such sentences as these, where 'the butler' and 'the murderer' are not mutually substitutable *salva veritate*, we have intensionality. The butler is the same person as the murderer, but when Sleuth remembers that that person had a heavy cold, his memory is of that person *under a particular description*, namely as the butler. What makes it impossible to substitute 'the murderer' for 'the butler' in the sentence 'Sleuth remembers that the butler had a heavy cold' is that, although the descriptions 'the murderer' and 'the butler' refer to the same person, they do not have the same meaning. Intensionality enters into our discourse when what is important is not simply the people, things, events and qualities that we are talking about, but the descriptions under which we talk about them. This is often the case when what we say concerns people's knowledge, attitudes, desires, emotions, and so on.

The intensionality of desire

Desire is intensional. Suppose I am a great fan of Brahms, and I have recordings of most of his chamber music, except the string quintets. I have heard the quintets and like them very much. So I want to buy a recording of them. In these circumstances, if I want to buy some recording of the string quintets of Brahms, then it is under the description 'recording of the string quintets of Brahms' that I want it. That normally implies at least that a recording's being of the string quintets of Brahms is a necessary condition of my buying it; if it isn't of the Brahms string quintets, I won't buy it. So I go in search of a recording. Now it happens that the particular recording I light upon and decide to buy has a picture of trees on the case. But I do not therefore desire it under the description 'recording with a picture of trees on the case'. It is not a necessary condition of my buying it that it have a picture of trees on the case; it may be a matter of complete indifference to me what picture is on the case. I desire the recording as a recording of the Brahms string quintets, not as a recording with a picture of trees on the case. To put the same point in another way, what stirs my desire, what moves me to want to buy the recording, what interests me about it, is that it is of the Brahms string quintets, not that it has a picture of trees on the case. Though the recording which is of the Brahms string quintets is the very same recording which has a picture of trees on the cover, it interests me under the description 'recording of Brahms string quintets', and not under the description 'recording with a picture of trees on the cover'. What my interest is, the description under which I am interested in this recording, I will call the point of my desire. The point of my desire can be discovered in a number of ways. For instance, I can be asked about it. If I am asked what kind of recording I want, I will answer: 'a recording of the Brahms string quintets' and not: 'a recording with a picture of trees on the cover'. If when I have bought the recording I am asked why I bought that particular recording, I will answer: 'because it is of the Brahms string quintets' and not: 'because it has a picture of trees on the cover'. Even without asking me on this occasion, an observer might be able to make an intelligent guess as to the point of my desire. If I listen regularly to the music of Brahms, if on suitable occasions I wax lyrical about it, if I never show any particular interest in pictures of trees or in the cases of recordings, then anybody in a position to see is also in a position to see that it is very likely indeed that on this occasion, when I buy this recording, what interests me is that it is a recording of Brahms quintets, and not a recording with a picture of trees on the cover. It is possible in certain cases to work long and hard in order to discover the point of somebody's desire, rummaging through libraries, interviewing acquaintances, and so on; but the quickest, surest and simplest way, if available, is to ask the interested person himself. Then, in the normal case,[8] that person's answer settles the question. The question would normally take the form 'Why do (did, will) you want to ... ?' and the answer the form 'Because I (you, he, she, it, we, they) ... '. Take the example of the recording. The basic question you need to ask to discover the point of my desire, what I am interested in, is 'Why do you want to buy that disc?' Then my answer will be something like 'Because I need a recording of the Brahms string quintets.' That answer establishes definitively (subject to correction only by myself) that this is why I want to buy the disc. You cannot reasonably say to me, unless accusing me of lying or forgetting: 'No, you are wrong. You want it because of the trees on the cover.' Nevertheless, it remains true that the recording I want does have a picture of trees on the cover. This means that there is an ambiguity in the sentence 'I want a recording with a picture of trees on the case.' What it would normally be taken to mean is that I am in search of, have set my desire on, am interested in, a recording with a picture of trees on the case. In that normal sense, the sentence is in this case false.[9] But it could also mean 'The recording I want has, as a matter of fact, a picture of trees on the case.' In that sense, the sentence is true. It is true if taken as a statement about one of the qualities that the recording I want happens to have, but false if taken as a statement about the nature of my desire, or about what I am interested in, or what it is about a particular recording that makes me want it.

Homosexual desire

I have already suggested above that the word-pair homosexual/ heterosexual might be less useful that we sometimes think it is. This is because if we are told that Christopher and Anne both experience what we call homosexual desire, this does not tell us that they have any common experience, but rather experiences the objects of which are quite different. But we can now see another reason for being careful about 'homosexual' and 'heterosexual'. Suppose, again, that Christopher desires David sexually; this is a form, no doubt very complicated, of desire. We have seen that intensionality is often at work in desire, and so it is here. There are those who believe that the essence of homosexual desire is that one desires another instance of the same: man desires man, woman desires woman; same desires same, and for some theologians that is what is wrong with homosexuality, for we are made to desire the other (or the Other).[10] This is certainly suggested by the term 'homosexual'. But in a case of homosexual desire do we really have same desiring same? Of course, Christopher desires David, Christopher is a man and David is a man, so the person desired is of the same sex as the person desiring. But does this tell anything substantial about the desire: that it is a desire for the same? Remember that in cases of desire, because intensionality is central, we need to establish what I have called the point of the desire. We need the answer to the question 'Why do you want ... ?' and the easiest way to find that is to ask the person desiring. In this particular case, if we ask Christopher why he desires David, his honest answer would have to be, if homosexual desire were desire for the same, something like: 'Because he is a person of the same sex as myself.' But this would surely be a most unlikely and puzzling, even impossible, answer. Christopher knows or knows of many people of that description – all his male friends and acquaintances, all the men he passes on the street, all those he sees on television, etc. Yet, though they are of the same sex as himself, he does not desire them as he desires David; to most of them he is indifferent, by some even repelled. Christopher's answer is likely to be much more specific, perhaps one dwelling on David's fine qualities: his kindness and generosity, his intelligence, his patience, and so on; or perhaps Christopher himself will be mystified as to the reason for his desire. At any rate, it is his answer that settles the question, and that answer will almost certainly not be couched in terms of desire for the same. The conception that homosexual desire is desire for the same (David is after all of the same sex as Christopher) tells us nothing about the nature of the desire, and so nothing about those who have homosexual desires; it is uninformative and misleading.[11] We have found several reasons to be dissatisfied with the term 'homosexual', in more than one context. Nevertheless, since it is current I will continue to use it, but bearing in mind the reservations arising from our investigation. And, in order to show that I sit lightly to it, I shall use other terms as equivalents; the reader will already have noticed that I use 'gay' and 'same-sex'. I am not arguing the equivalence of the three terms, merely stipulating it in this book as a reminder of the inadequacy of 'homosexual'.

The intensionality of condemnation

Ambiguity is important in several ways in a Christian discussion of homosexuality. One situation in which it arises is in the discussion of the attitude expressed in biblical texts towards homosexual acts, as we shall see later. But intensionality and the ambiguity surrounding it are not confined to desire; they turn up in many situations. To take one important one, there is condemnation. Suppose I condemn a particular French novel. I might condemn it for its use of language, whereas you, who do not know this, may believe I condemn it just because it is French. Now, as a matter of fact, the sentence 'The book I condemn is French' is true. Nevertheless, your belief would normally be taken as false, because you have caught on to the wrong description under which I have condemned the book, for I condemned it not under the description 'French', but under the description 'misusing language'. So to be correct, you have to find out the point of my condemnation, what it is in this book that I find objectionable. Note that you may be particularly disinclined to undertake the necessary labour if you yourself are francophobe; in that case, it may seem obvious to you that a book should be condemned just because it is French. Now think of the 'condemnation of homosexual acts' in Leviticus 18:22. Certainly, the act of which the author speaks is what we would describe as a homosexual act, but does he actually condemn this act under the description 'homosexual' or something so close to it as not to matter? It may seem obviously so to many, but that appearance may be due more to the preconceptions of the readers than the intentions of the author. Truly to understand the text we need to forget readers' preconceptions and do what we can to discover the author's intentions (which may of course turn out to be the same as the preconceptions). This will be a large element of our approach in the following chapters. After this second rather long and technical prologue, we now turn at last to the study of those biblical texts reputed to concern homosexuality.

CHAPTER THREE

The Bible Against Homosexuality?
I: Introduction and Old Testament Texts

Introduction

The Bible has always been an important factor in Christian moral thinking. There have been disagreements as to what its exact place should properly be. For some, it has been the source of morality as well as of doctrine; for others, it has been rather an aid to moral discernment. In the Protestant tradition, the former position has tended to dominate, at least in theory. Among Catholics, the picture is more mixed. Thomas Aquinas held that all the necessary ethical principles were – in principle – discernible by human reason alone, Christ and the apostles merely adding a few details to the moral law;[1] the moral norms of the Bible serve simply to make morality clear to those – the vast majority of humankind – unable to work it out for themselves.[2] More recently, accompanying the revival of biblical studies in the Catholic Church, there has been a renewed emphasis on the Bible as the basis of morality.[3] There are several aspects to a proper examination of the relation between the Bible and homosexual acts. There are texts which, it is often claimed, explicitly condemn these acts; so we need to examine those texts in some detail to find out what they say; that will be the task of this chapter and the next. Again, it is claimed that there are also texts which do not mention homosexual acts but which propose a vision of human sexuality which excludes homosexual acts because they run counter to the values expressed in that vision. So these texts also have to be examined carefully, to see whether they do indeed propose any vision of human sexuality and whether homosexual acts are incompatible with that vision; this we will do in Chapter 5. But we also have to ask some wider questions: Should we expect to find a condemnation of homosexual acts as such in the Bible? If there are texts which, in one way or another, imply a negative attitude towards some or all homosexual acts, what is the value of these texts for us, and what do they imply for our own attitude towards same-sex activity? There are many biblical texts and biblical attitudes which we happily ignore; should we ignore the ones which seem to exclude homosexual acts as well? If so, why? Or should we take them seriously? If so, why?

Dangers in reading the Bible

The first step will be to look at the texts often claimed to condemn same-sex practices. The texts most often cited in this connection are Genesis 19, Leviticus 18:22 and 20:13, Romans 1:26–7, 1 Corinthians 6:9 and 1 Timothy 1:10; it will be necessary to look at each of these in turn, to see what they actually say and do not say. There are exegetical problems with some of these texts; sometimes it is just not clear what they are saying. But there is another kind of difficulty, which lies on the side of the reader rather than of the text itself. Few of us are neutral when it comes to the question of same-sex practices. For some of us, they are fine and natural; for others, inadmissible and even abominable. Whatever our view, we may be inclined, if we take the Bible at all seriously, to want to find that view expressed in biblical texts. At the very least, those who look unfavourably on same-sex practices will want to find a condemnation of them in the Bible, while those who see them positively will want to find, if possible, a positive endorsement of them, and if that is not possible, then at least the absence of a clear condemnation. Such attitudes as these are almost bound to hinder an objective reading of what the Bible actually says. Another, related difficulty is that authoritative voices in the church have put their weight behind an interpretation of these texts which sees them as condemning same-sex relations. Thus *HP* §6 cites all the texts I have listed, and interprets them all as in one way or another expressing a negative attitude towards homosexual people and acts; and the 1992 *Catechism of the Catholic Church* claims that the Bible 'presents homosexual acts as acts of grave depravity' (§2357), citing most of the same texts appealed to by *HP* §6.[4] Anybody concerned to uphold authority in the church may be inclined a priori to think that the authoritative voices must be right, and that our texts must mean what the authorities say they mean. To suggest otherwise would be to question authority; and if those who speak authoritatively for the church can have been wrong on this matter, they might have got other, more central points wrong as well, which is not to be contemplated. Unfortunately there is also sometimes a climate of fear in the church, which makes people unwilling to contemplate an interpretation of these texts which is at variance with the official interpretation, for fear of being accused of dissent, and of any negative consequences they might suffer. Such fear is not conducive to an honest and objective reading of the relevant texts. There are thus factors which incline anybody in this debate not to let the texts speak for themselves; and, whatever side we take in the debate, we must be constantly on our guard against our own presuppositions, prejudices and fears. An honest reading of the texts presupposes that, while we may indeed hope they support our position, we are prepared to acknowledge that in fact they do not; while we may hope that they do not speak against our position, we must be prepared to accept that in fact they do. I can do no better in this connection than to quote Enzo Cortese, Professor of Old Testament Studies at the Studium Biblicum Franciscanum, Jerusalem:

> It sometimes happens that in today's heated discussions of homosexuality we see somewhat hasty references to the Bible, which after a rigorous analysis prove rather unconvincing and somewhat simplistic. The Old Testament has also been used in this way, as often happens, on the basis of a certain predetermined understanding of the text, i.e., from a preconceived starting point. In our case, such prejudices are sometimes motivated by a benevolent attitude which, even if partly justifiable and proper, cannot do away with the need for honest objectivity, to avoid being influenced by any prejudice in interpreting the Bible's moral teaching.[5]

Cortese's insistence on rigorous analysis independent of any preconceived starting point should always be borne in mind when reading our texts. But his remarks need some amplification. He suggests that one temptation seducing us away from a rigorous objectivity may be 'a benevolent attitude'. Given the context in which he writes his article, and that article's content, we may guess that he means a human sympathy with homosexuals which might make the exegete reluctant to see them condemned by Scripture. If so, his warning is surely correct. But there is another side to the coin. One's understanding of a text may be predetermined by, for instance, the fact that the CDF has already published an opinion on the meaning of the text, and by a desire, from whatever motive, to support the Congregation's interpretation. Objectivity may also be compromised by the feeling that one must support an official view of the text, out of fidelity to authority or out of fear of voicing a contrary opinion. For some, a temptation in this direction will undoubtedly be greater than a temptation do undue sympathy for homosexuals. But if there is an official interpretation of a text, and if it is a sound one, it will need no biased exegesis to support it. If, on the other hand, unbiased exegesis does not support the official interpretation, then the official interpretation needs to be challenged and revised. Before coming to a study of the relevant texts, it is necessary to say a few words first about the use of the Bible, and then, since we are concerned with purported biblical condemnations of homosexual acts, about the logic of condemnation.

Use of the Bible in discussing homosexuality

There are several points to be borne in mind when reading the Bible in connection with homosexuality. First, talk of unanimity presupposes that we can actually understand adequately all the texts in question. But understanding biblical texts, even at the surface level, can sometimes be very difficult. The social, political, cultural and religious contexts within which these texts were written are not ours, and are often very foreign to us. It is often the context of a text – not only the literary context in which the text is embedded but also and more importantly the culture which author and readers share and which enables so much to be left unsaid – which makes it readily intelligible to its original audience, and the lack of that context that makes its original meaning difficult for us to grasp. Even if the meaning seems fairly obvious, we can still get it wrong. One reason why the meaning of a text might seem obvious to us is that we as readers have our own social, political, cultural and religious contexts, which may make a certain way of reading a text appear natural, even compelling. But in view of the huge gulf between biblical times and our own age, this impression can be very deceptive. This is a reason why we should tend to be modest in our claims to understand a given text, initially at least. Secondly, suppose we do feel confident about our understanding of a text and are justified in that confidence, and suppose we understand that text as condemning a particular activity. It is then important to know also, as best we can, *why* the text in question condemns that activity, what it is about the activity that makes it objectionable according to the text. For rational human beings, if an activity is objectionable it is for a reason, and one which can in principle be stated. If the activity is objectionable, that is because there is something about it which is objectionable. If we are to see the Bible as in any sense a guide to behaviour, we must, if we are reasonable, suppose that biblical attitudes to activities are not arbitrary; that the Bible does not condemn certain acts and recommend others for no reason at all. So if a given biblical text condemns an activity, it is for a reason or for a number of reasons. If we see the Bible as, at least some-times, expressive of God's will for how we, whom he has created as rational, are to live, this criterion amounts to saying that we cannot conceive the will of God for us as arbitrary; if God condemns an activity, it cannot be for no reason at all. If for us a biblical text that condemns an activity expresses the fact that God forbids us to engage in that activity, God's interdiction must be intelligible to us; we must be able to give some reason why God forbids us to do this particular thing. But, if the meaning of a particular text – what it says – can be obscure, so, by the same token, can the reason why it says what it says. So, even if we can establish beyond reasonable doubt that a given text condemns a particular activity, we are still left with the task of understanding *why* it condemns it. If we cannot understand why, then the condemnation appears unintelligible to us, and we cannot incorporate it into any ethical system which appears rational to us. This point also has a bearing on the question of biblical unanimity. It is often alleged that the texts in question form a significant group, in the sense that they are all the biblical texts which mention same-sex practices, and that they all agree in condemning them. There are, it is said, no biblical texts which speak of such practices in a positive way. Thus, so the claim goes, not only are these texts unanimous in condemning homosexual acts, but, as the sum total of what the Bible has to say in connection with those acts, they show that the Bible condemns them clearly, firmly, unwaveringly and unanimously. There may be areas of human life in which the biblical witness is uncertain or divided, or where the New Testament corrects the imperfect vision of the Old. But in this particular case there is no doubt, no hesitation and no division; Old and New Testaments speak with one, clear voice. The implications for the modern church are obvious: in the face of this biblical unanimity, anybody who pretends to take the Bible seriously – and surely all faithful Christians do – has no option but to adopt the same attitude and condemn homosexual acts. The question of what counts as unanimity does not seem much to trouble those writers who claim that the Bible unanimously condemns same-sex activity. Often, a brief survey of the texts in our group, with the observation that they all condemn homosexual activity, seems to suffice. Thus, for example, Lawler, Boyle and May, in the course of their short discussion of the morality of homosexual acts, say simply of these texts: 'there are specific biblical passages referring to homosexual acts, and in each of these passages such acts are unambiguously condemned'.[6] Again, *HP* asserts simply:'[T]here is ... a clear consistency within the Scriptures themselves on the moral issue of homosexual behaviour. The Church's doctrine regarding this issue is thus based, not on isolated phrases for facile theological argument, but on the solid foundation of a constant Biblical testimony' (§5). But, despite this confidence, there are real difficulties here.

To establish that the Bible speaks with one voice on a particular subject – say, homosexual acts – it is not enough to establish that all the relevant texts condemn homosexual acts; we also have to understand why each text condemns them, for apparent agreement can hide deeper disagreement. Suppose that, in a small, far-away republic, the Centre Party is in power and proposes a modest land-reform measure. The proposal is attacked both by the People's Revolutionary Socialist Party and by the National Front for Patriotism, Law and Order. They both agree in condemning the government proposal, so a foreigner, unaware of local political issues and ignorant of why the various parties condemn what they do, may assume there is unanimity between the PRSP and the NFPLO. But in fact the PRSP condemns the government proposal because it finds that the CP is refusing to put an end to the exploitation of the peasants by the landowners, while the NFPLO condemns it as a destabilizing attack on property rights and social order. The surface unanimity between the two parties hides a deeper difference. In the same way, it cannot be assumed without more ado that if two biblical texts condemn homosexual acts, they do so for the same, or even compatible, reasons. They may well do, but they may not, and only further investigation will tell. Even with further investigation we may be left in ignorance as to the reasons why the various texts condemn what they do, so that it may be impossible to discover whether we are dealing with a real unanimity or not. A third point concerning use of the Bible is the question of what importance we should attribute to the views of biblical texts, even if we can establish that they all adopt the same stance and for the same, or at least complementary, reasons. Suppose that a biblical text, as we understand it, condemns an activity for a particular

61

reason or complex of reasons. Stating those reasons gives the reason why, in the view of the text, the activity is objectionable. But stating those reasons does not necessarily convince us, today's readers, that that activity is objectionable. For a variety of reasons, modern Christians do not always have the same moral outlook as the authors of the Bible, particularly of the Old Testament. To take an example at random, suppose it turned out that an activity was clearly condemned in the Bible, and that it became apparent that the reason why it was condemned depended on a world-view which saw pigs as ritually unclean and rendering those who ate them unfit to take part in worship. Then the condemnation of that activity could not carry conviction for us, because we just do not, as Christians, think that pigs are unclean in this way. Or suppose it turned out that a biblical text condemned an activity for reasons closely tied up with the view that women were intrinsically inferior to men. Not all Christians have always rejected this view, but in modern mainstream Christianity it is quite unacceptable; so, for modern mainstream Christians, the fact that this text condemned the activity would be no reason at all for us to condemn it. In general, what counts as a reason for a biblical text to condemn an activity need not count as a reason for us. Indeed, the condemnation of a particular activity in a biblical text may be based on reasons we actively reject and find repulsive. In such a case, the fact that the text condemns a given activity gives us *no reason at all* to condemn it ourselves. This does not mean that it is perfectly acceptable to engage in that activity. We may have many perfectly good reasons to condemn it, but the fact that the text condemns it will not be one of them. To see whether and how a particular text's condemnation of the activity in question is pertinent to our moral evaluation of that activity we need to examine the reasons for the condemnation, the values that lie behind it, to see whether they are consonant with what we count as authentic Christian values. (And, of course, our sense of what are authentic Christian values will be shaped in some measure by the Bible and the way we read it.) So it could be that, for example, a careful reading of the story of Sodom and Gomorrah in Genesis 19 really did show that it condemns all same-sex activity. This would not by itself be a reason why modern Christians should also condemn all same-sex activity. We should also have to enquire into the reason behind this condemnation. If we could not find a reason why the text condemned it, then the text's condemnation would remain unintelligible to us; it would appear totally arbitrary. So it would be impossible to adduce it in support of a reasoned, non-arbitrary condemnation of same-sex activity. Or suppose that we could find out with reasonable certainty why the text condemned same-sex activity, and it turned out that the text's condemnation was founded upon reasons compelling at the time but indifferent to us, or that it presupposed views that were actually repugnant to us, then Genesis 19's condemnation would give us no reason at all to condemn same-sex activity. The same considerations apply to any number of texts. If there are, say, six texts that clearly condemn same-sex practices, and if each one of them does so for reasons which, as far as we can discern them, are irrelevant or antithetical to a modern Christian outlook, then none of them entails that modern Christians should evaluate these practices negatively; and the fact that these texts are unanimous in their condemnation (if they are) and represent the sum total of what the Bible has to say on the subject adds no weight to them at all. Biblical passages may be liable to misinterpretation if we are blind to the fact that the concerns of biblical authors are sometimes very different indeed from our own. If we are inclined to think in modern Christian terms and hold modern Christian values, and if we think of the Bible as basically a Christian book, we may assume automatically that a passage like Leviticus 18:22 expresses a condemnation of what the church condemns, and that it condemns it for reasons broadly similar to those for which the church condemns it. This *may* be so, but a study of the Bible reveals that the values of the biblical authors are sometimes far removed from and incompatible with the values of the modern church. This should give us pause, and make us at least wonder whether the standard 'anti-homosexual' texts give genuine support to the church's position, or whether the support is more apparent than real.

The logic of condemnation

Condemnation, like praise and all evaluation, is intensional. That is to say, acts (or relationships or people, or whatever it may be) are condemned under a particular description. We have already met the intensionality of condemnation briefly in the previous chapter. To see its relevance here, we need to take a closer and longer look at a simple example. Suppose I drive into town to shop. I see a space conveniently near the shop I wish to visit and park there. So intent am I on my shopping, and so glad to find a space, that I do not notice that I park on a double yellow line. A traffic warden sees my car parked on the double yellow line and gives me a parking ticket. Let us say that her giving me a ticket is a kind of legal condemnation of my act. Now my act of parking on this double yellow line is one and same act as my parking in a space conveniently near the shop I wish to visit. That is to say, there are (at least) two perfectly good descriptions of what I am doing when I park where I do: I can be described as parking conveniently near to the shop I wish to visit, and I can be described as parking on a double yellow line. In some kinds of sentence these two descriptions can be substituted one for the other without loss of truth. For example, if it is true that I park in the space conveniently near to the shop I wish to visit at 1:02 pm, then it is also true that I park on the double yellow line at 1:02 pm. These are extensional sentences. Sentences expressing condemnation are, by contrast, intensional. If we ask why, for what act, the traffic warden condemns me in this way, a true answer would be to say that she condemns me because I parked on the double yellow line. But it would not be true to say that she condemns because I parked in a space conveniently near to the shop I wish to visit. She may not have the least interest in whether I park in a space conveniently near to any shop; what she cares about is that I have parked on a double yellow line. She condemns, not simply my act however described, but my act *under a particular description*. In condemning my act, she condemns an act which is, as a matter of fact, an act of parking conveniently near to the shop; but she does not condemn it *as* an act of parking conveniently near to the shop.[7] As well as saying that she condemns my act, we can say that she condemns me. We might say: she condemns me *for* parking on a double yellow line. Though it is true that I park conveniently near to the shop, she does not condemn me *for* parking conveniently near to the shop. Since it is true of me that I have parked conveniently near to the shop, the traffic warden, in condemning me, condemns a person who has parked conveniently near to the shop. Nevertheless it would in most circumstances be highly misleading to report that she condemns somebody who has parked conveniently near to the shop, for this would normally give the impression that the parking near the shop was the reason for her condemnation, whereas in fact it is quite irrelevant to it. A further important point is that of the two descriptions of my act one gives access to the rationale of the condemnation, while the other will not. The traffic warden condemns my act as an act of parking on a double yellow line. Parking on double yellow lines is illegal, and that for a variety of reasons: double yellow lines are put down where parking would clog up the road and make life miserable for all local motorists, or in order to keep an entrance free for essential vehicles, and so on. The warden does not condemn my act as an act of parking conveniently near to the shop. It is not illegal to park conveniently near to shops one wishes to visit. There is no general puritanical sentiment that such parking is self-indulgent and that all self-indulgence should be discouraged by law. To have a hope of understanding the reasons behind the condemnation, we need to start off from the correct description, the description under which the act is actually condemned, rather than some possible alternative description. But starting with the correct description is not enough if we want to understand the reasons behind it. In the parking case we need to know the system of traffic signs of which double yellow lines form a part, and we need to know the prevailing traffic and road conditions in Britain which make it useful to have this system of signs and useful to forbid people from parking in particular places at particular times. This knowledge is essential for a correct and adequate understanding of what the traffic warden is doing. Somebody ignorant of British life may be perplexed about this; in an attempt to understand it, he may develop weird hypotheses about the British mentality. He might think the British hold the colour yellow to be sacred, and that parking on anything yellow is a kind of sacrilege; or he might think that the British hold it unclean for cars to come into contact with double lines of any colour. He would be particularly prone to do this if in his own society certain colours were held to be sacred, or if double lines were thought unclean.

When we are looking at biblical texts which condemn certain acts, we need, in order to understand those condemnations correctly, to be clear under what description the acts are condemned, what they are condemned *as*. We then have to understand correctly the rationale for the condemnation. The second task in particular is difficult. Biblical texts tend not to state explicitly why they condemn what they do; such explanations may well have been unnecessary, as the rationale of the condemnation may have been obvious to contemporaries. But to us, who live a long time afterwards and in a very different culture, the lack of explanation is a bar to understanding. We have to guess at the explanation, as intelligently as we can, by looking around the text concerned at other texts which will illuminate for us the culture and the mentality in which the condemnation had its original home.

The concept of homosexuality in the Bible?

What would make the task of understanding and evaluating biblical texts easier, in the context of a discussion of homosexuality, would be if there were in biblical Hebrew or Greek a word that was unproblematically translatable as 'homosexual'. Then Lot could have said to the men of Sodom: 'Don't do this thing; it is homosexual and therefore wicked'; the law of Leviticus could have run: 'With a man you shall not lie the lyings of a woman; it is homosexual and an abomination'; St Paul could straightforwardly have condemned all homosexual activity instead of resorting to neologisms and circumlocutions. But none of this occurs in the Bible. Notoriously, there is no word in biblical Hebrew or Greek which is the equivalent or near equivalent of our 'homosexual'. This has a bearing on the present discussion, for we have said that condemnation of an act is condemnation under a particular description. If there is no biblical word which can correctly be translated 'homosexual', then no biblical description of an act as homosexual is possible; but that seems to mean in turn that no biblical condemnation of an act under the description 'homosexual' is possible; and that means that, while some of the acts the Bible condemns can be correctly described as homosexual (by us who have the word), no biblical text can condemn any act *as* homosexual. So it would seem that any attempt to show that the Bible does condemn homosexual acts is doomed to failure before it begins. But this is a little hasty. We sometimes have a place for a word in our discourse without having the word itself. We find that we categorize people, things or events in a new way which our present vocabulary allows us to express only clumsily; we can then invent a new word to do the job more elegantly. This is presumably how the word 'homosexual' itself came about; certain people wanted to group people in general into those who were sexually attracted to people of the same sex as themselves and those who were not, and looked for a word to enable them to do this in an elegant way, rather than having to talk all the time about 'people who are sexually attracted to people of the same sex as themselves'. So, it has been argued, it is possible to have the *concept* 'homosexual' without having the word itself.[8] Then it would be possible that the biblical writers had the concept of homosexuality even though they had no word for it. This is indeed possible, though one could equally argue that if we generate words to satisfy such a need and when our discourse has made a place for them, then the fact that there is no equivalent of 'homo-

sexual' in the Bible is an indication that the biblical writers had no
need for it and therefore did not think about sexual behaviour in
such a way as to make the word useful, so that the absence of the
word would after all indicate the absence of the concept.

There is another indication, apart from the lack of a certain
vocabulary, why there is no concept of homosexuality in the Bible.
Our word 'homosexual' when applied to acts groups together certain kinds of activity. We can easily list the central ones:

> anal penetration of one man by another (using the penis);
> fellatio performed on one man by another;
> manual stimulation of one man's penis by another;
> stimulation of one woman's clitoris by another, using her
> hand or some instrument;
> cunnilingus performed on one woman by another;
> passionate embracing and kissing between two men;
> passionate embracing and kissing between two women.

This list can be added to, and maybe some would like to shorten it.
No matter. The point is this: to have the concept of homosexuality
is to think of these activities as forming a group, and perhaps to
think of other activities as closely related to them. If there is evidence, say from the way a person writes, that she does think of these
activities as forming a group, that is also evidence that she has the
concept of homosexuality, or one closely related to it, whether she
uses the word or not. Similarly, if we wanted to know whether
somebody condemns certain acts because they are homosexual, we
would be interested in whether he grouped together just the acts in
our list under one condemnation. Somebody may well disapprove
of anal sex between men, but if he disapproves of anal sex between
men *because he disapproves of homosexual acts*, we should expect
him also to disapprove of one woman stimulating another's clitoris,
for that also is a homosexual act. Similarly, we would expect him to
disapprove of the other items on the list, for they are all homosexual
acts. He might disapprove of some more than others, for other
reasons, but if he disapproves of any one of these acts on the
grounds that it is homosexual, he will, on the same grounds, disapprove of the others. If he disapproves of one of these acts but not
of the others, then he does not disapprove of that one act because it
is homosexual. If, for instance, he disapproves of anal sex between
men but not of oral sex between men, then he does not disapprove
of anal sex between men because it is a homosexual act, but for

some other reason. It might turn out on further investigation that he disapproves of anal sex between two men and of anal sex between a man and a woman. In that case his disapproval is entirely unrelated to homosexuality, and we might surmise it has something to do with the sexual use of the anus. Again, if he disapproves of the mutual masturbation of two men but not of the mutual masturbation of two women, then he does not disapprove of male mutual masturbation because it is homosexual, but for some other reason, perhaps because he disapproves of wasting semen or of sex between two males. And so on.

So we can ask: do biblical writers group together sexual acts according to this list, or something substantially like it? Suppose, for example, that the author of Leviticus disapproves of anal sex between males. (It will be argued later that this is the sense of 18:22 and 20:13.) Is there any evidence that he also disapproves of any of the other activities on our list? The answer has to be negative. There is no mention of cunnilingus between two women, or of mutual masturbation between two men, or indeed of any other activity that we think of as homosexual. There are neither laws forbidding these activities, nor narratives expressing a negative attitude towards them; there is no reference to them at all, however oblique. A fortiori there is no evidence at all that the author of Leviticus considers these activities related. Hence there is no evidence at all that he has the concept of homosexuality. This result does not show that he did not have the concept of homosexuality, only that we have no reason to believe that he did. So while it is clear that he condemns one sexual act – the anal penetration of one male by another – that is a homosexual act, we have no reason to think that he condemns it *as* homosexual. Throughout the Bible, in fact, we nowhere find the activities in our list treated as a group. This is partly because most of them are not treated at all. So there is no evidence that there is a concept of homosexuality in the Bible. Certainly, some biblical authors are concerned with acts that we would call homosexual, and they condemn those acts; but there is no reason to believe that they are concerned with them or condemn *as* homosexual. To approach the relevant texts with the pre-conceived idea that they are about homosexual acts considered as homosexual is unwarranted. It is also likely to be a bar to understanding the real rationale behind the condemnations that these texts contain, by leading us to start our investigation at the wrong point, with the wrong description of the acts; it would be like trying to understand the condemnation of my parking offence on the basis of a description of it as parking conveniently near to a shop. With these points in mind we can turn to a discussion of the specific biblical texts usually held to condemn homosexual practice. These texts are spread over both the Old and the New Testaments. The New Testament passages form a natural group, in that they are all by Paul or followers of Paul. For reasons which will become clear, the Old Testament texts also form a group, so I shall treat them together, and turn to them first. We will come to the New Testament in the next chapter.

THE OLD TESTAMENT

Genesis 19:1–11

The story of the destruction of Sodom and Gomorrah features in many official church treatments of homosexuality, and was until recently often held to furnish biblical condemnation of homosexual acts. *HP* says of Genesis 19:1–11: 'There can be no doubt of the moral judgement made there against homosexual relations' (§6). As already noted, in the *Catechism of the Catholic Church* this passage is referred to, along with Romans 1:24–7, 1 Corinthians 6:10 and 1 Timothy 1:10, in support of the contention that the Bible 'presents homosexual acts as acts of grave depravity'.[9] The document *Homosexual Relationships*, issued by the Church of England's Board for Social Responsibility in 1979, asserts that the story of the destruction of Sodom and Gomorrah expresses 'abhorrence of homosexuality',[10] though this judgement is absent from the treatment of the same story in the 1991 document *Issues in Human Sexuality*. This difference between the two Church of England documents perhaps reflects a tendency on the part of some churches to distance themselves, in the light of recent biblical scholarship, from the earlier interpretation. As the above quotation from the *Catechism* indicates, however, the official Roman Catholic view is still that this text implies a condemnation of homosexual acts. Does an examination of the text support this judgement? Several considerations lead to a strongly negative answer. First, this story actually begins at Genesis 18:1, rather than at 19:1. Here the Lord appears (mysteriously, in the form of three men) to Abraham by the oaks of Mamre. In the verses that follow, Abraham invites the three strangers to sit and refresh themselves and eat a morsel of bread. When the strangers accept, Abraham goes and tells his wife Sarah not to bring some bread for the strangers, but to bake cakes from fine meal for them. He then runs and fetches a fat calf from his herd and tells his servant to prepare it for the visitors. He then serves them himself, giving them milk in addition, and standing in attendance like a servant while they eat (vv. 1–8). Abraham is the very model of humility and generous hospitality, and he is rewarded by the promise that his wife Sarah will bear him a son (vv. 9–15). It is at this point that two of the men leave to make their way to Sodom. The one that remains, now identified as the Lord, reveals to Abraham that he is going to Sodom to see if the city really is as wicked as people say: 'And the Lord said: "Because the outcry against Sodom and Gomorrah is great and because their sin is very serious, I will go down and see whether they have done altogether according to the outcry coming to me; and if not, I will know." And the men turned from there, and went to Sodom; but Abraham was still standing before the Lord' (vv. 20–2). There then follows the well-known dialogue between the Lord and Abraham in which Abraham gets the Lord to promise not to destroy the cities, despite their wickedness, if even ten good men are found in them (vv. 23–32). In this way the stories of Abraham's hospitality and the destruction of Sodom are closely linked. We are meant to see a connection and a contrast between the two episodes. Just as Abraham is rewarded for his hospitality by the promise of posterity, so, we are led to understand, the cities of the plain are completely destroyed, without hope of posterity, because of their flagrant inhospitality. This reading is confirmed in chapter 19 itself. When the two men (now identified as angels) arrive at Sodom they are again offered hospitality, this time by Lot, Abraham's nephew, who is not a citizen of Sodom but a resident alien. Like his uncle, Lot greets the angels (who, as verse 8 makes clear, he takes to be men) by humbly bowing to the ground. He invites them to lodge in his house for the night and offers them a feast. It is at this point that all the men of Sodom surround Lot's house, calling to him: 'Where are the men who came to you tonight? Bring them out to us, that we may know them' (v. 5). In context, this is almost certainly not, as Bailey claims, a demand to know the identity of the visitors, but a demand that Lot deliver them up that they might use them sexually.[11]

It is here that readers, including those in positions of authority in the churches, have sometimes seen a reference to homosexuality: the men of Sodom want to have sex with the two visitors, who are themselves men. (The men of Sodom, like Lot, are unaware that they are in reality angels.) The men of Sodom are, it is sometimes claimed, expressing homosexual desire (they never actually get to have sex with the visitors), and it is for this that they and their city, as well as the neighbouring city of Gomorrah, are destroyed. But this interpretation is inadequate, for several reasons. Note first Lot's reaction to the men's demand. He does not reply in the vein: 'Do not do this, for it would be homosexual'; or even: 'Do not do this, for it is a forbidden form of sex.' He says rather: 'Do nothing to these men, for they have come under the shelter of my roof' (v. 8). He appeals, that is, not to the sinfulness of (male) homosexuality, but to the fact that the men are his guests. Hospitality demands that the visitors be treated with honour, in fact as superiors; Lot, like Abraham, has bowed to the ground before them. To use them for sexual pleasure would be to dishonour them, to treat them as inferiors, and thus humiliate them. The behaviour of the inhabitants of Sodom is the very reverse of the hospitality that Lot, like Abraham, has shown. And as Abraham has been rewarded for his hospitality by the promise of a child, so the citizens of Sodom will be punished for their infringement of the hospitality due to guests. It is in order to carry out his obligations to the visitors whom he has brought under his roof that Lot seeks to protect them now from the sexual predations of the citizens of Sodom, and he will be rewarded in his turn by being warned to escape the city before it is destroyed.[12]

Secondly, it is clear that what the citizens of Sodom have in mind is rape; that is their projected evil deed. They do not want to share sexual activity with the visitors, but to subject them to sexual domination. They do not knock politely at the door to ask whether the visitors would care to partake in some sex play with them. They demand that Lot bring them out to them that they may 'know' them. The visitors themselves are to be reduced to a state of passivity. They are not asked to come out; Lot is to bring them out. That is, they are not even humanized by being addressed directly, they are treated as a commodity to be handed from Lot to the citizens. They are not invited to get acquainted; they are to be known. Their wishes are not consulted; they are to be treated as mere objects for the pleasure of the citizens. To be reduced to passivity is, according to the outlook of this story, to be humiliated. The humiliation is all the more marked since the two (supposed) men have enjoyed the status of honoured visitors. It is in the context of protecting the honour of his guests, those who 'have come under the shelter of my roof', that Lot offers the crowd his two virgin daughters to do with as they please. We are no doubt to believe that he loves his daughters, but they are subordinate members of his family, subject to his authority, effectively owned by him; they are not guests whose honour he is bound to protect. As virgins (as all unmarried girls were supposed to be), they are in a way part of Lot's economic assets. If they are raped by the crowd, this will imply suffering for them; but it will also imply an important economic loss for Lot. They will be practically unmarriageable,[13] so he will have to remain permanently responsible for their upkeep. Lot's gesture in offering the crowd his daughters is not, then, an effort to get them to commit a relatively acceptable heterosexual sin as opposed to an abominable homosexual sin; it shows the lengths to which he is prepared to go, what he is prepared to sacrifice, in order to protect the honour of his guests.[14] In short, what we have in Genesis 19 is not a story of homosexual desire punished by the destruction of the cities of the plain.[15] It is the story of inhospitality punished, in contrast with the preceding chapter, which shows us hospitality rewarded. It is not true, as *HP* claims, that 'there can be no doubt of the moral judgement made there against homosexual relations' (§6).[16]

Inhospitality always takes a particular form. It can be verbal insult, failure to offer food, even violent attack. In the case of Sodom and Gomorrah, it takes the form of attempted rape. It would be setting up a false antithesis to say that this narrative either condemns inhospitality or it condemns some sexual act; it condemns a sexual form of extreme inhospitality. The act which the men of Sodom perform can be described in (at least) two ways: as an act of inhospitality and as an attempt at committing a certain kind of sexual act. But it should be clear by now that it is for that act, considered as grossly inhospitable, that the men of Sodom are condemned, and not for that act considered as a homosexual act; they are condemned for being inhospitable, not for being homosexual. Because the visitors are angels, visitors from another world, the attempted rape is tantamount to sacrilege. Just as Abraham entertained angels unawares (see Hebrews 13:2), so the men of Sodom fail, unawares, to entertain the same heavenly beings, but outrage them. So it is fitting that they be visited with punishment from heaven, a rain of fire and brimstone (Genesis 19:24). The crime of the men of Sodom is, then, a complex one; it is at once a sexual form of inhospitality and a sexual insult to the divine. This is why the Epistle of Jude can say that they were punished for 'going away after different flesh' (v. 7).[17] But whatever it is, the crime is not one of attempted homosexual rape, except that the men *believe* that the angels are men like themselves. Though they may think that they are about to rape two men, we, the readers, know better.

Anti-homosexual interpretations of the story ignore this central and obvious point. Let us for the sake of argument ignore it too, and treat the story as one of a simple attempted homosexual rape. If we understand it in this (defective) way, then we can say that it expresses a condemnation of male homosexual rape, and not just of this particular attempted rape, but of male homosexual rape in general. But, of course, a condemnation of male homosexual rape is not a condemnation of all homosexual acts, not even of all male homosexual acts; there are many people who approve of some kinds of homosexual act but strongly condemn male homosexual rape. To condemn male homosexual rape is not to condemn homosexual acts in general, any more than to condemn heterosexual rape is to condemn heterosexual acts in general. Any act which is a homosexual rape is also a homosexual act, but to think that a condemnation of all homosexual rapes is therefore the condemnation of all homosexual acts is to commit more than one logical fallacy, including the fallacy of neglecting the intensionality of condemnation. This consideration suggests a simple thought experiment: in the place of the two angelic and apparently male visitors at the centre of this story, put two female visitors. If the story were of two women menaced with rape, followed by the destruction of the cities, nobody would dream of reading it at as a condemnation in narrative form of heterosexual acts. It would be plain to all that it was a story of attempted rape, with no evaluative implications beyond that for other forms of heterosexual behaviour. To understand the story in its actual form as a condemnation of homosexual acts in general is to read into the text something that is absent. The only reason for its being read as such is that readers have already, prior to reading, been determined to condemn homosexual acts and to find a biblical justification for their attitude. That justification is not to be found in the narrative if, following Cortese's advice, we read the text objectively. *HP*'s claim that '[t]here can be no doubt of the moral judgement made there against homosexual relations' is simply false; there is no such judgement.

Leviticus 18:22 and 20:13

If the story of Sodom and Gomorrah is not about same-sex activity, it is nevertheless significant that the visitors whom the men of

Sodom wish to rape are taken to be men. This can best be brought out by a look at the next Old Testament text often cited in support of a Christian condemnation of same-sex activity, Leviticus 18:22. It runs: 'With a male you shall not lie the lyings of a woman; it is an abomination'; or, in the less literal but more elegant rendering of the Revised Standard Version: 'You shall not lie with a male as with a woman; it is an abomination'.[18] This is a very short, and apparently clear, legal text. If in reading Genesis 19 one has to extract a moral from the narrative, so that it may remain doubtful whether one has extracted the correct moral, here there is no narrative veil covering the message. It is plain for all to see, and its meaning is apparently obvious: it condemns homosexual activity. And this condemnation does not come from the mouth of a minor Old Testament character; it is part of the law given by God himself to Moses to be handed on to the people of God.[19] The condemnation is repeated in oblique form in 20:13: 'A man who lies with a male the lyings of a woman, they have done an abomination, the two of them. They shall be put to death; their blood is upon them.'[20] But the meaning of 18:22 (and so also of 20:13) is not as clear as it might at first sight seem; at least, if some see it spontaneously as a condemnation of same-sex activity, it is not obvious that such an interpretation can be sustained. We may start with the observation that this law, like the narrative of Genesis 19, concerns only men. It is with a male that 'you' must not lie the lyings of a woman,[21] and the 'you' is a masculine singular pronoun.[22] What is forbidden here is what two men might do together. It does not concern women at all. This is not necessarily significant in itself. After all, the law generally speaks in masculine terms, whether in the second or in the third person. The law 'You shall not murder' (Exodus 20:13) is similarly addressed to a man, but this does not mean that women were permitted to murder. Though the laws are written in the masculine, that is, we might say, merely their literary form; they are actually applicable to women as well.

Sexual inequality in Israel

Such a response has much sense in it. From a Christian point of view, too, given that in Christ there is neither male nor female, it would be natural to say that the law – if applicable at all – is applicable to people without distinction of sex.[23] But not all Old Testament laws can be so easily generalized to those to whom they are not explicitly addressed. This is particularly true of laws concerning sexual behaviour, and one reason for it is the great institutionalized inequality between the sexes in ancient Israel.

For example, already in the law normally translated as 'You shall not commit adultery' (Exodus 20:14) things are more complicated. In Old Testament terms, male and female adultery are not the same offence. In our modern understanding of the term, adultery is a breach of marriage vows made by a married person who has sexual relations outside the marriage, and can be committed equally by a married man or a married woman. This was not the case in the society to which the law of Exodus 20:14 is addressed. As is well known, in ancient Israel marriage was not an equal partnership, a relationship between two equal people who had equal status even if they had different roles. Married women were considered as, roughly speaking, the property of their husbands. This is already indicated by the law of Exodus 20:17: 'You shall not desire your neighbour's house. You shall not desire your neighbour's wife or his male slave or his female slave, or his ox or his ass, or anything that is your neighbour's.' Here, the neighbour is masculine, and his wife is counted, along with his house, his slaves and his livestock, as his property. So it is that a man may repudiate his wife,[24] just as he may dispose of his property. But there is no provision for a wife to repudiate her husband; property cannot free itself from its owner. The idea of a wife as her husband's property cannot be pushed too far; she could not be sold or killed like a sheep. But there was a strong sense that a wife belonged to her husband as a husband did not belong to his wife. So a wife was praised for being useful to her husband and bringing him profit,[25] but there is never any indication that a husband ought to be useful to his wife. One special way in which a wife is useful is in providing her husband with children, especially sons. This inequality within the marriage relationship is only a special instance of a general inequality between the sexes in ancient Israel. Whatever the realities of private domestic existence, public discourse was dominated by men, and in this discourse, largely carried on by men, men dominate. Men and their interests are the centre of attention. Generally speaking, men are important in their own right, women in so far as they are important to men. Power was in the hands of men; the political leadership was almost always male-dominated, and the powerful priesthood was the exclusive preserve of men. In general, it was considered the role of men to be active, to lead, to command, to be strong, to possess, and of women to be passive, to follow, to obey, to be weak, to be possessed. While it was the lot of many to die in battle, at the hands of other men, it was considered shameful to be killed by a woman.[26] There are, of course, exceptional stories of women to be found in the Old Testament: one thinks immediately of Deborah, Esther and Judith. But part of the interest of these figures and their stories is precisely that they are exceptional; they show how God can act even through the weakness of women.[27]

Inequality between the sexes was part of the social structure of ancient Israel. The history of more recent times, particularly the last century or so, has made us very aware how contingent social structures are and how much they can be changed, even if they are of their nature resistant to change; we also know that there are explanations of particular social structures in terms of history, economics, and so on. 'Nature' is not an Old Testament term but to the people of ancient Israel their particular social structures were not contingent, appearing rather, as we would say, to be natural. That was how things were, and how they ought to be. Indeed, these structures were attributed to God himself. In particular, it was God who, according to their Scriptures, created and ordained sexual hierarchy. In the beginning, Adam and Eve were not created together for mutual help and comfort; Adam was created first, to serve God by tending the garden, and Eve was created afterwards to be a helper to Adam, to make life easier and more pleasant for him.[28] He exists for God, she exists for him. We will look at this story more closely later, in Chapter 5. We have noted the existence of Old Testament laws and narratives expressing a sense of sexual hierarchy. We, who are conscious of the contingency of social structures, might be inclined to see the origin of these laws precisely in that hierarchy, for laws are shaped by and express the public values of the society which frames them. But those who gave us the Old Testament did not believe that these laws were framed by their human governors or by their social institutions; they had their origin rather in God himself, who gave the law to Moses and to Israel through him. It was thus rather these laws that were believed to shape Israelite society rather than the other way round – or shape it to the extent that Israel was faithful to them. Thus any threat to this social order was not a sign of progress or a result of the play of economic forces or social pressures; it was an abhorrent rebellion against the 'natural' order of things, the order which went back to the very creative act of God himself.

In this society, where there was severe institutionalized and – so it was believed – divinely ordained inequality between the sexes, this inequality had its effect on how sexual activity was conceived. Sex took on a certain symbolic significance. Because, in a sexual relationship, the man was considered superior to the woman, their sexual activity was thought of as embodying this. Sex was conceived, not surprisingly, as basically penetrative. (That is, there hardly seems to have been a concept of 'sex', covering a range of different possible acts; but there was a preoccupation with penile-vaginal intercourse.) If a man sexually penetrated a woman, that meant that he subordinated her to himself, that he took her and treated her as his own.[29] If she was a willing partner, she effectively gave herself to him, acknowledged herself as his, and as subject to him, under his authority.[30] Sexual penetration was a symbolic taking and giving of possession. For a man to commit adultery was not for him to violate his marriage vows by having sex with another woman; it was for him to penetrate another man's wife; and that in turn meant that he treated her as his own, and so infringed the other man's property rights over her.[31] On the other hand, when a married woman committed adultery by having sex with a man who was not her husband she acted as if she were not her husband's, and so again infringed his property rights. Thus the victim of adultery, the one sinned against, was always a married man. A married man could not offend against his wife, for she had no rights over him.[32] Thus the Old Testament concept of adultery is markedly different from ours, because the Old Testament social structure was very different from ours, to the extent that it is possibly more misleading than helpful to use the word 'adultery' to translate the Hebrew term. Given that Israel had a deeply institutionalized sexual hierarchy, dominated by men, and that sexual activity was understood as an expression of this hierarchy, we should not assume that all Old Testament laws addressed to men applied equally to women, or can be applied to women without distorting the sense of those laws. This is particularly true where those laws concern sexual behaviour. Where there is a sexual hierarchy, and where sexual behaviour is held to express that hierarchy, there is liable also to be an asymmetry in the ways the sexual activities of men and of women are viewed. Certain things may be permitted to men that are not permitted to women, and vice versa. We have already in effect seen an example of this: while it was a serious offence, punishable by death, for a married woman to have sex with anybody but her husband,[33] there is no corresponding restriction on the sexual activity of a married man. He is, as far as the law is concerned, free to behave sexually practically as he wishes; all he has to avoid is sex with a woman who belongs to another man. Again, a girl was expected to be a virgin at the time of her marriage; if she is discovered not to be, the punishment is death.[34] But there is no legal obligation on a young man to remain a virgin before marriage.

Leviticus 18:22 and sexual hierarchy

There are reason for thinking that this asymmetry of sexual concern is at work in Leviticus 18:22 also; that is why there is no corresponding law prohibiting women lying together, and why it distorts the sense of this law to treat it as if it were applicable, *mutatis mutandis*, to women as well as to men. If we read it in the light of the above brief remarks on the sexual hierarchy that existed in ancient Israel, we can immediately see the possible significance of a law that forbids, not homosexual activity, but, as the law precisely says, lying with a man *the lyings of a woman*. The act forbidden might be one which is abhorrent because it violates the divinely ordained sexual hierarchy by putting a man in the position of a woman, the superior in the role of the inferior, the possessor in the place of the possessed. To see that this is in fact the case we have to ask first precisely what the act in question is: what is it to lie with a man the lyings of a woman? Evidently, it is not simply one man lying down with another, sharing the same bed. Some kind of sexual activity – as we would call it – is involved. But is 'lying with' engaging in any kind of sexual activity, such as kissing, embracing, stroking or mutual masturbation? Nowhere does the Old Testament evince concern with such activities. The act indicated by 'lie with' is almost certainly sexual penetration. This is strongly suggested by texts such as Genesis 19:30–6, where the daughters of Lot lie with (the same verb is used as in Leviticus 18:22) their drunken father and both become pregnant as a result. But we probably need not look that far. The verse immediately following the one which concerns us says: 'You shall not lie with any animal so as to defile yourself by it; and a woman shall not stand in front of an animal so that it lies down: that is confusion.' The language of this verse is not easy. The phrase I have translated 'lie with' is not the same as that in verse 22; a more literal translation would be 'You shall not set your lying on'. But the verb 'lie' corresponds to the same Hebrew root in each case. The difference in the phrases in the two verses suggests a reciprocity in the act of verse 22, where the Hebrew equivalent of the preposition 'with' occurs. In verse 23 it appears to be rather something that is imposed on the animal; there would of course be no question of seeking an animal's consent. It is difficult to imagine what might be envisaged in verse 23 if it is not sexual penetration of the animal. This impression is strengthened by the contrasting vocabulary of the rest of the verse, which forbids a woman, not to do the same thing, but to do a different but related thing. Here the woman is obviously being forbidden to offer herself for penetration by an animal. The verb I have translated 'lie down' (*raba'*) is quite different from the one translated 'lie with' (*shakab*). It is a relatively rare verb, but is used in the following chapter to denote the sexual coupling of animals.[35]

The evident fact that verse 23 is concerned with sexual penetration – by a man in 23a and of a woman in 23b – together with the similarity of vocabulary between 23a and 22, as well as the close proximity of these two laws, suggests very strongly that what is being forbidden in verse 22 is not just any sexual contact between men, but the sexual penetration of one man by another, anal intercourse.[36] The connection between 22 and 23a suggests, too, that it is the one who 'lies' who penetrates. This conclusion comes as no great surprise. But this little inquiry underlines the fact that the concern of this law is not all possible forms of what we would regard as sexual contact between men – 'male homosexual activity' in general – but the specific act of sexual penetration.[37] We have seen that penetration was not just 'having sex': it was a symbolic subordination, a taking possession. To penetrate a man was to do that to him. It was not to 'have sex' with him; it was to put him in the inferior position of a woman. The problem with this was not that it was a personal humiliation to the man concerned; he presumably was a willing partner to the act: 20:13, which prescribes the death penalty for this behaviour, appears to be concerned not with an act of rape but with a consensual act.[38] Certainly, the point of 20:13 is not to right a wrong done to a penetrated man who feels himself to have been humiliated. The offence is rather against the order of things. A man, who is, by the creative will of God, one who occupies a position in the social hierarchy superior to that of a woman has been symbolically put in the inferior place of a woman. The act has a symbolic sense which contradicts the divinely ordained sexual and social hierarchy. It is a breach in the hierarchical order of the world as created by God; hence it is an offence against God himself. It is now clear, I hope, that the concerns of Leviticus 18:22 are not with people behaving in a 'homosexual fashion', as *HP* suggests. The concern is with the maintenance of a sexual hierarchy conceived as divinely ordained. This law is not one expressed in masculine terms but applicable to all as an interdiction of same-sex activity whether between men or between women. On the contrary, it expresses a sense of a vast and vertical difference between the sexes; it cannot be extended to women without entirely destroying its sense. The act of anal penetration of one man by another which is forbidden here can be described in (at least) two ways. It is a homosexual act, and this might be the description of it that comes first to our minds, since the homosexual/heterosexual distinction is central to our classification of sexual acts. But it does not follow that this text condemns this activity *as* a homosexual act. Much more probably, given the Old Testament context, the text condemns the activity as one which undermines the God-given sexual hierarchy. So, when *HP* says that the author of this verse and 20:13 'excludes from the People of God those who behave in a homosexual fashion', this is quite correct if it means that the people condemned by these verses are ones who engage in a particular sexual practice which is in fact homosexual. But that does not show that, as *HP* appears to believe, these verses form part of a biblical condemnation of homosexual practices. That would only be so if the people excluded in these verses were excluded *for* engaging in a homosexual act, and we have no reason to think that is so. This point is of course related to the by now familiar theme of intensionality. If, in saying that the author excludes from the People of God those who behave in a homosexual fashion, *HP* wishes to say that in this law the author excludes people who behave in a way which is in fact homosexual, that is correct. But what it needs to say in order to makes its case is that the author excludes them *for* behaving in a homosexual fashion; that the ground of their exclusion is that their behaviour is homosexual. And that is false; or, at the very least, we have no reason to suppose it true, and much reason to prefer a different understanding of the text. This law has, then, nothing to do with same-sex activity as such. It is about what it is permissible for men to do to men and with men; what it forbids is, as it says quite clearly, a man treating a man sexually as he would treat a woman. What is at stake here is not a supposed divine plan of heterosexuality, but a supposed divine plan of male dominance. What this law depends on, and what it expresses, is the idea that God wills male superiority over the female; it also depends upon and expresses a conception of sexual penetration as a symbolic actualization of that superiority. Most modern Christians reject absolutely both of these ideas, officially at least. Not only does this law not support, *pace* a large number of Christian writers on sex, including the CDF, a condemnation of same-sex activity, but it is based on assumptions which are incompatible with modern Christianity. It is therefore quite inappropriate to appeal to this text in support of the thesis that God wants heterosexuality for us all. God may well want heterosexuality for us all, but Leviticus 18:22 has not the least tendency to show that he does.

The importance of quantifiers

There is a further, related difficulty about *HP*'s language here. When it says that 'the author excludes from the People of God those who behave in a homosexual fashion', there are four things this might mean, depending on what quantifiers we assume to be implicit in it:

1   the author excludes from the People of God *some* of those who behave in *some* homosexual fashion;
2   the author excludes from the People of God *all* those who behave in *some* homosexual fashion;
3   the author excludes from the People of God *some* of those who behave in *all* homosexual fashions;
4   the author excludes from the People of God *all* those who behave in *all* homosexual fashions.

HP uses Leviticus 18:22 and 20:13 as part of a general biblical case against homosexual acts in general; that is, against *all* homosexual acts committed by anybody whatsoever. So 4 must be the proper interpretation of *HP*'s claim.[39] In order for the text of Leviticus to support *HP*'s thesis, then, it has to exclude from the people of God all people who perform any homosexual act whatsoever. However, the text licenses at most, even if all my other arguments are wrong, interpretation 1. It is not about all people, but only males, and it is not about all forms of homosexual behaviour, but only homosexual anal intercourse. Standard anti-homosexual treatments of this text also illustrate the danger and inappropriateness of imposing the modern category of homosexuality on an ancient text like Leviticus 18:22. As we saw earlier, in Chapter 2, to think in terms of homosexuality is to think in terms of a single basic phenomenon with male and female instantiations. It treats the question of whether one is dealing with a male–male practice or a female–female practice as irrelevant, or at best secondary. What is important is only that the partners to whatever sexual act it may be are of the same sex. In societies where there is an important social distinction between the sexes, and where particular sexual acts are conceived of as expressive of social structure, the sex of each person concerned and the exact nature of the act are likely to be of capital importance. To think in terms of homosexuality is therefore a recipe for missing the point of a text like this.

Back to Genesis 19

And so we now finally have the explanation of the significance of the fact that men of Sodom want to rape *male* visitors. Not only do they commit, in seeking to perpetrate this rape, a gross violation of the law of love in the specific circumstances where people (as they believe) are seeking hospitality; they also seek to reduce Lot's male guests symbolically to the status of women, contrary to the will of God as expressed in creation. Their desire is not just for sex; this they could have had with Lot's daughters or with their own wives. They don't just want an orgasm; this they could have got by masturbating. They don't just want homosexual activity; this they could have got among themselves. They want to humiliate the (supposed) men sexually. And that is an offence not only against the men themselves as those to whom hospitality is due, but against God as the author of the sexual hierarchy. As we have already seen in Chapter 2, desire is intensional. The act whereby the men of Sodom seek to inflict this humiliation on their visitors is a homosexual act, a rape of men by men. But they do not desire to perform this act *as* a homosexual act; they desire to perform it under a different description, as an act which humiliates. So it is seriously misleading in this context to say without more ado that the men desire to perform a homosexual act, for that would normally be understood as asserting, falsely in this case, that the homosexuality of the act desired is part of the intensionality of the desire; it would imply that what the man are after, what they want to do, is to commit a homosexual act, whereas what moves them to want to commit the act is that it will humiliate the visitors, not that it is homosexual; their attack does not spring from homosexual desire.

Cortese and the men of Sodom

In the light of these remarks it is instructive to look at Cortese's treatment of this passage in his *Osservatore Romano* article. He writes:

> Now it is true that Lot's reason for opposing his fellow residents' demand to treat his two guests as they pleased does not exactly concern the vice in itself but only his duties of hospitality. Nevertheless, the attitude that the Sodomites resent is precisely Lot's opposition to their homosexual demands, to the point that he is paradoxically prepared to offer them his own daughters (cf. 19:8); this can only involve a condemnation of what is commonly called a sin against nature.

Despite showing awareness of the considerations of hospitality that I and many others have put forward, he concludes that this text does after all express disapproval of same-sex practices. (Given the context, this must be what he means by 'sin against nature'.) But his reasoning is fallacious. In saying that the attitude that the Sodomites resent is Lot's opposition to their homosexual demands, there is once again the attempt to smuggle in homosexuality where it does not belong. Of course, the citizens resent Lot's opposition to their demands, and of course we can describe their demands as homosexual, because we can describe the act they are demanding to perform as a homosexual act. But that does not imply that they resent Lot's opposition to their homosexual demands. Demand, like desire, is intensional.[40] The men of Sodom demand to be allowed to perform not a homosexual act but an act which will humiliate the visitors. This demand is opposed by Lot. Opposition, it will be no surprise, is also intensional.[41] Though the proposed act which Lot opposes can be described as a homosexual act, Lot does not oppose it *as* a homosexual act, but under a different description, as an act of gross inhospitality to his guests. Cortese's way of putting the matter implies wrongly that the resentment of the men of Sodom has something to do with the nature of their demands as homosexual, as if they would be less resentful if their demands were not homosexual. More importantly, it wrongly implies that Lot's opposition has to do with the homosexual nature of the demands. It is this that apparently licenses Cortese's conclusion that 'this can only involve a condemnation of what is commonly called a sin against nature'. But in reality the conclusion is not licensed. Cortese has indeed himself just conceded that Lot's refusal to accede to the demand is based 'only [on] his duties of hospitality'. If his reason is only his duties of hospitality, it is not an opposition to same-sex practices. Cortese's conclusion is conjured up out of nowhere, and rests on no more secure foundation than a fog of words. We may note also that it is misleading to say, as Cortese does, that the reason for Lot's opposition does not *exactly* concern 'the vice in itself'; rather, it does not *at all* concern same-sex practices. Cortese's language here gives the impression that though Lot's words are not exactly a condemnation of same-sex practices, they are pretty nearly so. But they are not; as Cortese concedes in the following phrase, they are *only* about his duties of hospitality. This is not a substantive point; it concerns only the rhetoric of Cortese's article. But it is not unimportant, for Cortese's language here is just one example of a quite common tendency among writers in this area to use misleading language, an implied or explicit misdescription of a text or a situation, in order to beg questions or to imply points that are not gained by argument.

What about the women?

There is a further important question concerning this story: what is the role of the inferiors in the sexual hierarchy, of the women? What, to begin with, about the women of Sodom? These, we are to presume, share in the general fate of the inhabitants of the cities of the plain. Since only Lot and his family are spared, we must believe that all the wives and daughters of the men of Sodom perish along with the men in the fire and brimstone. We have already noted how this story is couched in such terms as to justify the destruction of Sodom in the light of Abraham's dialogue with God: all the men of Sodom, young and old, take part in the attempted gang rape (19:4), so that not even ten righteous men are to be found in the city. But what about the women? They do not share in the assault on the visitors. Might not some of them be just? For the author of the story, it obviously does not matter. As far as this narrative is concerned, it is only male righteousness and male wickedness that count. (And this makes us sensitive now to the fact that, in that earlier dialogue, Abraham uses only masculine forms when he wonders whether there might be fifty, or even ten, righteous in the city.) The language of 19:4 is also revealing here. It emphasizes that the house was surrounded by 'the men of Sodom, from youth to old man, *the whole people*'. The men and youths of the town are equated with the whole people, and this without any kind of reserve or sense of irony. The entire female population of the city – surely at least half of the total – are simply not counted. It is as if they did not exist; they are silently written out of the story. Such women as appear are entirely passive. Lot offers his daughters to the crowd in an effort to save his male guests, and he does this, as we have seen, at considerable potential cost to himself. But the daughters themselves have nothing at all to say about this kind offer of Lot's. They are not consulted, not asked if they are willing to suffer gang rape. Perhaps they would be willing to suffer this fate to protect their father's guests, but we don't know. The narrative obviously considers it not an important question. As far as the author is concerned, the daughters have nothing to say. The very way this story is told, therefore, indicates a preoccupation with males, their value and their behaviour to the total exclusion of females. This way of thinking plainly comes naturally to the narrator, and we can only suppose that it came naturally to his audience, too. The society which gave birth to this narrative in its present form is sexist and patriarchal in the extreme, just as is the society which lies in the background of Leviticus 18:22. These two texts encapsulate and express those values. Take away those values, and we can no longer understand the texts. Those values are repugnant to modern Christians – or at least they ought to be. Rejecting them means that there is no Christian sense to be found in either of the texts, if we take them at face value. It may be that we can read them in some other way, for instance as indicating that we should not degrade others, or that the duty of hospitality is to be respected,[42] but they cannot be used by Christians in any straightforward way as an indication that same-sex activity is to be avoided. We can only treat these texts as expressing the will of God in sexual matters if we regard the sexual hierarchy which lies behind them as also ordained by God, if we regard the particular – and unjust – social structure of ancient Israel as God-given and willed by God for all nations at all times. But we cannot do that. God is not the author of any sexual hierarchy. Not only does the narrative of Genesis not imply a condemnation of same-sex activity in general, but only of the rape of men, but part of what lies behind this attitude is the idea of male superiority, which Christians reject. Genesis 19 condemns male rape, quite rightly, but partly for the wrong reasons. Thus, while there may be many good reasons for urging people not to engage in same-sex activity, the narrative of Genesis 19 does not furnish one, and neither do the laws of Leviticus 18:22 and 20:13.

CHAPTER FOUR

The Bible Against Homosexuality?
II: New Testament Texts
and Summary

Romans 1

Perhaps the most important single text appealed to in support of a moral condemnation of all same-sex activity is Romans 1, where Paul paints a very unflattering picture of Gentile society, including the alleged fact that 'their females exchanged the natural use for that which is against nature, and the males likewise abandoned the natural use of the female and burned in their desire for each other, males committing what is shameful with males and receiving among themselves the due reward for their delusion' (Romans 1:26–7). This text is important first of all because it is a New Testament text. Appeal to it is an appeal to the new dispensation inaugurated by Jesus Christ, not to the old. Use of Genesis 19 and Leviticus 18:22 may run into problems about the applicability of Old Testament law to Christians, or indeed to anybody since the coming of Christ. Use of Romans 1 avoids any such problems. And it apparently shows quite clearly that, in the new dispensation as under the old, same-sex activity is unacceptable. Further, and very importantly, Paul seems to refer to sex between women. The Old Testament texts we have examined are concerned exclusively with the sexual conduct of men, and with possible breaches of the sexual hierarchy ordained by God. Paul apparently redresses the balance. He is concerned with men and women equally, even speaking of women first. This suggests even before we look at the text in detail that his argument does not get its force from a sexist conception of society supposedly ordained by God, a conception unacceptable to modern Christians. This impression is strengthened further when we remember that it is this same Paul who writes that in Christ Jesus 'there is neither male nor female' (Galatians 3:28). Further, the fact that he is concerned both with women having sex with women and with men having sex with men means that what he is condemning here really is homosexual practice. If that description of what Genesis 19 and Leviticus 18:22 and 20:13 condemn is misplaced, it surely is not inappropriate here. Paul is concerned not with what men do to men, but with what people of the same sex do together. The 'likewise' connecting verses 26, which mentions the conduct of women, and 27, which is concerned with the conduct of men, shows clearly that Paul regards what the women do and what the men do as two manifestations of what is basically the same phenomenon, the phenomenon that we call homosexuality. If Old Testament writers classify sexual acts differently from us, in accordance with their conformity or nonconformity with the sexual hierarchy of their society, Paul categorizes as we do, in terms of the sameness or difference of sex of the sexual partners. Even if he doesn't have the words, he thinks in terms of heterosexuality and homosexuality. And he clearly condemns the latter.

Crime or punishment?

So it seems, but, once again, things are not quite so simple. There are several factors which should make us hesitate to embrace this way of understanding the text. To begin with, this part of Romans 1 is not primarily an attack on people who go in for same-sex activity, but on Gentiles, the vast majority of humanity who do not worship exclusively the one true God, the God of Israel. The wrath of God 'has been revealed against all the impiety and injustice of those people who unjustly suppress the truth' (v. 18). The true nature of God is apparent to them through the created things they see around them (vv. 19, 20), but though they knew God they did not glorify or thank him as they should, but they became vain, their senseless hearts were darkened (v. 21). Claiming to be wise, they became stupid and exchanged the glory of the imperishable God for images in the likeness of perishable animals (vv. 22–23). This is basically what is wrong with the Gentiles: that they have abandoned the one whom they knew to be the true God in order to worship idols. They are not idolaters out of ignorance, but have deliberately suppressed what they knew to be the truth. Because of this, God has given them up, by means of the desires of their hearts, to uncleanness, so that they dishonour their bodies among themselves (v. 24) – those who exchanged the truth of God for a lie and worshipped the creature instead of the creator (v. 25). This is the background to the two verses which, according to many, amount to a clear condemnation

of same-sex activity, and which follow immediately. It is because of
their exchanging the truth for a lie that God has given them up to
dishonourable passions, so that their women exchange the natural
for the unnatural, and the men burn for men. Thus, as has often
been pointed out, if Paul thinks the Gentiles typically engage in
same-sex activity, this is for him not a sin that demands punishment, but is a condition that God has put them in because of their
suppression of the truth about him; if anything, it is itself a punishment for a crime.[1] We need not think that Paul attributes a
personal and conscious rejection of the true God to every individual
Gentile. Rather, such rejection is the explanation why Gentile
civilization exists at all, why it began. At some point in the past,
some deliberately turned away from the creator; and so their mind
was darkened and they worshipped the creation instead.[2] Subsequent members of Gentile society are caught up in this darkness
and this idolatry by virtue of their birth. So Gentiles are by nature
incapable of seeing the truth about God or of acting righteously. As
Eugene Rogers puts it:

> 'Nature' works differently for Paul than for us. For him, nature
> and morality can be intertwined among Gentiles, slaves, and
> women, and it comes as a surprise to him and to the circumcision
> party that holiness appears among the Gentiles, precisely
> because they regard the Gentiles – in what we would consider a
> category mistake – as *morally inferior by nature*. For 'nature'
> applies in Paul's vocabulary not only to male and female, but
> also to 'Jew and Greek,' which is the most important case of all.
> And in that case, the Gentile nature proves no barrier to God's
> grant of holiness in the Spirit. 'Jew or Gentile' is for Paul both a
> natural and a moral distinction.[3]

Let us for the moment grant that what Paul is talking about here
amounts to same-sex practices as we conceive them. Even so it is
clear that Paul's target here is Gentiles, those who, because of their
benighted minds, do not recognize the true God. It is this suppression of the truth that has provoked God's wrath. The sexual
practices typical of Gentiles are attributed to the action of God,
who has 'given them up . . . to uncleanness so that their bodies are
dishonoured'. This dishonouring of their bodies is the recompense
of their delusion – that is, of their idolatry. The Gentiles themselves
do not, of course, recognize this as any kind of punishment for
idolatry. To begin with, they do not regard their idolatry as

something which should be punished; to them, it is true religion, and the gods might well punish them if they abandon their cult. Secondly, they do not see their sexual practices as a punishment, because they do not see their bodies as being dishonoured by them. They think these sexual practices good; they find them natural and pleasing. It is only somebody outside Gentile civilization, somebody who does not suffer what Paul calls the Gentiles' darkening of the mind but who recognizes the true God – in short, only a Jew – who sees that these sexual practices are shameful and that they dishonour the body.[4] In the picture that Paul paints there is a certain poetic justice about the way God has treated the Gentiles: because they exchanged the truth for a lie, the imperishable God for images of perishable creatures, God has brought it about, by giving them up to uncleanness through their desires, that in their sexual desires and behaviour they have exchanged the 'natural' use for what is 'against nature', so that one exchange is punished with another. The sexual practices of the Gentiles are, then, not a sin, a crime against God to be punished; they are themselves the 'recompense' inflicted on the Gentiles for their deliberate turning away from the truth. Thus, if this passage of Romans can be used today to show anything at all about same-sex practices, it is not that they are sinful, but that they are the punishment for sin, the sin of deliberately refusing to recognize the true God. Paul certainly speaks of these practices in disparaging terms: they are a form of uncleanness, and are a dishonouring of the body. This is no surprise; we would certainly expect him to speak negatively about them if he regards these practices as some kind of divine punishment for idolatry. Punishments are supposed to be negative, something to be regretted, and so avoided if possible. If prison were spoken of in glowing terms, it could hardly be presented as a punishment for crime. Paul does not here use the vocabulary of sin when describing same-sex practices.[5] This again is what we would expect if he sees them rather as a punishment for sin. If prison is a punishment for crime, to be in prison is not itself a crime. He speaks of dishonour and shame, just as prison might bring dishonour and shame. In the case of the Gentiles, of course, the dishonour and shame are not imposed on them against their will; God has shamed them by bringing it about that they desire practices that bring shame upon them, so that they effectively bring shame upon themselves.

But Paul does not speak of same-sex practices as he does of Gentile idolatry, which he describes as impiety and injustice (v. 18). These are the things which call for punishment, and they are the reason why God has shamed all the Gentiles. He does not say of these practices, either, as he does of the long list of 'things which are not to be done' in verses 29–31, that those who practise them are worthy of death (v. 32). That is, Paul does use the language of sin in this later part of Romans 1, but he refrains from using it precisely where he speaks of same-sex practices. This analysis does not show, of course, that same-sex practices are not sinful; nor does it show that Paul did not think them sinful. It does show, however, that he does not present them in Romans 1 as sinful. He calls them unclean, shameful and dishonourable, but not sinful. This is not a matter of mere words: the essential point is that he presents them not as practices provoking the wrath of God and calling for punishment, but rather as a result of the wrath of God, as a punishment for sin. It could of course be the case that God, to punish them for their sin of idolatry, causes the Gentiles to commit further sins. This is in fact what Paul seems to be saying in vv. 28–32, particularly in v. 28, where he says that 'just as they did not see fit (*ouk edokimasan*) to recognize God, God gave them up to an unfit (*adokimon*) mind, to do those things which are not to be done'[6] – things which are deserving of death (v. 32). But he does not say this with respect to same-sex practices; he does not say that God punishes one sin by leading the sinners to commit other sins. Those readers of Romans who believe on other grounds that same-sex practices are indeed sinful may well think that in this case, too, God has punished sin by leading the sinners into more sin, but this is not what Paul says, and Romans 1 is not evidence for that view.

Sin and shame

Just to rub this point in, let us consider the following. Paul does clearly say that same-sex practices are shameful, so it is natural to ask: does this not imply that they are also sinful? After all, shameful things are not to be done, and sin is also what is not to be done. Therefore, though Paul does not say explicitly that these practices are sinful, we are nonetheless entitled to draw that conclusion from what he does say. There are two answers to this. The first, short, answer is to note that it involves a logical fallacy. If the shameful is not to be done and the sinful is not to be done, it does not follow that the shameful and the sinful are one and the same. If gluttony is dangerous to health, and if under-eating is dangerous to health, it does not follow that gluttony and under-eating are one and the same; it is simply that they have a common property, that of being dangerous to health. Similarly, all we can say about the shameful and the sinful is that they have a common property, that they are both to be avoided. But it may be that they are each to be avoided for quite different reasons. In particular, there is no reason to think that what Paul implies is that what is shameful is to be avoided because it is sinful. Certainly, some shameful things may be sinful, and sin may sometimes or always be shameful, but the shameful and the sinful remain different concepts.

The second answer is to look more closely at the language of shame that Paul uses here. The Greek word which I have translated 'what is shameful' (*aschemosyne*) and its cognates are used a number of times in the Bible, both in the New Testament and in the Septuagint version of the Old. The way they are used in the Septuagint reveals the body as a locus of shame for Jewish culture. For example, a law in Exodus says: 'You shall not go up by steps to my altar, lest your nakedness (*aschemosyne*) be exposed upon it' (20:26). It is used regularly in Leviticus to translate the Hebrew *'erwah*, rendered as 'nakedness' in the standard English translations. This is particularly striking in the laws forbidding 'uncovering nakedness' in 18:6–21; for example: 'The *aschemosyne* of your father and the *aschemosyne* of your mother you shall not uncover; she is your mother, and you shall not uncover her *aschemosyne*' (18:7). In these texts, though the uncovering of the *aschemosyne* may be sinful, the *aschemosyne* itself certainly is not. Its use here reveals a sensitivity about the human body, with the Exodus text focusing particularly on the sexual organs. The root is used in a similar way in Ezekiel, who speaks of Israel as a girl 'naked and bare' (*gymne kai aschemonousa*; 16:7.).[7] There is no suggestion here, either, that the *aschemosyne* is at all sinful. It is rather that to have one's nakedness seen by others brings shame. A different though related use is to be found in Deuteronomy 23:14–15, which prescribes that faeces (*aschemosyne*) be covered over so that the Lord, who walks in the Israelite camp, may see no *aschemosyne*. Once again, no sin is involved in producing faeces. Deuteronomy 25:3, while perhaps not directly concerning the body or excreta, confirms that what is at stake is how the person concerned is looked upon by others. It limits corporal punishment to forty strokes, lest 'your brother be shamed[8] (*aschemonesei*) before you'. The Levitical laws concerning uncovering nakedness also, at least in part, point to the shame involved in having one's naked body seen by others.

One more, quite different, example shows again the distance

between shame and sin. In 2 Maccabees 9:2, Antiochus is said to lose a battle and to 'beat a shameful (*aschemona*) retreat'. There is of course no suggestion here at all that Antiochus's retreat is sinful. Rather, it brings dishonour upon him; because of this action, he is not viewed by others with respect, but with contempt or ridicule. In none of these texts is there a connection between shame – *aschemosyne* – and sin. The word has to do rather with how one is looked on by others, and so is closely related to the ideas of honour and dishonour. Its use reveals also that the body is a particularly sensitive locus of shame. The – rather rare – use of the word and its cognates in the New Testament points in the same direction. Apart from Romans 1:27, all the other uses except one are in 1 Corinthians (7:36; 12:23; 13:5). Of these, 7:36 and 12:23 clearly concern the body, and the latter equally obviously has nothing to do with sin. The only non-Pauline use – and the only other use of the actual noun that Paul uses in Romans – is at Revelation 16:15: 'Behold, I come like a thief. Blessed is the one who watches and keeps his robes, so that he may not walk naked and they see his shame.' This is plainly very closely related to Old Testament usage. It does not imply that walking naked is sinful, but associates shame with one's nakedness being seen by others.[9]

There is thus no reason at all on biblical grounds for inferring that Paul's description of same-sex practices as shameful implies that they are also sinful. The word 'shameful' is appropriate here because these practices closely concern the body. There may also be a hint that in the societies which Paul is criticizing these activities are not hidden. While they may be acceptable in those societies, in the eyes of Paul and of other Jews who contemplate them – and perhaps see them – they bring shame on those who practise them.[10]

Dishonourable passions

Paul speaks of God giving people over to 'dishonourable passions'. It might be thought that what makes these passions dishonourable is the fact that they are homosexual passions. It might seem as if he has a contrast in mind, between these dishonourable passions and some which are honourable, or at least not dishonourable, so that, while these particular passions are to be disapproved of, there would be others which were to be approved. But this is not Paul's meaning. The word in question is *pathe*. Every time this word and its cognates are mentioned in the New Testament in the sense of 'passion' rather than 'suffering' (and this is always in the Pauline corpus), it is used negatively.[11] To have passion is always to be subject to passion, and that is always, in the Greek philosophical tradition to which Paul is heir, shameful, for it is to be out of control; it is to be moved not by reason but by irrational forces. In addition, when a man becomes subject to his passions, he is like a woman, whose place is to be subject, rather than the man that he is, whose place is to dominate. This is a constant risk for a man, since he is constantly moved by passion, and it takes a constant battle against passion to be a true man. In *A Rereading of Romans*, Stanley K. Stowers puts it in illuminating and dramatic fashion:

> Life is war, and masculinity has to be achieved and constantly fought for. Men are always in danger of succumbing to softness, described as forms of femaleness or servility. In the ancient Mediterranean construction of gender, the sexes are 'poles on a continuum which can be traversed'. To achieve self-mastery means to win the war; to let the passions and desires go unsubdued means defeat, a destruction of hard-won maleness. The centrality of this gender defeat explains why leaving assigned gender roles for same sex love serves as the illustration in 1:26–27 of the extent to which gentiles have succumbed to passions and desires.[12]

So we need not think that in Romans 1, Paul has in mind passions which lead to particularly dishonourable behaviour; for him, all passions are dishonourable in this sense. What is dishonourable about the passions of which Paul speaks is not that they are homosexual passions, but simply that they are passions.

What homosexuality?

When we read Paul asserting that 'the males likewise abandoned the natural use of the female and burned in their desire for each other, males committing what is shameful with males', we may spontaneously read this as a straightforward allusion to male same-sex practices. It is that reading of the text which makes us think it relevant for a moral assessment of same-sex practices in our own day. But it is a legitimate question to ask whether this is in fact what Paul means. His language is very general; he speaks effectively of males having sex with males, in a way that seems to cover all male same-sex activity. However, the fact that his language is general does not mean that he did not have something quite specific in mind, which contemporary readers would have recognized immediately. Robin Scroggs in his interesting and illuminating study,[13] poses the question what kinds of same-sex activity Paul could have been familiar with, and so what activities he could be referring to in Romans. His conclusion, backed with a weight of evidence, is that the only publicly known and discussed form of male same-sex practice in the Jewish and Hellenistic civilizations of Paul's time was pederasty. If this is true, then Paul, despite the general nature of his language, is actually talking about something that we, who are acquainted with a broader range of male same-sex activity and relationships, would regard as a quite specific form, which for us carries with it its own particular moral problems.[14] Scroggs shows how Hellenistic Greeks in particular were also very aware of moral questions attending pederasty.[15] For them, as for us, the lack of equality, true consent and reciprocity were real problems. But, however real such problems then and now, pederasty is most definitely not at the centre of the modern Christian debate on homosexuality. Almost everybody, on both sides of the debate, would agree that pederasty is not an option for Christians, or indeed for anybody. The modern debate is about the admissibility of adult, consenting, reciprocal relationships. Scrogg's study makes it look as if Romans 1 is simply irrelevant to the modern question because, though its language is general and it looks at first sight as if it might be pertinent to the question of such relationships, it is concerned with a different practice. In matters historical it is often impossible to attain to complete certainty, and we may have doubts about the strength of Scrogg's case. In particular, though his claim that the pederastic relationship was by far the dominant form of male same-sex relationship seems well established, the further claim that it was the *only* model available for homosexual relationships is difficult to accept.[16] But it is, at the very least, cause for reasonable doubt as to whether Paul's words can legitimately be interpreted in such as way as to speak to the modern debate. I have argued above that Paul sees same-sex practices as a punishment for sin, rather than as sinful. If that is correct, what he says here cannot be enlisted as an argument against the admissibility of these practices. But even if I have misunderstood the text, Scroggs's argument indicates that Romans is at worst useless and at best a doubtful witness for those who wish to use it in a scriptural case against them.

'Against nature'

Much scholarly ink has been spilt over the question of what Paul meant by saying that same-sex activity is 'against nature'. There is first the question how to translate the Greek *para physin*. I have followed what has become the standard English translation, following the Vulgate's *contra naturam*. But *para* more often means 'beyond' rather than 'against' (as in 'paranormal'), and 'in excess of nature' is another possible translation of the phrase, adopted by Rogers;[17] Countryman suggests 'over against nature'.[18] Another, more important, question is what Paul means here by 'nature' anyway. Again, different interpretations have been proposed. There is not space to go into the question here. Though it has its own interest, it is, if my argument above is correct, of only subsidiary importance. If one thought that Paul was saying that same-sex activity was sinful, and that it was sinful because 'against nature', then it would be an important question as to what exactly the phrase signified, and what concept of nature Paul was using. However, if, as I have argued, Paul is not saying that same-sex activity is sinful, the question is, in the present context, less urgent. For the point of this examination of Romans 1 is to see whether it provides biblical authority for the view that same-sex activity is sinful. If I am right in saying that it does not, the major question is settled. We should, however, note an incidental corollary: if Paul is saying that same-sex activity is against (or some other preposition) nature, in whatever sense of the word, and is not saying that it is sinful, this text also gives evidence against the view that what is against nature is sinful, or at the very least gives it no support. It leaves with considerably diminished biblical foundation the idea that human conduct, in order to avoid being sinful, must be in some sense according to nature.

Heterosexuals playing at being homosexual?

It has been argued, notably by Boswell,[19] that in the verses under consideration Paul is condemning not all same-sex activity, but the same-sex practice of those who are basically heterosexual. The basis for this is the fact that Paul uses the phrase 'against nature'.[20] What Paul is complaining of, the argument runs, is people acting against their own sexual nature, those who are basically heterosexual going against their heterosexual tendencies by having sex with another person of the same sex. This, despite the evidence offered by Boswell, is unconvincing. It depends on the idea that Paul thought that each person had his or her own individual nature, including a sexual nature, but there is no evidence of this. It is true that Paul does not necessarily think that all human beings share the same nature: he speaks of some people as being 'by nature' uncircumcised (Rom. 2:27) and of himself and his fellow Jews as being 'by nature' circumcised (Gal. 2:15). But nowhere does he indicate that he thinks that each individual has a nature proper to himself or herself, which might include particular sexual proclivities. Indeed, the idea of a heterosexual or a homosexual as a kind of person with a particular sexual nature seems to be a recent one. In any case, the suggestion that the people of whom Paul is speaking here are not acting according to their true sexual inclinations does not ring true. For the whole point of the passage is that it is these people's deep desires that lead them to act as they do. God has delivered them to uncleanness by means of the desires of their hearts (1:24), so that the men burn for each other (1:27). Here Paul's language is very close to that of 1 Corinthians 7:9, where he counsels those men with strong desires for women to marry, 'for it is better to marry than to burn'. The men of Romans 1 are not men whose desires are basically heterosexual and who are just playing at sex with each other; they burn for each other, as a man might burn for a woman to the extent of marrying her.

What are the women doing?

There has never been much doubt expressed about what Paul is saying about the women who 'exchanged the natural use for that which is against nature'. It has, as far as I am aware, almost always been understood that they, like the men, burn for each other and do shameful things together. This may well be correct. But there is a doubt to be raised. While Paul says that the men, likewise, abandon 'the natural use', he says of the men alone that they burn for each other, and of the men alone that they do shameful things with each other. That the women do, *mutatis mutandis*, the same as the men seems to be implied by the word 'likewise' which joins verse 26 and verse 27: the females abandon the natural use for that which is against nature, and *likewise* the males abandon the natural of the female and burn for each other. But the 'likewise' seems intended to bring out the fact that both females and males abandon what is natural, rather than that they perform the same kind of act. If they both act unnaturally, there is perhaps more than one way to be unnatural. If the men are unnatural in burning for each other, may not the women have a different way of being unnatural? What prompts this question is that, if Paul is talking about sexual relations between women, it is curious that he should do so. Nowhere else in Scripture is there any allusion to sex between women; the laws and the stories are resolutely male-oriented. According to Scroggs, there is no evidence that Hellenistic culture ever thought seriously about it, either.[21] Why should Paul mention it, and that in first place, before he speaks of the men? There is also a tiny linguistic detail that points in the same direction: while Paul writes of *the* males, he writes of *their* females, suggesting (no more than that) a relationship of possession. It is not entirely clear to whom the females might belong, but females, in both Jewish and Hellenistic culture, normally belong to males. His use of 'their' casts doubt on the sexual egalitarianism of Paul in this passage. If Paul considers it natural for men to engage in sex with women, his culture also considered it natural for women to be sexually subject to their husbands, and perhaps he is here echoing and subscribing to that cultural assumption. The possibility arises that what the women are doing is not engaging in sex with each other, but engaging in sex with men who are not their husbands. If this is so, Paul's concern with the women becomes much more traditional and much more comprehensible: they are committing adultery. That this is a possibility, suggested by the text itself, again raises doubts about the suitability of using this text in support of a condemnation of same-sex activity.[22]

James E. Miller[23] has an interesting argument which points in the same direction. He begins by resuming briefly some of the conclusions to which I have come, transposed from Palestine to Rome: In the Hellenistic world to which Paul addresses himself there is a large and entrenched inequality of the sexes. For this reason female sexual activity is not understood in the same way as male sexual activity. There is not one 'homosexuality' of which there are two manifestations, one among men and one among women. Thus from the fact that when Paul is talking in verse 27 about men performing sexual acts together – for that is what he says – it cannot be concluded that when he is talking about the women in verse 26 he is doing the same – for he does not say so. What he says is that the women, like the men, act unnaturally. Importantly, Paul, when speaking of the women, does not speak of any change of sexual partner; he does not suggest that women act unnaturally with women, while he does say that the men act unnaturally with men. So it is legitimate, even natural, to suppose that the women commit their unnatural acts with men, not with women; that they are heterosexual, not homosexual. Miller goes on to show that ancient sources do in fact disapprove of women taking part in heterosexual non-coital sex,[24] then produces an argument that it is worthwhile to quote in full:

> If a woman wishes to have non-coital intercourse with a man her options are those of the homosexual male, for once the woman decides not to use her vagina she has no other gender-distinctive orifice. In other words, the remaining options for a woman are oral intercourse, anal intercourse and intercourse which does not involve penetration. Sexual activities of female homosexuals are quite different due to the radical difference in genitalia. Though either form of homosexual intercourse may each share some sexual practices with heterosexual intercourse, they have almost nothing in common with each other. It is significant that Paul refers to natural and unnatural function ... in verse 26 which is shared with homosexuals in verse 27. It is not male and female homosexuals who share common functions, but rather each shares some functions with heterosexuals engaged in non-coital intercourse. Thus the similarity in function described in Romans 1:26 refers to non-coital sexual activities which are engaged in by heterosexual women similar to the sexual activities of homosexual males. So females, described first, exchange natural function for unnatural, but an exchange of partners is not indicated. Males, however, to function like the females just described, exchange the natural partner for the unnatural. There is little reason to read Romans 1:26 as a reference to female homosexuality, and strong reason to understand Paul's comments as a rejection of some or all unnatural (non-coital) heterosexual intercourse, the type of intercourse used in verse 27.

Miller's argument is hard to understand unless one realizes that he is talking about 'passive' homosexuals, receptive partners in anal intercourse; it is these who share some similarity in their sexual activity to heterosexual women. It is also these who are feminized, so we are led back to see a connection with Stowers' insistence on the importance for men of self-mastery and the battle for masculinity. So it was above all these passive homosexual men who were despised. Hence the opprobrium heaped upon Julius Caesar when, having conquered Nicomedes of Bithynia, he allowed him to 'conquer' him sexually, the strong taking the part of the weak, the male of the female.[25] So Paul does not write having in mind the egalitarian category of 'homosexual' that we may think he does. He is not concerned with homosexuality at all, but with 'unnatural' sex, which in the case of women involves acts such as oral and anal intercourse with men – forsaking their 'natural' sexual instrument – and in the case of men a feminizing submission to a desire to play the role of the woman in sexual intercourse with a man. Therefore the idea that Paul is condemning homosexuality collapses.

Paul and the 'homosexual condition'

The common, though as I believe to have shown incorrect, interpretation of this passage of Romans has been that in it Paul condemns all homosexual activity. But this passage is relevant, too, to the distinction recently developed between homosexual activity and the so-called homosexual condition, which has already been mentioned. Paul says that God has brought the idolatrous Gentiles into uncleanness by means of their desires. In context these desires can be none other than the burning which leads the men into same-sex activity. Though the language is very different, these desires are thus close to the supposed homosexual condition, which is 'a more or less strong tendency ordered toward an intrinsic moral evil' – the moral evil of same-sex activity. So, if we can use such language in discussing Romans 1, Paul is saying effectively that it is God who has given the Gentiles this homosexual condition. Unlike some currents in modern moral theology, Paul makes no use here of the distinction between condition and practice, and between desire and activity. That distinction is what enables the theologians to say that those who suffer from this condition should nevertheless resist their desires and refrain from homosexual activity. According to the usual interpretation of the passage, Paul condemns same-sex activity. If this were the case, he would be imputing guilt to the Gentiles for not resisting but giving in to their condition, their desire for same-sex activity. In order for his thought to be in line with current ideas, it would be necessary for him to make some distinction between the desire, which is imposed by God, and the act, which is nevertheless to be resisted. But Paul does not argue like this. He does not say that, though God has given them the condition, the Gentiles are perfectly capable of resisting their same-sex desires, and what's more they ought to. If he locates guilt anywhere, he certainly does not locate it in their failure to resist their desires. He looks down not only on the behaviour of the Gentiles, but on their very desires, on the fact that the men burn for each other. If this passage can be read as a condemnation of same-sex activity, therefore, it must by the same token be read as a condemnation of the homosexual condition. It sits ill, therefore, with more modern thought. In terms of what *HP* wants to say, if it proves anything it proves too much. Indeed, rather than make a distinction between activity and desire in such a way as to suggest that the one need not follow from the other, the whole point of the passage is that the two go naturally together, and must do so in this case. For, if the behaviour did not flow unresisted from the desire, God would be unable to lead the Gentiles into uncleanness through their desires. If the Gentiles tried to resist their same-sex desires, and succeeded, they would actually thereby succeed in thwarting God's intention; he would have failed to punish them for their idolatry by handing them over to uncleanness.

Paul and (homo)sexual abstinence

This observation raises some much wider questions. If Paul does not suppose in this passage that people with same-sex desires can be expected to master them so as not actually to engage in same-sex activity, this is not because he does not think desires can be resisted; he often says or implies that they can and should be resisted; this is part of the programme of self-mastery which is essential for winning the battle against the passions. Interestingly, he counsels the Corinthians to resist sexual desire – heterosexual desire. For him, as for later Christian tradition, the proper place for sex is within the context of a marriage but, notoriously, he urges the Christians of Corinth to remain unmarried (1 Cor. 7:27–38), and hence to refrain from sexual intercourse. In this, they are to be like him (7:8). It should be noted, however, that he does not envisage people living a lifetime of sexual abstinence. He urges celibacy on them 'because of the present distress', (v. 26) a distress which is upon them because these are the last days, because 'the time has grown short' (v. 29). Paul does not expect that young people have many long years of sexual abstinence in front of them; celibacy and its collateral abstinence is an emergency measure enabling the Christians to concentrate on God, who will very soon bring the world to an end.

But, although he counsels celibacy, Paul does not think this possible for everybody, even for the short time he expects to have to wait before the end of the world. He describes as follows what a young man engaged to a woman should ideally do: 'He who stands firm in his heart, not under constraint, but who has mastery over his own will and has so decided in his own heart, to keep her as his betrothed – he will do well' (v. 37). But, while this is for him the ideal solution he realizes that not everybody is capable of it: 'If anybody thinks he is treating his betrothed shamefully, if he has strong passions and it must be so, let him do what he wants, he is not sinning; let them marry' (v. 36). A little earlier, he acknowledges the same reality: 'I want everybody to be like me, but everybody has his own gift from God, one this, another that. But I say to the unmarried and to widows that it is good for them to remain as I am. But if they cannot control themselves, let them marry, for it is better to marry than to burn' (vv. 7–9). People are different; when it comes to sex, not all have the capacity to master their desires, even for a relatively short time. This capacity is a gift from God. For those who do not have it, marriage is a possibility, giving them a place where they can act on their sexual desires. And married people must be careful not to abstain too much from sex, for this only gives an opportunity to Satan to work mischief, taking advantage of their lack of self-control (v. 5). Paul does not think, then, that when it comes to sexual desire everybody is gifted with the self-control that makes total and permanent sexual abstinence possible. Just as for the Gentiles whom God gives over to uncleanness through their desires, so for the Christians of Corinth, unless they have a special gift from God, sexual desire issues in sexual activity. There is no expectation that people universally will be able to master their desires so as to live in abstinence. And the inability to do so is not weakness or sin; it is a part of what it is to be human, even for those who are members of the church, even for those, that is, who have been cleansed, who have died to sin and been reborn in baptism, who are members of Christ and live by the Spirit of Christ. In 1 Corinthians Paul is addressing some problems which arise in the context of what we would call heterosexual relationships, and problems of how to handle sexual desire in the context of those relationships. Nevertheless, what he says here leads to some pretty obvious questions about the modern churches' attitude to gay men and lesbians. While Paul recognizes that, unlike other forms of desire, sexual desire cannot be mastered by everybody, but only by those to whom God has given the gift of such mastery, and that for a relatively short time and in expectation of the imminent end of the world, some modern churches think that all lesbians and gay men, without exception, can be expected to master their sexual desire and live in total sexual abstinence for all of what may be a long life, without expectation of the imminent end of the world. It is manifestly true that some can and do, just as some heterosexuals can and do. But why expect that all lesbians and gay men be able to live in this way? Is it that homosexual desire is supposed to be so much easier to master than heterosexual desire? There is no reason to believe that, and every reason to believe that homosexual desire is as strong and insistent and as difficult to come to terms with as heterosexual desire. Is it that God is supposed to have given a special charism to all gay men and lesbians which enables them to master their sexual desire as Paul mastered his? There is no biblical warrant for such a position; it is in apparent contradiction to the views Paul expresses in 1 Corinthians, and there is absolutely no empirical evidence to support the belief that lesbians and gay men find abstinence easier than heterosexual men and women. The only thing that might induce anybody to believe it is if he or she felt it theologically required to give coherence to a law of abstinence imposed universally on homosexuals. It is also clear that in this text Paul expects each individual to be the judge of whether he is strong enough to master his desire. He says simply that somebody (a man) is to abstain if he 'has so decided in his own heart'; on the other hand, he is to marry 'if he has strong passions and it must be so', and there is no hint that anybody else is to judge the strength of these passions but the one who experiences them. We may ask with what justification, in opposition to this text, some churches judge that homosexuals must all abstain, even without having so judged in their own heart; and with what justification, in opposition to this text, some churches take it upon themselves to judge that no homosexuals have passions sufficiently strong for them to say that 'it must be so'.

A remedy for homosexual sin?

Paul says to those who judge they are not strong enough to master their passions that they should marry. Marriage gives them a context in which they can follow their passions without Satan taking advantage of their lack of self-control – that lack of self-control which is not due to sin but, for those who have not received a special gift, part of the normal condition of regenerated humanity, part even of life in Christ. Marriage is for Paul, in the words of *The Book of Common Prayer*, 'a remedy against sin, and to avoid fornication; that such persons as have not the gift of continency might marry, and keep themselves undefiled members of Christ's body'.[26] There are those Christians who advocate what might be called gay marriage; even in the thorny domain of homosexuality, this is a question thornier than most. Leaving it prudently aside, it still has to be asked: If most heterosexuals are deemed to need such a remedy against sin – as they surely do – why are homosexuals not deemed also to need a remedy against sin? For they also surely do. If God provides marriage for those heterosexuals who 'have not the gift of continency', why should it be believed that he provides nothing, or wills that nothing be provided, for homosexuals who have not the same gift? Is God supposed to will that Satan take advantage of their human lack of self-control? This is hardly credible, unless one believes that God wills homosexuals in general to be lost. That is, if we do not believe that God wants homosexuals to be lost; then we cannot believe that he wills that Satan take advantage of their human lack of self-control; so we cannot believe that God gives homosexuals no remedy against sin; that he wills no provision to be made for homosexuals who have not the gift of continency to live in a way that avoids fornication. How can this conclusion be avoided? Until a credible answer is given to this question, and to the others posed above, it cannot be rational to believe that adherence to the will of God requires that no such provision be sought or provided. One further point: the remedy against sin of which Paul speaks is a particular form of relationship between persons – marriage. Such a form of relationship is at present not available to homosexuals in most churches. Perhaps it never will be, and perhaps there are good reasons why it should not be. But it is nevertheless significant that Paul sees the solution in terms of a personal relationship in which the partners commit themselves to each other for life. This is, of course, in full conformity with traditional Christian teaching on sex: that it has its proper place only within such a committed relationship. Paul's approach also provides a biblical justification, if one be needed, for avoiding the reductionist discourse of sexual 'acts' in isolation from human relationships, a discourse so prevalent in *HP* and elsewhere in the Catholic Church.

A Question of Truth

Gay Christians

The main argument of this section has been simply that Paul, as far as concerns what he says in Romans 1, does not say that homosexual practice is sinful; rather, one form of male homosexual practice, just like the adoption of non-coital sex by some women, is the result of the sin of wilful failure to recognize God. Let us suppose I am wrong about this, and that 1:26–7 really does amount to a condemnation of all homosexuality. Still, it remains incontrovertible that for Paul in Romans the root of same-sex activity is the deliberate rejection of God. This fact alone raises difficulties concerning the use of this text in a modern Christian argument about gay sex. One of the most important reasons why this debate is going on, not between the churches and the rest of society but within the churches themselves, is that there are not inconsiderable numbers of Christians who wish to overturn the traditionally negative Christian attitude to homosexuality. A large percentage of these are themselves homosexual. There are many gay Christians who are quite happy to be both: who sincerely worship God, who believe that their sexuality is a gift of God, who celebrate it and give thanks for it, and who want the value of their sexual love to be recognized as is that of their heterosexual brothers and sisters. There are, that is, plenty of people in homosexual relationships who have not wilfully refused to recognize God, but who gladly honour him and give thanks to him (cf. Romans 1:21). Other Christians may believe that they are wrongheaded, but they have certainly not deliberately exchanged the glory of the imperishable God to serve images of creatures. As noted at the beginning of this section, Paul is arguing not against homosexuals, but against those who have unjustly suppressed the truth about God and turned to idols. That is, he is not in the least arguing against those who have seen and acknowledged the eternal power and divinity of God. In modern terms, he is not arguing against gay Christians. The argument of Romans 1 is simply not about them.

It is important to stress here that Paul does not single out same-sex desire as *the* consequence of suppressing knowledge of the true God. On the contrary, he lists a number of negative consequences. Those who deliberately abandoned God are 'full of all injustice, evil, greed, wickedness, full of envy, murder, quarrelling, treachery, malignity; whisperers, slanderers, God-haters, insolent, haughty, boasters, inventors of evil, disobedient to parents, senseless, disloyal, inhumane, merciless' (vv. 29–31). From this list, it is clear that, if

Paul does not think homosexual desires and acts sinful but merely shameful, due recompense for rejection of the true God, he does consider them a natural concomitant of the sinful and godless way of life that he outlines in these verses. For him, this godless way of life and this shameful sexual behaviour go together, the sexual behaviour functioning as a kind of emblem or symbol of the way of life. But for gay Christians, this sexual behaviour does not go together with that way of life. They behave this way sexually, but they do not lead that godless way of life. On the contrary, they reject that way of life as part of their acknowledgment of the true God. With gay Christians, the link that Paul fashions between recognition of God, sexual desire and behaviour, and way of life breaks down. If Paul thought it impossible to acknowledge the true God and give thanks to him and at the same time be a partner in a homosexual relationship, then he was wrong. If he thought it impossible to be in a same-sex sexual relationship and yet not be full of all injustice, evil, greed, wickedness, and the rest, then he was wrong. More likely, he just did not consider the possibility of people full of love of God and of their neighbour who are homosexual. If he did not, that is a good reason why we cannot understand the argument of Romans 1 to be about them. We have already seen that if he thought that all same-sex relationships were pederastic, his argument, which appears at first sight to be about same-sex relationships in general, does not in fact apply to non-pederastic relationships. In the same way, if he thought that all homosexuality was due to a conscious rejection of God, then his argument, which appears at first sight to be about same-sex relationships in general, does not in fact apply to people who do not reject God. It may be that he did indeed consider the possibility that there might be homosexual relationships among those who acknowledge God, and that he carefully framed his argument to exclude them from its scope, not wishing to argue against them; but we have no reason to think so. On the other hand, it may be that he considered this possibility and rejected it; he may have thought not only that wilful rejection of God leads to homosexuality, as he asserts in Romans 1, but also that *all* homosexuality is due to the wilful rejection of God. Again, as far as I can see, we have no reason at all to think that he did so; certainly, he does not say so in Romans. Equally certainly, if he did think this, he was wrong, for there are as a matter of fact such relationships. In either case, homosexual relationships between devout Christians are simply not a possibility envisaged by the text we have, and the argument of the text therefore does not and cannot apply to them.

1 Corinthians 6:9–10

In these verses Paul presents a list of those who will not inherit the kingdom of God:

> Do you not know that the unjust will not inherit the kingdom of God? Do not be deceived: neither fornicators, nor idolaters, nor adulterers, nor *malakoi*, nor *arsenokoitai*, nor thieves, nor the greedy, nor drunkards, nor slanderers, nor robbers will inherit the kingdom of God.

There are difficulties in translating more than one term in this list, but for us the chief concern, and the chief difficulty, is with the words I have left untranslated. There is no commonly accepted translation of either.

Malakos

The less problematic word is *malakos*. This often means simply 'soft' when applied to inanimate objects.[27] It can also be applied in a metaphorical way to people. In 1 Corinthians 6:9 it is applied to people, and clearly in a pejorative sense. Throughout this list, Paul uses unambiguously masculine forms, though feminine forms were available. For the most part, this is unimportant; the masculine was simply the default gender. Paul certainly objects to female drunkards as well as to male ones, even if he does not supplement the masculine form of the word with a feminine one. But in talking of *malakoi*, 'the soft', he almost certainly has males alone in mind. In the Hellenistic world, as often in ours, the soft is associated with the feminine, while men are supposed to be in some sense hard. The *malakoi* are probably men who are not behaving as men should, but as women stereotypically do. But is the 'feminine' behaviour of these men a matter of general comportment, or a specifically sexual one? There seems to be no general agreement; so while the King James Version translates 'effeminate', the New Revised Standard Version has 'male prostitutes'. While there is some evidence that *malakos* and its cognate *malakia*, 'softness', were sometimes used with overtones of 'feminine' sexual behaviour, their use was certainly not confined to that.[28] That Paul disapproved of male *malakia* is not in doubt but, taking the word on its own, it seems difficult to go further. We cannot say exactly what *malakia* con-

106

sisted in for him, and even less can we identify it with some specific form of sexual behaviour. One way in which it seems possible to go further is to ask: What reason would Paul have to disapprove of the *malakoi* if he does not have some sexual practice of theirs in mind? And what kind of sexual practice could this be but homosexual practice? To us, who are preoccupied with homosexuality and who readily see softness or effeminacy in men as a sign that they are homosexual, the link may seem obvious, but our preoccupations are not those of all ages and all societies. In the Hellenistic world masculinity – associated among other things with strength and self-control – was much prized, and femininity and its associated qualities correspondingly disparaged. Softness in men could itself be derided and despised, apart from any association with 'feminine' sexual behaviour. So Paul Veyne writes:

> The passive homosexual was not rejected for his homosexuality but for his passivity, a very serious moral, or rather political infirmity. The passive individual's effeminacy was not the result of his perversion, far from it: it was simply one of the results of his lack of virility, and this was still a vice, even where no homosexuality was present. Roman society never bothered to ask if people were homosexual or not, but it devoted an excessive scrutiny to tiny details of dress, speech, gesture, and deportment in furthering its contempt for those who showed a lack of virility, whatever their sexual tastes.[29]

It is quite possible that Paul disapproves of exactly what he says he disapproves of, softness in men, without the implication of any particular sexual behaviour, homosexual or otherwise. If, on the other hand, he does have some kind of homosexual behaviour in mind, it is quite possible that he disapproves of it not as homosexual but as 'feminizing', or unfitting precisely for a man, because it makes him soft. If this is so, then there is no distaste for homosexual acts underlying his condemnation of the *malakoi*, but rather a particular vision of what it is to be a man and a concern for 'masculine' qualities. Such a concern for masculinity would explain why Paul does not bother to include in his list a term to cover female homosexuals. It would also fit in very well with the concerns of those whose importance in the ancient world Stowers reminds us of. In short, there is uncertainty about exactly what Paul means by *malakoi*, and there is certainly no reason to think that he is condemning any kind of homosexuals.

Arsenokoites

One reason why it is tempting to see homosexual overtones in the word *malakoi* is the fact that the next word in Paul's list is *arsenokoitai*. This word is obscure, and apparently of Paul's coining. It is almost certainly inspired by the Septuagint version of Leviticus 18:22, and so in all likelihood Paul has in mind those who perform the activity or activities he understands to be banned by that verse; this can only be some sexual activity between males. This fact has caused many to see the two terms *malakoi* and *arsenokoitai* as forming a pair. It then becomes possible to see the *malakoi* as those who take a passive or feminine role in sex between men, and the *arsenokoitai* as those who take an active or masculine role.[30] This is not impossible, though it needs some justification, as the list as a whole does not seem to be constructed out of pairs of terms; a reason has to be given why just these two should be understood as a pair. Whether or not *malakoi* is to be understood in the light of *arsenokoitai*, there can hardly be any doubt that the latter term refers to men who perform some kind of sex act with other men. But we know by now that this is far from sufficient to make it a condemnation of homosexual acts. Once again, condemnation is intensional. That the act these people perform can be truly described as a homosexual act does not imply that Paul excludes them from inheriting the kingdom of God *for* committing a homosexual act. He may not be at all concerned about sex between two people of the same sex but by, for instance, behaviour which in his eyes and the eyes of his culture feminizes a man, one of which happens to be taking the passive role in a sexual act between two men. If so, his concerns are not far from those of the author of Leviticus 18:22. Further, if he is not concerned with homosexual acts or people as such, this would again explain why he makes no reference to lesbians here, an omission that would otherwise be curious.

How is Paul likely to have thought about these matters? One way to answer this question is to ask how he understood the word *arsenokoites*. Nobody knows for sure. Certainly, we cannot discover how Paul or anybody else understood the word simply by looking up its etymology.[31] We discover how words are understood – that is, what they mean – by discovering how they are actually used, and there is no established use of the word in Paul's period. It is inspired by Leviticus 18:22, but whatever we may say about the actual meaning of Leviticus 18:22 at the time it was written, we have no direct evidence at all about Paul's understanding of it hundreds of years later. However, we can get a clue by looking at how Philo, his contemporary and the foremost thinker of Hellenistic Judaism, understood that law. He treats it in his work *The Special Laws*, where he without hesitation sees it as referring to pederasty. He objects to pederasty partly on the grounds that it is sterile, but it is clear that for him the great and distinctive defect of this kind of sexual activity is that it feminizes one of the partners, or rather, that it is an element of his effeminacy. For Philo reserves his greatest condemnation for the wider 'feminine' behaviour of the younger, passive partner, behaviour which marks the corruption of his male nature, so that he becomes a 'man-woman' (*androgynos*):

> Mark how conspicuously they braid and adorn the hair of their heads, and how they scrub and paint their faces with cosmetics and pigments and the like, and smother themselves with fragrant unguents ... These persons are rightly judged worthy of death by those who obey the law, which ordains that the man-woman who debases the sterling coin of nature should perish unavenged ... And the lover of such may be assured that he is subject to the same penalty. He pursues an unnatural (*para physin*) pleasure and does his best to render cities desolate and uninhabited by destroying the means of procreation. Furthermore he sees no harm in becoming a tutor and instructor in the grievous vices of unmanliness (*anandrias*) and effeminacy (*malakias*) by prolonging the bloom of the young and emasculating the flower of their prime, which should rightly be trained to strength and robustness. (*Special Laws*, III.37–39)[32]

And there is more in the same vein. In sum, the young passive partner debases his masculinity and effectively becomes a woman, while the older active partner encourages and teaches him. This is not all that is wrong: Philo remarks that the pleasure of the active partner is sterile and *para physin*, but clearly the chief defect of this pederastic relationship is that it corrupts the masculinity of one of the partners, making him soft and effeminate; his sexual passiveness is but one element of his emasculation. What is important is that a male be masculine. This involves, to be sure, taking an active sexual role and avoiding sexual passivity, but it also involves strength and the avoidance of self-adornment and other 'feminine' ways of behaving. We are not far from Veyne's characterization of the sexual concerns of the ancient Romans. What we have here is Philo's view, not Paul's, but, apart from the fact that Philo is a leading Jewish contemporary of Paul's, it accords well with the picture that Scroggs paints of how male–male sexual relationships tended to be conceived at the time. So we have reason to think that this is how Paul may have understood Leviticus 18:22, and we have no reason to think he understood it differently. If Paul did understand the word *arsenokoites* in this way – and that is our best guess – then he is concerned here with a particular kind of pederastic relationship that flourished in the Hellenistic culture of his time, but which is marginal in our own day. Though the sexual activity involved in that relationship is indeed homosexual, Paul does not condemn the *arsenokoites as* taking part in homosexual activity, but as taking part in the feminization of men. And perhaps he condemns the *malakos* for being happily feminized. The sexual relationship involved is rendered even more specific, and even more marginal to our own day, if we follow Scroggs when he argues that the relationship is basically a commercial one, that the *malakos* is a boy prostitute and the *arsenokoites* his customer.[33] But even if Scroggs is wrong here, the most probable understanding of Paul's vocabulary leads to the conclusion that he is not condemning homosexual relationships or homosexual activities. Rather is he denouncing one very specific form of male–male sexual relationship which is part of the feminized way of life of one of the partners, and condemning it because of the effeminacy involved. Apart from the fact that this has nothing at all to do with female–female sexual relationships, it is irrelevant to the majority of male–male sexual relationships that occur in modern societies, for these are not pederastic, and neither do they depend on or encourage the effeminacy of one of the partners.

The context of this list is also important for a correct understanding of what Paul is saying here. In 6:1 Paul complains that the Corinthian Christians are taking each other to court to settle disputes, and going to court means standing for judgement before the unjust (*tôn adikôn*). They should seek one among themselves to judge between them (v. 5). In fact, it is already a defeat for them that they litigate at all; they should rather be prepared to suffer injustice (*adikeisthe*) (v. 7). But instead of that they actually commit injustice (*adikeite*) and defraud their fellow Christians (v. 8). A theme running through these verses is injustice, doing wrong to another. This theme is continued in our list, which begins: 'Do you not know that the unjust (*adikoi*) will not inherit the kingdom of God' (v. 9). Then follows the list of ten kinds of people who will not inherit the kingdom. In context, it looks as if the list is an expansion of the original 'the unjust will not inherit the kingdom of God': the ten kinds of people in the list are all in their way *adikoi*. But the sense of *adikos* in this passage, repeated several times, is committing an offence against another person. Here, as so often in the New Testament, the criterion of uprightness before God, fitness to inherit the kingdom, is how one treats other human beings. Paul is not entirely consistent about this, for he includes idolaters in his list, and idolatry appears to be purely an offence against God, doing no harm to others. (Though this is a debatable point; remember how in Romans 1, Paul thinks that idolatry engenders a whole list of kinds of injustice.) Nevertheless, it is reasonable to say that the context creates the presumption for each of the members of our list that the people involved inflict some kind of wrong or injustice on some other or others. This element of injury to others is easy to see in most cases, but difficult in the case of the *malakoi* and the *arsenokoitai*. Perhaps Paul thinks, like Philo, that they harm society by failing to procreate; but he certainly does not say so. Perhaps he thinks that the *arsenokoitai* take advantage of an unjust slave trade;[34] but again, he does not say so. We simply have to guess, and much uncertainty must surround any conclusion we come to. But the context of the list strongly suggests that in including *malakoi* and *arsenokoitai* Paul is thinking of practices which do injury to others and will be recognized as such by his readers. That is, he does not condemn these practices as homosexual, but as unloving and harmful. He is not talking about 'homosexual acts' in general – there is no indication here that he had such a concept – but about practices, including certain specific homosexual practices, which harm others. So it implies no condemnation at all of any homosexual practices which do no harm to others.

There is one further point to be made about Paul's list. The individual items on it seem to be of little importance; he lumps them all together at the head of the list under the term *adikoi*, and again at the end when he tells the Corinthians: 'Such were some of you' (v. 11).[35] Paul seems to be envisaging a godless way of life in global terms, a life of which the activities of the *malakoi* and the *arsenokoitai* form part. I have argued that Paul is not referring to and condemning homosexual acts in general, but even if I am wrong on this point we still have to grapple with the fact, already mentioned in the discussion of Romans 1, that in the case of many modern homosexuals, and specifically Christian ones, their sexual activity is most definitely not part of such a life as Paul depicts. We know that such homosexuals are not idolaters, drunkards, greedy or robbers.

If for Paul it was natural to lump all these ways of living together, we do not do so, and we cannot do so without doing violence to what we actually know to be the case. We have to say once more either that, as I have suggested, Paul is talking about very specific sexual practices important in the culture of his day, or that he did not envisage the possibility that people in homosexual relationships be not godless, a possibility which we know to be realized in our society.

1 Timothy 1:10

In 1 Timothy, Paul[36] gives another list, this time of people against whom the law is intended. It is laid down

> not for the just, but for the lawless and disobedient, the impious and sinners, for the irreligious and godless, for parricides and matricides, for murderers, fornicators, *arsenokoitai*, slave traders, liars, perjurers and whatever else is contrary to sound teaching.

The word *arsenokoitai* crops up again here, and that is the reason why this text is sometimes cited as a condemnation of homosexual activity. But all the uncertainty which attends this word in 1 Corinthians 6:9 attends it here as well. We just do not know what kind or kinds of people Paul is talking about, which of their practices he has in mind, or the precise nature of his objection to those practices. All the remarks made above about this word in the context of 1 Corinthians 6 apply here too, along with the conclusion that to interpret its inclusion in this list as a condemnation of homosexual activity in general is unwarranted. There is, though, one piece of speculation, due to Scroggs,[37] which may help shed some light on Paul's target here. The following word in the list is *andrapodistes*, here translated 'slave trader'. The word can equally be translated 'kidnapper', and it is easy to see how the two translations might be related. If the translation 'slave trader' reflects Paul's intention, then it is a pertinent fact that one aim of the slave trade was often to provide prostitutes to work in brothels. In this context Paul might well have had in mind when speaking of *arsenokoitai* clients of brothels who bought the sexual services of boy slaves. If this is correct, it underlines the point that Paul is not here condemning what we would recognize as homosexual practices in general, but a very specific and exploitative sexual system. But there seems to be no way of verifying Scroggs's hypothesis, which must remain speculative. All we can say with certainty is that we do not know with any precision who and what Paul is talking about.

Further Remarks

What unanimity?

Our examination of the biblical texts most frequently claimed to express condemnation of same-sex activity has shown that the picture is not as clear as it is often presented. Certainly, the contention that these texts all condemn all homosexual activity is false. Despite *HP*'s assurance concerning Genesis 19 that '[t]here can be no doubt of the moral judgement made there against homosexual relations', no judgement is made there at all against homosexual relations. If there is a moral judgement, it is against homosexual rape; but a condemnation of homosexual rape is evidently not a condemnation of all homosexual relations, any more than a condemnation of heterosexual rape is a condemnation of all heterosexual relations. Leviticus 18:22 does not condemn homosexual relations, either. It condemns men who treat men sexually as women and men who allow themselves to be so treated; and it does this not because such behaviour is homosexual but because it degrades men to the status of women. This verse probably concerns consensual sex between men, not the rape which is attempted in Genesis 19, and to that extent it is less irrelevant to the modern Christian debate about the morality of same-sex relationships. But its judgement is based upon a supposed sexual hierarchy which modern Christians do not believe in (officially), and loses all sense when separated from the sexist society which is its background. While it condemns one specific form of male–male sexual activity, it does so for reasons which are, to Christians, not reasons at all; so it cannot furnish any support for a modern Christian condemnation of same-sex relationships, not even a condemnation of male–male sexual relationships. In the New Testament, the most significant text, Romans 1, is difficult to understand in some ways, but if it is a condemnation of anything it condemns deliberate rejection of God, and describes homosexual desire and activity (perhaps, rather, noncoital sex and hence 'unnatural' sex) as a kind of punishment for that rejection. Even if it can be shown, despite the arguments in this chapter, that Paul really is talking about homosexuals and their behaviour, those of whom Paul speaks are not condemned *because of* their homosexuality; because of their rejection of God, they are condemned *to* homosexuality. The clear link Paul makes between refusal to acknowledge God and the sexual practices of which he speaks also makes it difficult to see how this passage can be pertinent to a discussion of Christian homosexuality. Further, if Scroggs is right (though he may well not be), the form of homosexuality Paul has in mind – at least when he is speaking of males – is basically pederastic, and so he does not in any case have in mind the adult same-sex relationships which are the subject of debate in the modern church. As for 1 Corinthians 6:9–10 and 1 Timothy 1:10, though the occurrence there of the word *arsenokoites*, with its obvious links to Leviticus 18:22, at first seems promising, both texts turn out to be impossible to understand with any reasonable precision, so they can hardly be used to contribute to the current debate on homosexuality. The unanimity among these Old and New Testament texts which is often so easily assumed does not in fact exist. In so far as we can understand them, they are not all concerned with the same things, they do not all condemn the same things, and they do not all condemn what they do for the same reasons. Most importantly, they do not all condemn same-sex activity, some of them do not condemn same-sex activity, and *none of them* clearly condemns homosexual relationships or activity of a kind which is pertinent to the modern Christian debate.

An inconsistent approach?

It is a disquieting aspect of the way the texts we have been examining are sometimes used as part of a case against same-sex activity that their authority is invoked in a way which is internally inconsistent. Those who appeal to the authority of these texts at the same time treat these same texts as non-authoritative. To illustrate this I will look at the use made of three of these texts in *HP*. First, let us return to the following statement in §6: 'In Leviticus 18:22 and 20:13, in the course of describing the conditions necessary for belonging to the Chosen People, the author excludes from the People of God those who behave in a homosexual fashion.' We have already seen reason for thinking that *HP* misdescribes 18:22: it does not condemn people who behave in a homosexual fashion, but men who behave in a treating-men-as-women fashion. We have not so far looked closely at 20:13: 'A man who lies with a male the lyings of a woman, they have done an abomination, the two of them. They shall be put to death; their blood is upon them'. This verse adds little to our understanding of the kind of activity involved in 18:22, to which verse it is closely related, except that it perhaps makes clearer that the activity is a consensual one. But the law is not in fact a proscription of (penetrative) sex between men, but a prescription of how the community is to treat both men who treat other men sexually as women and men who allow themselves to be so treated. Now, *HP* invokes both 18:22 and 20:13 as showing that homosexual relations are condemned in the Bible, and that therefore we ought to condemn them. But if 20:13 shows that we ought to condemn homosexual relations, it shows by the same token that we ought to put to death those who are known to have had homosexual relations. There are, happily, few Christians today who press for the death penalty for people who engage in same-sex activity, and no doubt the authors of *HP* would be appalled at any such suggestion. Indeed, they seem to distance themselves from the full implications of 20:13 by stating that 'the author' of the verse excludes from the People of God those who behave in a homosexual fashion, rather than that it is God's will that they be so excluded; this is one man's opinion, not the revealed will of God. They also use the relatively soft 'exclude', from which those not already familiar with the verse would hardly conclude that it in fact prescribes death. This distancing is understandable, indeed laudable; but what is its justification? If the author of this inspired text excludes practising homosexuals from the people of God by prescribing their execution, ought we not to do the same? In fact, not only do we feel free to ignore the prescription of 20:13, most of us also would be strongly opposed to any suggestion that we should obey it. But it is inconsistent to treat 20:13 as having authority in so far as it is deemed to express a negative attitude towards same-sex activity and to treat it as having no authority in so far as it prescribes how the community should treat the people involved. Given the close relationship between this verse and 18:22, to which we have devoted more attention, it is also inconsistent to treat the interdiction of 18:22 as authoritative while not similarly treating the prescription of 20:13 as binding. Either both are authoritative for us, or neither are. Those who – surely rightly – refuse to recognize the binding nature of the prescription must equally refuse to recognize the binding nature of the interdiction. In short, if we do not think, on the basis of 20:13, that God wills that men who have sex with men and women who have sex with women should be put to death, then we *cannot* think, on the basis of 18:22, that God wills that men should not have sex with men or women with women. (This of course does not preclude us from thinking this for other reasons.) Secondly, a similar inconsistency also lurks in *HP*'s treatment of Romans 1, though I think a less serious one. It speaks of the disharmony between Creator and creatures wrought by idolatry, and says: 'Paul is at a loss to find a clearer example of this disharmony than homosexual relations' (§6). *HP* nowhere tries to justify this very strong statement. It is a remarkable thing to say in the light of the long vice list which Paul gives in verses 29–31: those who have deliberately denied God are 'full of all injustice, evil, greed, wickedness, full of envy, murder, quarrelling, treachery, malignity; whisperers, slanderers, God-haters, insolent, haughty, boasters, inventors of evil, disobedient to parents, senseless, disloyal, inhumane, merciless'. That is quite a list. Are we really to believe that Paul thinks that a same-sex couple having sex together is a clearer example of disharmony with God than murder, treachery or inhumanity? Surely not. But suppose it should turn out to be true, and that Paul really does think it more sinful,[38] as *HP* implies, for one man to have sex with another than for one man to murder another. What consequences does that have for our attitude today? Does the putative fact that Paul thinks this indicate that we should think it too? This would surely go against any sense of moral proportion, and most Christians would reject it without hesitation or apology. We do not here feel bound to agree with Paul, if indeed this is his attitude. But it seems *HP* is committed to saying that we are bound to agree with Paul, because the whole point of its appeal to this passage of Romans is to say that the attitudes Paul expresses here have authority for us. However, if we can permit ourselves not to share this particular view attributed to Paul – that same-sex activity is worse than murder, hating God, and the rest – then it seems we can also permit ourselves not to share other views he expresses here; in particular, we are under no obligation to adopt his negative attitude to same-sex desire and activity.

This instance of inconsistency is not so serious, because the authors of *HP* can escape it simply by dropping the claim that Paul can find no greater example of disharmony than same-sex relations. The difficulty we encounter with *HP*'s reading of a third text, 1 Corinthians 6:9–10, is not so easily evaded, for it is a difficulty posed by the very words of Paul rather than by a gloss on them. *HP* interprets this passage, as we have already seen, as saying that

'those who behave in a homosexual fashion [are included] among
those who shall not enter the Kingdom of God'. We have found
reason to find this interpretation more than doubtful. But suppose
it is correct: what then? *HP* cites this text in support of the claim
that homosexual acts are universally condemned in Scripture. But
this passage is not about acts, it is about people; according to *HP* it
is about, among others, 'those who behave in a homosexual fashion'. It does not merely condemn certain acts, it says that those who
commit them shall not enter the Kingdom of God. Well, do we
believe this? And do the authors of *HP* believe it? Do they, and do
we all, believe that, for example, a pair of male social workers, who
dedicate their lives to looking after the poor and deprived, who visit
the sick and those in prison, and who give of their time and money
to the needy, who worship God devoutly, who love each other and
thank God for that love, and who have sex together – who 'behave
in a homosexual fashion' – are excluded from the Kingdom of God?
Of course not. But if we feel free not to believe, on the basis of this
text, that they are not excluded from the Kingdom of God, then we
cannot consistently think we are constrained to believe, on the basis
of this same text, that their sexual activity is sinful. So our study
appears to show not only that the biblical texts used as a standard
appeal in support of a condemnation of homosexual activity do not
in fact support it, but also that in at least two of those texts, from
Leviticus and 1 Corinthians, the appeal to biblical authority contains an internal contradiction; it is incoherent. This, together with
the detailed study of all the standard texts that we have undertaken,
shows that this part of the biblical case against same-sex activity is
specious. The supposed biblical condemnations of same-sex activity
either do not exist or, where they may be thought to exist, cannot be
supposed to have authority for us. But appeal to these 'proof texts'
is only one aspect of the modern case made against homosexual
practice on the basis of the Bible. In view of the doubts frequently
raised about the interpretation of these texts, and which are
beginning to be shared even by conservative theologians, less weight
has been put on them in recent times, and another line of argument
has been developed, one based not upon isolated texts held to
condemn homosexual practices but upon a positive vision of human
sexuality to be found, so it is claimed, in Scripture; a vision with
which homosexual practices are allegedly incompatible. We must
now turn to an examination of this.

CHAPTER FIVE

The Bible for Heterosexuality?

In addition to the texts we have just looked at, attempts have been made recently to construct an anti-homosexual argument from texts which do not mention homosexuality at all, but in which there is either a non-sexual theme or a supposed reference, taken as normative, to heterosexuality. *HP* is an example of this kind of argumentation. It claims to find a basic divine plan for sexuality in the opening chapters of Genesis, one which sets up heterosexuality as the norm and which therefore excludes homosexuality. Examination of arguments of this kind, and particularly of the argument to be found in *HP*, will make up the second stage of our discussion of the Bible. Thirdly, we will turn to some other biblical texts which may be of help in structuring a Christian attitude towards homosexual acts and relationships, texts which tend not to feature in arguments on this subject. This third stage, which will follow in the next chapter, is an attempt to broaden the biblical base of the discussion of homosexuality and so to avoid putting excessive weight on those few texts which are normally at the centre of the biblical debate.

Genesis 1

Genesis 1, the story of the world's creation, is for many the essential basis of any Christian understanding of sex, and therefore of same-sex activity. This chapter shows the antediluvian world, the pre-lapsarian world, the world upon which God looked and saw that it was very good (Genesis 1:31). This is a vision of the world uncontaminated by human sin, the world which is exactly as God wants it to be. If there are any clues to be had in the Bible as to the essential nature of human sexuality as willed by God, we will surely, they think, find them here.

Lawler, Boyle and May

I start the discussion of this chapter with some remarks of Lawler, Boyle and May, who find Genesis a very significant text indeed for a Christian understanding of sexuality in general. While their discussion is short and happily untechnical, what they say represents fairly what has become a standard view of this chapter in Catholic discussions of sex in general and of homosexuality in particular. They claim that it teaches four great truths about human persons, human sexuality and marriage. There is not space to examine all four of these alleged truths, and not all of them are relevant to our purposes. The most important is the first:

> it unequivocally affirms the fundamental equality of man and woman as persons made in the image and likeness of God ... 'So God created man ... in his own image, in the image of God he created him; male and female he created them' (Gen. 1:27). Each is a different but complementary epiphany or revelation of God himself, whose full image is found in their communion.[1]

Here the authors refer in particular to Genesis 1:27. This verse is apparently the basis for their claim that Genesis 1 teaches this 'great truth'. There is no doubt that much of what they say in this short passage is admirable; but is it really what is taught by this verse, or by Genesis 1 as a whole? The first obvious thing to note is just how much of what they say is absent from the text they cite. Genesis 1:27 does indeed say that God created men and women in his own image. But it does not say that men and women have a fundamental equality; neither does it say that men and women are complementary revelations of God; nor does it say that God's full image is to be found in the communion of male and female. Some or all of these things may be true, but it is another thing to claim that they are asserted by this verse of the Bible. Let us look at the claims in a little more detail. First, Lawler, Boyle and May claim that this verse 'unequivocally affirms the fundamental equality of man and woman as persons made in the image and likeness of God'. Let us take it that the text does imply that both men and women are made in the image of God. But what about their fundamental equality? We may believe that men and women are fundamentally equal, but that does not oblige us to think that this text says so, or even that it implies it. The text of Genesis 1 states effectively that males and females have a quality in common, that of being made in the image of God. But having a quality in common, even an important quality, does not imply equality. All that can be said about this text is that it does not make any explicit statement of inequality; but not asserting inequality is not the same as asserting equality, still less affirming it unequivocally. We have also, of course, to ask what is meant by equality here. We might think of equality in the eyes of God: that God treats all people the same regardless of who they are, and in this case regardless of what sex they are. On the other hand, there is social equality. Even if all people have equal value in the eyes of God and are treated impartially by him, they are certainly not treated equally in human societies; cases of discrimination and inequality are too numerous to need documenting here. For Christians it is how God views people that is determinative, not how they are seen in any particular human society. If we are trying to understand the thought of Genesis 1, however, this distinction between the divine and the human, the eternal and the social, is not so easy to draw; for, as we have seen, according to the ideology of the Pentateuch, certain social patterns are found in Israelite society just because God wills them. Social structures are expressed and confirmed through law, and according to the Pentateuch the law governing Israelite society is no mere human invention but of divine origin. If one thing is certain about ancient Israelite society, it is that there is a huge inequality between men and women. And this inequality is inscribed in law, a law purportedly imposed not by the dominant males but by God himself. Thus, according to the dominant ideology of the Old Testament, laid out in the Pentateuch, there is a God-given inequality between male and female. The author of Genesis lived in and was formed by this society. Genesis 1 is part of the Pentateuch, in which that ideology finds expression. Further, it is almost universally agreed among biblical scholars that it is closely related to the so-called Priestly school responsible for much of the legislation to be found in the rest of the Pentateuch, including that of Leviticus, and which enshrines sexual inequality in law. It is thus practically inconceivable that the author of Genesis 1 would want to assert the sexual equality that Lawler, Boyle and May claim to find in the text. Not only is there no explicit assertion of equality; if anything is implicit, it is much more likely to be an assumption of inequality, and of God-given inequality at that. There is thus no warrant at all for the claim that Lawler, Boyle and May make at this point. Though we may all want to say that there is a fundamental equality between men and women, such a doctrine cannot be read out of this text. Lawler, Boyle and May assert, too, that according to Genesis 1:27 men and women, though different, are complementary epiphanies of God. Now, if the text says that both are made in the image of God, it is fair to interpret this as saying that each is an epiphany of God (taking epiphany as equivalent to image). And since there is a difference between male and female, we can say that each is a *different* epiphany of God. But we have to be careful here. There are different sorts of difference, and images can be different in more than one way: among others, there are differences of medium and differences of content. For example, take two images of the same person, one a photograph, the other an oil painting. There will be large physical differences between the two, just because they are very different media. But in another way, from the point of view of content, they might be the same, because they are images of the same person made from the same angle. (The painting might even be painted using the photograph as model.) Again, two images might be the same materially, if they are both photographs or both oil paintings, but differ in content; they might be images of different people, or images of the same person from different angles. Or two images might be different in terms of both medium and content.

Now, if Lawler, Boyle and May want to say that men and women are different images of God, what sort of difference do they mean? Is it that men and women, being materially (and perhaps also psychologically) different from each other, are as it were different media in which the same divine stamp is imprinted, so that the content of the image is the same? Are they like an oil painting and a photograph of the same person from the same angle? Or is it rather a difference of content that is being asserted? Is it that, while both being images of the same God, they are images of different aspects of God, like images of the same person made from two different angles? There does seem to be support in the text for saying that men and women are different images of God in the sense of being images in different media. Men and women are by definition different physically in particular ways, and it might be that one can point also, in a general way, to other physical differences and to certain psychological differences. But there is nothing in the text to suggest that the content of the image is different in each case – say, that men and women are images of different aspects or qualities of God. If anything, the fact that God is simply said to make human beings generically (*ha'adam*) in his image rather suggests that the sexual difference is not relevant to the content of the image. The text, then, seems to license saying that men and women are different images of God only in the sense that they are the same image stamped on different materials. But what then is the warrant for saying that they are *complementary* epiphanies of God? Complementarity is not the same as difference. In recent Christian thinking about sex, particularly in the Catholic Church, the term has acquired increasing importance, and it is difficult to read a book or even an article on human sexuality or on homosexuality without coming across it. Its precise meaning is not entirely clear; we shall have to devote some time to this question later. But if we come across the term in recent writings, we do not come across it, or anything like it, in the Bible, let alone in Genesis 1. Though it preoccupies modern theologians, we have no reason for thinking that it was of concern to biblical writers. This is one reason for thinking it not altogether licit to interpret Genesis 1 as speaking of complementarity. But there is a further reason. There is an obvious sense in which men and women might be said to be complementary: they can fit together in such a way as to reproduce. That kind of complementarity relates to their material differences. But if we are thinking of men and women specifically as different and complementary *images*, what seems to be required is some kind of complementarity with respect to the *content* of the images. For it is hard to see how a material difference, a difference in the medium, could be of such a kind as to make two images complementary precisely as images. An oil painting and a photograph of the same person from the same angle are certainly different, but this difference hardly licenses calling them complementary. On the other hand, we can easily make sense of the idea of complementary contents of images; for example, we might call a front view of a person and a rear view of the same person complementary images of that person, or a front view and a profile, as in police photographs. Genesis 1 licenses speaking of men and women as complementary only in the material sense, and gives no indication at all that they are complementary with respect to the content of the image of God. So while it may make sense to speak of men and women as in some sense biologically complementary – we might want to call them 'complementary reproducers' – there is no scriptural warrant here for calling them complementary images of God. Neither does the text hint that, as Lawler, Boyle and May claim, the full image of God is to be found in the communion of male and female. It does not mention communion at all. Further, speaking of a 'full image' of God supposes a distinction between a full image and a partial or defective image. That distinction is quite foreign to the text, which says simply that God made human beings in his image. It does not say that he made men and women each as partial images, and that his full image is to be found in their communion. Since the text makes no distinction between partial and full images, that can only mean that each person, male or female, is a complete image of God in his or her own right;[2] and this is in any case the natural way of reading the text.

HP

HP also attaches great importance to Genesis 1; indeed, though its treatment of the text is as brief and dense as is that of Lawler, Boyle and May, it takes it as the very starting point for its discussion:

> Providing a basic plan for understanding this entire discussion of homosexuality is the theology of creation we find in Genesis. God, by his infinite wisdom and love, brings into existence all of reality as a reflection of his goodness. He fashions mankind, male and female, in his own image and likeness. Human beings, therefore, are nothing less than the work of God himself; and in the complementarity of the sexes, they are called to reflect the inner unity of the Creator. They do this in a striking way in their cooperation with him in the transmission of life by a mutual donation of the self to the other. (*HP* §6)

This is a noble vision, linking human procreation to the very nature of God himself. It may be the basis of a truly Christian vision of humanity's calling. But what has this vision to do with same-sex relationships or same-sex activity? How might it be a basis for a theological understanding of homosexuality? In the same section, §6, *HP* refers to what is traditionally known as the Fall, the events described in Genesis 3. The breach with God caused by our first parents' disobedience causes in turn a rupture in human relationships. This is followed by a progressive deterioration which is traced, it is implied, in the succeeding chapters of Genesis. The story of Sodom in Genesis 19 is to be understood, according to this same section, as part of that deterioration, and that story expresses a clear condemnation of same-sex activity. So such activity is to be understood as a result and symptom of human degradation from its original perfection, a consequence of the Fall. If we now ask why we should understand same-sex activity in this way, the answer comes in §7:

123

To choose someone of the same sex for one's sexual activity is to annul the rich symbolism and meaning, not to mention the goals, of the Creator's sexual design. Homosexual activity is not a complementary union, able to transmit life; and so it thwarts the call to a life of that form of self-giving which the Gospel says is the essence of Christian living.

In short, same-sex activity cuts across God's design as expressed in Genesis 1. This approach has the great advantage that it does not treat homosexuality as an isolated phenomenon, to be discussed and evaluated independently of other biblical considerations. Such a treatment would run the risk of reaching conclusions that appeared arbitrary, unconnected to wider values. The approach of *HP* seeks to avoid this, aiming to place homosexual activity firmly within the context of a biblical view of human sexuality as a whole, so that its judgement on homosexual activity is situated within a broader context and given sense and force by that context. But is this vision of human sexuality, outlined in §6, actually to be found, as *HP* claims, in Genesis? Can it be read out of the text, or only read into it by those who for other reasons subscribe to it? *HP* does not explicitly state what part of Genesis it has in mind, but it clearly refers to Genesis 1. Within that, the focus is mainly on verses 26–8, the creation of and blessing of human beings. The text runs as follows:

And God said: 'Let us make humankind in our image and according to our likeness, and let them dominate the fish of the sea and the birds of the sky and the cattle, and all the earth and every creeping thing that creeps on the earth.' And God created humankind in his image; in the image of God he created it;[3] male and female he created them. And God blessed them and God said to them: 'Be fruitful and multiply and fill the earth ... '

As *HP* implies, this text shows us God creating men and women in his image.[4] It goes on to speak of human fruitfulness, what *HP* refers to as 'transmission of life'. But does this text say essentially what *HP* says it does? Does it say that men and women 'in the complementarity of the sexes ... are called to reflect the inner unity of the Creator'? Does the text say essentially that men and women 'do this in a striking way in their cooperation with him in the transmission of life by a mutual donation of the self to the other'? There are number of points which cast grave doubt on this view of the text. *HP* quite rightly states that according to Genesis God creates men and women in his image. It goes on to claim that 'therefore ... in the complementarity of the sexes, they are called to reflect the inner unity of the Creator'. Let us note first that nowhere is this said in the biblical text itself. Genesis does not make any explicit link between people's being created in the image of God, on the one hand, and their being called to reflect the inner unity of the Creator in the complementarity of the sexes, on the other hand. What we have in *HP* is not a straightforward exposition of the biblical text, but a theological interpretation of it. There is nothing wrong with that. But the fact that it is a theological interpretation raises two important questions. First, is it a plausible interpretation? And second, is it the only possible or plausible interpretation? The first question is of obvious importance: if *HP*'s interpretation of the text should turn out to be implausible, then the basis of *HP*'s position on homosexuality crumbles, for Genesis was meant to provide 'a basic plan for understanding this entire discussion of homosexuality'. But the second question is also an important one. Even if *HP*'s interpretation of the text should turn out to be sustainable, other interpretations might be equally possible; interpretations which are at least equally faithful to the biblical text but which do not have the implications for human sexuality in general and for homosexuality in particular that *HP* claims its own interpretation has. If other interpretations are possible, at least equally faithful and at least equally plausible, then *HP*'s own interpretation becomes but one among others. Adopting it or preferring some other interpretation becomes a matter, not of fidelity to the Bible, but of theological choice. *HP*'s own interpretation cannot be properly presented as necessary. But if that is so, those who honestly prefer a different interpretation are entitled to part company with *HP* at the very first step of its argument. They are entitled to say to the CDF: 'No, Genesis does not mean what you think it means, so it does not have the implications for human sexuality in general and for homosexuality in particular that you think it has; effectively, Genesis does not provide a basis for understanding homosexuality, or at least not the basis you think it provides.' So, in order to assess the force of *HP*'s appeal to Genesis, we need both to assess *HP*'s own interpretation of the biblical text and to see whether there are any other possible interpretations which are at least as faithful to the text.

Is *HP*'s interpretation of the text of Genesis 1 plausible in itself? There are several considerations which may lead us to have grave doubts. The first major apparent difficulty is that most of the key ideas behind *HP*'s interpretation are simply absent from the text of Genesis. We have already seen that the same difficulty confronts the assertions of Lawler, Boyle and May about what Genesis 1 says. The text does of course say that God created humankind in his image, and that he created them male and female, and this seems to imply that both men and women are created in the image of God.[5] But, as we have already seen, the text does not talk about any complementarity between male and female. Neither does it say that men and women are called, on the basis of this putative complementarity, to reflect the inner unity of the Creator. Indeed, there is no mention at all of the inner unity of the Creator. Still less does the text imply in any obvious way that men and women reflect this inner unity in a striking way 'in their cooperation with him in the transmission of life by a mutual donation of the self to the other'. But we have to ask how far this is a real difficulty. Though the vocabulary of *HP* is absent from the text of Genesis, that does not necessarily mean that the ideas behind the vocabulary are not to be found, or that they are not strongly implied. For example, Genesis 1 does not speak of people being called to do anything; they are simply created in God's image. But we can reasonably argue that being created in God's image implies a call to live in a certain way. In the Sermon on the Mount, Jesus is clear that we are, as a matter of fact, children of God; God is our heavenly father. But this fact implies the call to behave in certain ways, and so to be like God our father: 'I say to you, love your enemies and pray for those who persecute you, so that you may be sons of your father in heaven' (Matt. 5:44–5). Living up to the name of Christ means pursuing some kinds of behaviour and avoiding others. Similarly, we can say, the fact of being made in the image of God implies a call to live up to what we are by our actions. Again, though the text does not speak of the complementarity of men and women, there is an obvious biological sense in which men and women are complementary: they are fitted to reproduce together by their joint sexual activity. This biological complementarity is suggested by the text itself when it speaks of God creating people, not as men and women, but as male and female. 'Male' and 'female' are impersonal, biological terms, applied in the Old Testament to animals as well as to people.[6] So it is possible to say that the text does imply the complementarity of men and women, if by this is meant that biological complementarity which is a feature of sexual reproduction.

The image of God

There are, therefore, reasons for accepting certain elements of *HP*'s interpretation, despite the distance of its language from that of the text itself. But there remain problems concerning other, more central, elements, in particular *HP*'s conception of the image of God. The phrase 'image of God' is vague and enigmatic, and has been the object of much speculation. It is far from clear what is the meaning of the phrase in the thought of Genesis 1, and any interpretation runs the risk of appearing to impose a meaning alien to the text. This is not a risk *HP* escapes. Indeed, *HP*'s interpretation of the text at this point is vulnerable for several reasons, both exegetical and theological. First, *HP* seems to be using the idea of the image of God in a way similar to Lawler, Boyle and May: men and women are complementary, in the sense that they can reproduce together, and they are also both images of God; so they are complementary images of God. But, as we have seen, while there is a point in calling men and women complementary reproducers, the text of Genesis 1 does not license calling them complementary images of God. Secondly, while there might be reason for saying, as indicated above, that humankind's being created in the image of God implies a call to live in such as way as to image God, there is no suggestion anywhere in the text, or beneath the surface of the text, that this image has anything to do with the unity of God. If people are in some way called to show forth God in the world, there is no reason at all to think that, according to the text of Genesis, what people are to show forth is precisely the inner unity of God. Christians do of course believe that God is one, not only in the sense of there being only one God, but also in that God is a union of three divine Persons, conventionally called Father, Son and Holy Spirit. But this Christian belief is not expressed in the text of Genesis 1; it may be read into the text, but cannot legitimately be read out of it. The doctrine of the Trinity is not to be found in the text, even if Christians can and do read it with this doctrine in mind. In its own terms, the text not only does not speak of the Trinity, it does not speak of the unity of God at all. Thirdly, and this is again an exegetical point, *HP* links people's being created male and female with their being created in the image of God. This is a connection not made by the text of Genesis 1:26–8 itself, or by the immediate context. The text does seem to say that both men and women, male and female, are created in the image of God. But it does not say that their being in the image of God consists of their being sexually differentiated, or that it consists in the sexual complementarity of male and female. On the contrary, there is every reason for thinking that this is not what the text intends to say. For if it is in their being sexually differentiated that their being in the image of God consists, we would expect human sexual differentiation to be a reflection of sexual differentiation within God. But nowhere in Scripture is it stated or implied that sexual differentiation is an element of the divine nature itself, that God is both male and female; God is mostly spoken of as male, rarely as female, but never as male and female. It would be surprising indeed if any idea of internal sexual differentiation in God underlay the text of Genesis 1. And if the text does not state or imply any sexual differentiation in God, it cannot be thought, either, to imply that sexual differentiation between human beings is any element of the meaning of their being created in the image of God. Fourthly, *HP* says that men and women reflect the inner unity of God 'in a striking way in their cooperation with him in the transmission of life by a mutual donation of the self to the other'. Clearly, what *HP* here calls a 'mutual donation of the self to the other' is an act of sexual intercourse resulting in conception.[7] Now, it is hard to see how a woman's engaging in a sexual act of this kind makes her reflect in a striking way the inner unity of the Creator, and equally hard to see how a man's doing the same makes him a striking image of the inner unity of God. What might be claimed with less difficulty is that it is the couple, the man and the woman together, who reflect the inner unity of God. But if that is what is being claimed here, then it is the couple that is held to be the image of God, not the individual male and female human beings. Exegetically speaking, this is perhaps not an impossible reading of Genesis 1:26–7, but there is little to support it. It runs up against the difficulty that in 5:1–3 the male individual Adam, formed in the image of God, appears to transmit this image to an individual, his son Seth, and not to any couple. More seriously, in 9:5–6 God imposes the death penalty for the killing of human beings, and the rationale given for this is that God made people in his own image. It is clearly individual human beings that are meant here, and this gives strong support to the interpretation of Genesis 1 that makes the individual, not the couple, the bearer of the divine image. From a wider Christian point of view, the interpretation which makes the couple the bearer of the divine image is also incompatible with the Christian and biblical doctrine that the individual Jesus Christ is the image of God par excellence (see Colossians 1:15). A fifth problem is that it seems to be a mistake to link the idea of the image of God to that of reproduction. There may appear to be a case for saying that people's being created in the image of God has something to do with their capacity to reproduce sexually, and hence with the biological complementarity of the sexes, in that in 1:28, immediately following the statement that God created people in his own image, we read: 'And God blessed them, and God said to them, "Be fruitful and become numerous and fill the earth and subdue it."' The blessing 'be fruitful and become numerous' may at first sight seem to be a consequence of people's being created in the image of God and so an explication of what the expression 'image of God' means. But further examination of Genesis 1 shows this to be unlikely. For in verse 22 God blesses the fish in the same way, and there is no suggestion that fish are created in the image of God. We should understand rather that people's being created in the image of God is logically prior to their ability to reproduce sexually:[8] if there is something especially important about human reproduction, it is because human beings are already the bearers of the image of God. A sixth difficulty is the interpretation itself that *HP* proposes of the term 'image of God' and its relation to the Christian tradition. It relates this term, as applied to human beings, to the complementarity of the sexes and the ability to procreate, as if this were unquestionably the Christian understanding of it. But throughout almost all of Christian history the term has actually been understood quite differently. To take just two examples, but two important ones, both St Augustine and St Thomas Aquinas understand the relevant text differently from *HP*. Augustine, commenting on Genesis, says:

> [W]hen he said 'in our image' he immediately added 'and let him have power over the fish of the sea and the birds of the air', and other animals which are devoid of reason. Thus we should understand that man is made in the image of God in virtue of that by which he is superior to irrational animals. But that is reason itself, or mind, or intelligence, or whatever else it might more fittingly be called. So the Apostle too says 'Be renewed in the spirit of your mind, and put on the new man,[9] which is renewed in knowledge according to the image of him who created it', amply showing in what respect man is created in the image of God, that it is by virtue not of bodily shape but of some intelligible form of illuminated mind.[10]

For Augustine, then, people's being created in the image has nothing to do with the difference, complementary or otherwise, of the sexes, still less with their ability to reproduce sexually. Indeed, in his reference to Colossians he expressly rules out any connection with bodily form: it is mind that makes us the image of God, not body.

In article 2 of question 93 the first part of the *Summa Theologiae*, St Thomas Aquinas discusses the question 'whether the image of God is to be found in irrational creatures'. He frames his reply in terms of similitude to God. In a very basic sense, he concedes, everything that exists resembles God simply because, like God, it exists. There is a second, more important sense in which living creatures in particular are like God. But there is a third sense in which those creatures resemble God which have discernment and understanding. He quotes with approval Augustine, who says that in all creation nothing more closely resembles God than such creatures. So he concludes that 'only intellectual creatures are, properly speaking, in the image of God'.[11] So at least two central witnesses to the Christian tradition interpret the concept of the image of God not only differently from *HP* but in a way incompatible with it. *HP*'s interpretation does not, then, represent the consensus of the tradition. I know of no patristic or medieval text which understands the idea of the image of God in the same way as *HP*, so as far as I know *HP*'s understanding of it is quite untraditional. This may just be my ignorance; there may be significant contributors to the tradition who do support *HP*'s view. But the fact that figures of the stature of Augustine and Aquinas have a quite different understanding of the image of God shows at the very least that there is another stream to the tradition, and this seriously undermines any idea that *HP* gives *the* Christian, or even *the* Catholic, understanding of what it means to be created in the image of God.

Seventhly, from the point of view of Christian theology, it is traditional to say that the unity of the Trinity is constituted by love. But this love has nothing to do with sexual complementarity. The Persons of the Trinity are not, as traditionally conceived, of different sexes, and the love that unites them is not sexual love. If the love uniting the divine Persons is in some way analogous to human love, it is not primarily analogous to the mutual sexual love of a man and a woman. Given that this is so, it is not easy to see how human mutual sexual love can be thought of as a particularly apt or striking image of the mutual love of the divine Persons. Certainly, Jesus never uses such imagery, whereas he constantly uses the imagery of father and child to express the close relationship between God and himself and between God and the disciples. Christian theology does relate love to the concept of the image of God in that it urges people to be like God by loving. I have already cited Matthew 5:44–5 as an instance of this.[12] In John 13:34 and 15:12 Jesus similarly urges his disciples to love each other as he has loved them. Other passages to similar effect are Ephesians 5:1–2 and 1 John 4:7–11. But this love which is an imitation of God is always an imitation of the love of God *ad extra*, the love of God for the world, and not an imitation of the love of the divine Persons for each other. We are held to be like God if we love human beings as God loves human beings, not if we love human beings as God loves God. Nor is this human love by which people imitate God a sexual love; it is never held in the Bible that sexual intercourse is a particularly striking expression of this love. Christians are not urged to make love; they are urged to love their enemies and pray for those who persecute them (Matt. 5:44), to give to those in need (Matt. 5:42), to forgive without limit those who wrong them (Matt. 18:21–35), to be humble and to prefer others to themselves (Phil. 2:3), and so on.

There is thus little to recommend *HP*'s understanding of Genesis 1, just as there is little to recommend that of Lawler, Boyle and May. Here, as there, several exegetical difficulties attend the proposed reading of the text. Not the least of these is that the key ideas of this reading are all absent from the text itself; they are not there explicitly and they are not there implicitly, either. The theology of creation, with its implications for the understanding of human sexuality, which *HP* claims we find there, is simply not there to be found. If we read the text, particularly verses 26–7, in a wider Christian theological manner, in the light of the New Testament, *HP*'s interpretation of what Genesis 1 says about the image of God fits uneasily with the conception of Jesus Christ as the image of God. If, on the other hand, we as Christians read Genesis 1 in the light of that conception, we are impelled towards a different understanding. If we can interpret its image-language as a call, then it looks more like a call to act as our heavenly father acts, to be like God in selfless and forgiving love. The definitive image of God, the one who shows us what it really is to be in the image of God, is Jesus, and it is in modelling ourselves on him that we answer the call to be like God. So Genesis 1 is to be read not in terms of a recipe for human sexuality, still less as a text prescribing compulsory heterosexuality, but as one pointing us towards Jesus Christ, the true image of God, so that we in turn, looking at him, may be remade in his image (2 Cor. 3:18), shot through with love. Genesis 1 does not, therefore, furnish us with a starting point for a Christian understanding of human sexuality, unless we understand it to be saying that our sexual behaviour, like the rest of our activities, is to manifest or at least be compatible with that love that makes us children and images of God. So neither does it give us a key to understanding homosexuality and same-sex activity in the way *HP* claims it does. It does not reveal to us the Creator's sexual design, or even that the Creator has a sexual design, so neither does it in any way imply that homosexual activity runs counter to any divine design, as *HP* claims. This does not show that God has no sexual design, and it does not show that homosexual activity does not run counter to any sexual design God may have. God may well have such a design, and homosexual activity may well run counter to it; but this biblical text gives us no reason to think so. There may be any number of reasons why people should not engage in homosexual activity; only, what Genesis 1 says is not one of them.

The logic of the argument

These difficulties with what *HP* says, which I have presented as problems to do with *HP*'s interpretation of the text of Genesis, have another aspect: there is a difficulty regarding the logic of *HP*'s assertions, apart from its exegetical claims. This part of *HP* has the form of an argument. A premiss is laid down and a conclusion or series of conclusions is drawn from it. It has the form *P, therefore C*. Once we understand *P*, we should be able to see that *C* follows from it. Once we admit the truth of *P*, we are led to admit the truth of *C* also. We can schematize the argument in this way:

P: God fashions humankind, male and female, in his own image and likeness.

Therefore,

C_1: Human beings are nothing less than the work of God himself; and

C_2: In the complementarity of the sexes, they are called to reflect the inner unity of the Creator.

It is possible that we should also add:

C_3: They do this in a striking way in their cooperation with him in the transmission of life by a mutual donation of the self to the other.

It is not entirely clear whether this last sentence is intended to represent part of the conclusion drawn from the premiss, or whether it is to be seen rather as an independent assertion which will serve as a premiss in the argument of the following paragraphs. Given this doubt, I exclude C_3 for the purposes of what I have to say here. Though the text here is in the form of an argument, what logical relation do C_1 and C_2 actually bear to P? Do they follow? We can see at once that C_1 is closely connected to P: if God fashions humankind in his own image then human beings are clearly, a fortiori, the work of God. C_1 follows from P quite formally, as a matter of logic. This is incontrovertible. Further, for any Christian understanding of humanity, it is incontrovertibly important to assert that human beings are the work of God. But that does not get us very far in developing a Christian understanding of same-sex activity, which is the theme of *HP*. That work is done by C_2. It is here that we start to see a theory of human sexuality which will later be used to pass judgement on homosexual activity. C_2 is tacked on to C_1 as if it were the same thing, as if, once we have arrived at C_1 we have also arrived at C_2. Rhetorically, there is an obvious advantage to writing in this way. Since C_1 so obviously follows from P, we are given the impression that C_2 is equally a clear logical consequence of P. So we are led to accept the view of human sexuality proposed in C_2, and to accept it as a supposed consequence of P. C_2 gets in on the coat-tails of C_1, as it were. But, obviously, C_1 and C_2 do not say the same thing. If C_2 follows from P at all, it follows as a separate conclusion. The argument would then become in effect: God fashions humankind, male and female, in his own image and likeness; *therefore*, in the complementarity of the sexes, they are called to reflect the inner unity of the Creator (*P, therefore C_2*). It is obvious, however, that there is a huge gap between the premiss and the conclusion that is supposed to follow from it. While C_1 follows from P logically and unproblematically, it is difficult to see how one might even begin to think that C_2 follows from P. The premise P contains nothing about complementarity, nor about the inner unity of the Creator, nor about any call to reflect such unity. But if that is so, no conclusion that follows logically from P can contain any assertions about these things. What is presented here as a logical argument is in fact not one. It may have the appearance of such an argument, but the appearance is specious.

It has to be said that this is not a fair conclusion as it stands. For one could reply that there is an argument here, only it is hidden, that there are a number of suppressed premises which, when made explicit, form a cogent argument. And it is true that there are suppressed premises, which we have in fact examined above. One can construct more of an argument by adding the premises that men and women are complementary, that being made in the image of God implies a call to live in a certain range of ways, that being in the image of God means reflecting God's unity, and that it is together, and by reason of their complementarity, that men and women are in the image of God. Given these additional premises, the conclusion C_2 would seem to follow. But these premises need to be established. We have already seen that there is no reason to suppose that they can be drawn from the text of Genesis itself. *HP* makes no attempt to do this, nor to justify the additional premises in any other way. In short, a lot of work needs to be done in order to make *HP*'s argument convincing, or even to show that an argument exists at all, and *HP* itself does none. As a result, its argument can only appear defective and unconvincing. Those who are already convinced of the truth of *HP*'s conclusions do not need this argument. Those who are not already convinced should not be convinced by it. In effect, this supposed argument is superfluous; it does not work at all.

Genesis 2

The standard view

Most of us know, at least in outline, the story of the creation of Adam and Eve which occurs in Genesis 2. Here is one way that the story can be read. Towards the beginning of the chapter God is shown creating Adam from the dust of the earth (v. 7); at the end of the same chapter he creates Eve from one of Adam's ribs. When Adam sees her, he exclaims: 'This at last is bone of my bones and flesh of my flesh' (v. 23), and the narrator comments: 'For this reason a man leaves his father and his mother and cleaves to his woman,[13] and they become one flesh' (v. 24). Here we have the first human beings, Adam the first man and Eve the first woman. They are created by God for each other, and the joyful acceptance of Eve by Adam leads to what is in effect the first marriage; and their marriage relationship, as the comment of the narrator makes clear, is the model for subsequent relationships between men and women. What happened then, at the dawn of humanity, is not simply a past event like other past events; it shows a truth about humanity in general. (Indeed, 'Adam' just means 'human being'; what is true of the first human beings, it seems to be implied, is also true of us today.) Not just then, but also now and for all time, men and women are made for each other. Men are made to find their joy in women, and women in men, and this joy is meant to lead to that permanent relationship, that cleaving, that we call marriage, a relationship so close that the Bible can talk of the two becoming one flesh. It is clear also that this is a sexual relationship, one in which the personal intimacy between man and woman finds its expression in an easy physical intimacy: 'And the two of them were naked, the man and his wife, and they were not ashamed' (v. 25). This intimacy will bear fruit later with the birth of their sons Cain and Abel (4:1–2). That is how God created the first human beings, and that is how he continues to create us all now. God makes us, in other words, to find our fulfilment in a permanent heterosexual union of the kind we call marriage. There are those who remain unmarried: those who dedicate themselves to God by vows which include a promise of celibacy, such as priests, nuns and monks; those who are unable to find a suitable marriage partner; those whose filial duties to sick or ageing parents keep them from founding a home of their own; and so on. But the model of heterosexual marriage remains clear; that is what the exceptions are exceptions to. Equally clearly, this model excludes homosexual relationships and all homosexual activity. To be sure, homosexual activity is not excluded explicitly, but the narrative of this chapter shows unmistakably that God created us for heterosexual marriage, and so for heterosexual activity. Some among us may not engage in any sexual activity at all, but if we do, it must be, according to the plan of God, with a member of the opposite sex and in a permanent married relationship. Homosexuals do not fit into this divine plan; they are unable to establish themselves in a heterosexual marriage. For many, that is a misfortune which brings unhappiness, but they are not alone: heterosexuals who are unable for one reason or another to find a marriage partner are in the same situation. Like them, homosexuals are called to that form of chastity which fits their unmarried state, that is to say, complete sexual abstinence. In outline, it is in this way that Genesis 2 is often read, and this reading used to establish the divinely willed pattern of human sexuality;[14] this pattern is heterosexual and excludes all homosexual activity.[15] Put briefly, God made Adam and Eve, not Adam and Steve. But now, is this a fair and accurate way to read this chapter? Are other readings possible?

Might other readings even be truer to the chapter as a whole? It is to be hoped that other readings are possible, for the interpretation of this chapter which reads it as revealing a divinely established universal heterosexuality in fact suffers from serious difficulties.

Difficulties in the standard view

First, there is an asymmetry between the roles of Adam and Eve in this story which makes it clear that its view of the relationship between men and women is one in which the male is socially superior to the female. The story has its origin in an Israelite society in which, as in most societies we know of, there is no equality between men and women, but rather a radical inequality, men being dominant and women subservient. The story reflects and uncritically accepts this social hierarchy as natural and God-given. There is perhaps already an indication of this in the structure of the chapter. As already remarked, God creates Adam in verse 7, towards the beginning of the chapter, and Eve in verse 22, towards the end. In Genesis 1 we have the impression that men and women are created together; at least, no stress is put on their being created in any particular order. This creates an impression of equality between the sexes, or at least does not suggest any inequality. This impression of equality is strengthened by the fact that the text appears to imply that both men and women are created in the image of God. I have argued that this impression is a superficial one, and that there is in fact no assertion or presumption of equality between the sexes in Genesis 1; but at least there is no assertion of inequality. In Genesis 2, on the contrary, there are several indications of such a presumption. The man is definitely created well before the woman. This may be of little or no significance; it may mean nothing that the author does not show God making Adam and Eve together at the same time. But in at least one New Testament interpretation of the story, in 1 Timothy 2:11–15, the simple fact that Adam is created before Eve is understood as implying that men are to have authority over women and not vice versa. More telling is the way and the circumstances in which Eve is created. Adam is first created alone. God then puts him in the garden he has planted, to tend it, and gives him the liberty of the whole garden, except that he is not to eat of the fruit of the tree of the knowledge of good and bad (v. 15–17). Verses 8–14, which describe the garden and the rivers that water it, make it clear that, though he is there to work, it is a thoroughly pleasant place for Adam to be in: it contains every tree which is attractive to look at and good for food (v. 9); there is gold, bdellium and onyx (vv. 11–12). But all is not perfect: God says: 'It is not good that the man should be alone; I will make him a help fit for him' (v. 18). Though it is not stated explicitly here, it becomes clear from the subsequent course of the story that the reason why it is not good that Adam should be alone is that it is not good *for* Adam to be alone; we will come back to this later. There is nothing lacking in the man's surroundings; it is the fact that he is solitary in those surroundings that is the problem. It is as a solution to that problem that Eve is finally created in verse 22. Eve is created for Adam, then; she exists to solve the problem of his solitude. He, on the other hand, is not created for her. Whereas he has value in himself, she has value in her relation to him and because she is good for him. We hear nothing in this story about whether he is good for her. Indeed, nothing at all is said about what might be good or bad for her; all that we need to know about Eve – about woman – is that she is there to be a companion to Adam, the man. When Adam sees Eve for the first time, he reacts to her with a joyful exclamation. Eve, however, remains silent; if Adam receives her with joy and wants to take her as his companion, his wife, the question is not even posed whether she is filled with joy at the sight of him, whether she wants to take him for her companion. While he is active, she remains utterly passive; he desires, she is desired; what counts in the formation of this relationship is the will of the man, to which the woman acquiesces in silence. The narrator links Adam's acceptance of Eve with the institution of marriage: 'For this reason a man leaves his father and his mother and cleaves to his woman, and they become one flesh' (v. 24). In the same way, it is the man who is presented as active in the formation of the marriage relationship: it is he who acts, who leaves father and mother and cleaves to his wife; her part is simply to accept.

The dominance of Adam over Eve, of the male over the female, is further expressed in the act of naming. The creation of Eve is in fact only the final part of a longer experimental process. Having noted that it is not good for the man to be alone, God first of all creates the various animals and brings them to Adam, and Adam gives them names (vv. 19–20). The imposition of a name is a sign of superiority, of authority, even ownership.[16] Adam's naming of the animals is an expression of that domination of the animals which is referred to in Genesis 1:28. Just as Adam names the animals who have been formed from the dust of the earth, so he names the creature taken from his rib: 'This one shall be called woman, for this one has been taken from man' (v. 23). The conclusion is unmistakable: Adam exercises the same domination over Eve as he does over the animals. Note too that it is a generic name that he gives her, not a personal name. He names her just as, we are to suppose, he gives the animals generic names. While Adam does greet her joyfully as his companion, this naming strikes a strangely impersonal note, suggesting a distance between himself and her similar to that between himself and the animals, an authority over her like his authority over the animals. The woman will not get a personal name until after they have both received God's punishment for eating the forbidden fruit; and then it will again be Adam who gives her the personal name, Eve (Gen. 3:20). None of this is difficult to notice, and none of it is surprising, given the sexually hierarchical nature of Israelite society, upon which we have already remarked. Yet these obvious features of the text are often overlooked by Christian writers in an attempt to ground here a Christian view of marriage. For an example, we may turn again to Lawler, Boyle and May. They note that the giving of a name is a sign of superiority and authority. Commenting on the naming of the animals, they say that Adam is 'utterly different from and superior to the other animals. None of these is his equal; he exercises authority over them all. This authority is symbolized by his being given the power to name all the animals.'[17] But they unfortunately forget this when it comes to the naming of Eve. They note that he names her too,[18] just as he names the animals, but do not draw the appropriate conclusion. Instead, they claim that the woman created for Adam is 'a person equal to the man'.[19] But this is a gratuitous assertion, without basis in the text; indeed, it flies in the face of the plain implication of the text. Of course, one has every sympathy with what they want to say here; equality of man and woman is part of modern Christian doctrine, and happily so. The modern Christian doctrine of marriage is predicated upon that equality. But the text of Genesis 2 does not express modern Christian doctrine; it expresses a view which is, in this respect, antithetical to modern Christian doctrine. It thus hardly recommends itself as a text on which to base Christian teaching on the nature of marriage, on the relationship between the sexes and on sexual relationships.

An alternative view

Nevertheless, one cannot abandon a text of Scripture because it has its origin in and reflects values which are very different from our own. The reason why we call Scripture the word of God is because we believe that we have something to learn through it, that God has something to teach us through it. Texts of Scripture, even difficult ones, are precious gifts which must not be thrown away. Only, the above remarks establish that we cannot swallow whole this particular text's vision of the relationship between the sexes and of marriage. What, then, can we legitimately get out of the plain meaning of this text from a Christian point of view? I will attempt to answer this question from the standpoint of the specific concern of this book, the appropriate Christian attitude towards homosexual relationships. Let us go back to the situation which leads to the creation of Eve. Adam is alone, and this is not good. God reacts to this by resolving to create a help for him. From the story so far, given that Adam has been put in the garden to tend it, we might imagine that what God wants to create is a help who is fit also to tend the garden. But no, he wants to create a help fit for the man, a partner, as we might say.[20] This is to be a help in a deeper sense than a mere assistant, one to lighten the workload; by the end of the story, it will have become clear that the help is to be a life-partner, and a sexual partner, but that is not yet in full view. It is in an attempt to make this help that God sets about creating the animals. It is they whom he makes first as projected partners for the man, not the woman; the woman is created only when all the animals have been tried and have failed. So why do all the animals fail to fit the bill? Why does a giraffe or an elephant or a beetle not end up as Adam's partner? The text tells us: 'The human being gave names to all the cattle and to all the birds of the air and to all the wild beasts, but for the human being he did not find a help fit for him' (v. 20). Here we have very much the picture of God improvising: he tries one thing, then another, the camel then the snake, trying to find the appropriate partner for the man; but he does not succeed. This raises the question: what counts as success, and what is the sign of success? When God makes an elephant and brings it to Adam, why is that not the end of the matter? Why does not God effectively say to him: 'Here is the help I have made for you; now get on with it'? God has after all in one sense succeeded: he has made what he wanted to make – an elephant – and he has made it for the purpose of being a help to the man, in the sense of a companion, because it is not good for him to be alone. If God has made the elephant for the man, then it seems to be the divine will that the man is to have the elephant for a companion. If we were still in chapter 1, there would be no question of divine failure. God would simply have said 'Let it be so', and it would have been so; God would have created the elephant as the man's partner, and the elephant would therefore have been the man's partner. The man would have been obliged, on pain of frustrating God's will and disobeying his implicit commandment, to accept the elephant as his partner. But we are not still in chapter 1, and the atmosphere is very different. Here God can fail, and does. The idea of an elephant as Adam's partner is of course absurd. But why is it absurd? Surely because we cannot imagine the intimate communion between a man and an elephant that the term 'help' comes to signify by the end of the story. We cannot imagine an elephant as a man's – or a woman's – life partner in that sense. That *cannot* be God's will for Adam, or for us. This little elephantine fantasy establishes two things about this part of the story. First, in making the animals one after the other and bringing them to Adam, God is imposing nothing on Adam. Rather, he is trying them out, suggesting. If one thing doesn't work, he is willing to try another. Secondly, we get the distinct impression that the criterion of its working is Adam's reaction to the animal God presents him with. Success does not depend on God's own reaction. He does not put Adam and the elephant side by side and as it were say to himself: 'They make a fine pair' or: 'No, that won't do.' When God brings the newly created animals to Adam to see what he will call them, he submits them for his judgement. It is because *Adam* does not react to each one positively as a prospective life partner that God goes off and makes the next one.

This point is for the moment only an impression, but it is strikingly confirmed in what follows, when God makes Eve for Adam. This time, of course, God is successful. But he is not the judge of his success; Adam is. Success is not signalled by God putting Adam and Eve side by side and saying: 'Now, these two really do go well together.' It is quite explicitly *Adam*'s reaction that signals the success of the attempt. It is because *he* reacts positively to Eve, because *he* receives her with joy, that we know the quest for a partner has reached a successful conclusion.[21] And so it is at this point that God ceases looking for a partner for Adam. He quite simply accepts Adam's judgement, never even expressing his own. Or perhaps as far as God is concerned it is not up to him to judge in this area of human life. The fitting partner for the man, then, is the one that he, the man, receives with joy, the one whom he himself recognizes as a partner fit for him. In this story God imposes nothing; he is the servant of the man's need, and submits his attempts to the man's judgement. He recognizes that it is not good that the man live in solitude, and that this solitude can be alleviated only by a 'help' that gladdens the man's heart, by one he actually wants. Any partner whom God imposed regardless of the man's reaction or, worse, despite the man's negative reaction, would thereby fail to be the kind of partner the man needs. That it is Adam himself who decides on the companion he will have should be no surprise, for that is just the sort of thing a companion is. A companion, in the sense of companionship which is in view in this text, is somebody you actually *want* to be with and to share your life with. An imposed companion would be no companion at all. That is why God can only propose, suggest, and wait upon the man's reaction, for it is only in this way that God can succeed in doing what he wants: to give Adam a companion that Adam wants to be with. If he imposed his own will by imposing a partner of his choice rather than Adam's choice, God would frustrate his own project. In creating Adam as one for whom it is not good to be alone, God creates him as one whose heart needs to be gladdened by another, one who needs to delight in another, and he puts himself at the service of that need, seeking again and again one who will indeed make glad his heart, for it is thus and only thus that God fulfils his own project, too. That is why Lawler, Boyle and May's description of Adam's reaction to the creation of Eve is misleading. They say that his first words are 'a short poem expressing, in wondrous delight, a vision of the relation meant to exist between man and woman'.[22] We have already seen that the misdescription of what a biblical text says can lead to a false comprehension of the values behind the text, and what Lawler, Boyle and May say here is a further illustration. Their description is a misdescription first because it suggests that Adam delights, not in the companion God has created for him, but in a vision of a relation. Secondly – and more dangerously because less obviously – it suggests that Adam recognizes here a relation that is *meant* to exist between man and woman, with the implication that he also recognizes that it is meant to exist. This is dangerous because Adam is the representative human being. If he recognizes that this relation is meant to exist, then so ought we, if we are to be true to our humanity. Now we may be prepared to follow Lawler, Boyle and May in saying, though it is contrary to what the text implies, that what Adam delights in is not a woman but a vision of a relation. We may well also think, with them, that the relation established in this story between Adam and Eve is one that is meant to exist between men and women in general (if we ignore its sexist aspects); though some of us, if we are homosexual, may disagree with this. But the text gives no justification at all for suggesting that Adam recognizes that things are *meant* to be like this; that they should not be otherwise.[23] And so it gives no justification either for the implication that we all ought to recognize that things are meant to be like this. This story is not a tale of Adam recognizing a moral truth; it is a tale of human delight. There is no 'meant to be' about the relationship between Adam and Eve, no preconceived divine model of who or what is meant to be Adam's companion, a model to which Adam is somehow duty-bound to conform. All depends on Adam's reaction. Indeed, to suppose that God in this story does have a preconceived idea of Adam's partner is to make a nonsense of the whole dynamic of the story. For it renders superfluous the attempt of God to find a companion for Adam by making the animals. If God already knows that it is the woman he is going to create as Adam's partner, this episode becomes a mere charade. But there is no reason to believe it a charade; nothing about the way the story is told suggests it. Indeed, when the narrator remarks that among all the animals he did not find a help fit for him (v. 20), the impression is given that there might have been, that this is a genuine attempt to find a help fit for him. Further, Adam's joyful reaction to Eve, which is in a way the climax of the story, becomes redundant if God has already decided that Eve is going to be his companion. If it is God's prior decision that Adam will have Eve, then Adam's reaction to her is irrelevant to the outcome of the story.

Adam and us

Adam is in this story not merely a man, but *the* man, the representative of all men. If we can abstract from the unchristian sexism which is also expressed in this story, and which makes the woman find her reason for existing only in satisfying the man's need, then Adam becomes the representative human being, and we can say that God is at the service of *our* delight, of the delight of all of us, men and women. It becomes true of each of us that it is not good that we should be alone, and God seeks for us a help, a partner. But God seeks for each of us, not the partner that pleases God, but the partner that pleases us, for it is only thus that he can fulfil us as the needy creatures he has made us, and only thus that he can succeed in his own project of providing us with a companion. We are here far from the 'compulsory heterosexuality' interpretation of this story, the interpretation that says that God made Eve, not Steve, for Adam, and that is how it must be. Yes, Adam ends up with a woman for his partner, but not because God imposes a woman on him. Adam has a woman, not because that is how God wants it, but because that is how Adam wants it, and God is at the service of Adam's delight. Adam is delighted by Eve, a woman. That is apparently how most men are; it is with a woman that they enjoy or wish to enjoy an intimate partnership. And most women apparently enjoy or seek to enjoy an intimate partnership with a man. But there are exceptions. Apart from those who do not enjoy or particularly seek an intimate partnership with anybody, there are men who delight in another man, and there are women whose heart is gladdened by another woman. Because God is at the service of the delight of Adam, the representative human being, we must suppose that he is also at the service of the delight of men whose heart is gladdened by a man and of women who delight in a woman. Just as God is shown here taking seriously the need of Adam for a fit partner, a partner whom he will receive with joy, so, we must suppose, he takes seriously the need of lesbians and gay men for a partner whom they will receive with joy. When God notices that it is not good that Adam be alone, he does not simply remark 'Too bad; he will just have to put up with it.' Because Adam is the representative human being, God does not say either of homosexuals that it's just too bad, they will just have to put up with their solitude. It is here that we see the final bankruptcy of the compulsory heterosexuality interpretation of the story of Adam and Eve. Not only does it misrepresent God as one who imposes his will regardless of human delight, but, in the case of lesbians and gay men, it completely undermines the dynamic which leads to the creation of Eve. That dynamic has its starting-point in the perception that it is not good that the man should be alone. It is for that reason that the animals are created, for that reason that Eve is created, for that reason that marriage is created, that a man leaves his father and his mother and cleaves to his wife. But the compulsory heterosexuality interpretation would have it that it is after all good that homosexuals should be alone. It would have God shrug his shoulders at their solitude and say 'Too bad.' But the whole story expresses the belief that God does not say 'Too bad.' He does not say 'Too bad' when he sees that Adam's solitude is not good. When Adam receives the elephant as his prospective partner with less than perfect joy, God does not say 'Too bad; either Adam takes the elephant or he remains alone.' The whole point òf this story is that God does not want Adam to remain alone, because it is not good. We cannot suppose, consistently with this story, that God effectively presents a gay man with a woman and says: 'Here is your partner. If you don't like it, it's too bad; you'll have to remain alone.' We cannot suppose, consistently with this story, that God presents a lesbian with a man and says: 'Here is your partner. If you don't like it, you'll just have to remain alone.' But this is a little hasty. Adam does after all welcome a woman as his partner, not a man. Is this not a model for us? Are we not presented here with a model of humanity such as God wills it, and are we not therefore obliged to follow it? No. We are not disciples of Adam, but of the second Adam, Jesus Christ. What is essential for us here is not the will of Adam but the will of God. And the will of God shows itself here as the will to serve, just as Jesus Christ came to serve. Here, he is shown serving the needs of those he has created needing to delight in and to enjoy intimate companionship with another. Adam is left free to accept or refuse, and his acceptance follows not from obligation but from delight. We respect the role of God in this story if we say that, like Adam, we too are left free, that we too are to accept the partner in whom we delight. Indeed, the idea that we *have* to follow Adam here is not only false in itself but would lead to unacceptable conclusions. For what Adam does is *delight* in Eve. The obligation to follow Adam would be not the obligation for men to refrain from sexual relations with men, but the obligation for men to delight in women (and so, by analogy, for women to delight in men). The mere failure to find the opposite sex attractive, or to want to take as partner a particular member of the opposite sex, would be enough to condemn gay men and lesbians, and indeed people who just do not delight in anybody in particular. No responsible Christian community would want to assert that. The example of Adam would also seem to make marriage compulsory, and to make marriage based on delight compulsory. No Christian community in which celibacy has an honoured or even a tolerated place can contemplate that.

Why a woman?

We surely cannot ignore the fact that God does after all create for
Adam a woman as his partner, and that Adam accepts her; it is an
element of the scriptural text, to be received with gratitude and
pondered. But we do not have to resort to making a heterosexist
theology of sexuality in order to give full value to Adam's choice (and,
once again, it is Adam's choice, not God's) of a woman as his partner
in this story. There are sufficient other ways in which this can be
appreciated. First, Adam, as the representative man, is also the typical
man. Typically, men do want a woman for their partner, not another
man. We have every reason to believe that this was as true in the
ancient Israel that gave birth to this story as it is in most places today.
It is therefore quite natural that the story should be told in those
terms. But a story framed in terms of the typical does not of course
morally exclude the atypical. Any story which seeks to represent all
human beings, or even simply all men, in just one man must perforce
paint with an exceedingly broad brush, taking no account of all the
variety that arises when there is a multiplicity of people. Adam's
accepting a woman as his partner no more excludes another man's
taking a man as partner than Adam's speaking Hebrew excludes
another man's speaking French, or than Adam's being a gardener
excludes another man's being a violinist. Secondly, this is also supposed to be the story of the first man, the founder of the human race,
from whom we are all descended. But the history of the human race, if
it is to take into account at all the conditions of human existence,
cannot be traced back just to a first man; it has to be traced back to a
first couple. And if we are to have a story in which the human race is
traced back to a single couple, it must be a mixed-sex couple, for, as a
matter of fact, that is how the human race propagates. A story of two
men or two women could not be the story of our first parents. Because
of this aetiological aspect of the story, Adam *must* have a woman as
partner. But the fact that a story about the originators of the human
race has to be a story about a mixed-sex couple does not in any way
show the illegitimacy of same-sex couples who are not originators of
the human race. Thirdly, the status of Adam as the representative
man – *the* man – excludes a second representative man and also calls
for somebody to fulfil the role of *the* woman. Fourthly, if this story is
of the beginning of the human race, it is also of the origin of marriage,
the institution which binds a man and woman together. This is made
clear by the narrator in verse 24. For it to be this, it must be the story
of a man and a woman; Adam must delight in a woman.

Sexism and homophobia

There is another, less reputable reason for Adam's accepting a woman as his companion, a reason why it is impossible that God be shown presenting him with a man as his partner, and Adam accepting him joyfully. The relationship between Adam and his partner is plainly conceived as a sexual one. It is generally recognized that ancient Israelite society was patriarchal and sexist, and undervalued women. As far as we can gather from the story of the destruction of Sodom and Gomorrah and the laws of Leviticus 18:22 and 20:13, it was also a society which disapproved in the strongest possible way of sexual relations between men. Our investigation has indicated that these two facts are not unrelated: the reason why sex between men is so abhorred is that it is conceived on a penetrative model and *reduces* one of them to the role of a woman. As in other societies, antipathy to sexual activity between men (particularly sexual penetration) is closely connected to an undervaluing of women. Sexism and what is often today called homophobia go naturally together. The reason this story, the product of ancient Israelite society, shows Eve created to occupy a position inferior to Adam is the same reason why it is unthinkable that the same society produce a story in which Adam is given a male partner. Lawler, Boyle and May draw attention to the fact that ancient Israel was a sexist society.[24] They note, as we have done, that, while men were permitted to repudiate their wives, wives were not permitted to repudiate their husbands, that women were regarded as inferior to men, and that there was a double standard for adultery. What they do not say explicitly, perhaps because it is too obvious, is that the way we know this is through Old Testament writings. The Old Testament is by far the most important source of our knowledge of the society which produced it. The reason we know that the society was sexist and patriarchal is that what we have of their writings, where it treats or alludes to relations between the sexes, is sexist and patriarchal. If it is through the writings that we know of the society, the nature of the society explains the nature of the writings. A Christian society is (or would be) different, and so we discount the sexist aspect of Old Testament writings as due to human imperfection; these attitudes represent not divine gold but human dross, even though they are presented there as divine law. But then it seems equally true, from the writings we have, that ancient Israelite society was violently opposed to sexual relations between men, for reasons closely related to its sexist attitude to women. Logically, therefore, we ought also to put the 'homo-phobic' attitudes expressed in the Old Testament down to human imperfection, even though it is presented as divine law.

The story of the creation of Adam and Eve does not, then, contrary to what is sometimes asserted, provide a universally applicable heterosexual blueprint for human sexuality. It does not show God expressing his will that we all be heterosexual. On the contrary, if – despite its obvious adherence to an ideology of male superiority – it shows us anything at all, it shows that God recognizes that it is not good for us to be alone, and that he wants for us the partner that we can receive with joy, as Adam receives Eve. It shows us that there is no divine blueprint; there is only what makes glad the heart of each of us. Or rather, it shows that the divine blueprint is that each of us should have the companion that delights our heart. There may be all kinds of good reasons why everybody should avoid homosexual relationships, but one is not to be found in this story.

The two texts we have studied are the ones commonly supposed to ground a biblical vision of sex, one which puts heterosexual marriage and excludes all homosexual relationships. If the approach adopted here is at all correct, they provide no foundation for such a vision. They rather invite each one of us to live in love, in a way consonant with our status as images of God, in imitation of Jesus Christ who is *the* image of God. And they invite us to recognize that God has created us such that it is not good for us to be alone, that God puts himself at the service of our need and wills that we find a companion in whom our heart delights. If we start here, and let the texts speak for themselves, we will not get the results that so many Christian moralists think we get.

Why start here?

This prompts the question: why start here anyway? Why think that it is these Old Testament texts that will provide the foundation of a sexual ethic for Christians? Would not some New Testament text or texts be a more appropriate starting point? I will take up this question more fully in the next chapter, but one or two remarks on the subject are in order here. One reason why one might be tempted to start with the first pages of the Bible has already been suggested: in the world of Genesis 1 and 2 we have nature, and in particular human nature, as God wanted it in the beginning, and so wants it now. It gives us a picture of humanity, and perhaps even human sexuality, before the corruption of sin distorted it. This is an important idea, and we shall come back to it in Chapter 7. But there is one reason that is properly explored now. It has been argued that, though Genesis 1 and 2 are indeed Old Testament passages, they are important, too, in the New Testament. For example, Paul quotes 2:24 in 1 Corinthians 6:16 when explaining why Christians should not use prostitutes. Again, the author of Ephesians uses it to speak of the union between Christ and the church (5:31). More centrally for our purposes, we know that both 1:27 and 2:24 had an importance for Jesus himself, and that in connection with human sexuality. He clearly refers to both verses in his dispute with the Pharisees over the practice of repudiation (Matt. 19:1–9). When the Pharisees ask whether it is lawful for a man to repudiate his wife, Jesus replies: 'Have you not read that he who created them at the beginning made them male and female and said "For this reason a man will leave his father and mother and be joined to his wife, and the two shall become one flesh"?' (vv. 4–5).

So there is a New Testament reason for looking seriously at these Old Testament texts. I have tried to show that Genesis 1 and 2 do not have the importance often attributed to them in theological discussions of sex, but the fact that Jesus himself refers to them, and thinks them of decisive importance in resolving a question about marriage, should perhaps make us think again. So we have to ask: if these verses of Genesis were important for Jesus, what kind of importance did they have for him, and what does this imply for our view of human sexuality in general and homosexuality in particular? It is clear from the context in Matthew's Gospel that it was important to him as a means of combating the idea that husbands could dispose of their wives at will, as if wives were mere property. The desire of a man to rid himself of his wife by repudiating her (as permitted by Deuteronomy 24:1–4) was for Jesus nothing but hardness of heart (Matt. 19:8). One can only suppose that hardness of heart is, in this context, the indifference of the man to the wishes, welfare and happiness of the wife he repudiates; in repudiating her he breaks faith with her and abandons the responsibilities he undertook towards her in marrying her.[25] In appealing to the text of Genesis in order to combat the practice of repudiation, Jesus is not trying to impose a harsh, unbending law, to force couples to live together in bitterness because they cannot or are not allowed to separate, but to urge men not to behave harshly towards their wives. In opposing repudiation, Jesus is not being hard-hearted, but opposing hardness of heart in others. The fundamental enemy here is hardness of heart, as is only to be expected given Jesus's general teaching that human relationships are to be founded on love. What relevance, then, does Matthew 19:1–9 have for a Christian discussion of homosexuality? One obvious implication is that homosexuals, like everybody else, are to avoid hardness of heart, and to avoid it in their sexual relations as well as in all other aspects of their life. (It remains a question to be asked whether avoiding hardness of heart in sexual relations also implies, for homosexuals, avoiding all sexual relations.) But some have seen a further and more specific relevance in what Jesus says here. This view is stated succinctly by John F. Harvey:

> In the New Testament Jesus Himself reaffirms the norm of Genesis ... [In Matt. 19:3–8] Jesus reaffirms the monogamous, heterosexual norm of sexuality found in Genesis. Note that He quotes both Genesis 1:27 and 2:24, thereby repeating their teaching about the meaning of human sexuality.'[26]

By the 'monogamous, heterosexual norm of sexuality found in Genesis', Harvey means effectively the interpretation of the relevant verses found in *HP*, to which he refers a couple of paragraphs earlier and which he uses to expound the biblical text. We have already seen reason to question the interpretation of *HP*, but independently of that, there are major problems with Harvey's claim. First, that Jesus combats repudiation, saying that men may not put asunder those whom God has joined in marriage,[27] does not imply that he affirms a heterosexual norm of sexuality. His debate with the Pharisees is about an aspect of the heterosexual institution of marriage, namely about whether it can be brought to an end by a man's repudiating his wife. But to engage in a debate about an aspect of a heterosexual institution is not to affirm a heterosexual norm of sexuality. Jesus does not even affirm marriage here as a norm for human beings; he merely says that if a man marries a woman, then that marriage is permanent, and he may not repudiate her. If Jesus is affirming a norm here at all, it is a norm about marriage, that it should be lifelong, not a norm about sexuality, that it should be heterosexual. Still less is what Jesus says here a rejection of homosexuality; there is no affirmation of the value of heterosexuality *as opposed to* homosexuality. That is simply not in question here; the debate is not about homosexuality. If Jesus says that marriage should be lifelong, there can be no doubt that he approves of the sexual activity of people within a context of mar-riage. But this gives us no indication whatever of what he thinks about the sexual activity of unmarried people, whether heterosexual or homosexual. (There might be indications of what he thinks about this elsewhere in the Gospel, but that is another matter.) The fact that Jesus quotes Genesis 1:27 and 2:24 makes no difference to this result. *Pace* Harvey, his use of these two texts does not imply that he thereby repeats their teaching about the meaning of human sexuality. He uses them for a very specific purpose: to combat the practice of repudiation, not to affirm any general teaching about sexuality. The importance of Genesis 2:24 in this context is not that it teaches a view of human sexuality (if it does), but that it implies, as Jesus understands it, the permanence of the marriage relation-ship and hence the inadmissibility of repudiation. Further, even if one could maintain that Jesus's repetition of these verses implied an affirmation of their teaching, it would imply an affirmation of their teaching as understood by Jesus, not as understood by Harvey or *HP*. We do not know how Jesus understood these verses, beyond saying that he understood them to rule out repudiation. We cer-tainly cannot assume that he understood them as Harvey or *HP* understands them; we have no evidence at all for this. Jesus's reference to these verses therefore does nothing either to reinforce Harvey's or *HP*'s understanding of them,[28] or to justify using them as a starting point for a discussion of homosexuality. We can say that it adds nothing to the Christian understanding of homo-sexuality, beyond emphasizing the general point that in all our dealings, including our sexual dealings, and indeed including our debate about homosexuality, we must avoid all hardness of heart.

CHAPTER SIX

The Bible, Love and Experience

In the last three chapters we have looked at two different approaches to how the Bible might help us to think as Christians about same-sex relationships and same-sex activity. In Chapters 3 and 4 we looked at the texts most often thought explicitly to condemn same-sex activity, and we found that many difficulties attend what has been in recent times the usual interpretation of these texts. If I am right, they do not all yield a condemnation of homosexual acts, none of them yield a condemnation of all homosexual acts, and even where there is condemnation of some kinds of homosexual acts, it is for the wrong reasons; so they give us today no reason whatsoever to condemn all homosexual acts ourselves. But perhaps I am not right. Perhaps I have misconstrued the biblical texts and overlooked or misinterpreted other evidence. Even if that is so, there remains a problem. Even if these texts do show convincingly, despite all arguments to the contrary, that the Bible condemns all same-sex activity as such, the question remains: why? The condemnation – if such there be – appears disturbingly arbitrary. We are given no reason for this condemnation. The Bible might as well condemn the eating of oysters – as indeed it does.[1] The one appears as arbitrary as the other. Any Christian who is happy to ignore the interdiction on eating shellfish should, apparently, be equally happy to ignore any condemnation of same-sex activity. In Chapter 5, we looked in a broader way at a picture of human sexuality which, it is alleged, is to be found in Scripture, and in particular in the opening chapters of Genesis. Here again we found reason to doubt the cogency of the interpretation often put on these texts; the theology of human sexuality which, it is claimed, is to be found in the accounts of creation is just not there to be found. We might note in passing that even if such a heterosexist account of creation were to be found, it would make little difference. No amount of saying how good heterosexual sex is can make it amount to another, homosexual, kind of sex, just as no amount of praise of French Chardonnay amounts to a condemnation of Australian Chardonnay; one may like both. The fact is, Genesis 1 and 2 make no reference to homosexuality. But to make no reference is just that; it is not to condemn. What is needed to exclude homosexuality is a direct condemnation. However, as we have seen, we as Christians can read no biblical text as such a condemnatory text. The second, more positive approach is fundamentally defective about it. But this second approach nevertheless has something right about it too, from the point of view of a Christian understanding of homosexuality. It does not treat same-sex activity as something which might be condemned in certain biblical texts; it rather seeks to provide a context for such a condemnation. To put the matter more neutrally, it seeks to develop an understanding, based on the Bible, of human sexuality in general, and to place an evaluation of homosexuality within the context of that understanding. A vision is offered of what human sexuality is about, and it is in the light of that vision, it is said, that we are forced to make a negative evaluation of same-sex activity. Even if, as we saw, the early chapters of Genesis do not in fact embody this vision of sexuality, as is alleged, this approach has the merit of starting from a broader view of what the Bible teaches. In this way it aims to give a context and an explanation. But we can ask whether that view, though broader than a simple appeal to proof-texts which allegedly condemn same-sex activity, is itself broad enough. To explain this, I must go back to look again at the idea of biblical unanimity. Suppose it were the case that there were biblical texts that mention homosexual acts and that they all condemned them. Suppose again that texts such as Genesis 1 and 2, which do not mention homosexual acts, clearly put forward what we would call a heterosexual view of human sexuality, and that in such a way as to exclude all homosexual activity. That would not be enough to establish a *biblical* unanimity on the subject of same-sex activity. For we would then have to ask whether these texts are themselves compatible with other biblical texts which do not mention homosexual activity directly and which do not mention sex at all. Pauline texts say that women must keep quiet in church (1 Cor. 14:33f.; 1 Tim. 2:11); there is no Pauline (or other) text that says that women may speak in church. Only men can do that. That's a kind of unanimity. But Paul also says there is a radical equality between male and female. There seems to be a tension, even contradiction, here: if men and women are equal, it at least appears prima facie that women should be allowed to speak in church just as men do. Either it has to be argued that the contradiction is specious, or we have to evaluate ourselves which texts carry the greater weight, and act in accordance with those and not the others. Many Christians claim that, whatever some biblical texts might say, the New Testament makes love the sole criterion for the moral evaluation of human acts. If that is true then, if homosexual activity is compatible with the criterion of love, it must be acceptable by Christian standards, regardless of what some texts say. If there is an apparent conflict among biblical texts, we have either to show that the conflict is only apparent or we have to choose which ones carry the greater weight. What is at stake here is not the alleged unanimity of a few texts, or even an alleged biblical doctrine of sex, but the overall coherence of our reading of the Bible. This problem needs to be spelled out in a little more detail.

The claim that love is to be the guiding principle in the life of Christians is surely incontrovertible, and few would dispute it. New Testament texts supporting it explicitly or implicitly are easy to find, and have long been held central to the tradition. Here are a few:

> You have heard that it was said 'You shall love your neighbour and hate your enemy'. But I say to you: love your enemies and pray for those who persecute you. (Matt. 5:43–4)

> One of them, a lawyer, to test him, said: 'Which is the greatest commandment in the law?' And he said to him: 'You shall love the Lord your God with all your heart and with all your soul and with all your mind; this is the greatest and first commandment. And a second is like it: You shall love your neighbour as yourself.' (Matt. 22:35–9)

> This is my commandment, that you love one another as I have loved you. (John 15:12)

> Owe nothing to anybody except to love each other; for he who loves another has fulfilled the law. (Rom. 13:8)

> Faith, hope and love abide, these three; and the greatest of these is love. (1 Cor. 13:13)

> The whole law is fulfilled in one word: 'You shall love your neighbour as yourself'. (Gal. 5:14)[2]

These texts all lay emphasis on love of neighbour, but there is another facet to the life of love that human beings are called to lead, the love of God. However, the love of God is not a separate, independent love; love of God and love of neighbour are inseparable. Hence the way Jesus yokes together in Matthew 22:35–9 the command to love God and the command to love neighbour, and hence also John's affirmation: 'If any one says, "I love God", and hates his brother, he is a liar; for he who does not love his brother whom he has seen, cannot love God whom he has not seen' (1 John 4:20). The criterion of whether we love God is whether we love our neighbour; there is no separate criterion; that is why, though the law says 'You shall love the Lord your God with all your soul . . . ', Paul can say repeatedly that love of neighbour is the fulfilling of the law. Love of God implies keeping God's commandments,[3] and it is thus that we honour him, as Paul says we should (Rom. 1:21); but his commandment is that we should love each other.[4] However, we have seen that some recent attempts to establish a Christian sexual ethic take as their starting point not the God-willed law of love as expressed in the teaching of Jesus and the apostles, but a theology of creation allegedly found in the opening chapters of Genesis. I have tried to show that this theology of creation is in fact not to be found there. But I might be wrong about this, and the exegesis I have spent so much time questioning might in fact be sound. Suppose it is, and that the alleged theology of creation really is to be found, and that it really does have the consequences for our sexual behaviour that its proponents think it has. Suppose, in particular, that it really does rule out homosexual relationships and same-sex activity. We would then be in the position of having two separate principles governing Christian life: the law of love, as expounded in the New Testament, and the theology of creation found in the early chapters of Genesis. The problem then would be that these two principles, if they are independent of each other, could well, when applied to particular questions of human conduct, give conflicting results. It might be, for example, that a certain kind of sexual behaviour was in accordance with the law of love, but not with the biblical theology of creation, or vice versa. In this way an internal conflict or incoherence would arise in our reading of the Bible. Some texts would pull us one way, others another way. A similar problem would arise if I turned out to be wrong in my understanding of the proof-texts sometimes adduced in condemnation of same-sex activity. Suppose that Genesis 19, Romans 1 and the rest really do condemn all homosexual behaviour as such. It might be that a sexual act between two people of the same sex can be a genuinely loving act, in the Christian sense, so in accord with the law of love and the biblical texts that proclaim it, and therefore acceptable, yet not in accord with the texts that forbid homosexual activity, and so unacceptable. We would then again be in a contradictory position and faced with an incoherence in our reading of the Bible. So even if contrary to what I have been arguing, there really is a group of biblical texts which are unanimous in condemning all homosexual behaviour, and even if there really is to be found in Genesis 1 and 2 a theology of sex which excludes all homosexual activity, we do not necessarily have a real biblical unanimity on the question of homosexuality, if it should turn out that at least some homosexual activity is consonant with the law of love. And prima facie at least some homosexual activity is indeed consonant with the law of love. While there is no doubt a good deal of fairly loveless gay sex going on, there is also gay sex between people who love each other. For there are, it seems, homosexuals who do love each other, just as there are heterosexuals who love each other. There are certainly people who live in same-sex couples and who profess to love each other; and they see their exclusive sexual activity together as a natural part of their life together.[5] If they love each other, have they not fulfilled the law? But if Leviticus really does forbid them to do it, and Genesis 1 and 2 really do imply that they shouldn't, it looks as if they have not fulfilled the law. We have potentially a very big problem here. There seems to be at a deep level not merely a lack of biblical unanimity, but a contradiction. We can react to this situation in several ways.

First, we can admit that there is a contradiction and reject one set of texts or the other. For a Christian, there is no doubt which set of texts carries more weight and is to be adhered to. Love carries the day. The order that God desires is love, and it is only where there is lack of love that there is disorder. We have to say that at its deepest, when it is concerned for that divine order, the Bible does not condemn homosexuality, even though at its more superficial moments it does. (We might then, as a further step, attribute the existence of those more superficial moments to the fallen and fallible humanity of the texts' authors, rather than to divine inspiration.) Secondly, we can say that it is unacceptable to hold that the Bible contradicts itself, and that there is no contradiction here because the biblical texts that might seem at first sight to condemn homosexuality do not in fact do so. The treatment of the apparently relevant biblical texts in the preceding chapters may tend to favour this path. Thirdly, we can claim again that there is no contradiction, but this time not because the relevant texts do not condemn homosexuality but because they do, and in so doing are in conformity with the law of love, so that there is a real and profound biblical unanimity on the subject. This is so, it might be said, because homosexuality is of itself contrary to love; this we know, not because the Bible says that homosexual activity is contrary to love (although it can be argued that some texts, particularly the New Testament ones, presuppose a view of gay sex as loveless), but from the nature of homosexual desire, which is fundamentally narcissistic and selfish. It is this third way that is generally taken, either explicitly or implicitly, by most writers who wish to maintain the habitual Christian hostility to homosexuality. And it is surely a reasonable path to take for those who remain convinced that texts like Genesis, Leviticus and Romans really do express or imply a condemnation of same-sex activity and want to take that seriously, for it betokens a commitment to maintain, as far as possible, a coherent reading of the Bible as a whole. But this option puts an onus on its proponents to show that homosexual activity necessarily is contrary to love. And here I mean not just that homosexual activity which is aggressive, like the rape of men by men; that, like all rape, is obviously contrary to love. And I do not just mean either that which is apparently loveless, like anonymous gropings in dark places where there is little or no personal contact between the participants and little apparent mutual concern. I mean that homosexual activity which takes place between two people who say they love each other, and who apparently do love each other. To show that the worst of homosexual behaviour is contrary to the will of God is not to show very much. If we are to believe that homosexual behaviour is always unacceptable in God's eyes, then it has to be shown that even the best homosexual behaviour is contrary to love. And it has to be shown because it is not obviously so. This takes us outside the Bible, outside the realm of revelation, into the domain of human experience and natural reason. We begin to move away from the exegesis of particular scriptural texts to what we can all know, if we look and think. We begin to move, that is, towards the realm of ordinary human experience and of natural law. This might be considered a typically Catholic move, softening the traditionally strong Protestant emphasis on the centrality of Scripture. And it is true that in the rest of this book the focus will be more on what might be called questions of natural law. But what has led us to this is the importance we attach to the Bible itself. We are faced with the possibility of contradiction and incoherence in our reading of the Bible, and the question of human experience arises in our attempt to evade this difficulty. This move away from the Bible is necessary in order to read the Bible properly, to see whether, and if so in what way, we can read it in a coherent manner.

Can gays love?

Many questions arise if we try to answer the question what the love of God and the love of neighbour imply for gay men and women and for their sex lives. For them, can sex be an element of love? Can it be a physical expression of love? Can they make love? Or does the fact that the person they think they love is of the same sex mean that they do not really love at all? Or if they can love, does the fact that they love somebody of the same sex somehow prevent them from making love? If they think they are making love, are they necessarily deluding themselves, just because the one they are doing it with is not of the other sex? Does the fact that they engage in sexual activity with another of the same sex actually diminish their capacity to love? Can gay people, as such, regardless of their sex lives, really love at all? Or does the fact that they are sexually attracted by members of their own sex close them off to real love, and so close them off to God? Many people, gay or not, will regard such questions with bemusement. Of course, they will say, gays can love, and of course they can make love. They fall in love, just as straight people do, and this love has a natural sexual expression, just as it does for straight people; that's why we can call it making love, regardless of whether the couple are of the same sex or not. And of course gay people love in a non-sexual way. Of course they are capable of giving themselves to others, even to the point of self-sacrifice. Of course gay people are not closed to God; many are deeply devout and prayerful, and try to live as faithful disciples of Christ. You only have to open your eyes to see that this is so. The above questions are ridiculous. Other people, however, have not found them ridiculous. Indeed, they have wanted to assert that gay sex cannot be an expression of any love but a narcissistic pseudo self-love, that it is necessarily self-centred and self-indulgent and does not reach out in love to another, and that it does not even express genuine love of oneself. According to this point of view, indulging in sex with another person of the same sex therefore strengthens self-centredness and weakens one's capacity to love. Being against love, such activity is also against God. The homosexual condition is a tendency to be self-centred and hence turned away from love and from God, so that people who have this condition can only turn towards God and towards genuine love of others and appreciation of themselves by fighting against it. These are bold assertions, and they are necessary if homosexual acts are to be shown contrary to love; but why believe them? What are the arguments involved?

Love and observation

Before turning to these, it is necessary to say a few words about the importance to this question of empirical observation – of ordinary human experience and perhaps also of scientific studies. In almost all areas of life we learn from experience: from our own personal life and observation, and from other people's experience passed on to us orally and in writing. So, if I want to know whether a given triangular object has a side seven centimetres long, I measure it, or I ask somebody else who is in a position to know or to find out. Again, if I want to know whether it is raining, I look out of the window, or I ask somebody else who is in a position to observe whether it is raining. But some questions, such as the truth of mathematical theorems, are not settled by observation. Pythagoras's theorem is not a generalization based on observation of large numbers of triangles; it and other mathematical theorems are the results of calculations based on definitions, and to that extent independent of experience. Religious dogmas are not the result of empirical observation, either; Catholics do not have the doctrine of transubstantiation because they have observed that Christ is really present in the Eucharist, and Protestants do not reject that doctrine because they have observed that Christ is not really present there. It is reasonable to believe that people's experience has something to do with the formation of religious doctrines, but not in this direct way. But most of the things we want to know do not depend on calculation or on religious authority or tradition; they depend on our senses, and on other people's senses.

At tea with Lady Marchmain, Father Mowbray recounts his attempts to instruct Rex Mottram in the Catholic faith:

> I asked him: 'Supposing the Pope looked up and saw a cloud and said "It's going to rain", would that be bound to happen?' 'Oh, yes, Father.' 'But supposing it didn't?' He thought a moment and said, 'I suppose it would be sort of raining spiritually, only we were too sinful to see it.'[6]

It is obvious that Mottram's answer is absurd, because rain is not spiritual. Rain is an empirical concept. We do not need virtue, spiritual insight, popes or bishops in order to know whether it is raining; we need only to look with passable eyes and in reasonable conditions, or to ask somebody who can look. And once we have looked, it doesn't matter what the popes or bishops say. If Mottram looks out of the window and can see that it isn't raining, then it doesn't matter if a hundred bishops or popes contradict him. Or rather, it only matters if they too have looked to see whether it is raining. This is not because popes and bishops have never claimed authority in this area of life; it is because the question whether it is raining or not is an empirical question. Love also is an empirical matter. If we want to know whether one person loves another, we observe. But love is a good deal more complicated than rain, and the observation involved is much more complicated than the observation we need in order to know whether it is raining. If we want to know from observation whether Andrew loves Jane, we may need to watch for a long time. We will need to see whether, over a sustained period, he seeks her good, is attentive to her needs and to her wishes, tends to overlook or forgive her failings, takes pleasure in doing things that please her, speaks well of her to others, enjoys doing the ordinary things of life with her, and enjoys or even delights in being with her. If Andrew and Jane are both sexually mature, we may also be interested in whether Andrew loves her erotically; then, even if we do not have access to their private behaviour, we will want to observe as far as we can how he looks at her, whether and how he touches her, and so on. If we are not in a position to make any of these observations, we can ask somebody who is or has been, such as a close friend of Andrew's who is able to see how he speaks to and of Jane, and how he behaves towards her. We can love more or less deeply, and our appreciation of what love of another involves deepens with experience. If we or other observers are experienced and sensitive enough, we can say whether Andrew loves deeply or shallowly. Our understanding of love will also deepen through meditation on the love that God has shown us through Jesus, and through pondering what the apostles and Jesus himself have to say about love. But love remains fundamentally an empirical concept. We can tell whether people love or not, and whether they love deeply or shallowly, by observation, if we are in the position to observe. And we can understand discourse about love too, independently of any religious revelation or authority. Jesus's audience could already understand it before he taught them.

If it were not so, Jesus could not have talked intelligibly to them about love. Whether one person loves another is a question to be settled by looking, not by calculation or by appeal to religious authority.

We can now return to consider directly the question of homo-sexuals and love. *HP* contains the following assertions:

> To choose someone of the same sex for one's sexual activity is to annul the rich symbolism and meaning, not to mention the goals, of the Creator's sexual design. Homosexual activity is not a complementary union, able to transmit life; and so it thwarts the call to a life of that form of self-giving which the Gospel says is the essence of Christian living. This does not mean that homo-sexual persons are not often generous and giving of themselves; but when they engage in homosexual activity they confirm within themselves a disordered sexual inclination which is essentially self-indulgent. (§7)

There is a great deal going in this paragraph; I will need to return to it at several points throughout this book. But for the moment I am interested only in those elements that touch on the question of homosexuals, their capacity to love and the relationship between love and homosexual activity. It is the final sentence which expresses most clearly the document's beliefs on this subject.

First, there is an admission, perhaps even an assertion, that homosexuals are 'often generous and giving of themselves'. Now generosity and self-giving are aspects of genuine love. One of the things we will look for in trying to observe whether Andrew loves Jane, to whom he is married, is whether he is generous towards her with his time and material resources; we will also want to see whether, when Jane needs it, he is prepared to give up for her sake things he considers important. (Andrew is a social worker. He may well be generous and self-giving in different ways to those who need his professional help; and this would be a sign that he loves them, though we might well want to make a distinction between his love for them and his love for Jane.) So the words of *HP* here amount to saying that homosexuals are often loving people. If we find that the homosexual Christopher is generous with his time and money to David, his partner, and that when David needs it Christopher will give up his own plans and desires, then this is an indication that Christopher loves David. (Christopher, like Andrew, is a social worker. He may, like Andrew, be generous in different ways to those with whom he comes into professional contact, and this will be a sign that he loves them, but in a different way from David.) So *HP* does not subscribe to any view that all homosexuals are, as such, self-centred and opposed to love. It does not even regard generous, self-giving homosexuals as rare exceptions; in its view, homosexuals are often like this. If *HP* admits that homosexuals can be genuinely loving people, it is not this admission that licenses Catholics or any Christians to say that homosexuals can love. We do not and cannot affirm that it is possible for homosexuals to love merely on the basis of documents and theological theories. The fact is, anybody who has any serious contact with homosexuals at all – for example, homosexuals themselves, friends of homosexuals, parents, siblings and children of homosexuals, lovers of homosexuals, colleagues of homosexuals, neighbours of homosexuals, and so on – can *see* that homosexuals are capable of love, moved by genuine concern for others in their professional, social and private lives. It is experience, not theory, that must have the dominant voice here. Indeed, it is simple empirical observation that makes it possible for the authors of *HP* themselves to say that homosexuals are often generous and self-giving; either they or the informants on whom they rely have had close enough contact with homosexuals to see that this is true. Perhaps they have in mind the notoriously high percentage of homosexuals in the 'caring professions', such as nursing, social work and the clergy. We perhaps also see here the result of the experience of the early years of the Aids epidemic in Western Europe and North America. Many clergy and religious at the time testified to the fidelity and devotion with which gay men cared for their sick and dying lovers.[7] Whatever the experiences *HP* has in mind, we can say, on the basis of experience, that *HP* is correct in its implication that homosexuals can love.

We can also tell by empirical observation that there are selfish, self-indulgent, unloving homosexuals. That being so, the one observation does not annul the other. If we observe that some homosexuals are selfish and unloving, that merely confirms the fact that homosexuals are a mixed bunch, just as heterosexuals are. There are relatively loving and relatively unloving homosexuals, just as there are relatively loving and relatively unloving heterosexuals. But being self-centred does not, as is shown by ordinary observation, follow from being homosexual. It is simply one of the sins to which humans as such are prone, and has nothing particularly to do with being homosexual. *HP* appears to acknowledge this implicitly; its authors do not appear to believe that gays as a group are any more self-centred, because of their homosexuality, than heterosexuals. If homosexuals can love just like everybody else, that should not be in the least surprising, and is only what we might expect in view of the gospel call to love. When Jesus calls people to love, we cannot understand him as excluding homosexuals from that call. No Christian body, as far as I am aware, interprets Jesus as excluding them. Everybody, regardless of sex, colour, race and sexual orientation, is called to love. This is never stated by Jesus explicitly, but the whole of the Christian tradition understands his call to love as a call to human beings as such, not to only a small group of disciples, or to those of a certain race, or indeed those of a particular religious conviction. Jesus calls *all* human beings to love. In the modern context, Christians understand that French people are not excluded from this call, or Cambodians, or Muslims, or people with light brown skin, or homosexuals. But if we must understand that gay people are called by Jesus to love, we must also believe that they are capable of love; that Jesus does not address to them a call to which they are incapable of responding. Here, theological necessity conforms, as all true theological necessity must, to the facts. Jesus calls gays to love, and as a matter of fact, gays are capable of loving.

Can gays love without struggling against being gay?

Now if we can see empirically that it is true that gay people can love and do love, we can see also that their loving does not of itself imply any struggle on their part against their sexuality. That is to say that, for example, a lesbian who devotes herself generously to the service of the poor, the sick and those in need of spiritual support, who gladly gives of her time and money to help her neighbours, and who rejoices in the well-being of her friends – such a woman does not succeed in doing all this only on condition that she struggles against being lesbian. This again is a matter of empirical observation. Lesbians do not universally (or, as far as I know, at all) report that on account of their homosexuality they find it difficult to be generous, and that they have to struggle against their homosexuality in order to succeed in being generous and giving of themselves. Neither is it a matter of common experience that generous lesbians show other, non-verbal signs of having to struggle with their lesbianism in order to be generous. Experience shows that there are lesbians and gay men who are generous and self-giving, but who are very happy being homosexual and do not struggle against their sexuality at all. A fortiori, their being generous and self-giving is not dependent on any such struggle. An important conceptual point follows from this fact: it would be wrong to characterize homosexuality partially as a tendency not to be generous and self-giving, that is to say, as a tendency not to love. If to be homosexual were of itself to have a tendency to be unloving, then, in order to love, any and every homosexual would have to fight against his or her homosexuality in order to love. The stronger a person's homosexual tendencies, the stronger would be that person's tendency to be unloving, and the greater the struggle necessary in order to perform a loving act. But no such struggle is, as a matter of observable fact, necessary. It is no doubt quite correct to say that homosexuals sin by not loving their neighbour sufficiently; but this is so because it is correct to say of *everybody* (except, perhaps, very heroic lovers) that they sin by not loving their neighbour sufficiently. It is true of homosexuals, just as it is true of heterosexuals. That is part of the fallen condition of humanity, a condition in which homosexuals share, but they share in it by virtue of being human beings, not by virtue of being homosexual. Indeed, there are obvious reasons for thinking also that happy homosexuals – those who are happy to be homosexual – are more likely to be loving than those ill at ease with themselves and struggling to overcome their homosexual nature. Struggling against oneself is a kind of preoccupation with oneself which can easily lead to self-absorption to the detriment of that benevolent attention to others which is essential to love. It is those who are at ease with themselves who are likely to be more easily able to devote their attention to others.

Is homosexuality a tendency ordered towards an intrinsic moral evil?

If the law of love is the fundamental law, underlying all other real laws, then if one transgresses any law at all one transgresses the law of love, for if a putative law does not follow from the law of love it is not a law at all, and there is nothing to transgress. This means that fundamentally the only transgression is a transgression against the law of love, and the only sin is a sin against love. If this is so, then another important theological and moral point follows. We have already seen that homosexuality (being homosexual) is not of itself a tendency to be unloving. In other words, it is not a tendency to sin against love. But if the only sin is sin against love, it follows from the fact that homosexuality is not a tendency to sin against love that it is not a tendency to sin *at all*. From which it follows in turn that homosexuality is not 'a more or less strong tendency ordered towards an intrinsic moral evil', *pace HP* (§3). It is not immediately obvious how to evaluate the implications of this observation. It could be seen as a merely conceptual point. The authors of *HP* could still argue that homosexual acts are intrinsically evil; they need only drop the characterization of homosexuality as a tendency ordered towards this evil, as a tendency to perform homosexual acts. This would fit in well with my earlier criticism of this way of describing homosexuality (see Chapter 2). If it is true, as I argued, that homosexuality is not well described as a tendency to commit homosexual acts, it would seem to follow that it is not well described either as a tendency ordered towards an intrinsic evil, provided that the 'intrinsic evil' the authors of *HP* have in mind is homosexual activity, as seems obvious. On the other hand, there may be a more substantial moral point at stake here. While homosexuality (again, being homosexual) cannot properly be reduced to a tendency to have sex with a member of the same sex, such a tendency is far from irrelevant to being homosexual. If being homosexual is more adequately described as a tendency to form (or to want to form) a sexual relationship with a person of the same sex, such relationships include by definition a sexual element, and that sexual element includes sexual activity; that is what makes them sexual relationships. If there is no sexual element to a relationship between two people of the same sex, then it is not a sexual relationship, and a fortiori not a homosexual relationship, even if both the people involved are homosexual. It is a tendency to form specifically *sexual* relationships with another of the same sex that makes a person homosexual. Now if, as argued above, being homosexual is not of itself a tendency to sin against love, and therefore not a tendency to sin at all, it follows that to tend to form specifically sexual relationships with another of the same sex is not a sin at all. If, further, a relationship is sexual if one of its elements is sexual activity, it would appear to follow that sexual activity within such a relationship is not a sin at all, either. Following the same chain of reasoning in the opposite direction, if homosexual activity were of itself sinful, then homosexual relationships would be of themselves sinful, since by definition they contain a sexual element which is sinful. If homosexual relationships were of themselves sinful, then being homosexual would be a tendency to sin, since it would be a tendency to form such sinful relationships. Since the only sin is sin against love, it would follow that being homosexual is a tendency not to love. But ordinary observation shows that this is not the case. Hence the initial premise is false: homosexual activity is not of itself sinful; it is not 'an intrinsic moral evil'. Which is the correct way to interpret the conclusion that homosexuality is not properly characterized as a tendency ordered towards an intrinsic moral evil? Is it a merely conceptual point, a consequence of the observation that homosexuality is not properly described as a tendency to perform homosexual acts? Or is it a substantive moral point, implying that homosexual activity is not of itself sinful? Two considerations (at least) point in the latter direction.

First, the argument of this chapter is fundamentally not based on the definition of what it is to be homosexual, but on empirical observation. We can *see* – at least, those who are prepared to look can see – that to be homosexual is not as such to have a tendency to be unloving. It is from this observation that it follows that to have a tendency to form homosexual relationships is not to have a tendency to be unloving. So it also follows from this observation that to have a tendency to form relationships with an element of homosexual activity is not of itself to have a tendency to be unloving. So it also follows from the same observation that to engage in homosexual activity is not to be unloving; from which it follows that homosexual activity is not of itself sinful. Secondly, the interpretation of our conclusion as a conceptual point, maintaining the sinfulness of homosexual activity while ceasing to characterize being homosexual as a tendency to engage in such activity, implies an unacceptable separation between being homosexual and an interest in homosexual activity, While the one cannot be reduced to the other, they cannot be separated, either. Being homosexual does imply a sexual interest in a member or members of the same sex. We seem compelled, therefore, to interpret our conclusion as a substantive moral conclusion. It implies that homosexual activity is not of itself sinful. If this reasoning is correct, it does not of course mean that no homosexual activity is sinful, merely that not all homosexual activity is as such necessarily sinful. There may be all kinds of sinful homosexual activity going on, just as there are all kinds of sinful heterosexual activity going on, but homosexual activity is not sinful simply by virtue of being homosexual. In cases where it is sinful, that is for other reasons. So we seem already to have settled, on empirical grounds, the Christian moral question concerning homosexuality, and to have settled it in a way which appears to run directly counter to the Christian moral tradition.

That our conclusion contradicts so flatly the traditional Christian position should give us pause. Perhaps we have gone too quickly. There are almost certainly errors in the argument leading to the conclusion, because there are errors in most moral arguments that pretend to be deductive. In the present case, one or more of these errors may turn out on examination to be fatal. This is the kind of error best discovered by hostile critics. But fidelity to the empirical method of this chapter demands also that the conclusion be tested empirically. If it is true that homosexual acts are not intrinsically sinful, intrinsically contrary to love, then it ought not to be an empirically observable fact that all homosexual activity makes its practitioners unloving, or more unloving than they would otherwise be. If it is empirically clear that homosexuals can and do love, is it also empirically clear that sexually active homosexuals can love? Or is there any empirical evidence that sexually active homosexuals are, as such, unloving?

Can sexually active gays love?

Homosexuals can, then, most certainly love, and do, and in order to love they do not have to struggle against being homosexual. But what of the sexual activity and sexual relationships of gay people? Do homosexual relationships militate against a person's capacity to love? If a homosexual is as such not unloving, is a homosexual engaged in a sexual relationship necessarily unloving, or at least less loving than he or she would be if not involved in a sexual relationship? Though I have argued that it is quite illegitimate to reduce homosexuality to a tendency to engage in homosexual acts (Chapter 2), we could also ask the question: does engaging in a homosexual act of itself make a person less loving, less generous and giving of self, as *HP* claims? If empirical observation shows that gay people are capable of love, and that they are not so capable because they struggle against their homosexuality, it does not show that homosexuals engaged in sexual relationships are any less loving than homosexuals who are not engaged in sexual relationships. This is partly because of our ignorance. We often do not know which people are homosexual and which are not, since in many societies gay people have an interest in not being known to be so. That implies in turn that we often do not know which homosexuals are engaged in sexual relationships and which are not. Discretion and even secrecy about being homosexual is still prevalent in many societies, and so, a fortiori, are discretion and secrecy about being involved in homosexual relationships. An additional difficulty is that one and the same person may at one time be engaged in a sexual relationship, at another not, and it may be difficult, even for the person concerned, to know whether at any given moment he or she is or is not engaged in a sexual relationship. If that is so, it is impossible to tell whether the person concerned is or is not more generous and self-giving when engaged in a sexual relationship than when not. We can say more easily in most cases whether a person is or is not taking part in sexual activity, to the extent that we are clear what counts as a sexual activity. If it is inadequate to speak simply of sexual activity without reference to the relational context in which it occurs, talking in terms of sexual activity at this point rather than of sexual relationships at least enables us to search more easily for an answer. And if a sexual relationship is not reducible to sexual activity, it is still a defining characteristic of a sexual relationship that sexual activity has a place in it. So we can ask the question: does engaging in homosexual activity of itself make or tend to make a person less loving, less generous and giving of self?

This, remember, is the claim of *HP*: 'when they engage in homosexual activity [homosexual persons] confirm within themselves a disordered sexual inclination which is essentially self-indulgent' (§7). The logic behind this claim, in the context of the paragraph in which it occurs, seems to be as follows: we are all, including homosexuals, called to a life of self-giving; we can all, including homosexuals, respond to this call, as indeed many homosexuals do. The nature of homosexual activity, however, is such that it tends to make people self-indulgent and thereby militates against a spirit of generosity; that is, it militates against love. So that somebody who takes part in homosexual activity – quite regardless of the relational context of the activity – performs an act which is of itself contrary to love. All homosexual activity is therefore contrary to the call which we have all received, and so to be avoided. It therefore makes (or tends to make) the people who do it unloving as well. *HP* has to be interpreted in some such way if its characterization of the tendency produced by homosexual acts as self-indulgent is to be relevant to its argument against those acts. How do we go about assessing such a claim? Note, first, that it is, or implies, an empirical claim. It implies a claim to the effect that a person who takes part in sexual activity with another person of the same sex thereby becomes less loving than he or she would otherwise have been. That person will not perform as many acts of love, because he or she will find it more difficult to do so and will have to struggle against a stronger inclination to act selfishly. If this turns out not to be true as a matter of empirical fact, then the theological claim is shown to be false. As far as I know, no scientific studies have been done to discover whether individuals become more or less loving when they engage in homosexual activity than when they do not, nor to discover whether individuals find it more difficult to act lovingly when they have recently engaged in homosexual activity than when they have not.[8] The claim that people become less loving when they engage in homosexual activity appears to be without scientific foundation. If engaging in homosexual activity makes people less loving we would also expect that, on the whole, and other things being equal, people who did so would be less loving than people who did not. That is, we would expect all sexually active homosexuals to be *ceteris paribus* less loving than homosexuals who are not sexually active, than heterosexuals who engage in heterosexual activity and than heterosexuals who do not; and we would expect the difference to be more marked in the case of those who engaged in homosexual activity relatively frequently. Once again, there have been, to my knowledge, no scientific studies which show that this is the case, and we have to say once more that the claim that people become less loving when they engage in homosexual activity appears to be without any scientific basis.

Nevertheless, we do not live entirely by scientific studies. We also have anecdotal evidence, our own experience of ourselves and other people, and the witness of others. But evidence of this kind is by its nature informal and unsystematic, and we can wonder whether it is at all suited to support the thesis that *HP* needs to uphold. For that thesis is not merely that some sexually active homosexuals are made less loving than they otherwise would be by some of the sexual activity in which they engage, but that *all* sexually active homosexuals are made less loving by the fact that they engage in *any* sexual activity at all. Anecdotal evidence will not serve to establish this; we need something much more systematic, like the kind of scientific study which has not been done. But if anecdotal evidence is not sufficient to establish *HP*'s case, it is enough to refute it. All that is needed to refute the hypothesis that all homosexuals are made less loving by engaging in any sexual activity at all is to produce one case of a homosexual who we would not say has been made less loving by engaging in some homosexual activity. If that can be done, that will show that it is not the simple fact of engaging in homosexual activity that makes people less loving. But such cases are not difficult to find. Indeed, it does not appear to be a matter of common experience that sexually active homosexuals are less generous and self-giving than sexually inactive homosexuals or than heterosexuals, sexually active or not. If anything, the high proportion of homosexuals, who we have no reason to believe are not sexually active, in the caring professions points in the opposite direction. *HP* itself seems unwittingly to endorse the same conclusion. It speaks of homosexuals as often generous and self-giving, while claiming that when they take part in same-sex activity they strengthen their tendency to self-indulgence. But if they really strengthened any such tendency by the mere fact of engaging in same-sex activity, we should expect them not to be generous and self-giving, or at least noticeably less loving than heterosexuals. That they are nevertheless generous and self-giving indicates that their sexual activity has, *pace HP*, no tendency to make them otherwise.

Pleasure and selfishness

If we ask whether we would say of a homosexual man and woman who we know or know of, and who takes part in homosexual acts, that they are less generous and self-giving than we would otherwise expect them to be, we would only be inclined to give a positive answer if their generosity had markedly declined since they engaged in some homosexual act or series of homosexual acts. While this may be true of some homosexuals, it is not true of all. This in itself makes implausible the claim that homosexual activity strengthens unloving tendencies. Further, we would also only be inclined to give a positive answer if we had some reason for thinking that their generosity had so declined *because* they engaged in that homosexual act or series of homosexual acts: not only *post hoc*, but also *propter hoc*. What reason could there be to believe this? What possible connection could there be between having gay sex and being unloving? *HP* seems to believe that there is such a connection. Why? The belief seems to be rooted in the observation that homosexual activity can be a great pleasure.[9] Doing it, the inference is, makes people more inclined to seek pleasure, more self-indulgent. This is a bad thing because it makes people more selfish, and so less open to the needs and wishes of others; and this means they are less loving. And this is contrary to God's call to human beings, which is to give themselves in love. As the same paragraph of *HP* says, '[h]omosexual activity . . . thwarts the call to a life of that form of self-giving which the Gospel says is the essence of Christian living'.[10] There are plainly important concerns here. It is obvious that Christian living is based on love, and that love includes generosity, thinking of the needs and desires of others. It is equally clear that selfishness is incompatible with this spirit of generosity; to be selfish is to look to one's own needs and desires rather than thinking about the needs and desires of others. So selfishness is incompatible with Christian living, and any selfish act can only be regarded as at best a failure to live up to the call of the gospel.[11] It is also true that there is a connection between selfishness and the seeking of pleasure. We think of somebody who lives for pleasure as one who lives for his or her *own* pleasure. Such a person seeks primarily his or her own pleasure, does things in order to procure pleasure for himself or herself, rather than to benefit others. And this is a selfish way to live; it puts self before others, and is thus incompatible with that 'self-giving which the Gospel says is the essence of Christian living'. So there are real Christian concerns at work here. But we still have to ask whether homosexual activity of itself, because it is often pleasurable, is therefore necessarily a selfish act, and so contrary to love and unchristian. For some, it is easy to jump to this conclusion, since they conceive of all sexually active homosexuals, particularly gay men, as selfish hedonists. But this is a caricature, and false. When 'respectable' people think of gay men, they often seem to think of men who devote themselves to a life of drugged disco dancing and uncontrolled, self-centred, anonymous sex. They forget that the man who spends his evening dancing and looking for sex is also the man who, during the daytime, works as a conscientious bank clerk, bus driver, architect, nurse, teacher, social worker or priest. They also forget that there are very many gay men who never go near a disco, take drugs or search for anonymous sex, and they seem unaware that lesbians have dropped out of their consideration altogether.[12] What is needed here is not caricature but argument; and argument will not, I believe, support the view that there is good reason to think homosexual activity necessarily unchristian.

Note, first, that if same-sex acts are unloving because pleasurable, that conclusion does not apply only to same-sex activity. If same-sex activity is selfish because it is pleasurable, then any pleasurable activity is *eo ipso* selfish, and so unchristian. Eating, when pleasurable, would be selfish and unchristian. Dancing, reading a favourite novel on a sunny beach, listening to Bach, giving a gift to a loved one, teaching one's child to read, going to mass, the sexual intercourse of man and wife, gardening, playing rugby – all these things, if pleasurable, would be selfish and unchristian. But such a conclusion would be absurd. That homosexual acts are pleasurable to those who perform them cannot, then, be the real objection to them. We have to look for that elsewhere. But before going on to try to locate it more exactly, we need to dwell a little on the above remarks, for they contain an important point. Human pleasures are many and various, and this variety is closely linked to the variety of human acts. Typically, a pleasure is the pleasure of doing something. One can get pleasure from cultivating roses, and pleasure from cooking. These two pleasures are necessarily different, because the one is the pleasure of cultivating roses, the other the pleasure of cooking. We cannot get the pleasure of cooking by cultivating roses, nor can cooking give us the pleasure of cultivating roses. To get pleasure from an activity is, in general, simply to perform that activity with pleasure. The activity in question might be a selfish one; for instance, if Christopher takes pleasure in eating to excess, and if he eats to excess when he knows that others around him have not enough to eat, then his activity is selfish, and we may also want to say that his pleasure is selfish. But the pleasurable activity may on the contrary be a very generous one: Sophie may take great pleasure in providing food for those who have not enough to eat. The fact that she gets pleasure out of her activity does not turn that activity into a selfish one. There is an asymmetry between these two cases. If Christopher eats to excess when he knows that others have not enough to eat, his reason for doing so is likely to be that it is a pleasure for him to eat to excess. But if Sophie provides food for the hungry, her reason is likely to be that they need food, not that it gives her pleasure to feed them. Christopher's reasons for action are likely to be self-regarding, while Sophie's are not. The target of *HP*'s remarks cannot be pleasurable activity in general, but only pleasurable activity which is undertaken for reasons which are self-regarding.

But this is still not precise enough, for it is possible to perform pleasurable activities for self-regarding reasons without rendering that pleasure either self-indulgent or selfish. For example, if Christopher decides to take a long, cool gin on arriving home after a long, hot, wearying and frustrating day at work, his reason for doing so is likely to be that he finds a long, cool gin in those circumstances very pleasurable. But that hardly makes his pleasure a self-indulgent one. A pleasure is not self-indulgent when sought and enjoyed for the pleasure it brings. It is only self-indulgent when it betokens an inordinate preoccupation with pleasure, when it forms part of a pattern of behaviour which reveals the person as overly concerned with his or her own pleasure. If Christopher lives in a pleasure-seeking way, if he takes too many occasions to do things because they are pleasurable, or if he seeks to do pleasurable things at inappropriate moments, then we would say he is self-indulgent, and we would also be likely to call many of his pleasures self-indulgent. (Not necessarily all of them. He might still seek pleasures in circumstances where we judged it reasonable to seek them: even if he is a pleasure seeker, we might still think it appropriate for him, and not a self-indulgence, to take a long, cool gin after a long, hot, wearying and frustrating day at work.) That is, it is primarily people, not pleasurable activities, who are self-indulgent. Activities cannot be judged self-indulgent in themselves, without reference to the pattern of life of the people who perform them. That Christopher performs an act because he finds it pleasurable to do it does not, then, make him a self-indulgent person, and neither does it make his act self-indulgent. Nor does it strengthen in him a tendency to become self-indulgent. Indeed, Christopher may have no such tendency. He may be very dedicated and disciplined in his life as a whole, including his work, and it may be precisely because of his dedication and discipline that he has long, hot, wearying and frustrating days at work. The fact that Christopher likes a long, cool gin after such days would then be understandable in the light of his dedication and discipline, and not of any putative tendencies to self-indulgence. The importance of self-indulgence is that a self-indulgent person is liable to be also a selfish person. A self-indulgent act is not of itself a selfish act. What makes a self-indulgent act selfish is the circumstances. If Christopher eats to excess for the pleasure of eating to excess, that may, in the context of the way he lives, be a self-indulgent act. If he does so in isolation, where he is confronted by nobody else's needs or wishes, his act remains at the level of self-indulgence. But if he eats in this way when surrounded by those who have not enough to eat, who need to eat more and wish to, and if he can share his food but will not, then his self-indulgent act becomes also a selfish act. Selfishness arises when a person thinks of himself in a context where he or she ought to be thinking of others. But if Christopher is self-indulgent, if he habitually takes occasion to do things because they are pleasurable to him, regardless of context, then he is likely to end up acting like that in contexts where his so acting leads him to disregard the needs and wishes of others. If he is self-indulgent, he is likely to be selfish also. So it is important from the Christian point of view that people avoid becoming self-indulgent, for one who is self-indulgent is liable to be one without love, and to commit acts which are contrary to love. But, to repeat, to perform an act for the pleasure it will bring is not of itself to perform a self-indulgent or a selfish act, or to strengthen any tendency to perform such acts.

The pleasure of shared sexual acts

Sexual acts are often pleasurable; they are performed with pleasure. Because, like many other pleasurable acts, they are often shared acts, they can be pleasurable in more than one way. When Andrew plays tennis with his wife Jane, whom he loves, part of the pleasure will be the pleasure of reasonably strenuous exercise, and part will be the pleasure of competition. But part of the pleasure will also be doing all this together with one whom he loves. People who love each other, like friends, like to be together; they take pleasure in each other, and in each other's company. This means that they enjoy doing things together, even, or especially, quite ordinary things, such as playing, or going for a walk, or drinking, or watching television. Even activities which can be irksome when performed alone, like washing up or shopping, can be pleasurable when done with a friend. Part of the pleasure of these shared activities depends on the belief that the activity is a pleasure also for the friend, the belief that this activity is a shared pleasure. If one believes that the other takes no pleasure in such shared activity, one's own pleasure will be blighted. So part of the concern of friends in their shared activity is to make the activity pleasurable for one another. Each seeks not only his or her own pleasure, but that of the friend. When Andrew has sex with Jane, part of the pleasure he experiences will no doubt be the pleasure of the bodily sensations he has during the course of the activity.[13] It may be also that one of the reasons why he in general wants to have sex with her is that he wants to have these bodily sensations occasionally. This does not imply that his sexual activity with Jane is self-indulgent on his part. This would be so only if he sought sex with her inordinately often or at inappropriate times, so that it betokened an excessive concern with his own pleasure and a disregard of her needs and wishes.[14] An additional part of his pleasure will be the same kind of pleasure he gets playing tennis with her: it will be the pleasure of being with her, of doing this together with her, the pleasure of taking part in a shared pleasurable activity. So it is an essential element of Andrew's pleasure that he believe it is also a pleasure for Jane. In order that this be so, part of his activity will be designed to give pleasure to her. Then it will be part of his pleasure to know that he is giving pleasure to her. (If he did not love Jane, this would not necessarily be so. He might enter on the sexual activity for the sole purpose of having pleasant sensations. In which case, the range of pleasures available to him will be much more limited; he cannot have – and does not seek – the pleasure of giving pleasure to Jane.) Andrew does not seek only his own pleasure, but that of Jane, and it gives him pleasure if he believes himself successful in giving her pleasure. Thus part of the pleasure of sex, for one who loves his or her sexual partner, derives from concern for the other and is not self-regarding. And of course exactly the same considerations apply to Jane and her sexual pleasure. She, too, may want to engage in this activity because of the pleasure it affords her, and part of that pleasure may well be the pleasure of having certain sensations. But that does not imply that she is being self-indulgent or selfish, either. If she loves Andrew, some of her pleasure will be the pleasure of sharing a pleasurable activity with him, some will be the pleasure of giving him pleasure, and some will derive from the belief that this is a pleasurable activity for him too.[15]

Are all homosexual acts contrary to love?

Suppose Christopher loves David, and David loves Christopher. They also both love others. They love their families and their friends. They are both social workers, and they both devote themselves far beyond the call of duty to the welfare of those with whom they work. They are typical of the generous and self-giving homosexuals of whom *HP* speaks. But their mutual love is special. They share their lives. They have lived together for a number of years, they share the cost and effort of maintaining a home together. Each looks after the interests of the other, sometimes at considerable cost to himself. They take pleasure in each other's company, and they like to do simple everyday things together. As part of their life together, they share the same bed, and sometimes they make love; they 'engage in homosexual activity'. Because they love each other, what is true of the sexual activity of Andrew and Jane is true of theirs also, for nothing said about Andrew and Jane and

174

their sexual pleasure depended on the sexual difference between them. There is no reason to think that either Christopher or David is being self-indulgent, unless the wider pattern of their lives indicates it. In this case it does not, since neither is a self-indulgent person and both live lives of self-giving generosity. They are not pleasure seekers, in the sense of tending to seek and do what gives them pleasure regardless of the needs and wishes of others. Their sexual pleasure is, apart from the pleasant physical sensations both may have, the pleasure of doing something pleasurable together. It is the pleasure of believing that the shared activity is pleasant for the other, and the pleasure of trying to make this so. There are, of course, homosexuals whose sexual activity is not like this at all, just as there are heterosexuals whose sexual activity is not like that of Andrew and Jane. There are no doubt homosexuals who are self-indulgent and who therefore risk being selfish. For these people, their sexual activity is liable to be self-indulgent too, and selfish. But, if so, it is the pattern of their lives that makes their sexual activity self-indulgent and selfish, not vice versa. It is because they generally think only of themselves and their own pleasure that they are likely to think only of themselves and their own pleasure in their sexual activity too. But the sexual activity of Christopher and David is not like that, because *they* are not like that. As already observed, homosexuals are a mixed bunch, like anybody else, and we should expect any evaluation of their sexual activity to reflect that diversity. There is, then, no reason to believe that the sexual activity of Christopher and David strengthens in either of them a tendency to self-indulgence. In it, neither seeks his own pleasure regardless of the other, or regardless of anybody else. The assertion of *HP* to the contrary is thus groundless. Not only is there a lack of empirical evidence supporting it, and some contradicting it, but the a priori reasoning which seemed to force such a conclusion on us is faulty. If their joint sexual activity tends to make neither of them self-indulgent, neither, a fortiori, does it tend to make either of them selfish, to indulge themselves in circumstances which call on them rather to attend to the needs and wishes of others. But if homosexual activity does not of itself tend to make Christopher and David selfish, it does not tend to make them unloving, either. This joint activity of theirs is no more contrary to love than their playing tennis together, or walking together, or doing the dishes together. That is, it is not contrary to love at all. It is not against the commandment to love which is the fundamental commandment of the Bible. There may be a case for saying that the sexual activity of some, self-indulgent homosexuals is contrary to love and so against the central moral principle of the Bible. If so, then it is because it is the sexual activity of self-indulgent individuals, not because it is homosexual activity.

This means that the attempt to salvage the coherence of the Bible with which this chapter started fails. The biblical passages alleged to condemn all homosexual activity directly and the biblical passages alleged to rule out all homosexual activity indirectly on the basis of a universally applicable heterosexual model of sex cannot be grounded in the commandment to love. We can arrive at a coherent reading of the Bible only by jettisoning the belief that these passages exclude all homosexual activity, and I have argued in previous chapters that this is a route which an attentive reading of such passages invites us to take.[16] If my arguments there turn out to be wide of the mark, and if these biblical passages really must be understood as excluding all homosexual activity, then we are left with a real tension between them and those dominical and apostolic sayings which establish the love of neighbour as the fulfilling of the whole law. In that case, the choice is clear for Christians: we must uphold that dominical and apostolic principle and jettison the rest, just as we have abandoned biblical injunctions against wearing clothes made of two kinds of material (Lev. 19:19), eating shellfish (Lev. 11:10–12) and charging interest on loans (Lev. 25:35–7) – even though it remains incumbent upon us to ensure that our wearing the clothes we do, our eating the food we do and our financial practices are compatible with the commandment to love. If there really are biblical passages which exclude all homosexual practice, they are, in the light of the law of love, no longer of interest to us.

CHAPTER SEVEN

Aquinas, Natural Law and Sexual Natures

'Nature'

People have often complained in a vague way that same-sex relations are unnatural, or against nature. The complaint was common in ancient and Hellenistic Greece.[1] Famously, St Paul speaks of same-sex practices as *para physin*, most often translated 'against nature', without clarifying what he means by the phrase.[2] Today, people sometimes still say that homosexuality is unnatural, though they might struggle to articulate what concept of nature, if any, underlies their attitude. In this chapter we shall look at some conceptions of nature and see what bearing, if any, they have on the question of homosexual relationships and acts. The word 'nature' can be used in several different ways. We particularly need to distinguish normative from non-normative uses of the word and its cognates. In one sense, we distinguish the world of nature from the human world. Nature documentaries on television are not about people playing football or about manufacturing cars; they are about lions or fish or spiders. The interest here is to observe, learn and wonder. In this sense, what is natural is just what is observed, what occurs in the world of nature, the non-human world; what happens in that world is *eo ipso* natural, and there is no such thing as the unnatural. We also speak in a closely connected way of the nature of an animal. What an animal does in the world of nature can never be unnatural; any one of its activities rather displays an aspect of its nature; we learn an animal's nature by observing how it acts. But once we have made this distinction between the natural and the human we can subvert it. We can speak and write about animals as if they were human, and more interestingly we can study human beings as if they were animals: we can observe the eating or mating rituals of people just as we can those of hyenas. This is in one way an obvious thing to do, as human beings are a kind of animal, and there are close connections between human behaviour and the behaviour of other animals. If we make this move, we end up with a view of humanity not as opposed to the world of nature but as part of it. And everything that humans do can be then seen as natural, just like everything gnus do; what a human being does is never unnatural, it simply displays an aspect of that person's nature, or of human nature in general. This concept of nature is entirely non-normative; it neither approves nor disapproves, but merely observes, and perhaps wonders. But there is another use or series of uses of 'nature' and its cognates which is normative. For example, people speak of some human attitudes and actions as natural in the sense of understandable: 'Tom gets very violent sometimes; it's only natural that Sheila should be frightened of him'; 'Anne and David work together all the time; it's only natural that they should have become close'; etc. Here the use of the word 'natural' seems to indicate not exactly approval but understanding, as if to say: 'I'd react in the same way myself' or 'I can see why he/she acts like this' or 'I could imagine myself doing that.' This understanding, it seems to be implied, has its source in our sharing the same nature. By contrast, saying of somebody's action 'That's unnatural' is to express disapproval, a certain distaste for the action in question, of a sort that puts a distance between the speaker and the person whose action is under discussion, as if they did not share a nature in common; as if the speaker were saying not merely 'He shouldn't do that' but 'How could he possibly do that?' or 'I can't imagine how anybody could do that.' Such distance is also expressed simply by saying of the act 'It's disgusting', which is often coupled with a rejection of the agent himself or herself as disgusting. It's the sort of thing many people are inclined to say when they hear of, for instance, a man having sex with another man, or of farmers feeding their cows with processed dead cows. It is important to note that such disapproval does not depend on the speaker having any theory of nature, of what counts as natural and unnatural. 'It's unnatural', like 'It's disgusting', can be, and often is, simply a verbal expression of disgust, rather than an observation on how the act in question relates to a particular conception of nature. It is in this sense a pre-reflective aesthetic response; which is not to say that it cannot be subsequently elaborated, but any elaboration is the further articulation of the response rather than the ground of the response. To say of same-sex activity that it is unnatural in this sense is not to offer an argument against it, but merely to evince more or less strong disgust at it. Again, we make a connection between the natural and the healthy; since health is good, the natural is good too. So the natural is to be sought out and cultivated; natural foods are to be eaten, and natural activities engaged in. The unnatural, by contrast, is associated with the unhealthy, and hence is to be avoided. This is clearly again an evaluative use of 'natural', but not one which is obviously related to the use which sees the natural as understandable and the unnatural as disgusting. It is possible that both these evaluative uses are involved in the popular complaint that homosexual acts are unnatural, and there may be other ways too in which 'natural' is used as an evaluative term, and other considerations behind the feeling that homosexual acts are unnatural. But there is little point in making a catalogue of such uses. To investigate the connection between homosexuality and nature, or whether there is such a connection, what is needed is a more developed conception of nature. This we can find by looking at the thought of St Thomas Aquinas.

Thomas Aquinas

Nature and rationality

Aquinas is the most eminent Christian theologian to bring conceptions of nature to bear on the question of the morality of homosexual acts. He attempts to bring some clarity to the common condemnation of these acts as unnatural, by giving an account of just what is, or should be, meant by the term 'nature' in this context. In order to understand his attitude, we need first to look at his use of the concept of natural law. He did not develop the idea of natural law, nor use it very much, but his views have had an enormous influence on moral thinking in the Catholic tradition. He uses the idea of nature, and correspondingly that of natural law, in two distinct but related ways, which can be summarized as follows. (In this section, unless otherwise noted, I am summarizing and paraphrasing *Summa Theologiae* 1–2.94.2c.) First, in Aquinas's view what is most distinctive about people is that we think; we are by nature rational, as other animals are not. Among other things, we can think about what we should do, and this is practical reason. Natural law, for rational creatures like people, is nothing less than practical reason; theologically speaking, we participate in the divine reason, and this enables us to see what is the right thing to do.[3] Aquinas likens the principles of natural law to the laws of logic such as the principle of non-contradiction: just as there are logical laws governing theoretical reason, the way we think about the things that are, so there are logical laws governing practical reason, the way we think about the things that are to be done. The most basic law governing theoretical reason is that we should not contradict ourselves; if we are not concerned to avoid self-contradiction, we can hardly be said to be thinking at all. Hence: 'the same thing cannot be affirmed and denied at the same time ... on this principle all others are based'. I may want to assert that my dog is a poodle, or I may want to deny that it is a poodle; but I cannot, on pain of unintelligibility, simultaneously both assert and deny that it is a poodle. Similarly, to be involved in practical reason means to be thinking about what is good.

> 'Good' is the first thing that falls under the apprehension of the practical reason, which is directed to action: since every agent acts for an end under the aspect of good. Consequently the first principle of practical reason is one founded on the notion of good, viz. that 'good is that which all things seek after'. Hence this is the first precept of law, that 'good is to be done and pursued, and what is bad to be avoided'. All other precepts of the natural law are based upon this: so that whatever the practical reason naturally apprehends as human goods belongs to the precepts of the natural law as something to be done or avoided. (*Summa Theologiae* I.94.2c)

The idea here is that to think an act good is to think of it as to be done; I cannot, on pain of unintelligibility, say in the same breath that such and such an act is good and that it is not to be done, nor that it is bad and is to be done. Nor can I say that a particular goal is a good one and not to be pursued, nor that it is a bad one and is to be pursued. We can think well or badly about what is; we can, for example, perform a mathematical calculation well and so arrive at the right answer, or perform it badly and so arrive at the wrong answer. Similarly, we can think well or badly about what is to be done. A right action is one that is truly rational; to act properly is to act in accord with right reason. A sin, by contrast, is an action that is irrational, not in accord with reason; it is an error. In this sense, every sin is a breach of natural law; it is against our nature as rational beings, a failure to think properly.

Just as theoretical reason is concerned with being, with what is, so practical reason is concerned with the good. The good is what all things aim at. By this Aquinas does not mean that all human beings seek what is actually good; it is part of our human condition, part of our problem, that we often seek what is not good. What he means is rather that, when we seek anything at all, we seek it *as a good*. If Brian wants to rob Matilda of her handbag, what he wants to do is, the rest of us would agree (unless there are special circumstances), a bad thing. But he sees it as a good thing to steal Matilda's handbag; that is what it is for him to want to do it. Conversely, the bad[4] is what people shun; we want to avoid doing those things we see as bad; it is another question whether they are actually bad. It may be, and in all normal circumstances would be, a good thing for Brian to return Matilda's handbag to her with an apology, once he has stolen it. But he will probably, and wrongly, see that as a bad thing to do, and so will not want to do it. This will be a failure of practical reason on his part, a failure either to think about the matter at all or to think about it properly. His not returning Matilda's handbag is a sinful omission. In failing to think properly, Brian is being untrue to his nature as a rational being; he is acting against nature.

Nature as teacher

But what gives Aquinas the confidence that, if Brian did think about things properly, he would see that it is really a bad thing to steal Matilda's handbag? Here we come to the second aspect of his idea of natural law. As well as being thinking creatures, we have other aspects to our nature. In particular, we have natural inclinations. We naturally want certain things, so we naturally see those things as good. (Let us call such things natural human goods.) We also naturally want to avoid certain things, so we naturally see those things as bad. It is these inclinations that, for Aquinas, give content to natural law. As he puts it: 'the order of the precepts of natural law is according to the order of natural inclinations'. What are these natural inclinations? First, there is the natural desire for self-preservation. Secondly, there are certain natural instincts such as the coupling of male and female and the raising of offspring. These we have in common with animals, but there is a third group of natural desires that belong to us specifically as rational beings: desire for the knowledge of God, and to live in society; and this implies that, for example, we shun ignorance and avoid offending those with whom we have to do. (It is perhaps to these instincts that we might appeal in trying to persuade Brian to return Matilda's handbag.) If we reason correctly about the good on the basis of these natural human goods, of those things that people, because of the kind of nature they have, see as good, we can, according to Aquinas, reach certain conclusions about the goodness or otherwise of human acts. Broadly, those acts which lead to the attainment of natural human goods will be good. They are in accordance with nature, and in conformity with natural law. Those acts which are necessary for the attainment of natural human goods will be obligatory, and these will be what Aquinas calls the precepts of natural law. Those acts which prevent the attainment of natural human goods, or which bring about any of those things which humans naturally regard as bad and to be avoided, will be bad. They are against nature, and are breaches of natural law.

General difficulties

Multiple difficulties attend Aquinas's concept of natural law. This is not the place to go into them in detail. I will merely mention briefly two objections which seem fundamental. First, there is a question about the status of the sentence 'The good is to be done and pursued, and what is bad to be avoided.' Aquinas characterizes this as the first precept of natural law, the source of all the other precepts of natural law. But it is not a precept at all. Aquinas has introduced it as a proposition whose truth is evident once we understand the terms used. As such, it is akin to 'triangles have three sides'. This tells us nothing about all the triangles that exist, or indeed whether any triangles exist, but is rather a kind of definition of the word 'triangle'. It amounts to a claim (true or false) about how we use the word. That is why we are supposed to be able to see that it is true immediately we understand the terms involved. It says that faced with a three-sided figure I (or anybody else) will, provided I am a competent user of English, call it a triangle. Similarly, 'The good is to be done and pursued, and what is bad to be avoided' does not tell us anything about what we are to do; it is a comment (true or false) on how we use the words 'good' and 'bad'. When we say that something is good, we mean it is to be done and pursued; when we say something is bad, we mean it is to be avoided. That is why we are supposed to be able to see the truth of the proposition once we understand the terms involved. But a grammatical remark of this kind is not a precept. It tells me nothing, not even in the most general terms, about what I should do. It says only that, if I (or anybody else) see something as to be done and pursued, I will (provided I am a competent user of English) call it good, and if I see it as to be avoided, I will call it bad. Secondly, no precept whatever follows from this grammatical remark. In particular, it does not follow 'that whatever the practical reason naturally apprehends as human goods belongs to the precepts of the natural law as something to be done or avoided'. One might raise difficulties here about the idea that we naturally apprehend things as good. There is also a crucial ambiguity in the notion of a human good. Does 'human good' mean that which a human being sees as good, or which all human beings see as good, or is it that which is good for a human being, or which is good for all human beings? These are certainly not equivalent. For example, I might, as a human being, see a particular human action as good, not because it is good for human beings but because it is good for whales. I might see a particular human action as bad, even though it is good for human beings, because it is bad for whales. Now it looks as if Aquinas means by 'human goods' what is good for human beings; his whole moral theory is centred on what is good for people. But from the fact (if it is a fact) that people see certain things as good, even that they naturally see them as good, it does not follow that those things which are good for human beings are to be done and pursued. And since 'the good is to be done' is a grammatical remark asserting that the word 'good' is used in connection with what is seen as to be done, it has no obvious connection with what is good for people.

Specific problems

But let us leave these general objections aside, or assume they can be dealt with, and address the specific question whether this theory of nature and of natural law shows that same-sex relations are indeed unnatural, against nature. It has certainly been taken to do so. When the *Catechism of the Catholic Church* asserts baldly that homosexual acts are contrary to the natural law (§2357) it is basing itself fundamentally on Aquinas. Aquinas himself clearly thinks this conclusion follows from his natural law theory. His claim is, put shortly, that if, in conformity with our rational nature, we think properly about homosexual acts we will see that they are against nature in that they prevent the attainment of natural human goods. He locates the discussion of homosexual acts firmly within the context of human sexuality in general. In the second part of the

Summa he discusses the virtues, and among these chastity, the right – the truly reasonable – ways of acting sexually (*ST* 2–2.151). It is as a pendant to this that he discusses those ways of behaving sexually which are contrary to the virtue of chastity, summarized as the vice of *luxuria*[5] (*ST* 2–2.153–154). All the behaviour which falls under *luxuria* is sinful because it is, he holds, unreasonable, against the order of reason which it is our nature to follow (*ST* 2–2.153.2c). These include, among other things, rape, adultery and incest, and finally what he calls the sin against nature. In a certain sense all sins of *luxuria*, indeed all sins of any kind, are sins against nature in the sense of being against reason; but he uses the term 'sin against nature' to designate sexual behaviour which is contrary to nature in another sense: it is that sin which is not only against reason but against 'the natural order of the sexual act which is fitting for the human species' (*ST* 2–2.154.11c). Under this head come masturbation, sex with animals, 'copulation with an undue sex, male with male, or female with female', any unnatural mode of copulation (*ibid.*).

Although the fourth item is vague, it is clear from the rest of the list, and from what he says elsewhere, that what he thinks is wrong with these kinds of sex is that conception cannot follow from them. In the natural order, what sex is for is procreation. The reason why human beings are sexual is so that we might reproduce and the species be conserved. Just as food is necessary to the preservation of the individual, so sex is necessary to the preservation of the human race (*ST* 2–2.153.2c). Sex is, then, by nature procreative, and any form of sexual activity which is non-procreative is therefore not in conformity with nature; it is against nature. And that, of course, includes all sexual activity between two members of the same sex. Here is the essence of the habitual natural law argument against same-sex practices: they are unnatural in that they go against the natural purpose of sex, which is procreation. To put the same point using a couple of medieval technical terms, sex naturally has procreation as its end; it is of its nature ordered towards procreation. But homosexual acts cannot have procreation as their end; they are therefore *dis*ordered. Hence the judgement, more than seven hundred years later, of *Persona Humana*:

> ... according to the objective moral order, homosexual relations are acts which lack an essential and indispensable finality ... homosexual acts are intrinsically disordered and can in no case be approved of. (§8)

184

HP adopts and reaffirms this judgement (§3). But is Aquinas right here? Does his argument convince, once we look at it critically? Apart from the general difficulties concerning natural law mentioned earlier, there are a number of specific points at which his treatment of same-sex activity fails. Here I mention only some. Following the headings which Aquinas establishes, it seems that there are three ways in which homosexual acts might be against nature. First, they might be against nature in the sense that they frustrate that desire which, according to Aquinas, is natural to human beings just because they exist, the desire for self-conservation. Second, they might be acts which go against some desire which people have because they are animals, one or more of those desires which 'nature has taught all animals'. Third, they might go against desires which people have because they are rational. In the following discussion I leave aside such fundamental questions as whether the existence of a desire can entail moral conclusions, and if so how. I concentrate rather on two questions: for each of Aquinas's three headings, does the desire (or desires) he claims exists actually exist? And, if it does exist, does it imply a negative judgement on same-sex activity?

Self-preservation

First, self-preservation. The continued existence of the species is, according to Aquinas, a natural good of the species, for he believes, as we have seen, that all things naturally seek to conserve themselves (*ST* 1–2.94.2c). But this belief is not true; things in general do not seek to conserve themselves. Animals, including human beings, very often do, but not always. Inanimate things do not seek to conserve themselves at all, for the reason that they do not seek anything.[6] The fact that human beings on the whole seek to preserve themselves was meant to be equivalent to their naturally seeing their own survival as good, since for human beings to desire something is to see it as good. But things which are not animals do not desire anything, and things which are not rational animals do not see anything as good. Now the human race is not an animal and not a rational animal. It therefore does not seek anything, and does not see anything as good. But still, it might be thought that we could generate an argument against homosexual acts by slightly adjusting Aquinas's claim. We can fairly safely assert that, on the whole, the human beings who are members of the human race at any one time want the human race to survive and thus see its continuation as a good. There is surely some truth in this; it is probably true that the great majority of human beings alive at any one time would say if asked that they would prefer the race to continue rather than to perish. Now it begins to look as if the continuation of the species is a common human good. But to act against a common good, or to fail to support that good, is surely a failure of charity; and homosexual acts, being infertile, do fail to support that good and are therefore to be avoided. However, this reasoning is specious. As a goal which most human beings share, the continuation of the species is, we can say, commonly seen as a good; but this does not license us to say that it is a common human good. We see here an instance of the confusion, noted earlier, between what people see as good and what is good for people. If most people want the human race to continue, that means that they see it as a good that the race continue, but it does not imply that it is good for them that the race continue. An act is a failure of charity towards people only if it implies a neglect of what is good for them; it is not against charity to fail to pursue an end that others, even all others, see as good.

Sex necessary for the conservation of the species

But let us say, for the sake of argument, that it is indeed a good of the species that it be conserved. It is, then, in Aquinas's theory, a good *of the species*. It is not a natural good of any individual human being as such; each individual human being is supposed naturally to see his or her own survival as a good, not that of the species. If we mean by the species simply the generality of individual human beings, and if most of them do in fact want the species to continue, then it is up to the generality of human beings together to manage things so that the species survives; it is not an end which any individual human being necessarily must play a part in achieving.[7] How is humankind in general to achieve this common good? It is clear that, for the human race to survive, it is necessary that men and women have sexual intercourse in such a way as to allow procreation, and that they do this on a sufficient number of occasions. (Modern reproductive technology, not available in Aquinas's time, makes a certain amount of reproduction possible without intercourse, but it hardly seems likely, even at present, that if we relied on this alone it would produce people in sufficient numbers to keep the species going.[8]) This is the basis of Aquinas's argument that *luxuria* is a sin. He claims that sex is necessary for the conservation of the human race (*ST* 2–2.153.2c and 3c),[9] and so it is, in one sense. But this is an ambiguous assertion, and the ambiguity centres on the use of the concept of necessity. Taken in one way the assertion is true, but it does not imply the exclusion of homosexual acts. Taken in another way it would, if true, exclude homosexual acts, but it is not true. The sentence can mean, first, that the race cannot be conserved without some acts of penile-vaginal intercourse, and that it is therefore necessary to the continuation of the species that a sufficient number of people engage in penile-vaginal intercourse in such a way as to produce offspring; in this sense the assertion is true. But, evidently, it does not follow from this that this good, if it is a good, cannot be attained if some people, as well or instead, engage in other sexual activities, ones which are not of a kind to produce offspring. So it does not follow either that homosexual acts are to be avoided. But the sentence can also mean that each and every sexual act that takes place, without exception, is necessary for the continuation of the species. If we interpret it in this way, then clearly any sexual act which is not procreative would impede the attainment of this good, and so would be against nature. And this would include all sexual activity between two men or between two women; homosexual acts would be against nature. But, understood in this sense, the sentence is clearly false. The species can and does survive quite well, even though much of the sexual activity that goes on is not procreative; there are even those who argue that it survives better, that we avoid damaging over-population, if much of the sexual activity that goes on is *not* such as to produce offspring. In particular, we know as a matter of fact that the species survives well even with all the same-sex activity that goes on. We can imagine circumstances in which this would not be the case. After some catastrophe numbers of people might be so reduced, or their fertility so impaired, that it becomes vital to the continuation of the species that there be as much penile-vaginal intercourse as possible. In those circumstances any non-reproductive sex – masturbation, bestiality or same-sex activity – would endanger the continuation of the species. In Aquinas's terms, since the conservation of the species is a natural good, it would be contrary to right reason and against nature, and so a bad thing. But such are not our circumstances. In our circumstances – and this has pretty much always been the case – there is enough procreative sexual activity going on to ensure the survival of the species, so all the non-reproductive sexual activity that goes on, including homosexual activity, does not endanger that common natural good. So we cannot conclude from this that same-sex activities are to be avoided.[10]

What nature teaches

Now we come to the second class of natural human goods, those natural human goods which human beings putatively seek because they are animals and in common with the other animals, such as the conjunction of male and female and the raising of offspring. Such things belong to the natural law, according to Aquinas, because they are 'what nature has taught all animals'. The assertion that human beings naturally seek the conjunction of male and female seems likely to have a direct relevance to the discussion of homosexual acts. This desire is said to belong to our animal nature; it is part of 'what nature has taught all animals'. A couple of preliminary remarks need to be made about this phrase. First, it seems that the term 'nature' does not have the same sense in this phrase as it has had in the discussion up until now. Until now, talk of nature has served as a way of referring to those qualities something has, just because it is the sort of thing it is. For example, human beings are by nature rational: any human being is said to be rational just because he or she is a human being; to be rational is part of what it is to be a human being. Again, human beings are said to have a natural desire for self-preservation. Andrew does not have this desire as he might have the desire to go to China, play the cello or be a millionaire. These desires are contingent, accidental; they are the sort of desire that anybody might or might not pick up during the course of a lifetime. The desire for self-preservation is something Andrew has, according to Aquinas, just because he is an existing thing; it is part of his nature, as it is part of the nature of every existing thing. In this sense of the word 'nature', there is no such thing as nature *tout court*; there are natures, and every nature is the nature of a thing. In speaking now of what nature has taught all animals, Aquinas[11] seems to be speaking of nature in some absolute sense, not of the nature of this or that being, or of this or that animal or species. But it is not clear what such a sense might be. The difficulty is compounded by the idea that nature teaches; what sense can we give to 'nature' which would make it intelligible to say that nature has taught something to all animals? Many animals are capable of learning, but then they learn from their parents, or from people, or from experience, not from anything we might call nature.

I am not sure that these are serious difficulties; it could be that Aquinas is simply using a bit of picturesque language here, which we need not take too seriously. He may be saying only that all animals have certain desires – for, among other things, the coupling of male and female and for the raising of children – as part of their nature; that they have them, that is, just because they are animals. If this is what Aquinas is saying, it is certainly false, in being too general. There are species of animal in which male and female do not couple, and in which there is no nurturing of the young. So Aquinas is not entitled to say that human beings naturally desire the coupling of male and female just because they are animals. In saying that animals naturally desire the coupling of male and female, Aquinas is obviously thinking only of those species of animal where male and female do in fact mate. (Though he thinks, erroneously, that all animals are like this.) When they do this, he is saying, it is obviously because that is what they want to do, for it is desire that moves animals. And this desire is natural to them; they have it because they are the kind of thing they are. To what is Aquinas contrasting the notion of natural desire here? He seems to mean that these desires are not contingent or accidental to these animals. They are not desires that each animal of a given species may or may not acquire, and they are not desires which they have been taught to have. They are desires which we would probably call instinctual; the animals in question do what they do by instinct, without having had to learn anything, without compulsion or prompting, spontaneously. This is perhaps what Aquinas's curious phrase is getting at: to say that nature has taught all animals certain things is perhaps to say simply that all animals do those things without being taught anything.[12] Taking the phrase in this sense, what all animals do naturally includes, according to Aquinas, the sexual coupling of male and female. All animals naturally aim at that coupling, so that all male animals naturally aim to couple with female animals, and vice versa. For example, when a male lion and a female lion mate together, this is not because they have been taught this behaviour or are coerced into it; under certain conditions, they do it spontaneously. It seems that Aquinas wants to say that this is true of human beings as well as lions, just because they are animals. Aquinas's claim that the desire for sexual coupling is natural to all animals is, as we have noted, too sweeping; it is not true of all animals. Since there are species of animal in which there is no mating of male and female, it cannot be true of human beings that they desire this mating just because they are animals, because it is part of their nature as animals. But, clearly, human beings are among those species of animal in which there is mating of male and female, and in which there is desire for this mating. However, the question immediately arises: is this desire natural, in the sense in which it is natural for lions? This involves the further question: if leonine sexual desire is untaught, spontaneous, instinctual, is this true of human beings too? This does not seem to have been a question at all for Aquinas; he appears to have taken it for granted that it was so. But it is a large and important question. We shall have to go into it later. For the moment, I want to bracket it out and simply ask: how do homosexuals fit into Aquinas's picture?

Homosexuals and nature

Human beings are animals; therefore, according to Aquinas, all human beings naturally couple male with female, and they all naturally aim at that coupling. So if Christopher is a male human being, he naturally, without being taught, seeks sexual union with a female human being, for that is what nature teaches him. And if Sophie is a female human being, she naturally, without being taught, seeks sexual union with a male. But Christopher is homosexual, and so is Sophie. They both actually seek sexual union with a person of the same sex as themselves, and neither seeks union with somebody of the other sex. How do they fit into Aquinas's picture? If they both, as taught by nature, seek union with somebody of the opposite sex – if they are both naturally heterosexual – it ought to be impossible for them not to seek union with somebody of the opposite sex. The sheer existence of homosexuals appears to contradict Aquinas's theory, and to show that it is false. There are two kinds of move that might be made in defence of Aquinas here. First, it could be claimed that Christopher and Sophie are not the exceptions they appear to be. They are really heterosexual, and they do in fact desire union with the other sex; they have this natural, innate desire just as everybody else has. What they have done, we could say, is to overlay this natural sexual desire with another, non-natural, artificially constructed, learnt desire for their own sex, to the point where they are barely, if at all, conscious of their natural desire. Or we could say, as a variant, that they have deliberately and unnaturally perverted their natural heterosexual desire into a homosexual desire.

This kind of move can be made, but it does not of itself resolve the difficulty. For it is not enough merely to assert that people like Christopher and Sophie are really heterosexual; the assertion has to be shown to be actually true. It depends on hypotheses as to what Sophie and Christopher have in fact done. Suppose Christopher said sincerely: 'No, honestly, I am not really attracted to women. I have not deliberately constructed a sexual desire for men. I have always wanted men, and I have never wanted women.' Suppose Sophie said sincerely: 'Really, I did not start off with a sexual desire for men which I have moulded into a desire for women. My desire for women is as natural and spontaneous as some women's desire for men.' Such responses, which are certainly roughly what many homosexuals would say sincerely in reply to these hypotheses, indicate strongly that the hypotheses are false. Normally, when sane, mature adults speak sincerely about the nature and history of their desires, we accept what they say. If we do so in this case, we have to abandon our hypotheses, and Aquinas's theory falls. We can, of course, refuse to believe replies of this kind. But for the refusal to be reasonable we have to come up with credible explanations of how Christopher and Sophie can be mistaken as to their own sexual desires, whereas heterosexuals are not. Some further hypothesis has to be true which would account for the mistake. But now we seem to be in the business of the multiplication of hypotheses. Not only do we have the as yet unproven hypothesis that Christopher and Sophie are really heterosexual, we also now have an additional hypothesis which we have to prove; and all this to defend Aquinas's as yet unsubstantiated hypothesis that all animals, and so all human animals, are heterosexual. Before us is a quagmire; this is not the way to go.

Another possible move that might be made to defend Aquinas's idea in the face of the existence of homosexuals is to admit that they really are homosexual, but because something has gone wrong. Christopher and Sophie are not deluding themselves, we might propose, when they say they really are and always have been homosexual, that their sexual desire for others of the same sex is quite spontaneous and as natural to them as is heterosexual desire for the majority of people. But this is because there is some deformity in their nature. This is the kind of explanation of deviant desire and activity that Aquinas gives when discussing the question whether there is any pleasure that is not natural. He argues that there can be unnatural pleasures. He first of all distinguishes two senses in which something can be natural to human beings. First, since reason is proper and specific to human beings, we can mean by natural pleasures those that have to do with the exercise of reason, such as contemplating the truth and doing works of virtue. But secondly, we can call natural to human beings what is not specific to them, but what they have in common with other animals. In this sense, natural pleasures include food, drink, sleep and sex (*ST* 1.2.31.7c). But, he continues, it can happen that the natural principles of a species can be corrupted in individual cases. For example, at a sheer bodily level, sweet things can taste bitter to people with a fever, and people with a 'bad temperament' can enjoy eating earth or coals. On the level of the soul, it can happen that some, owing to custom, enjoy eating people, or having sex with animals or (and here he is thinking of men) with men, such things not being according to human nature.

Now we are familiar with the idea that things can go wrong with nature. It makes sense to say, for example, that people naturally have a certain number of limbs and a certain bodily form. But babies are sometimes born misshapen, or with limbs missing. In such cases, doctors can sometimes identify what has gone wrong; it might be the result of a defective gene, or of a drug taken by the mother during pregnancy. They can find out, that is to say, what has gone wrong in those instances with human nature, and why what we call the natural course of development has been disrupted. It might seem reasonable to say, in similar fashion, that in the case of homosexuals something has gone wrong with them, that they would naturally be heterosexual but for some disruption of their development. But, again, this will not do. In the first place, such a move would here be a *petitio principii*. We can only speak of homosexuality as a result of some kind of interference with nature once we have already established that all people are by nature heterosexual; and that has not yet been done. Secondly, and this is a related point, Aquinas does not consider the possibility that the pleasures he attributes to corruption of nature are part of normal human variety. Some people enjoy eating mushrooms but will not touch lamb; others enjoy lamb but not mushrooms, and we do not regard one class of people or the other as indulging in unnatural pleasures. If we regard such differences as normal variations of taste, why should we not adopt a similar attitude when confronted with people's varying sexual inclinations, including in particular heterosexual and homosexual attraction? Thirdly, we are once again involved in the multiplication of hypotheses. Not only is there the as yet unvalidated hypothesis that all people by nature seek the conjunction of male and female, but there is also the additional hypothesis that, for each homosexual, something has gone wrong in his or her development; this supposition has to be shown to be valid in each case. A fourth difficulty here is that the concept of nature that Aquinas uses in his discussion of homosexuality and its relation to 'what nature has taught all animals' is different from that which we use when we speak of people naturally having, say, a certain number of limbs. The latter is to do with people's physical and biological constitution. Aquinas's theory of nature, on the contrary, is – at least when he is talking about what nature has taught all animals – not to do with how people are constituted biologically, but with what they spontaneously want and do, and what they delight in; it is a concept centred not on the biological processes which go on within organisms, but on untaught human desires and acts. The fact that one can talk of deformities of nature in the one case does not license a similar discourse in the other. A much simpler way out of these difficulties is to reject the original premiss that leads to them: the premiss that all animals, and so all human beings, naturally desire union with one of the other sex, and are naturally heterosexual. It is, after all, obviously false that all human beings are actually heterosexual. If what is meant by being naturally heterosexual is being taught by nature to be heterosexual, and if that means being heterosexual without being taught at all, then it is clearly false that all people are naturally heterosexual; for some people are, without being taught, not heterosexual but homosexual. There is no good reason to believe, as Aquinas seems to, that homosexuals have deliberately perverted a sexual desire which was innately heterosexual, or that they suffer from some condition which has led to their developing homosexual rather than heterosexual inclinations. In short, appearances suggest very strongly that some people are spontaneously homosexual. If this is actually true, the fact disproves Aquinas's thesis that nature teaches all animals the coupling of male and female. It has every appearance of being true, and the attempt to show otherwise is fraught with difficulties.

Exclusion of same-sex activity a non sequitur

But let us suppose that I am wrong about this. Let us suppose that it is possible to establish Aquinas's point that nature has taught all animals the coupling of male and female. What then? Aquinas's argument, even if correct, will not do what he and those who follow him want it to do as far as concerns same-sex activity. Even if it can be shown that all animals, including human ones, naturally seek the union of male and female, and that that union is therefore a natural human good, this tells us nothing at all about the moral status of the coupling of male and male or of female and female. No amount of proof that heterosexual coupling is naturally a good thing implies that homosexual coupling is naturally a bad thing. For Aquinas, a natural *malum* is that which all animals, including human ones, naturally shun. What he has to argue is not that all animals naturally seek other-sex coupling, but that they all naturally shun same-sex coupling. This he does not even try to argue. He perhaps took it for granted that there is no same-sex coupling among non-human animals. If he did, he was wrong; there is in fact plenty of evidence that not all non-human animals do shun it.[13] And of course not all human animals naturally shun it, either. From all the evidence, same-sex coupling just is not a natural *malum*. If, as Aquinas maintains, other-sex coupling is a natural good, then when people engage in same-sex activity they do not thereby realize that natural good, any more than they do when playing tennis or drinking coffee. But that does not imply that they are doing a bad thing, any more than it implies that they are doing a bad thing when playing tennis or drinking coffee. People who, when they engage in sexual activity, always do it with a member of the same sex, never realize the natural good of other-sex coupling, any more than do other people who for whatever reason – perhaps solitude or religious vows – never engage in sexual activity with a person of the other sex. It might be possible to argue, on the basis of Aquinas's theory, that it is a bad thing never to realize this good, and sinful if deliberate. Such deliberate refusal to realize that which nature teaches all animals to seek is, one could argue, perverse, and the sexually abstinent would be as guilty of it as any active homosexual who never mated with a member of the other sex.[14] But one cannot draw from Aquinas's argument to the effect that other-sex coupling is a natural good the further conclusion that same-sex coupling is a bad thing. In any case, as we have seen, it is not true that all animals seek the coupling of male and female. It is not obvious that it is possible to formulate a coherent and convincing theory of natural law of the kind Aquinas sketches in *Summa Theologiae*. That is a question I have not gone into here. My contention, based on the arguments presented above, is that, even if it is possible to formulate such a theory, it does not imply the exclusion of homosexual acts as against nature. The arguments Aquinas presents to that effect simply do not show what he takes them to show. This means that there is in fact no conflict between natural law, as understood by Aquinas, and same-sex activity. Hence it is possible to affirm, if one is so inclined, both that there is a natural law to which we ought to conform and that homosexual relations are in conformity with it. Just as natural law does not entail the rejection of same-sex practices, so acceptance of those practices does not entail a rejection of the concept of natural law. Hence it is possible not to reject homosexual practices and still to remain faithful to a long theological tradition of the church.

Knowledge of God and life in society

The third class of inclination Aquinas attributes to human nature consists of those desires which he claims we have specifically as human; those which we do not share with all beings, such as self-preservation, nor with all animals, such as the coupling of male and female, but which are proper to human beings as such:

> Thirdly, there is in man an inclination to good, according to the nature of his reason, which nature is proper to him: thus man has a natural inclination to know the truth about God, and to live in society: and in this respect, whatever pertains to this inclination belongs to the natural law; for instance, to shun ignorance, to avoid offending those among whom one has to live, and other such things regarding the above inclination.

What does Aquinas mean when he says that it belongs to our nature as rational social animals to avoid offending those among whom one has to live? He points perhaps to the fact that any society develops codes of conduct, codes of manners which may in a sense be arbitrary but which make social life possible. Societies tend to have rules regulating the ways their members dress, eat, address each other, and so on. While there may be no one natural set of such rules, it is difficult to imagine any society functioning without some such code. In that case, the failure of any individual to observe the code can upset normal social functioning, and hence impede social life; it may also, depending on the rigour with which the code is enforced, be disadvantageous or even dangerous for the individual concerned. For these reasons, it makes sense to avoid such infringements. But if his observations here are to have any relevance to the question of homosexual acts, Aquinas cannot mean simply that it is against natural law to fail to observe one's society's code of manners. For then it could be against natural law to say or do unpopular things, or things which offended people. It cannot be, for instance, that it is against natural law to perform homosexual acts in a society in which most people find such acts repulsive or offensive, for this would leave out of account the question of the justice of the prevalent attitude. It could be argued that in such a society the majority ought not to be offended by homosexual acts, or that they ought to allow other citizens to act in ways which they find themselves repulsive. The notion of offence at work here has to be more substantial. The act in question has to be one performed with the intention of offending, or one which offends by doing harm. That is, it must, in one of these ways, be contrary to love.

We have already, in the previous chapter, seen reason to believe that homosexual acts are not contrary to love, in the sense that they are not necessarily selfish or self-indulgent. Here we have to see whether it is really true at a social level: what is a homosexual's attitude, in performing a homosexual act, towards other members of his or her society, and what is the effect of that act on them? If homosexual acts are against natural law because of our nature as social animals, it must be because these acts are performed with the intention of offending, or because they in some way result in harm to other members of society. The first of these possibilities can be dismissed immediately. There is no reason to believe that homosexual acts are always, or at all frequently, performed with a view to offending others. Perhaps this happens sometimes, but if so this has more to do with the particular circumstances of the people concerned and with the particular institutions of their society than with the nature of homosexual acts. In the same way, it may be that heterosexual acts are sometimes performed with a view to offending others, but this tells us nothing about the nature of heterosexual acts. Does a homosexual act actually harm members of society who are not party to the act? It is not easy to see how this could be so; at least, it is difficult to see how a homosexual act could directly harm another member of society. Aquinas himself appears to believe that homosexual activity does no harm to others. In discussing the 'sin against nature' in general, he asks whether it is the greatest of the sins of *luxuria*. He considers the following argument to the effect that it is not:

It would seem that the unnatural vice is not the greatest sin among the species of lust. For the more a sin is contrary to charity the graver it is. Now adultery, seduction and rape which are injurious to our neighbour are seemingly more contrary to the love of our neighbour, than unnatural sins, by which no other person is injured. Therefore the unnatural sin is not the greatest among the species of lust. (*ST* 2–2.154.12.1)

He is not convinced by this argument. But he does not reply that in some deep or hidden way homosexuality is contrary to charity, that it works to harm people. Instead he argues as follows:

Just as the ordering of right reason proceeds from man, so the order of nature is from God Himself: wherefore in sins contrary to nature, whereby the very order of nature is violated, an injury is done to God, the Author of nature. (*ST* 2–2.154 *ad* 1)

Aquinas appears to accept, then, that non-procreative sex, including same-sex activity, of itself does no direct wrong to one's neighbour. Unlike rape, it is not an attack on an unwilling victim. Neither does Aquinas suggest that it might directly harm those who willingly engage in it. Instead, he introduces a totally new consideration: he who acts against nature acts against God.

An offence against God?

This appears to carry us away from Aquinas's third division of natural inclinations (unless perhaps an offence against God can be seen as contrary to the supposed natural desire to know the truth about God). But in introducing this consideration Aquinas displays a lively sense of God as the author of nature. He taps into the very strong Christian feeling that in dealing with nature, particularly human nature, we are not dealing merely with an assemblage of objects governed by physical laws but are confronted with the work of God. It is this that inspires the Christian sense of awe and respect that is the proper response to the created world and to human beings as part of it. Aquinas asserts that the sin against nature injures God, not in the sense that it harms God but in the sense that the failure to respect God's work is also the failure to respect God; non-procreative sex – including same-sex activity – is, as a failure to respect the reason why he has created us sexual, an insult to God himself.

Now it is certainly true that if God is in this sense injured by homosexual activity, there is no way that any Christian can take part in or in any way approve of it; and that includes any homosexual Christian. We live to the glory of God, and so of course cannot approve of, let alone take part in, any activity that dishonours God. However difficult it may be to resist such behaviour, that is what we are and should be all committed to. But does homosexual activity injure God in this way? The injury is done to God, so he says, as Creator, the author of nature, and it is done because homosexual acts do not respect nature but are against it. We have seen, though, that he has failed to make out a case for saying that they are against nature. They do not impede or destroy that common natural good which is the continuation of the human species. They do not run counter to any natural inclination to seek heterosexual union, nor to any natural inclination to avoid homosexual union. They do no harm to a neighbour. So, in terms of Aquinas's own threefold division of natural inclinations, they run counter to no natural human inclination; and since it is natural human inclination that determines the content of natural law, they are not contrary to nature. So neither are they against God, the author of nature. Something that Aquinas says elsewhere leads towards the same conclusion. In the *Summa Contra Gentiles* he asserts that 'God is not offended by us except by what we do against our own good' (*CG* III.122, with reference to III.121). If God can be said to be the author of nature, and so to be offended by any act that is against nature, it follows that for Aquinas it is a necessary condition of an act's being against nature that it be against our own good. Since Aquinas agrees that homosexual acts are not against our own good – against the good neither of those who perform them nor of other members of society – he is in fact committed to the view that they do not offend God.

Neighbours again

In the *De Malo* Aquinas does argue that all acts of *luxuria* are harmful to one's neighbour.

> Sometimes, along with disorder of concupiscence, there is also a disorder of the external act in itself, as happens in every use of the genital organs outside the marriage act. And that every such act is disordered in itself is apparent from the fact that every

human act is said to be disordered which is not proportioned to its due end, just as eating is disordered if it is not proportioned to the health of the body, to which it is ordered as to an end. But the end of the use of the genital organs is the generation and education of offspring, and therefore every use of the aforementioned organs which is not proportioned to the generation of offspring and its due education is disordered in itself. Every act of the aforementioned organs apart from the intercourse of male and female is manifestly not fitted for the generation of offspring. (15.1)

According to this, the end of the use of genital organs is the generation and education of offspring. Once again human good is central to Aquinas's thought, this time the human good of the generation and education of offspring. His comparison of sex to eating points in the same direction: just as an act of eating should be ordered to the human good which is the health of the body, so sexual acts should correspondingly be ordered to an appropriate good. Aquinas seems to take for granted that there is only one such possible good, and that is the generation and education of offspring. Here we might raise the question whether joint pleasure or mutual consolation might not be possible ends of the act; but let that too pass for the moment. What cannot be delayed is some comment on Aquinas's notion of the ordering of an act to its due end. Take again the example of eating. This, he says, is disordered if not proportioned to the health of the body, to which it is ordered as an end. But what is it for an act of eating not to be proportioned to the health of the body, and so disordered? It is easy to see that an act of eating might be called disordered if it is deleterious to bodily health – if, for example, one eats poison. But it is not evident that an act of eating which has no effect whatever on bodily health is also to be called disordered. One might, for example, eat something which has no nutritional value. One might even deliberately eat it because it has no nutritional value, to satisfy one's pangs of hunger while not adding to one's weight. (And it might not be for reasons of health that one wanted to avoid adding to one's weight.) It would be hard, I think, to call this act disordered. It does not benefit the health of the eater, but is not detrimental to it either. Certainly, it is not a *malum*, an act to be avoided because it damages a human good. Now Aquinas wants to say that a disordered act is a *malum*; that is why a disordered act is one which is not to be performed. In the light of this, it seems that we have to say that such a nutritionally neutral act of eating, since it is not a *malum*, should not, in Aquinas's terms, be called disordered, either. If, then, the fact that an act is disordered is to have any moral import, if it is to be seen as a bad thing, we should only call those acts disordered which are actually detrimental to the good to which they are held to be ordered. Acts which are neutral, which neither serve nor damage the good to which they are ordered, cannot be held to be disordered. An act of penile-vaginal intercourse between a man and a woman who are not sterile may serve the end of generation and education of offspring. Any other kind of sexual act, including homosexual acts, cannot serve this end. It does not follow, however, that they are disordered, or that they damage that end. They might rather be neutral with regard to the end. They might even be chosen because they do not result in generation. But it is difficult to see how a sexual act might damage the end of generation and education of offspring. While there may be the sexual equivalent of eating something with no nutritional value, it is not easy to imagine the equivalent of eating poison. We might perhaps think of an act of intercourse involving a pregnant woman and which put an end to the pregnancy, or any non-procreative act engaged in at a time when one ought to be educating one's offspring. But ordinary non-procreative sexual acts performed at most times – and among these are most homosexual acts – do not appear to fit the bill. Thus it appears problematic, to say the least, to speak of homosexual acts as disordered. Whereas in the *Summa Theologiae* Aquinas appears to accept that the 'unnatural sin' – any form of sexual act which is by its very form non-procreative – does no harm to a neighbour, in the *De Malo* he takes a different position. In question 15.2 he wants to show that every act of *luxuria* is a mortal sin. An objection is made to this thesis, an argument very similar to one we have already seen:

> Every mortal sin is contrary to charity ... But simple fornication is against neither the love of God, as it is not a sin against God, nor the love of neighbour, because it does no injury to a neighbour.

Aquinas replies:

> All the vices of lechery which are beyond the legitimate use of marriage, are sins against a neighbour, inasmuch as they are against the good of the offspring to be generated and educated. (*De Malo* 15.2)

Aquinas's reasoning here seems to be problematic on several grounds.[15] It is possible that if a sexual act which might result in the generation of a child is engaged in when a decision has been taken not to provide for the upbringing of any such child, or in the knowledge that no such provision could be made, then this can be regarded as a sin against that child. But this is a rare case. In any case, Aquinas's argument plainly only applies to sexual acts which are potentially procreative. There can be no sin against any off-spring to be generated and educated if the sexual act is by its form non-procreative, as are all homosexual acts. So Aquinas does not show that homosexual acts involve any sin against a neighbour.

Sex and marriage

The failure of this argument is relevant to the objection sometimes made against homosexual acts that they take place outside marriage. Marriage, in the Christian tradition, is of its nature a permanent union between a man and a woman, and so unavailable to same-sex couples. Any sexual activity between same-sex couples is therefore necessarily non-marital. But since only sexual activity within marriage is legitimate, it follows that no homosexual act is ever legitimate. This is in fact the position of *HP*:

> The Church, obedient to the Lord who founded her and gave to her the sacramental life, celebrates the divine plan of the loving and live-giving union of men and women in the sacrament of marriage. It is only in the marital relationship that the use of the sexual faculty can be morally good. A person engaging in homosexual behaviour therefore acts immorally. (§7)

This position can be argued with in a number of ways. If Christian practice reserves, and always has reserved, marriage to heterosexual couples, practice can be changed, and some Christian communities have begun to admit homosexual marriage. But it remains a moot question whether Christians are free to change their practice in this way. As can be seen from this extract from *HP*, the Catholic position is that Christians do not have this freedom, since marriage is instituted as a sacrament by Christ himself. (For *HP*, this position is clearly linked to the divine plan for human sexuality that it detects in the opening chapters of Genesis; we have seen good reason, however, to doubt whether such a plan is to be found there.)

This position also appears to say to homosexuals: 'In order to be able to have a legitimate sexual relationship, you must marry. But you cannot marry. So there is no way your sexual activity can be legitimized.' There is something a little curious, even Kafkaesque, about this logic. One might reply that it is only reasonable to make marriage a condition of legitimacy in this way for people for whom marriage is an option. There would then be two directions in which such an argument could be pursued: either, since there is no such thing as homosexual marriage, the condition that homosexuals marry in order to have a sexual relationship must be dropped; or, since marriage is indeed the only legitimate context for sexual activity, we must make a place for homosexual marriage. The traditional position also appears vulnerable in the light of the fact that, as we saw in the previous chapter, St Paul sees marriage in part as a remedy for concupiscence. It seems odd that there should be such a remedy for the concupiscence of heterosexuals, but none at all for that of homosexuals. The debate over the question of homosexual marriage raises large questions. Here, I merely note some of them, without investigating them further. But one element of the tradition is closely related to the line of thought that we have been pursuing in Aquinas. *HP* notes that the Catholic Church celebrates the sacrament of (heterosexual) marriage. This does not of itself prevent it from approving, or even celebrating some homosexual relationships, whether they are called marriages or not. What can prevent it doing so is only that such relationships are just not to be celebrated, because they involve sexual acts that cannot be approved. And *HP* does indeed provide a reason at this point why such sexual acts cannot be approved: 'It is only in the marital relationship that the use of the sexual faculty can be morally good.' No rationale is given for this statement, which is after all quite traditional. But if we ask what such a rationale might look like, the law of love and Aquinas's thought as seen above might incline us to look in the direction of love of neighbour. For if the use of the sexual faculty outside marriage does no harm to a neighbour, then there is no reason why we should not think it morally good. As we have seen, Aquinas does provide an argument, based on the good of any possible offspring resulting from a sexual act, for saying that all sexual activity outside marriage is wrong. But, as we have also seen, this argument, even if sustainable, can only apply to sexual activity that is potentially procreative, and fails to catch homosexual activity in its net. This failure appears to leave the traditional Christian position, the one enunciated also by *HP*, without support and looking peculiarly arbitrary. Aquinas's argument seems aimed implicitly only at heterosexual activity outside marriage, and any conclusion based on it cannot be used to exclude the possibility of homosexual activity.

Sex, nature and nurture[16]

I remarked earlier that Aquinas's belief that nature had taught all human beings about the union of male and female (or, alternatively, that God had instilled in all people this precept of the natural law) was not borne out by empirical observation. The actual facts of human sexual behaviour create a problem for Aquinas and those who follow him, one which it is not possible to solve convincingly. But we can go further than this and say that the way in which human sexual behaviour varies undermines the whole idea of a determinate, God-given, and therefore constant, human sexual nature. Aquinas's view of sexuality (and he is not alone in this) is ahistorical and asocial; in his view, all people, everywhere and at all times, have the same natural knowledge of what kinds of sexual activity are good, and the same natural inclination towards that activity. But human sexuality is in fact highly malleable, and sexual behaviour and sexual norms depend heavily on social factors. There is little doubt that, as a matter of fact, human beings organize their sexual behaviour in a wide variety of ways. Different societies, and subgroups within societies, develop various values, rules and conventions governing the sexual behaviour of their members, and these values, rules and conventions differ widely from society to society, from group to group. Activities and relationships which are proscribed or ridiculed as unnatural in one society can be accepted as normal and natural in others. These varying sexual codes express differing sexual values. Whereas in our society we support the value of love and mutuality, other societies have seen sex simply as a source of pleasure in which one person (normally a man) uses another for his own pleasure, without particularly bothering whether the experience is pleasurable also for the other. As we have seen, in the Hellenistic world in which Paul was writing, this conception of sex was common. Whereas we tend to think officially of a sexual relationship as essentially a relationship of equals, other societies have laid more stress on sex as an expression of power and social hierarchy. This is plainly linked to the idea of sex as use: the stronger uses the weaker. The strong, the user, is also the active, while the weak, the used, is reduced to passivity. Where sex is seen in terms of penetration, the act of penetration becomes a symbol of power, and to be penetrated is a sexual expression of social weakness. We have already, in Chapter 3, seen that ancient Israel is an example of a society in which this view of sex was dominant. In ancient Rome too sex, that is sexual penetration, was symbolic of power, so it was considered acceptable for a householder to penetrate a slave, either male or female, but not for him to be penetrated by a slave.[17]

Such ways of thinking about sex are not entirely foreign to us who live in modern Western liberal democracies. But other factors enter into our attitudes to sex. Our societies tolerate wide differences in sexual attitudes, but for many of us difference or sameness of sex between sexual partners can be a crucial element in evaluating a sexual relationship or activity. To focus in this way on the sex of the partners may even seem to us inevitable, natural. But it is neither natural nor inevitable; it is a function of the values of our own particular culture. The examples just mentioned already indicate how little sameness or difference of sex was important in ancient Western societies. Greek and Roman references, of a quite matter-of-fact kind, to homosexual activity are numerous. Some of these juxtapose homosexual and heterosexual activity as if the distinction were of little importance. For example, in the *Republic* IX 574b, Plato says of the tyrannical man that he would strike his mother for the sake of a new girlfriend and his father for the sake of a new boyfriend; in *Laws* VIII 840a, he praises an athlete, one Iccus of Tarentum, because while he was in training he touched neither a woman nor a boy. While there were no doubt in ancient Greece men who preferred boys or men to women and men who preferred women to boys or men, and while this difference of desire was no doubt noticed, it was not one that seems on the whole to have excited much interest or to have evoked moral concern. There was no particular stigma attaching to men who loved men, nor were such classified as a particular type of man, different from others, 'homosexuals' different from 'heterosexuals'. Still less was it thought that there was something pathological about a man who loved men, that something had gone wrong with him, that he suffered from a 'condition'. Quite normal, ordinary, healthy men were expected to be attracted to people of both sexes, both younger and older. As Foucault sums up:

> To their way of thinking, what made it possible to desire a man or a woman was simply the appetite that nature had implanted in

man's heart for 'beautiful' human beings, whatever their sex might be.[18]

The Greeks did not generally classify men – still less women – into homosexuals and heterosexuals and the recently fashionable bisexuals any more than we divide people into those who like cabbage rather than carrots, those who prefer carrots to cabbage and those who are quite happy to eat either. Nor did they have a separate category for paedophiles, any more than we have a special class of bean-eaters. Nor were they upset in the same way as we are by sex between adults and children. This is not to say they had no difficulties with sex. They certainly did, but the problem, as we noted when looking at Paul's Letter to the Romans tended to be one of coping with and mastering sexual passion, rather than of ensuring it went in a particular direction.

A more modern, and much studied, example of a society whose sexual values are different from ours is Melanesia. Here there is a variety of institutionalized practices that we would think of as paedophile, homosexual and incestuous. The details vary from tribe to tribe, but generally boys are inducted into sexual maturity by having a fully sexual relationship with a maternal uncle or a sister's husband, a relationship that lasts many years. Sexual practices are also common between adult men. Greenberg, who gives an account of this institutionalized homosexuality in his *The Construction of Homosexuality*, describes the practice of one particular tribe:

An Etoro boy's career in homosexuality starts around age ten, when he acquires an older partner, ideally his sister's husband or fiancé (so that brother and sister receive semen from the same man). The relationship continues until the boy develops a full beard in his early to mid-twenties. At this point, the now mature young man becomes the older partner of another prepubescent boy, ordinarily his wife's or fiancée's younger brother. This relationship continues for roughly fifteen years, until the older partner is about forty. His involvement then ends, except for initiation ceremonies, which include collective homosexual intercourse between the initiates and all the older men or, if he takes a second wife, with her younger brother. Because taboos on heterosexual intercourse are extensive, while there are none on homosexual relations, male sexual outlets are predominantly homosexual between the ages of ten and forty.[19]

All this is very different from the way we do things, and very different too from the practices and attitudes of the ancient Hebrews and Jews whose writings still provide such a potent tool for the articulation of the sexual attitudes of many in the Church and of others in Western society. How are we to understand these great differences in sexual norms between our society and others? It cannot be done simply by disparaging the morals of those other societies. Neither ancient Greeks nor modern Melanesians are properly seen as libertines. In both societies there are sexual norms, activities prescribed and proscribed. And both also have their sexual worries. But their concerns are different from ours. What they consider it important to do and to avoid doing is different from what we think it important to do and not to do. There are no doubt many reasons for these differences of sexual practices and attitudes between us and societies such as these, including accidents of history. In the case of ancient Greece one important set of reasons centres on public attitudes to gender and power. As in ancient Israel and many other societies, men are dominant, women subservient. Men lead, women follow. Sex is enlisted to reinforce this basic social structure. As we have observed, sex is thought of in terms of penetration; to penetrate is to be active, dominant, like a man, while to be penetrated is to be passive, submissive, like a woman. But what is important is not so much the gender of those involved in the activity as their relative social status. A free man can penetrate a woman – so long as she does not belong to another man – because he is socially superior. But he is also socially superior to his male slave, so he can penetrate him as well. He is also, because he is an adult, socially superior to a freeborn boy.[20] The Greeks, then, would not be upset as we might be by inequalities of power in a sexual relationship. This connection between sex and power also helps to explain the obsession among the Greeks with specifically *male* sexual behaviour. The public discourse goes on between men; so it is the men who, at least as far as the public discourse is concerned, are dominant, the centre of attention; it is mostly their behaviour that matters and is the object of concern to men. The behaviour of women is of course important to a degree, but only in so far as they must remain subservient to the men. The reality may have been different in the privacy of the home, but in the public arena women are presented as important to men, while men are important in their own right. There are records of numerous other societies, both near to and far removed from our own in space and time, in which sexual values and the organization of sexual life are very different from our own. In particular, there have been many societies in which homosexual relationships of one kind or another have had an accepted place.[21] Faced with this diversity, we can no longer plausibly regard the sexual practices and values of our own Christian culture as the one and only natural way of doing things. We may certainly want to criticize the practices of other cultures. Where sex is conceived of in terms simply of using another for one's own pleasure, or as an expression of power over the other, we may want to say that this is incompatible with that love of neighbour to which we are all called (including ancient Greeks and Romans and modern Melanesians) by virtue of being made in the image of God. Particularly where children or slaves are involved, we need to be sensitive to the possibility of coercion and injustice. But we need no special theory of what counts as natural sex to enable us to be thus critical; we need only the central gospel value of love. And the sheer variety of sexual practices and values in different societies, and the dependence of those practices and values on other aspects of social structure, render implausible any claim that all human beings, regardless of the society in which they live, are 'taught by nature' to seek certain forms of sexual relationship and to shun others. In particular, given the wide distribution of homosexual practice, sometimes institutionalized, we have no reason to believe that all human beings naturally seek heterosexual intercourse, as Aquinas claims, and shun homosexual intercourse. It is still not impossible for modern followers of Aquinas to adhere to his claim, and to explain the wide distribution of 'unnatural' sex as due to some deformity in human nature, and they might want to use language unavailable to Aquinas to make their point, to talk in terms of oedipal conflicts, of gay genes, or of the homosexual condition. But given the fact, already noted, that Aquinas never establishes in the first place that all people are taught by nature to seek heterosexual intercourse, let alone to shun homosexual intercourse, such explanations of the supposed exceptions are redundant. Further, instances of homosexual practice, either institutionalized or transgressive, are so numerous and widespread that it is just not plausible to think of them as exceptions to or deformities of a basically heterosexual nature. We are surely not to explain differences from approved Christian sexual practices by supposing, for example, that ancient Greeks had more than their quota of gay genes, delighted in perversion, or had distant fathers and dominant mothers; nor can we plausibly think that all modern Melanesians suffer from an epidemic of the homosexual condition. Behaviour which might in some Western societies be generally branded as perverse or the result of a sickness or unnatural is in these societies, as in others, accepted as perfectly normal. We have no need of quasi-medical explanations of supposed departures from a supposedly natural norm. We already have perfectly intelligible explanations of human sexual variety to hand. People are inducted into these activities as part of their growth into their society; they learn that they are approved of, and learn to approve of them themselves; they learn to value them as good, normal and healthy, to think of them, as we might say, as natural. Aquinas was ignorant of this sexual diversity; we are not, and can no longer share his easy assumptions about the sexual behaviour natural to human beings.

Natural sex, natural language

Mary Douglas, discussing the work of the anthropologist Marcel Mauss, writes that

> in his essay on the techniques of the body ... [he] boldly asserted that there can be no such thing as natural behaviour. Every kind of action carries the imprint of learning, from feeding to washing, from repose to movement and, above all, sex. Nothing is more essentially transmitted by a social process of learning than sexual behaviour, and this of course is closely related to morality ... Mauss saw that the study of bodily techniques would have to take place within a study of symbolic systems.[22]

The brief comments I have made above may be taken to illustrate much of Mauss's point here, with which Douglas concurs. People learn how to behave sexually, and in learning what behaviour is expected of them they also learn what to value as good and normal. The situation is rather complicated by the fact of transgression. Young people do not always passively accept the values their parents and their wider society would have them adopt. Some of them do not or cannot learn the modes of sexual behaviour that others seek to teach them or that their surroundings tend to inculcate. People of all ages break sexual rules because they disagree with them or find them difficult, or because it is exciting to break rules, or because they want to rebel against an environment they see as oppressive. And societies, perhaps especially modern Western societies, are not monolithic; sometimes different sets of values compete for allegiance. It is nevertheless clear that social learning is essential to forming people's views of what is sexually good and normal and in getting them to behave in the requisite ways. But there is one important point at which I believe Mauss, as represented by Douglas, goes wrong. The point that sexual practices and values are learnt in whatever society one finds oneself I take as made; but does that really show that there is no such thing as natural behaviour? Does it, in the present context, show that there is no such thing as natural sexual behaviour? These queries prompt the following logically prior questions. What is this natural behaviour which is being ruled out? What conception of human nature lies behind Mauss's remarks and Douglas's approval of them? Both authors seem to put natural behaviour in opposition to socially learnt behaviour: because a piece of behaviour (as well as the values that go with it) is learnt it is therefore not natural. Here we seem to have a conception of nature and the natural not unrelated to that Aquinas uses when he speaks of what nature teaches all animals. The natural seems to be, for Douglas and Mauss, that which is unlearned, perhaps the instinctual, what we would do if we grew up alone and were left to our own devices, unshaped by parents and friends, uninfluenced by the societies in which we live. We need to look at this conception of nature a little more closely.

The word 'natural' is a very slippery one when we try to apply it to human beings. We do sometimes contrast natural with learnt behaviour. For example, an easygoing acquaintance of ours might get a job which requires her to behave very formally. It would make perfect sense to describe her formal behaviour as learnt, as opposed to her natural informal ways. Or we might think of Wittgenstein's idea of learnt pain behaviour replacing the natural expressions of pain.[23] But in these examples we are contrasting a person's way of acting at different times or in different contexts, one known behaviour pattern with another. And it all takes place within a social context. Society changes our behaviour. But to grow up apart from any society and not to learn any way of behaving, as seems to be envisaged in Mauss's conception of nature, is not a natural way to grow and live for human beings. We would not expect somebody who grew up in complete isolation to act naturally; on the contrary, we should expect their behaviour to be severely abnormal. To the extent that we may be said to have a nature, we are by nature social. We naturally congregate with others to whose behaviour we to varying degrees adapt our own; as children we are raised by others on whom we are dependent and from whom we learn by imitation and instruction. A human being who has not learnt from others how to behave, if such a person exists, is not one who has developed naturally, but one who has been removed from his or her natural human environment and therefore deprived of the opportunity to develop naturally. Whether such a person is to be counted as fortunate or wretched is another matter, but he or she is certainly not likely to behave in a way that we would describe as natural. Animals may perhaps be said to behave naturally if they behave independently of human interference, but humans do not in this sense interfere with one another; they do not by influencing each other *ipso facto* replace some supposed natural behaviour with learnt, artificial behaviour. We are made to be influenced by other humans.[24] It belongs to human behaviour to be moulded in particular ways. A human being is always a taught being, instructed formally and informally in the specific, contingent ways of the society around him or her. If we wish to retain the notion of nature here, then we have to say that human behaviour is naturally acquired, naturally learnt. We are given possibilities of behaviour, which become our nature (*not* second nature). These ways of behaving do not spring from some pre-social biological or psychic essence of the individual, with which nature tends so often to be identified.

It may be helpful here to compare sexual behaviour with language. It is in one sense obviously true that we are naturally linguistic creatures. To be linguistic has rightly been regarded as characteristically human, central to human nature. To have a language is a distinctively human thing; no other creature that we know of has language, except perhaps in the most rudimentary fashion. And all normal humans have language. But, while it is natural to us to have language, there is no such thing as a natural language, a language which we possess even in potential when we are born. All language is taught and learnt, and belongs to particular times and places and societies. As we learn different ways of speaking, so we also learn different ways of behaving sexually. Just as it is natural for us to be linguistic, so it is natural for us to be sexual, but there seems equally little reason to believe that there is a 'natural sexuality' as there is to think that there is a 'natural language'. There seems to be no natural sexual way of behaving, if by 'natural' here is meant a determinate sexual nature which pre-exists education and imitation in society. Or we might say that we acquire a determinate sexual nature by our life in society. Sex, like language, is always something that is learnt in a particular social context. Just as we can expect languages to differ from place to place and from time to time, and just as we expect other social customs to vary from society to society, so too we can anticipate that sexual *mores* will differ, and do so naturally. Sexual nature is a social and cultural matter, not merely biological; we can expect it to have all the variety that we find in other social matters, and it does.

Our own native language – that is, not the language which we were born speaking, but our first language, the language by learning which we learned to use language – can seem to us natural. Indeed, this language, in all its particularity, is natural to us. But this sense of its being natural is a result of linguistic socialization, of being steeped in the language of this particular society. We make a mistake if we then think that our language is the natural language in the sense of being natural to everybody, the natural vehicle of those thoughts which we all, as humans, have in common, as if all speakers of other languages laboured under a handicap because their language was less natural than ours, and so less apt to express thought. In the *Philosophical Investigations* Wittgenstein writes of the case

> in which someone imagines that one could not think a sentence with the remarkable word order of German or Latin just as it stands. One first has to think it, and then one arranges the words in that queer order. (A French politician once wrote that it was a peculiarity of the French language that in it words occur in the order in which one thinks them.) (§336)

It takes only some familiarity with foreign languages – with other people's native languages – to divest oneself of this illusion, and to realize that one language is no more natural, in some supposed absolute sense, than another. All languages are natural, but natural to their native speakers. Our own primitive sexual values, the values that we have absorbed from our infancy like our native language, can also seem natural, obvious, a matter of course. And so they are, to us. But since sense of the natural is again a result of socialization; nature is a social construct. We make the above French politician's mistake if we think them *the* natural values, natural for everybody, except that people from other societies unfortunately can't see it. The studies that have been carried out in the last century on the sexual customs and values of non-Western societies, and the renewed consciousness of those of biblical and ancient Greek and Roman societies, can help to dispel this notion, to make us see that one society's organization of sexuality is no more natural than another's. All are natural, but natural to the members of each society. The search for a natural sexuality which transcends all societies is the search for a chimera.

So it is a mistake to think that we have or might have a kind of pre-existent sexual nature, a set of natural sexual desires and inclinations with which we are born and which are then interfered with in various ways by those among whom we develop. We have still less reason to think that we are all born with the *same* set of desires and inclinations. We may, to be sure, be born with a capacity or disposition to develop sexual relationships and sexual desires of one kind or another, just as we are born with a capacity and disposition to learn language. If we all end up – and all want to end up – in permanent, heterosexual, monogamous relationships, and if we all meanwhile eschew all other forms of sexual partnership and gratification, that is not because in so doing we are being true to an inborn nature which we all share, but because we are all successfully socialized to live that kind of sexual life. The corollary of this is that where sexual differences occur, where the sexual desires and aspirations and forms of life of two people differ one from the other, this is not because at least one of them has corrupted his or her inborn sexual nature, or had it corrupted by others, or even necessarily because one has a different sexual nature from the other. It is because each has been sexually socialized in a different way, either because they belong to different societies or, if they live in the same society and have been brought up in the same way, because they have reacted in different ways to their sexual education. Thus the tendency in Christian theology, as exemplified in Aquinas but present also in some more modern authors, to assume that we do indeed all have a natural, pre-social sexual nature, and further that we all have the same – heterosexual – nature, is unwarranted.

The Bible again

We can now see further reasons why the attempt to derive information about our alleged sexual nature from a perusal of the early chapters of Genesis is suspect. In a previous chapter we examined the use to which *HP* puts these texts, but this document is far from alone in the emphasis it puts on them.[25] The frequent use of these verses is undergirded by and in turn reinforces assumptions which, as far as I can see, have been unexamined and are in fact misleading. First, the method of concentrating on the creation and subsequent early history of our first parents, or at least of what is presented as the archetypal human couple, as a means of finding out about everybody else assumes that we all have a common sexual essence; or at least, all men have one sexual essence and all women another, complementary essence. The Fall may have led to a number of deformities, creating some of the sexual variety we see about us, but basically we have one shared nature. A second assumption is that this nature is pre-social. Adam and Eve had their sexual natures created and defined by God before they entered into society; in any case, they did not at first live in society as we know it; their life in the Garden is life in a 'state of nature', naked amid the trees. This God-given sexual nature is what all later women and men too are born with, or at least grow up with if left to themselves. It is what they have before they get to the big city or the small village. It is what they have before they fall under the influence of parents, siblings and friends, or society. Third, this common, presocial sexual nature revolves around the difference between male and female, in the sense that perception of gender is seen as essential to sexual desire. One person's desire for another is inevitably bound up with the perceived gender of the one desired, indeed the perception that he or she is of the opposite gender. What belongs to our nature is that male is attracted to female and vice versa.

But, as I hope to have shown, none of this is right; or at least it is all very questionable. It is questionable in the first place because, as we saw in Chapter 5, the biblical exegesis on which it relies is seriously flawed. The concerns of the authors of these chapters of Genesis are not with nature, nor very much with sex. A theory about human sexual nature can only be read out of those chapters if it has first been read in. Secondly, as I have argued in the present chapter, our sexual natures are very largely social. If we are all born with the capacity for sexual desires, those desires remain amorphous or polymorphous[26] until we are inducted into our society's forms of sexual behaviour. Because those forms are so various, so are the kinds of behaviour that societies and individuals in them think of as natural, healthy and good. There are also a variety of concerns that go to shape the sexual customs of a given culture. There is no reason to believe in the kind of sexual nature that this kind of exegesis assumes. If we as individuals have a sexual nature, it is largely culturally formed, not determined by 'nature', presocially. Thirdly, the preoccupation with the gender of the sex object as a determinant of the moral value of sexual activity, which seems so natural to us, is itself a function of our culture. (Indeed, it is natural to us *because* it belongs to our culture.) It is not a necessary feature of human nature, but something we learn. It is not properly projected back into the Genesis narrative and attributed to characters who have had neither time to learn nor a culture in which to learn. The Genesis stories may or may not tell us something about the sexual preoccupations of their authors, by which we may have been much affected; but they do not therefore tell us anything about the essence of human sexuality.[27] Here again the analogy between language and sex is helpful. In chapters 2 and 3 of Genesis, Adam and Eve are seen speaking, with the serpent and with God. In the original Hebrew text of these chapters, they, like God, are presented, naturally enough, as speaking Hebrew: naturally enough, because the text was written for a Hebrew-speaking public. Where Adam and Eve are supposed to have got the capacity to speak this language is not explained. In fact, if there was an Adam and an Eve, and if they did speak some language, we can be sure it was not the Hebrew in which these chapters were written; that language is the product of a society which existed much later than any possible date for the first human couple. Rightly, nobody takes very seriously the fact that the Bible represents them as speaking Hebrew; it is taken as a mere literary device, and in translations no attempt is made to preserve the original language in which they are depicted as speaking: in English translations, Adam and Eve speak English. What matters in the text is not that they are portrayed as speaking this or that particular language, but that they are portrayed as language-speakers, for it is in their use of language, rather than in their use of Hebrew, that we recognize the humanity that they share with us. If the author of Genesis naturally makes Adam and Eve into Hebrew speakers, people who speak the language of his particular society, he also naturally makes them bearers of the sexual values of his particular society. But, once we recognize that sexuality is a diverse phenomenon, and shaped by society much as language is, we have no more reason to absolutize those particular sexual values, to try to turn them into *the* way of behaving sexually, than we have to regard the speaking of Hebrew as *the* way to speak. If Adam and Eve may be seen as embodying a particular set of sexual values, we have no more reason to regard as natural those particular values than to regard Hebrew as the natural language. Just as it is in their being linguistic creatures like us, rather than speakers of a particular language that we can recognize in them our shared human nature, so too we can recognize that shared nature in their being sexual creatures, like us, rather than their being bearers of sexual values which may be just as foreign to us as biblical Hebrew.

CHAPTER EIGHT

Homosexuality, Purpose and Happiness

When people complain that homosexual acts are unnatural, or that homosexuals are unnatural for wanting to indulge in them, it is often an element of the complaint that homosexuals use their organs, particularly their sexual organs, for purposes for which they were not made. In doing so they are not being versatile, they are misusing their organs. In so misusing their organs they end up performing unnatural acts. For example, an anus is an organ of evacuation; a man who uses his anus as a receptacle for another man's erect penis for the sexual satisfaction for one or both of them is using it for an unnatural purpose, and in contradiction to its natural purpose. In this chapter we shall be exploring some ideas of purpose, to see whether any substance can be given to this complaint. In addition, towards the end, we shall look at the connection between purpose and happiness and its consequence for homosexuals.

Purpose

Purpose and finality

The Catholic document *Persona Humana* asserts that 'homosexual acts are intrinsically disordered and can in no case be approved of' (§8); this is taken up and repeated in *HP* §3. One reason *Persona Humana* gives for this judgement is that 'according to the objective moral order, homosexual relations are acts which lack an essential and indispensable finality' (*ordinatio*). The essential idea here is that human acts have a finality. 'Finality' is not a word commonly met with. In its use here, it is taken from a Thomistic account of human action. Aquinas, basing himself on Aristotle (*Physics* ii. 9) believes that when we human beings act consciously and deliberately, knowing what we are doing, our act is always directed to some end

216

(*ST* 1.2.1.1c). This is practically equivalent to saying that deliberate human acts always have an aim or purpose, with one important caveat. Sometimes, we do things without purpose, just because we want to do them. Suppose I am running. I might be running with a purpose, say in order to catch a train, or in order to lose weight. But I might be running without any thought of achieving anything by running, just because I enjoy running. We might say in this second case that I am running without purpose, just for the sake of it. Aquinas, however, counts this too as a case of acting for an end; he says effectively that the act is its own end (*ST* 1.2.1.1 *ad* 2). So when he says that we always act for an end, he does not mean that we always act in order to achieve some purpose that lies beyond the act itself. Bearing this difference in mind, we can use 'end' and 'purpose' interchangeably. In most cases, the purpose of an act will simply be what the agent is trying to achieve by performing that act. If I am running in order to catch the train, then the purpose of my act of running is to catch the train. That is to say, the purpose of the act that I perform is simply my purpose in performing it. And if you want to know what the purpose is, you can find out by asking me; because it is my deliberate act, I know its purpose. When we do something for a purpose, in order to achieve an end, Aquinas says that the act is ordered towards that end. If I run in order to catch the train – if that is my end – then my act of running is ordered towards my catching the train. So, just as in most cases the purpose of my act is my purpose in performing the act, so in most cases the end towards which my act is ordered is my purpose, the end I have in mind when I act.

However, Aquinas appears to believe that some acts have a purpose in themselves, regardless of the purpose of the agent; that is, they are of themselves ordered to an end. Importantly for our purposes, these include sexual acts: ... just as the use of food is ordered to the preservation of life in the individual, so is the use of venereal acts ordered to the preservation of the whole human race (*ST* 2.2.153.2c). There is no reason to believe that Aquinas thinks that whenever anybody eats they do so in order to preserve their life, nor that whenever they engage in any sexual activity they do so in order to preserve the human race by procreation. Anybody who did think that would certainly be wrong; people often have sex just for the pleasure of it, just as they often eat simply for the pleasure of eating. In these cases, the end of the act is, in Aquinas's terms, the act itself, as far as the agents are concerned; they aim to achieve nothing beyond the performance of the pleasurable act. Aquinas was well aware of this. Indeed, one of his concerns is precisely that people commit acts of *luxuria*, sexual acts which by their physical structure are incapable of resulting in procreation, and that they commit such acts deliberately, in full knowledge of the fact that their activity is non-procreative. It is clear, too, that when he says that eating is ordered towards the preservation of the individual and sexual acts towards the preservation of the species, he means more than that these acts are, in normal circumstances, the ones we would be sensible to perform in order to achieve these ends. He does not mean that, if we want to preserve ourselves as individuals, it is a good idea to eat; and he does not mean that, if we want to preserve the human race, we will best achieve our end by copulating. He means, not that these acts may be fit for certain purposes of ours, but that they in some way have the purpose they do. And this, for Aquinas, has moral consequences; it is incumbent on us, in the way we act, to respect these inherent purposes. When he says that sex is ordered toward the preservation of the species, therefore, Aquinas means that such ordering is independent of the purposes of those who engage in sexual acts. Somehow, because they are the acts they are, sexual acts naturally have this purpose. So that when people, whatever their particular purposes, engage in sexual activity of such a kind or in such a way that this purpose cannot be fulfilled, they act contrary to the purpose of the act they are performing. They act in such a way that they cannot attain the end to which it is ordered, so that their act is disordered. This is, in broad outline, the thinking underlying the judgements on homosexual acts expressed in *Persona Humana* and *HP* with which we started this chapter, their assertions that these acts are disordered and lack an essential and indispensable finality. It will be the business of the first part of this chapter to explore further this way of thinking about purpose, and to see whether the attitude of *Persona Humana* and *HP* is well founded.

If it is proposed that there is a natural purpose inherent in an act, regardless of the personal purpose of the agent, the question arises as to how this can be so, given that we do normally associate the purpose of an act closely with the purpose of the agent. An answer that suggests itself is that an act can have a natural, inherent purpose because of its physical structure, because of the objects and the bodily parts involved in its performance. Such a response invites us to approach the question of the purpose of an act by thinking first about the purposes of things and organs. In the particular case of sexual activity, this approach suggests that we think about the purposes of human sexual organs. If sexual activity has an inherent purpose, if it is objectively ordered towards an end, this will be because human sexual and other organs have an inherent and natural purpose. If we can say, in addition, that the purpose of sexual organs is reproduction, then the purpose of sexual activity will then be to use those organs in accordance with that purpose, and any sexual activity which uses them otherwise, so that they do not serve their inherent purpose, will itself not be ordered towards its end. This will of course be true of (among others) all homosexual acts, in which the sexual organs are used in a way that is necessarily non-reproductive. All such acts, not being ordered towards the natural end of sexual acts, will be, in the terminology of *Persona Humana*, disordered. If homosexual acts are always in this sense disordered, this is not merely a philosophical observation of limited interest but a fact with important moral consequences. One of the images that, for Christians, gives the idea of the purpose of organs its power is the analogy between the human body and a machine. The parts of the body work together just as do the parts of a machine, in such a striking way that the body has often been called a machine. Just how far this analogy (for it clearly is an analogy) can be pressed is an interesting question, but not one we can go into here. One aspect of it is that machines are designed and made, sometimes by the same person. This fits with the Christian doctrine that the whole world, including the human body, is in some sense designed by God – this, despite the apparently well-established fact that the human body is also in some sense, through evolution, the product of 'blind' natural forces, and so not designed at all. Now, a machine's designer has a special authority when it comes to saying what are the purposes of the various parts of the machine. Other people may be able to deduce with a fair degree of certainty the purposes of the parts, but the designer does not deduce; he simply determines their purposes, and designs his machine so that the parts carry out those purposes. While others may go wrong in their deductions there is no question of the designer being wrong about the purpose of a part of a machine he has designed,[1] for he does not deduce. The part has the purpose it does just because the designer says it has. Others who work out the purpose of that part can perhaps do so with a high degree of certainty; in doing so, in gaining this insight into the structure of the machine, they also gain an insight into the mind of its designer. So, if we see the body as a kind of machine designed by God, then we can also see God as a special authority on the purposes of the parts of the body: parts of the body have the purposes they do because God says so, because that is how God has designed the body. We can often be certain, through observation, what those purposes are, and in achieving that knowledge we gain insight not only into the workings of the body, but into the mind of its designer, God. But what is in the mind of God, how God sees the world and in particular the human body, is not simply another interesting piece of information; it is normative for our own understanding of the body, and should inform our behaviour. So if, for example, it turned out that we could gather with a fair degree of certainty that the purpose of our sexual organs is reproduction, then that would show us what God himself designed those organs for, and it would be incumbent on us to use our sexual organs, when we use them, for that purpose, or at least not in a way that contradicts or nullifies the design and therefore the will of God. But homosexual acts, as inherently non-reproductive, would contradict the design of God. To use the language of *HP*, to choose someone of the same sex for one's sexual activity would 'annul . . . the goals of the Creator's sexual design' (§7).

The purpose of organs

But is all this in fact true? Let us begin by examining the idea that the natural purpose of the sexual organs is a reproductive purpose. When we ask for the purpose of an organ – or, for that matter, of a part of a machine – we are effectively asking questions such as 'What is it for?' or 'What does it do?' or 'Why is it there?' If we ask these questions about our sexual organs there is certainly a case for giving an answer in terms of reproduction. It is because we reproduce sexually that we have these organs, and they each have a function in the reproductive process. There is an obvious sense in this kind of answer: we would not find it easy to explain why we have the various organs we have, and which we call sexual, if we were not the kind of animal that reproduced sexually. Suppose we reproduced asexually; suppose, say, that buds periodically formed on the skin of every adult human being and developed into tiny children which became detached when sufficiently developed. In that case, if some people had testes and others ovaries, it would be difficult to see why. Sperm and ova would be superfluous, so it would be a puzzle why we had them. They would be oddities, because functionless. Our tendency would probably be to seek an explanation for them, and one in terms of function. Perhaps an explanation would be found in terms of a function they once had at an earlier stage in our evolution, when they did fulfil a reproductive function. To this extent, it makes clear sense to say that testes and ovaries have a reproductive purpose. If we say that the purpose of testes and ovaries is reproduction, we might go on to say that the reproductive process takes a certain natural course. Ovum and sperm have to meet and the fertilized ovum implant in the uterus. Given this, the erect penis, the vagina into which it is inserted, the vulva through which it is inserted, and the clitoris which it stimulates serve as means of bringing about the conjunction of sperm and ovum. So we can say too that penis, vulva and vagina have a reproductive purpose. (Though the male organ has at least one clear non-reproductive purpose, too: it figures in the passing of urine.) All this is a matter of observation. The purposes of organs are not secret, and they are not hidden in the divine mind, or accessible only to philosophers. In principle we can discover them by observation; perhaps we can simply look, or perhaps some kind of scientific study will be necessary. One way or another, we can examine the structure of an organ, and from that we can often ascertain how it functions. We can also observe its functioning; we can see what it does and how it does it. We can also remark how a particular organ is connected to others, and what differences its functioning makes to the organism of which it is a part. In making these observations we effectively observe the organ's function or functions; we discover its purpose or purposes. So we can establish the purpose or purposes of sexual organs in this way.[2] So much seems uncontroversial, but it is another question whether anything of moral significance follows from it. Importantly, if we say that a purpose of sexual organs is reproduction, we are not also committed to saying that they can only be legitimately used for this purpose. This is so for at least two reasons.

First, if there is a case for saying that sexual organs have an observable reproductive function, there is also a case for saying that they have an observable social function. Apart from sexual organs having a biological reproductive function, it is an important fact, and one that it takes little observation to discover, that people get pleasure from using their sexual organs, a pleasure related partly to the sensations that are to be had by using them sexually. (Though, as remarked in Chapter 6, the pleasure can go way beyond the sensations.) This raises the possibility that one of the purposes of our sexual organs is precisely to be a source of pleasure. Can we say this? Suppose we each had a patch of skin which gave us intense pleasure when it was rubbed, but which served no function other than to make us feel good: it played, for instance, no part in digestion, or in the elimination of waste products, or in perception of the environment, so that as far as the functioning of the individual is concerned, this pleasure patch might just as well not exist. Nevertheless, when we each rubbed our pleasure patch, we would feel good. This would give us a reason to rub our pleasure patch, for we like pleasure. But then we would feel good when somebody else rubbed our pleasure patch, too. Since we are social animals, we form friendships, and part of friendship is the desire to give pleasure to our friends; it gives friends pleasure to give pleasure to friends. So it would be natural for a friend to want to rub his friend's pleasure patch from time to time, in order to give him pleasure. This means that not just the pleasure patch but the friend's activity in rubbing it would become a source of pleasure. When friends are a source of pleasure for each other, this becomes a cause of bonding between them; it reinforces their friendship. So pleasure patches, though *ex hypothesi* they made no observable contribution to the functioning of the individual, would have an observable social function in binding individuals together into couples or into groups. (Because of this, we could imagine societies in which there were rules about who could rub whose pleasure patch.) Because we are by nature social animals, the idea of some part of the body which has no purpose at all but to give pleasure has a dynamism which carries beyond biology and beyond pleasure: while that part of the body would have no biological function, it would have a natural social function, reinforcing social bonds.

But there remains a problem behind this fantasy. Given that we had pleasure patches, the above reasoning shows they would have a social function; but would that explain why we had pleasure patches in the first place? It seems not. For such patches are not necessary to friendship or social cohesion, as is shown by the fact that friendship and social cohesion are possible among human beings, even though we have no such patches. Shared pleasure does play an important, perhaps essential, part in holding people together, but we get and share pleasure in all sorts of ways which do not depend on the existence of such patches: through games, music, painting, walking, sex, reading, lying on beaches, and so on. Since there are multiple sources of pleasure, pleasure patches are superfluous; and that means we could not give a good reason why we had them, if we had them. This does not mean that we could never have pleasure patches, for they might be thrown up by sheer chance, random genetic mutation.

But in that case we could not give an adequate explanation of them in terms of function, the part they play in our lives; we could not say what we have them for, as we can say what we have stomachs and kidneys for. For such an explanation to be possible, pleasure patches would have to play some essential role in human functioning; a role, that is, other than being a source of pleasure. Still, it remains true that if we did have pleasure patches they would have a social role, as a source of pleasure. What goes for pleasure patches goes for sexual organs, too. Sexual organs are not pure pleasure patches, for they do play an indispensable role in human reproduction, and that is why we have them. But, given that we have them for this reason, observation and experience show that, in addition, using them – and not necessarily for reproductive purposes – gives physical pleasure, just as rubbing pleasure patches would. This is an important fact about them. Because of this, and because we are social animals, it is fair to say that using them has a social function in strengthening relationships. Even if we reproduced asexually so that our current sexual organs had no observable biological function, there is every reason to believe that people would still have sex together, as indeed people do now have sex together, even when their sexual activity serves no reproductive purpose. Therefore, though non-reproductive, including homosexual, forms of sexual activity do not fulfil the reproductive purpose of sexual organs, there is a natural social function which they can and do fulfil.

A second reason why the fact that sexual organs have an observable reproductive function does not imply that sexual activity has to be at least of a potentially reproductive kind is that it is difficult to see a plausible principle from which such a conclusion might follow. We have seen that it is only by reference to their reproductive function that we can explain why we have sexual organs in the first place. But there seems to be no principle which allows us to assert that we can only legitimately use things – instruments or organs – in such a way as to fulfil the purpose in terms of which we explain why we have them in the first place. There is an argument for saying that we have teeth in order to be able to tear off and chew food. A carpenter hammering nails into wood may hold a supply of nails between his teeth. In doing so he does not use his teeth in a way that fulfils the purpose in terms of which we explain why we have teeth in the first place, but it would be absurd to claim that it is for that reason immoral for him to hold nails between his teeth. Similarly, it would be absurd to claim that non-reproductive sexual activity, including homosexual activity, is immoral because it does not display the reason why we have sexual organs in the first place. The reproductive function of sexual organs can only be fulfilled if they are used for one particular kind of sexual activity; to use them in any other kind of sexual activity is to use them in a way that does not make use of their reproductive function. But there seems to be no reason why we should not perform an act using anything, including our sexual organs, in such a way that it does not perform a function which, used in another way, it would perform. The example of the carpenter's teeth again illustrates this. When a carpenter holds nails between his teeth, he is not using his teeth in a way that makes use of their function as part of the digestive process. But we would not for that reason claim that it is illegitimate to hold nails with one's teeth. Similarly, a lesbian who uses her sexual organs in a way that does not make use of their reproductive function does not for that reason act illegitimately. So the fact that our sexual organs have a reproductive function has no tendency to show that non-reproductive, including homosexual, uses of those organs, is in any way illegitimate.[3] But this does not mean that there are no important differences between the various kinds of sexual activity. There is reason to think that penile-vaginal intercourse between a man and a woman has a special status.

The emblematic importance of penile-vaginal intercourse

The functioning of human sexual organs shares an important feature with some other organs. They do not perform their function automatically but only when people act in a certain way. The heart carries on beating regardless of what we do, or of whether we do anything (though the rate at which it beats will vary according to how energetic our activity is). But sexual organs will not perform their reproductive function regardless of what we do. Testes indeed produce semen automatically, and ovaries produce ova automatically, but in order for semen and ova to fulfil their reproductive function they have to be brought together. That, in human beings, does not happen automatically but only as result of a man and a woman performing a particular activity, penile-vaginal intercourse, together. While testes and ovaries simply function, in producing what they do, penis and vagina have to be used, deployed in a particular way, and such deployment is a human act. The fact that we can in an obvious sense observe that the reason why we have sexual organs is reproduction, and that this is in that sense their purpose, what they are for, and that the accomplishment of that purpose depends on an act of penile-vaginal intercourse (henceforth PVI for short), gives to PVI, among all the possible kinds of sexual activity, a special status. Suppose a child asked us what was the purpose of sexual organs. We could use a picture or a film of a man and a woman engaged in PVI as part of an explanation of the purpose of sexual organs, of why we have them. We could not in the same way use a film of the same man and woman engaged in anal intercourse, or of two men engaged in oral intercourse, or of one woman masturbating. Though sexual organs can certainly be used in these other ways, and often are, these other uses do not exhibit in the same way why we have them. These other activities do exhibit the fact that sexual organs can be put to use in various ways, given that we have them, but they do not feature in a functional explanation of why we have them in the first place. This is so because they all leave out of the account the function of the ovaries in producing ova, the function of sperm in fertilizing them, and the function of penis and vagina in bringing them together. While we might use, say, a film of two men having anal intercourse as one example among others of how people use their sexual organs, it would not serve as an illustration of what sexual organs are for.

Teeth

We can say a similar thing about teeth. If we ask what teeth are for, we can, as already noted, give an answer in terms of the tearing off and breaking down of food so that it can both be first processed by saliva and also be worked upon in the stomach. Given this purpose, it is an important fact about teeth that they are located in the mouth, the opening by which food enters the system. So we could use a film of an animal chewing its food as part of an explanation of why that animal has teeth. But teeth can be used for other purposes, too. Animals use them as offensive weapons, to inflict pain and injury on others, or to kill them. People sometimes do this, too. People also use their teeth to hold a supply of nails when doing carpentry. But there is a case for saying that these other uses are subsidiary, certainly in the case of humans; they show what uses people can put their teeth to once they have them, but they do not show why they have them in the first place. This is so because these other uses fail to account for the importance of the fact that the teeth are positioned in the mouth, where food starts to be processed.

Love and children

There is a further aspect of PVI, related to biological function, which differentiates it from any other kind of sexual activity, including same-sex activity; an aspect which, as far as I can see, has no dental parallel. Sexual activity can be a sign of love, of an intimate personal relationship, of a sharing of life.[4] When people fall in love, they typically want an intimate relationship with each other, and they typically want a sexual relationship. This is true of homosexual couples, just as it is for heterosexual couples. Like heterosexual couples, homosexual couples can have families; they can lovingly care for and raise children, and their joint love for those children can be to them a way of bringing others into the orbit of their mutual love, of widening their love for each other to embrace others. They can do this with children they adopt, or with children of one of them, the fruit of another, heterosexual relationship; and these children can be a source of great happiness to them. All this they have in common with heterosexual couples, for heterosexual couples also can adopt, or love a child of whom only one of them is the biological parent. But for heterosexual couples, because of the biological possibilities of PVI, their love-making can itself be the source of their family; it can be the very means of widening their love to embrace children, and of enjoying the happiness that children can bring. This means that, when a man and a woman have a mutual commitment which unites them closely in love, and when they are open to sharing that love with others by generating and lovingly raising children – when, that is, they have a relationship which approximates to how marriage is seen in modern Christianity – then their joint sexual activity can have a great richness to it. This particular richness is unavailable to homosexual couples, because their joint sexual activity does not have the capacity to generate children. This significant link between heterosexual love-making and procreation is what Pope Paul VI calls the 'connection ... between unitive significance and the procreative significance' of 'the marriage act'.[5] This link is of course not always realized. Heterosexual couples, even married ones, sometimes do not love each other, often their sexual activity does not result in the birth of a child, and it is often designed not to. Sometimes, when a child is born to them, they do not raise it lovingly. But the possibility of the link is there,[6] and its potential existence in the case of a heterosexual couple and its necessary absence in the case of a homosexual couple implies a real difference between their sexual activity, even if both couples enjoy committed and permanent loving relationships. How to assess the moral significance of that difference is another matter. Psychologically, if a heterosexual couple love each other and understand their sexual activity as an expression of their loving union, and if they want to generate and love children together, then it is hard to see how they could fail to see and prize that connection between the unitive significance and the procreative significance of their love-making of which Paul VI speaks, and how this could fail to enrich their understanding of their love-making. One can easily imagine that loving homosexual couples, contemplating that connection and its availability to heterosexual couples, might regret that it is not available to them. They might regret that by their love-making they are unable to generate others to share in their love, just as those loving hetero-sexual couples who are unable to generate children can and often do regret it. They might be willing to admit that, objectively, however rich and meaningful their own love-making, and however much they appreciate it, it lacks something by comparison with the love-making of loving and fertile heterosexual couples who are open to the procreation of children.

The difference between PVI and any kind of homosexual inter-course may, then, go way beyond the biological; because of the biological difference, there can be a real difference at the level of human relationships and the human significance of sexual activity within those relationships. Because of the way human reproductive biology works, PVI has potentially a whole dimension which is just not possible in homosexual intercourse. In the light of this differ-ence we might want to say that PVI is just *better* than any same-sex activity, not in the sense that every act of PVI is better than every homosexual act, but that an act of the one sort is potentially richer in meaning than any act of the other sort. If we do say this, how-ever, no consequences whatever follow immediately as to the moral status of same-sex activity. That one emblematic kind of hetero-sexual activity is better in the sense outlined does not imply that all types of homosexual activity are bad; it implies only that they are not as good. To put it another way, the argument implies only that, however good same-sex acts can be, PVI can be even better. In the same way, to say that the third symphony of Brahms is better than the third symphony of Saint-Saëns is to say (whether truly or not) nothing at all about how good the Saint-Saëns is, except that, however good it might be, the Brahms is better. Our argument does not imply, either, that every act of PVI is actually better than every homosexual act, only that the one kind of act has a potential the other lacks. Still less does it imply that all actual instances of homosexual activity are morally bad, but merely that some instances of PVI may, if all the right conditions are realized, be better. It might be that a particular homosexual act which realizes all of its human potential is considerably better than an act of PVI which realizes little of its human potential. In the same way, a good performance of the Saint-Saëns might be a much better piece of music-making than a bad performance of the Brahms. So nothing in what has been said so far indicates that all homosexual acts are in any way morally unacceptable. In order to arrive at a negative evaluation of homosexual acts, one so negative as to imply that they are absolutely inadmissible, some further step has to be made, some further argument produced. One might try to argue, for instance, that the unitive and procreative aspects of PVI not only make it potentially a richer experience than any other sexual activity, but that any sexual activity *must*, to avoid being sinful, also keep these two aspects together. This is indeed what Paul VI asserts in *Humanae Vitae*, and in the next chapter we shall look at length at an argument designed to prove it. Meanwhile, we may look more briefly at some other considerations.

Music and sex

The comparison between sex and music has its uses, but also some interesting limitations. Suppose Karen is a great fan of the third symphony of Brahms but not of the third symphony of Saint-Saëns, while Lawrence adores the Saint-Saëns and is not keen on the Brahms. Karen might be able to explain to Lawrence why the Brahms is better. She might point out the integrated nature of the work, the way Brahms exploits tiny melodic motifs to build huge structures, his use of counterpoint, and so on, as well as the fact that he writes superb tunes. She might point out that, by comparison, the Saint-Saëns is weak, that, though it has some nice tunes and some effective moments, it just does not have the richness or power of the Brahms – in short, that the Brahms is objectively better than the Saint-Saëns. Suppose Lawrence was able to see and appreciate everything that Karen said about the Brahms, agreed that these qualities were important, and that the Saint-Saëns lacked them. What we would expect is that he would come to agree that the Brahms is better, and begin listening to that rather than the

Saint-Saëns, becoming dissatisfied with the latter. It would be odd of him indeed, not to say irrational, if he continued to prefer Saint-Saëns to Brahms. Now suppose that the heterosexual Andrew, speaking with the homosexual Christopher, rehearses the argument we sketched above: that he discourses about the way PVI has objective human advantages over the sex Christopher enjoys with his partner David, asserting that the possibility of generating children opens up new horizons and new possibilities of love and happiness which are just not available to a same-sex couple. Now suppose that Christopher sees the points Andrew makes and agrees that they are important. As rationality seems to demand that Lawrence abandon Saint-Saëns in favour of Brahms, so it would seem to demand also that Christopher abandon his preference for homosexual acts and set out to find a heterosexual relationship instead. This, not because homosexual acts are necessarily bad, but just because acts of PVI are potentially better, for it is irrational not to prefer the better to the worse, even if the worse is not bad. But at this point the analogy between sex and music breaks down. The richness of PVI is not a matter of sheer biology; it depends on, among other things, a context of love, a committed personal relationship. If Lawrence switches allegiance from Saint-Saëns to Brahms, this is merely a matter of going to one concert rather than another, of buying one disc rather than another, and in such circumstances we say that he now loves Saint-Saëns less and Brahms more. But there is no switching of allegiance here; there are no questions raised concerning who Lawrence belongs to, who he is affiliated to, who he should be faithful to. It is a matter simply of a change of taste, effected by appreciation of certain objective qualities of music. But the love of people is different from the love of music; it involves fidelity, allegiance, belonging. Christopher cannot go off in search of a heterosexual relationship without abandoning David, in the sense of giving up his sexual allegiance and exclusive fidelity to him and his intimate personal relationship with him. If he is prepared to do that for the sake of potentially better sex, then he does not love David. But Christopher does love David; that is what gives their sex its quality of love-making and gives it whatever subjective and objective value it has. The very centrality of love which can make PVI so rich, and which implies that a married couple remain faithful to each other, implies also that Christopher remain faithful to David. It is the context of love, which makes it rational to believe that PVI is potentially objectively superior to any same-sex act, that also makes it rational for Christopher to prefer sexual activity with David, whatever its objective limits, to PVI with anybody else. It is rational because it is in reality not a matter of preferring one type of sexual activity to another. Christopher prefers David to all others; he loves him, so of course he will and should stay faithful to him. Added to this is the importance of sheer sexual attraction. Lawrence's view of the relative merits of Brahms and Saint-Saëns is changed by a series of cognitive considerations; he comes to see that certain elements are present in the Brahms which are lacking in the Saint-Saëns; it is Lawrence's opinion that is changed, and that is why his listening habits change. But in order for Christopher's sexual habits to change, for him to seek sex with a woman instead of David, it is not enough that he see the potential advantages of PVI over the kind of sex that he enjoys with David. He must also, regardless of questions of fidelity to David, be sexually attracted to women, or at least to a woman. Women have to get him excited, to turn him on, and he has to find a woman sufficiently attractive to want to build a permanent sexual relationship with her. But it is part of Christopher's being homosexual that he is on the whole much more likely to be sexually attracted to a man than to a woman. Christopher can perfectly rationally recognize the goodness of heterosexual love, and the potential superiority of PVI over any sex that he can have with David, and still say quite rationally that, because he is sexually attracted to men, or to one particular man, it is not for him.[7] In this section we have investigated one way of understanding the idea that sexual activity has, objectively and regardless of the intentions of the participants, the purpose of procreation. The upshot of our investigation is that, while it is not difficult to make sense out of the proposition that the natural purpose of sexual organs is reproduction, and while on the basis of this it is reasonable to say that among all kinds of sexual activity PVI has a special status, no argument can be drawn from this to show that homosexual acts are immoral. But the focus has been principally on the purpose of organs; it is now time to turn our attention to the concept of the purpose of a human act.

The purpose of human acts

As well as speaking of the purpose of organs, we also speak of the purpose of human activities. If things such as parts of machines and animal organs have purposes, people also do things for purposes.

We speak of people having purposes in what they do, and we say also that the things they do have purposes. Asking for what purpose somebody does something is one way of asking for an explanation of why they are doing it. There are several ways we can ask for somebody's purpose: 'What is the purpose of your doing that?', 'What are you trying to achieve by doing that?', 'What is the point of doing that?', 'Why are you doing that?' are all ways of asking for an agent's purpose. When we know somebody's purpose in performing a particular act, we have an explanation of why that person acts as he or she does.[8] But, though we use the language of purpose when we talk about people and their acts, just as we do when talking about organs and their functions, there are important logical differences between the purposes of organs and the purposes of people and their acts. The fact that we use the same word for both should not blind us to these differences. A fundamental difference is that, while the purpose of an organ is equivalent to its function,[9] as noted above, the purpose of a human act cannot be equated with function. To ask the purpose of an organ is to ask how it works and what it contributes to the organism of which it is part. To ask the purpose of a human act is to ask quite a different question; it is to ask what is the agent's purpose in doing it, why he or she does it. This kind of question expects an answer in terms of the agent's intentions, motives and desires, of his or her reasons for performing the action. Organs and parts of machines do not have intentions, motives or desires; they do not have reasons for doing what they do, they simply function, or fail to function. In the sense in which people and their acts have purposes, organs and parts of machines do not have purposes at all. We can make a good guess at people's purposes, why they do what they do, just by observing what they do, if we can observe them closely enough. In this respect, the purposes of people and their acts are similar to the purposes – the functions – of parts of machines and parts of animals. But we have another way of finding out the purpose of a human act: we can simply ask the agent what his or her purpose is in doing it. Generally speaking, the agent is the final authority on the purpose for which he or she performs a particular action. If we are perplexed as to why Anne did or is doing such and such thing, we can find out by asking her. If she answers honestly, her answer normally settles the matter.[10] If you perform an act, freely and intentionally, then you will normally have a purpose in performing it, and that purpose is your purpose, just because it is your act. The purpose of a person's action is the purpose of that person. You can have a purpose for your performing a particular act, but I cannot have a purpose for your performing that act. Your performing the act that you do may of course suit my purposes. Indeed, if I am an entrepreneur I may, in order to achieve my own ends, employ you to perform a particular kind of act. In such a case, you and your acts may be said to have a function in my enterprise, contributing to the working and success of the whole, somewhat as an organ and its functioning contribute to the well-being of the animal of which it is part, or as a machine part contributes to the working of the machine of which it is a part. But this language is somewhat metaphorical; if people can have functions as well as organs and machine parts, we must be careful to distinguish the way people fulfil their functions in organizations from the way organs fulfil their functions in organisms and from the way parts fulfil their functions in machines. People fulfil functions in organizations by acting, by performing free and intentional acts. So, in certain circumstances, a person might fail to fulfil a function by refusing to perform a particular act. An organ, on the contrary, does not perform any free, intentional acts, and so neither does it refuse to perform any acts. It simply works or fails to work. The same is true of a machine part. To say that people fulfil functions is not to reduce them to the status of organs of some super-organism or parts of a super-machine. People who fulfil functions in organizations remain agents who perform free and intentional acts, and who may perform them for their own purposes. Suppose I am your employer, and I offer you a large bonus if you complete a particular task ahead of schedule. I might have any number of purposes for making this offer: I might want the task finished early because that will substantially increase my profits, or because it will free me to go on holiday. Here I perform an act: I induce you to perform a particular task. This act is my act, and I do it for my purposes. You may or may not care about my profits or my holiday; you may care only about the prospect of a large bonus. If you accept my inducement, that suits my purposes, but you accept it for your purposes; if you have a reason for accepting it, that reason is your reason. My act of inducement is one I perform to achieve my end; your act of accepting my inducement is one you perform to achieve your end.

Divine and human sexual purposes

What is true of accepting the offer of a bonus is true of human acts in general, and human sexual acts in particular. If Anne performs a sexual act, of whatever kind, and performs it freely and intentionally and for a purpose, then the purpose for which she performs that act is her purpose. If she performs this act jointly with Brian, her purpose may or may not coincide with Brian's reason for performing it; but if it does, it remains her purpose for performing it. If human acts may be said to have purposes, then, this is because human agents have purposes, and the purpose of any particular act is the purpose of the agent who performs it. Purposes do not inhere in actions, regardless of the purposes of those who perform them. We do sometimes talk about the purposes of acts in a way that makes no explicit reference to the purposes of people, but when we do so there is always an implicit reference to people's purposes. Somebody may observe that people regularly perform a certain kind of act, and ask what is the purpose of that act. A reply to such a question may well take the form: 'The purpose of that act is such and such.' But this is simply equivalent to: 'People do that in order to achieve such and such ends' (just as the question is equivalent to the question: 'Why do people do that?').

In the light of these considerations it is difficult to make much of Aquinas's thought, which we saw towards the beginning of this chapter, that certain human acts are of themselves, regardless of the intentions and purposes of those who perform them, ordered towards certain ends. Human acts cannot have ends in and of themselves, independently of those who perform them, because the end of a human act is precisely the end of the one who performs it. It makes sense to say that the purpose of eating is to maintain health, if by that is meant that if people want to maintain their health it is important that, among other things, they have a diet sufficiently rich in essential nutrients, or that if people do not eat in this way they will find themselves in poor health. And we can speak in this way of the purpose of eating, without reference to the purposes of individuals, because we take it for granted that on the whole people are to an extent concerned about maintaining their health. But there is no way to support the contention that the act of eating in general somehow inherently has this purpose, a purpose which must moreover be respected in all individual acts of eating. If it makes sense to say that a good diet is essential to health, it hardly follows that it is always immoral to eat a meal which has low nutritional value. Even cardinals diet, and do so without sin. In the same way, it makes sense to say that the (or a) purpose of sex is to keep the human species in existence, if by that is meant that if we want to maintain the species in existence then it is essential that, among other things, a sufficient number of people perform sexual acts of a reproductive kind, or that if we all stop copulating the species will die out. And we can speak in this way of the purpose of sex, without reference to the purposes of individuals, because we take it for granted that most of us think it a good thing that the species continue in existence. But there appears to be no way to support the contention that the sexual act in general somehow inherently has this purpose, a purpose which must be respected in all individual sexual acts. If it makes sense to say that a certain amount of reproductive sex is essential to the maintenance of the species, it hardly follows that it is always immoral to engage in a non-reproductive sexual act. So we cannot find here any convincing argument to the effect that it is always immoral to engage in a homosexual act. If it is not possible to make sense of the idea of purpose inherent in an act, then the position of Aquinas is undermined, and so too is that of *Persona Humana*, which depends on it, for the latter speaks of an 'objective moral order', according to which homosexual acts 'lack an essential and indispensable finality'.

Do homosexual acts lack an indispensable finality?

As we have seen, it is one of the major complaints of the CDF against homosexual acts, in *Persona Humana*, and then again in *HP*, that they lack an indispensable finality. (The 'an' of *Persona Humana* becomes 'their' in *HP*.) How can it be that homosexual acts lack this finality? If we adopt the view that the ends of an act can be given, regardless of human intentions – that it is somehow there, just like the colour of a flower, essential to the act itself – then there is perhaps an argument to be made to the effect that this end can somehow go missing, and that it does so in the case of all homosexual acts.[11] But we have already seen, in the previous chapter, that this kind of objectivism is untenable. Nevertheless, it is instructive to try to see how such an argument might be constructed, so let us for a moment admit the possibility of such inherent purposes. We need to ask, first of all: if all homosexual acts lack an essential finality, what finality? Obviously, they do not have as their finality the goal of reproduction. But why should they have this finality? Why should it be thought essential and indispensable to them? Both 'essential' and 'indispensable', and particularly the former, have an ambiguity about them. In most ordinary usage, to say that something is essential is to say that it may not be omitted; it has to be included because its omission means the failure of the project of which it is part. For example, a cookery book may say: 'Before cooking the aubergines it is essential to salt and press them so that the bitter juice drains out'; it might explain by saying that if you do not do this, the dish will be spoiled, even uneatable. Or we could imagine a businessman saying to an employee: 'It is essential that you deliver this package before noon'; he might explain that he stands to make a lot of money if it is delivered before noon, but will lose this opportunity if it is delivered later. What is at stake is whether or not somebody achieves his or her purpose. What hangs on the essential element is the success of somebody's project; this may be either the project of the one who performs the activity (the cook), or the project of the one who causes the activity to be performed (the employer sending the courier). The element in question is essential in the sense of being a condition of the success of the project, or the realization of the purpose. We could substitute 'indispensable' for 'essential' in these cases without loss of clarity. It is important to note here that what is essential depends on the project: while pressing aubergines may be essential to producing a good ratatouille, it is not essential to our businessman making a lot of money. Conversely, rapid delivery of packages is not in general essential to producing a good ratatouille. In this sense, things are not essential in some absolute way; whether they are properly described as essential depends on the project in question. So when it is claimed that something is essential, we must always ask: essential to which project, for which purpose? And whose project is it? Can this be the sense of 'essential' in which homosexual acts are said to lack an essential finality? Hardly. There is first of all the difficulty that what is said to be essential is a finality, an end. But a finality is a purpose or project. In the current sense of 'essential', something may be essential in virtue of a project or purpose; projects and purposes are not themselves essential. It makes no sense to speak of the project itself being essential, unless what is meant is that it is essential to a larger project. It is the project of producing a ratatouille that makes pressing the aubergines essential. Producing the ratatouille is not itself essential, unless it is part of a larger or higher project. This project might be creating a meal pleasing to a friend who is pleased only by meals containing ratatouille, or carrying out the wishes of a customer who has ordered a ratatouille.

Now it might be argued that there is precisely a higher project involved in the case of homosexual activity; not the project of the people involved, but the project of God. What God wants is that those people procreate. The situation is analogous to that of the employer who sends the courier with a package. The courier, because he is an employee and a subordinate, adopts the project of his employer. It is his task to deliver the package quickly, and if he is a good employee he will make it his project to do so. He will organize his activity so as to get the package delivered. He will go directly to the package's destination, and not elsewhere; he will not tarry on the way. Similarly, it may be said, God wants Christopher and David to procreate. As creatures of God they are subordinate to God, and it is their duty to fulfil God's wish. Christopher should be having sex with Christine, and David with Daphne, so that God's project of children might be realized. If this account of God's will and its consequences for human sexual behaviour were plausible, it would give a sense and a weight to the assertion that homosexual acts, such as the anal intercourse of Christopher and David, lack an essential finality. Their having sex together would be like the courier spending his time visiting various entertaining places instead of going directly to deliver the package. But it is not a plausible account, there being a number of problems with it. First, there is no justification for the assertion that God wills that Christopher and David, or either of them, generate children. There is no evidence of any divine command enjoining everybody to have children,[12] and which would apply to Christopher and David. If there were, everybody who did not at least try at some time to have children would be guilty of infringing it. All sexually abstinent people, as well as those whose sexual activity was never of a kind apt to produce children, would be disobeying such a command. Secondly, a command to generate children is not a command to do nothing except generate children, to abstain from all activities which are not apt to generate children. If it were, it would be disobedient to such a command to play tennis or read a book, for these activities, like most of the things people do, are not apt to generate children; they do not have any procreative finality. But it is absurd to believe that all these non-generative activities are sinful. Being non-generative does not entail being sinful. When Christopher and David have anal sex together, they are not doing anything generative, either. But this gives no more grounds for saying that what they are doing is sinful than for saying that reading a book is sinful. If Christopher and David play tennis together, what they do has no procreative finality; the argument we have been examining gives us no reason to think that it ought to, and that it therefore lacks an *essential* finality. When they play tennis, what they do is just something different from procreating. Similarly, the same argument gives us no reason to suppose that when they have sex together what they do lacks an *essential* procreative finality. If they perform an act of, say, anal intercourse, they will not, unless they are very ignorant about biology, do so as part of a project of having children together; their act will not have that finality. But we may ask not only why it should have that finality, whereas their playing tennis together need not, but how it could have such a finality. How could an act of anal intercourse have such a finality, unless those who participate in it are sexually ignorant? But if the act cannot, given a modicum of biological knowledge, have this finality, then such a finality can hardly be said to be essential to it. So the principle that God wants everybody to procreate is not only dubious in itself; it will not do the work needed of it in this context; it has no tendency at all to show that homosexual acts lack any essential finality.

'Essential' as definitional

But there is another, more philosophical or definitional sense of 'essential'. In this sense, one thing is essential to a second thing in order for the second thing to be what it is. Explaining the concept of a triangle, a teacher may say that it is essential to a triangle that it has three sides. Here there is no question of a triangle succeeding in accomplishing its project; triangles do not have projects. What is meant is simply that it is part of the definition of a triangle that it have exactly three sides. Any geometrical figure which does not have three sides may be a perfectly good circle or hexagon or straight line, but it is not a triangle. It is impossible that there be a triangle which lacks the essential property of having three sides. There are plenty of things that do not have three sides but, precisely because they lack three sides, none of them is a triangle; so neither is any of them a triangle which lacks an essential quality. This point is not confined to geometry. In this sense of 'essential' it is impossible that anything, including a human act, lack something essential to it. It is in this sense clearly essential to a human sexual act's having the quality of being potentially procreative that it potentially lead to the conjunction of sperm and ovum. Any human act which cannot lead to that is by definition not procreative. Playing tennis is not procreative, and neither is anal sex. But that implies no kind of defect either in tennis or in anal sex. Further, being procreative is not, in the sense of the word being currently examined, essential to tennis. A human activity does not fail to be a game of tennis because it is not procreative. Similarly, a human activity does not fail to be sexual because it is not procreative, and neither does it fail to be an act of anal sex. Indeed, no human activity fails to be a homosexual act because it is non-procreative. Being procreative is not – in this sense of 'essential' – essential to anal sex, or to any other homosexual act, since it is not essential to any·sexual act whatever. So, once again, in being non-procreative same-sex activity does not lack any essential finality. What goes for qualities of acts goes for finalities in the sense of intentions. Take, for example, a murder. It is essential to any murder that it possess a certain finality; essential to every murder that, among other things, the agent intends to kill the victim. Where one person kills another without that intention, accidentally, this is not a case of a murder without an essential finality; it is not a murder at all. But an act does not fail to be a sexual act because the participants do not intend to procreate. The intention to procreate is – again, in this sense of 'essential' – not essential to sexual acts. It is a fortiori not essential to homosexual acts. So again these acts do not lack any essential finality.

Morally essential

There is a third sense of 'essential' in which one might well claim that a procreative finality, or at least a procreative possibility, is essential to sexual acts, namely, the sense of being morally imperative. This is after all the major sense the Christian tradition and the *Catechism* are interested in. What they want to say is that it is morally imperative that all sexual acts be at least potentially procreative. And it is true that nothing I have said above shows this to be wrong. If it is right, then clearly homosexual acts are morally unacceptable. But while taking 'essential' in this way gives it a clear sense, it deprives us of any argument tending to show why we should believe that sexual acts are essentially procreative. The appeal to essences is naturally at home in an argument about the nature of things. The whole vocabulary of essence and finality is normally rooted in some conception of how things naturally are, and so of how they ought to be. It belongs to a theory of natural law. Nature is taken as the foundation of morality. We have seen that in the end there appears to be no satisfactory way of showing on this basis that homosexual acts lack an essential finality, but at least this approach is an attempt to show that there is a reason why they are unacceptable.

Homosexual acts and homosexual happiness

We all know that having sex does not of itself make you happy and fulfilled. Sex can be joyless, empty and depressing. The argument of *HP*, however, is that Joe and Eric will not find the happiness and fulfilment they seek and expect in their relationship together, in their shared life, and they will not find it because they have sex together, and God did not intend that. Practising the wrong kind of sex means you do not find the happiness you are after. *HP* states: 'As in every moral disorder, homosexual activity prevents one's own fulfilment and happiness by acting contrary to the creative wisdom of God' (§7). Gay sex is said straightforwardly to prevent the happiness and fulfilment of those involved. Having a sexual relationship with a partner of the same sex actually has a detrimental effect on one's happiness and fulfilment. That is official church teaching. It actually has its roots deep in a strong and important current of Catholic theology. It is a central conviction in Catholic thought that the laws and commands of God are not arbitrary. We are creatures of God, and God made us to be and to flourish. We are animals, and it is essential to our flourishing that our organs function properly and do the job they were meant to do. My flourishing is dependent on my heart pumping blood efficiently to all the corners of my body. If it is not working properly, I will suffer and eventually die. Thomas Aquinas puts the point this way:

> God cares for each thing according to what is good for it. But it is good for each thing that it purpose its end, and it is bad for it to swerve from its proper end. As in the whole, so in the parts: each part of a man and all his acts should be allotted to its due end. (*Summa Contra Gentiles* III.122)

But our flourishing does not depend only on the state of our physical organs; it depends also on what we do. This is partly because what we do affects our organs: if I drink too much, I am going to ruin my liver, and if I smoke tobacco I am going to ruin my lungs and possibly give myself and others cancer. But it is also partly, and importantly, because we are social animals. We are not only physical bodies, but also members of various social bodies, and our flourishing depends on how we live together in society, what we do with others, what we do to others and what others do to us. It is not only bad livers that cause human unhappiness, but bad relationships. In order to be happy and fulfilled, in order to flourish, we need to live together in right ways, and avoid doing bad things with and to each other. What we call a law of God is not a law in a legal sense at all; it is simply a rule which tells us how to order our human relationships so that we can flourish, be happy and fulfilled as far as is possible on earth, and God forbids us nothing except what is contrary to our flourishing. Thus, as noted in the previous chapter, Aquinas says: 'God is not offended by us except by what we do against our own good' (*Summa Contra Gentiles*, III.122). We need rules like this, because as individuals we often do not see clearly; our desires get in the way. Even though we know tobacco is bad for us and may be killing us, we long for a cigarette. When we are in love, too, smoke gets in our eyes; though everybody else can see it's going to be disastrous, we can't. The rules that we call laws of God are the voice of reason, helping to clear away the smoke of our temporary desires so that we can find lasting happiness. This is an attractive and fruitful way to understand God as our creator, to understand our own nature and to understand the idea of a law of God. It is not in the least legalistic; at the heart of it is the conviction that God is our loving creator, who creates us for our own happiness. Understood in this way, we have every reason to embrace wholeheartedly the laws of God.

What *HP* says is that one of these laws of God is that homosexual acts are to be avoided. They are the moral equivalent of cigarettes. While they may be nice for a while, they end up being bad for you. God gave us lungs for breathing in air, and by doing that we flourish. Our lungs are not for breathing in tobacco smoke, and if we persist in doing that we are storing up trouble for ourselves. Though it seems so good now, it will become a source of unhappiness. Similarly, God gave us our sexual organs so that we might reproduce, and by doing that we flourish. Our sexual organs are not for indulging in non-reproductive kinds of sexual activity, and in particular they are not about men having sex with men and women with women. If we persist in doing that we are storing up trouble for ourselves. That is what people like Christopher and David and Sophie and Tanya are doing, according to *HP*. Of course they love each other, they want to make each other happy and to be happy together. Of course they will enjoy their sex together, they will delight in each other's body and in giving and receiving sexual pleasure, and they will see this delightful activity as an expression of their mutual love. But in the end it will turn to ashes; what seems so sweet to them now will be a source of frustration and unhappiness. Christopher and David and Sophie and Tanya are not evil, but they are unwise. And so is anybody else who, like them, engages in sexual activity with a member of the same sex. Doing things in a way that God does not intend means that they will end up unhappy and unfulfilled. So if we are ever tempted to engage in homosexual activity, we should resist the temptation, not because there is some celestial policeman who will punish us for it, but because straightforward prudence and good sense should make us want to resist it, just as good sense should make us want to resist the temptation to smoke tobacco. This is the theory. But is it true? It is based, after all, on an assumption which has yet to be justified. If we accept the idea that the laws of God are rules which guide us towards our happiness – and that is surely an attractive idea – it still has to be shown that the precept that we should avoid same-sex activity is indeed one of those rules, one of the laws of God. All kinds of argument have of course been put forward to show that this is so, and we have examined a number of them. Though arguments about the interpretation of the Bible and about the purposes of organs and acts can be and have been bandied back and forth in a way that can seem sterile, there is a way to test the theory currently under discussion in a way which short-circuits these arguments. In Chapter 6 we found that appeal to empirical observation was central in assessing the truth of the claim that same-sex practices make those who take part in them self-indulgent and selfish. We can use the same empirical method here. The theory says, in outline, that all sin prevents the sinner from being truly happy, and that since homosexual activity is sinful, it prevents those who engage in it from being happy. So this is not an abstract theological theory divorced from reality. It predicts that all those who have sex with a person of the same sex will end up unhappy. So we can test this theological theory by empirical observation. We can observe what happens and see if the actual facts bear out the theory. As in the discussion of same-sex practices and selfishness, there is an important asymmetry that needs to be pointed out here. It is easier for the facts to disprove a theory than to prove it. Suppose we have a theory which predicts that certain events will happen. Even if all the facts turn out to be as the theory predicts, that does not show the theory to be true, for there might be other explanations of why the facts are as they are. But if, on the other hand, there is a single genuine exception, if an event happens which the theory predicts should not happen, then that shows the theory to be false. So, in the present case, if all sexually active homosexuals are in fact unhappy in the long run, then the theological theory that predicts that they will be unhappy stands a chance of being true; it is perhaps true that it is a law of God that we should avoid homosexual activity. But even if all active homosexuals are unhappy, that does not *prove* that there is a divine law forbidding the activity, for there might be other explanations of that unhappiness. Even if sin makes the sinner unhappy, other things apart from sin might make a person unhappy; illness and loneliness can make you unhappy, but it is not a sin to be ill or lonely. If, on the other hand, we find that there are genuinely happy homosexuals, happy despite having an active sex life, that contradicts our theory and shows it to be false. So even without going into all the debates about the interpretation of the Bible and about natural law, we can test the truth of the theory. If it should turn out that there are happy, sexually active homosexuals, then the theory is false; whatever the arguments put up in its favour, we know that there *must* be something wrong with them, at least one of them must be fallacious, even if we cannot say exactly where the error lies.

So we have to ask: are things actually as the theory predicts they should be? Are all sexually active homosexuals unhappy and unfulfilled? We are straightaway in a difficulty here, because happiness is not a measurable quantity. The question whether somebody is happy is not like the question at what temperature a given liquid boils. Happiness, though an important concept, is a vague one. This vagueness means that two people (call them Alan and Brian) might in some circumstances disagree about whether a third person (Caroline) is happy or not. Alan might point to Caroline's constant smile as evidence that she is happy. Brian might say that, though Caroline sincerely believes herself to be happy and says so, since she has just been jilted by her lover she is really unhappy, and her smile is a desperate one, part of an attempt to defend herself against misery. Cases like this are not infrequent. In addition, people can be enigmatic and difficult to fathom, and we may in many cases be simply unable to say with any assurance whether a person is happy or not. Nevertheless, over time it normally becomes clear whether people are really happy or not, if we study them

closely enough. This reference to time is important. Happiness, in
the sense in which it is used in the Catholic tradition, is essentially a
long-term business. We can and do speak of people being happy or
unhappy for an evening, a day or a week. We may say of somebody
who is having a bad day at work that she is unhappy that day; the
next, when things are going better, we may say that she is happy
again. When *HP* claims that people's engaging in homosexual acts
prevents their happiness, it does not mean that they feel miserable
on the day they do it, or in the following week; that would be an
absurd claim. It is rather that, over periods of months or years,
engaging in this kind of sexual activity will lead to a lack of fulfilment, a frustration, which we would normally label unhappiness.
HP's assertion can perhaps be understood on analogy with the
claim that taking hard drugs is contrary to a person's true happiness: however good a dose of the drug may feel in the immediate
short term, and however positively the drug may seem to transform
a person's life at the beginning, in the long term the practice will, it
might be claimed, lead to degeneration and misery. Happiness, even
true happiness, is not, then, a mystical, hidden quality; it is normally open to discovery by observation, though perhaps over
considerable time.

With these points in mind, then, let us return to our question: is it
actually true that all sexually active homosexuals are observably
unhappy, in the long run? One thing we can say at the start is that
homosexuals are a pretty miserable lot by comparison with the rest
of the population; at least, the men are. One indication of this is
that, particularly among young gay men, rates of suicide and
attempted suicide are far higher than among young straight men. (I
can say nothing about lesbians, younger or older; on this question,
as on so many others, the attention of scientists, of theologians and
of the press tends to be concentrated on gay men almost to the
complete exclusion of lesbians.) And there are plenty of gay novels
about anguished gay men of all ages. But this does not prove the
CDF's theory. For one thing, there are many reasons of a quite
non-theological kind why we would expect this to be so. Many
young gay men feel, perhaps rightly, that to survive they have to
hide their sexuality from their friends and families. That does not
show them or their sexual acts to be sinful. Others live in openly
homophobic societies where gays are persecuted officially and
unofficially; it is surprising when people living in that atmosphere
are *not* unhappy. Jews were a pretty unhappy lot in Nazi Germany,
but that does not show that it is a sin to be Jewish; it shows rather

that the society in which they lived was very sinful. And so on. So the general unhappiness of gays is not a reason for thinking the Vatican is right. A second important consideration is that what is supposed to be a sin, against the law of God, is not being gay but engaging in homosexual acts. The people who are supposed to be unhappy, according to the CDF theory, are not homosexuals as such, but people who engage in homosexual acts. There is, as far as I know, no evidence whatsoever that gays who have an active sex life are unhappier than gays who do not. Even if there were, this would be far from showing that they are made unhappier by performing homosexual acts. In societies where homosexuals are unhappy because they have to lie and dissemble, their sexual activity is one more thing to hide, and is in itself a source of anxiety in that it can be difficult to hide and may lead to their discovery and disgrace. In such cases, it is not homosexual activity that leads to unhappiness, but homosexual activity in that kind of society.

If there is one thing we know about human nature and human happiness, it is that, on the whole, adults are made happier by having a successful relationship with a significant other – a husband, a wife, a partner. This is a significant component of happiness for most people, straight or gay. When adults pair off in this way, there is most often an important sexual aspect to their relationship; it is most likely sexual attraction that gets them together in the first place. This is as true of gays as of straights. So we have every reason to expect that a homosexual in a successful relationship will be happier than one in no relationship at all (or, even worse, in an unsuccessful relationship). We have every reason to expect this, even if the homosexual's successful relationship involves sex. I say we have every reason to expect this. But is it in fact true? Are there, as a matter of fact, reasonably happy homosexuals who have a close relationship with a partner, and who have sex as a part of that relationship? This is not a question we can decide a priori; we have to look at the evidence. I think I can affirm safely that, as a matter of fact, such happy, sexually active homosexuals do exist. Here I am not talking simply of people who are on a high because they have just fallen in love and are on a sexual roller-coaster. I am talking of people who have stable lives, stable sexual lives, and are happy. I am talking not of people who start off excited, but of people who actually end up happy, after years of relationship and years of sexual activity. Anybody whose familiarity with homosexuals is at all extensive, where the prevailing culture, including the prevailing gay culture, tolerates such relationships, is likely to know some such people. They certainly exist. What matters here is not that the members of CDF do not know of such people, but that others do. There are homosexuals with a fair idea of how to live happily, who know that the happy life involves generosity and self-giving love, who know what it is like to live with another in a relationship, who have found that their experience of living together, including their sexual activity together, contributes substantially to the happiness of each. They have found, by experience, that homosexual activity does not make them unhappy and unfulfilled. It is true that many relationships do end badly, gay as well as straight, and perhaps gay relationships have much more working against them than straight ones. But we do know, empirically, that there are people who are long-term happy in homosexual relationships. (And I have not even talked of the possibility that there are happy sexually active homosexuals who are not in stable relationships.)

So we can safely say that engaging in homosexual activity does not, as a matter of fact, prevent happiness and fulfilment. Now *HP* asserts that, since homosexual activity is sinful, it prevents happiness. But if its being sinful implies that all sexually active homosexuals are not happy, then, conversely, if it is not true that all sexually active homosexuals are unhappy, that implies that not all homosexual activity is sinful. Therefore, since we know from empirical observation that it is not true that all sexually active homosexuals are unhappy, we also know, from empirical observation, that not all homosexual activity is sinful. When *HP* claims both that every moral disorder prevents happiness and that homosexual activity is such a moral disorder, it is, as a matter of plain fact, wrong. This is not a matter of theological dissent, but of empirical observation, of facts which anybody can observe, if they will. This result does not show that *HP* is wrong in claiming that homosexual acts are always sinful. It shows only that it cannot claim, consistently with observable facts, both that homosexual acts are always wrong and that every moral disorder prevents one's own fulfilment and happiness. One of the two theses has to be given up. So it would be possible in the light of the facts to continue to maintain all homosexual acts are wrong, while abandoning the idea that moral disorder prevents one's fulfilment and happiness. But this course is unattractive, for various reasons. The belief that moral disorder prevents one's fulfilment and happiness is a principle which goes much deeper in Catholic moral thinking than the mere disapproval of a particular range of sexual practices. As noted earlier, it involves an important and attractive view of the relation between God and people, and furnishes a fruitful way of understanding the concept of a law of God. It also, by linking the will of God to human flourishing and happiness, makes it clear why it is in our interest to obey the will of God. These are important elements of any moral theology. In addition, the idea that God seeks human happiness, and that it is by living in accord with the will of God that happiness is to be found, is much more firmly attested in Scripture and tradition than any prohibition on all homosexual activity. (See, for example, Deut. 28–30, Gen. 2.) The more economical course to take in the light of the empirical observation that happy, sexually active homosexuals do in fact exist, and the less damaging course, is to abandon the doctrine that all kinds of homosexual activity, always, everywhere and in all circumstances, constitute a moral disorder.

CHAPTER NINE

Some Modern Arguments

While traditional natural law arguments tend to focus on the supposed objective purposes of sexual organs and sexual activity, in modern times a new kind of argument has come to the fore, at least in Catholic circles. This style of argument centres more on the meaning of sexual acts, and makes use of notions such as symbolism, complementarity and alterity. In this chapter we shall first look at a number of such arguments in their relationship to homosexuality, focusing principally on the work of Germain Grisez. Then we shall examine the idea that underlies most of these arguments, whatever the language they employ: that human acts, in particular sexual acts, have a meaning often labelled 'objective', a divine meaning, irrespective of the meanings that human beings give or fail to give them. An example of such an argument, or the outline of one, is to be found in *HP* §§6–7:

> Human beings ... are nothing less than the work of God himself; and in the complementarity of the sexes, they are called to reflect the inner unity of the Creator. They do this in a striking way in their cooperation with him in the transmission of life by a mutual donation of the self to the other.

> To choose someone of the same sex for one's sexual activity is to annul the rich symbolism and meaning, not to mention the goals, of the Creator's sexual design. Homosexual activity is not a complementary union, able to transmit life; and so it thwarts the call to a life of that form of self-giving which the Gospel says is the essence of Christian living.

We have already met both these paragraphs on more than one occasion, the first when looking at Genesis 1. We found reason there to doubt the claim that the theology of creation outlined in this paragraph was indeed to be found in Genesis. In the present context, that supposed theology serves as the basis for the argument against homosexual activity found in the second paragraph. That

247

argument is presented with such brevity as to render it obscure, but, if I understand it correctly, it can be fleshed out somewhat as follows.

God has created people in his image, and this image is displayed especially strikingly when a man and a woman, through sexual activity together, generate new life. One problem with homosexual activity, mentioned here in passing, is that it does not respect the ends of sexuality; this criticism we have looked at in an earlier section. More central here is a quite different, but related argument: because homosexual activity is, by its very structure, biologically sterile, not 'able to transmit life', it does not have the expressive potential of heterosexual intercourse; it does not show forth the divine image. But since, in creating people male and female in his image, God willed that men and women should display his image particularly in their procreative sexual intercourse, sexual activity which is of its nature not procreative, and so does not display his image in this way, runs counter to the symbolism inherent in creation and willed by God from the beginning. The main argument here, though intimately linked with traditional concerns about the procreative purpose of sex, is thus essentially concerned with sexual symbolics. In creation, by making people male and female in his image, God willed that sexual activity has, not a particular purpose, but a certain meaning. It has that meaning because it is by nature procreative; its meaning is rooted in and depends on certain objective biological facts. Because sex thus has an objective meaning, willed by God in giving us the possibility of procreating sexually, it is incumbent on human beings to respect that meaning; for not to do so is to go against the will of God. But any sexual activity that is of its nature non-procreative by that very fact lacks that meaning, and so is contrary to the divine will. And such, necessarily, is any and every homosexual activity. Hence a choice to engage in homosexual activity is, by its very nature, a choice to 'annul the rich symbolism and meaning, not to mention the goals, of the Creator's sexual design'. Further, respect for God's design is essential to living human life as it ought to be lived. God made us for love, to give ourselves generously to others and for others; even if this remains obscure in the Old Testament, including Genesis, it is revealed definitively in and by Jesus Christ, whose supreme example of loving self-giving and whose teaching are transmitted to us in the gospel. That love is the truest reflection of the inner life of the Creator. It is a common theme of the Christian tradition that it is love which binds together the Persons of the Trinity and constitutes their unity. This, it might be argued, renders any exegetical worries about the meaning of 'image' in Genesis 1 finally irrelevant; what truly matters is not the text of Genesis read and studied in isolation, but its meaning when viewed in the light of the gospel and the Christian tradition. Since it is heterosexual, procreative sexual intercourse which displays the image, and so the inner unity of God, it is this too which displays love. Such sexual activity is a physical symbol of love, it is naturally expressive of self-giving love, as is attested not only by Scripture but by common human experience. It is a total physical self-giving, which therefore has its natural place within a procreative relationship of total self-giving, that relationship which we call marriage. Homosexual activity partakes of none of this. Because it does not have the meaning which is essential to sex as willed by God, it is not a showing forth of the image of God, of the divine unity. That is, it is not an act which displays love, as sexual activity was and is meant by God to do. It is not a loving act. Therefore, far from expressing and being part of a life of total self-giving love – the life to which the gospel calls us – it actually runs counter to such a life, and is in opposition to the gospel. The gospel calls us to love and have concern for the other, but homosexual activity is essentially loveless and self-regarding. That is why *HP* continues: 'when they [*sc.* homosexual persons] engage in homosexual activity they confirm within themselves a disordered sexual inclination which is essentially self-indulgent' (§7). This is a reconstruction of the argument which lies behind the text of *HP*, and it may not correspond entirely to the thought of the authors; but the reconstruction does not, I think, betray it, either. In fact, this argument, or something substantially similar, is to be found in several modern Catholic texts. For example, Livio Melina, Professor of Moral Theology at the John Paul II Institute for Studies on Marriage and the Family in Rome, argues that

> human sexuality is included in that primordial and good plan of God the Creator, who called man and woman with their reciprocal complementarity to be an image of his own love and responsible collaborators in the procreation of new individuals. Therefore, objective meanings are inherent in the physical acts related to sexuality and represent as many calls to achieve the person's moral good.[1]

Melina's starting point is plainly related to that of *HP*. He continues:

Through the symbolism of the sexual difference which marks their bodily nature, man and woman are called to achieve two closely connected values: 1) the gift of self and the acceptance of the other in an indissoluble union (*una caro*), and 2) openness to the transmission of life. Only in the context of legitimate marriage are these values proper to sexuality adequately respected and achieved.

But homosexual activity

lacks that unitive meaning in which 'an authentic gift of self' can take place. In fact, only in the conjugal sexual relationship between a man and woman does their reciprocal complementarity, based on their sexual difference, allow them to become the 'one flesh' of a communion of persons who together constitute one and the same procreating principle. The gift of self and the acceptance of the other are real, because they are based on the recognition of *otherness* and on the *totality* of the act which expresses them. The gift of the body is a real sign of self-giving at the level of the persons. The meeting of one person with another is expressed with respect for the symbolism of the sexed body ... In the homosexual act, on the other hand, that true reciprocity which makes the gift of self and the acceptance of the other possible, cannot take place. By lacking complementarity, each one of the partners remains locked in himself and experiences his contact with the other's body merely as an opportunity for selfish enjoyment. At the same time, homosexual activity also involves the illusion of a false intimacy that is obsessively sought and constantly lacking. The other is not really 'other'; he is like the self: in reality, he is only the mirror of the self, which confirms it in its own solitude, exactly when the encounter is sought.[2]

Harvey argues in a similar vein. According to him, 'homosexual activity is objectively always seriously immoral, inasmuch as it in no way fulfills the essential purposes of human sexuality. The Catholic teaching flows *necessarily* from the *whole scriptural vision of the meaning of sexuality* and of the *complementarity* of man and woman.[3] Sex, [he continues,]

is life-giving by its very nature ... Genital activity also has a life-uniting meaning: it joins two persons by a special kind of love ... The man–woman relationship is in accord with the aspirations and needs of both sexes. This is the way nature's God meant things to be ... The complementarity between man and woman is physical (two in one flesh), psychological (the male's joy in the presence of the female), and spiritual (he leaves his own family to commit himself to her) ... The kind of complementarity, however, between two homosexual persons in a steady relationship is much inferior in terms of its structure, strength of commitment, and consequences ... Thus even the best homosexual genital relationship is seriously flawed.'[4]

He contends further that 'homosexual union lacks ... transcendent meanings' and that those who lead 'the active homosexual lifestyle' have a 'commitment to sexual freedom and sexual pleasure'.[5] Here again we see the same basic elements: by his creative act, God established the complementarity of man and woman. This gives sex an essential two-fold meaning: it unites a man and a woman in love, and it is procreative. By this objective standard, all homosexual activity, even that which takes place within a faithful, committed relationship, is highly defective, and is connected to a self-centred search for sexual pleasure.

Before we go on to analyse this style of argument in detail, note one common feature. Homosexual acts are to be judged by how well they fit into the divine plan revealed to us in Scripture, for it is that plan that establishes the true nature of sex. Scripture reveals that sex is of its nature heterosexual, an affair of men and women together. Homosexual activity is to be judged by how well it accords with that objective nature of sex. Thus homosexual activity is not to be looked at in isolation, but in its relationship to God's overall plan for sex. This approach therefore locates homosexual activity within a global vision of the nature of sex. This can be seen in one way as an advantage of this style of argument. It does not rely on individual isolated proof-texts, simple appeals to texts such as Leviticus 18:22 and Romans 1. This latter approach is in danger of making the biblical condemnation of such acts appear arbitrary. While it may succeed, if we are convinced by the exegetical arguments involved, in showing that the biblical condemnation may be clear, we are left wondering *why* homosexual acts are supposed to be wrong. The present approach, which locates the discussion of homosexual activity firmly within the context of God's overall plan for human sexuality, a plan which establishes the nature of human sexuality, tries to show that homosexuality is not consonant with

God's plan, that it is out of step with human nature, and thus that there is a strong reason for rejecting all homosexual activity. On the other hand, we have already seen that the alleged global scriptural view of human sexuality on which this kind of argument depends has rather less support in the actual text of Scripture than is commonly supposed. In particular, Genesis 1 and 2 will not bear the weight that is put upon them; the interpretation of them that the current argument requires goes far beyond the text in ways that are, to say the least, difficult to sustain. There is a further, more general difficulty about this approach. It is held that God establishes the nature of human sexuality, and that the nature that God establishes is essentially heterosexual, so that what sex is naturally about implies sexual relations between a woman and a man. Now it is clear at once, before any further argument, that homosexual activity does not fit into this schema, by the simple fact that it is not heterosexual. This is only to state the obvious, and for supporters of this kind of argument it is an obvious strength; for them, we have only to look at the God-given nature of human sexuality to see that homosexual acts won't fit in, that they are in an obvious sense unnatural. But those who look with a more critical eye may wonder whether the terms of the argument are not being set up to exclude homosexual acts by definition. Of course, they may respond, if homosexuality is judged in terms of heterosexuality it is bound to look defective. But why should it be judged in those terms? They may wonder, that is, whether the supposed God-given unified nature of human sexuality actually exists. They may point, as already noted, to the weakness of the scriptural interpretation alleged in support of it, and to the possibility of other interpretations that lead in different directions. They may argue that human sexuality is, in fact and by nature, more various than the current approach allows for, and that the restriction of human sexuality to a heterosexual model has not been justified. If the current approach is to carry conviction, it needs to be argued for in other ways; it needs to be shown, independently of weak scriptural arguments, that sexual activity does indeed of its nature have the symbolic structure it is claimed to have. A serious attempt to do this does exist, in the work of Germain Grisez. Grisez's argument is an influential one; his assertions, conclusions and terminology are echoed by numerous other writers on the subject, including those quoted above. So it is to an examination of Grisez's thought that I now turn.

Germain Grisez

Grisez treats of sexual matters most fully in his manual *The Way of the Lord Jesus*, volume 2, *Living a Christian Life*, and I will be concerned with the argument he develops there. His particular approach has the advantage that he develops a view of human sexuality which is more or less independent of Scripture and of other Christian authorities. As a Christian he is of course committed to the Bible as a place where God's word is revealed. As a Catholic, he also sees those who hold teaching office in the church as authoritative sources of doctrine. But it is for him an important exercise to see how much we can know about the nature of human sexuality on the basis of reason alone. If he can root Christian teaching about sex in reason independent of revelation, he thereby shows that it is not arbitrary and divorced from the realities of human life, but based on human nature itself. If he can do that, he also importantly makes his moral conclusions concerning sex available to everybody, regardless of their religion. Of particular concern to us here is that he will be able to demonstrate the immorality of homosexual acts to anybody, whether they accept Christian revelation or not, and whether or not they are convinced by any particular interpretation of a handful of biblical texts. He would thus avoid having to say that, while it is wrong for anybody, whatever their faith, to commit homosexual acts, only Christians – and perhaps only Catholics – can know that it is wrong. Grisez's particular approach, which may fittingly be labelled a natural law approach, promises to meet the objections raised above. For this reason, and because it is more fully expounded and closely argued than the other texts quoted above, it will reward close attention. Like the other authors we have looked at in this section, he locates the discussion of homosexuality firmly within the context of human sexuality in general, and his evaluation of homosexual acts cannot be understood without first grasping the broad outlines of his general theory of sex.

Human sexuality

Basic to Grisez's understanding of human sexual conduct is his idea of a one-flesh union. He introduces the term in his discussion of marriage, and he makes use of it in an argument designed to show that marriage is indissoluble and that the marriage relationship is the only legitimate context for human sexual activity. The term 'one-flesh union' is based on a biblical expression. In Genesis 2, when Adam joyfully receives Eve, exclaiming 'This at last is bone of my bones and flesh of my flesh', the narrator comments: 'Therefore a man leaves his father and his mother and clings to his wife, and they become one flesh' (Gen. 2:24). This passage is quoted by Jesus in a dispute with Pharisees about divorce (Matt. 19:3–9). These passages are not directly concerned with sex, but with marriage, and indeed, as I have said, Grisez's primary concern is also with marriage; it is marriage which he describes, borrowing from these biblical texts, as a 'one-flesh union'. But the way he fleshes out his use of this term refers essentially to the human faculty of reproduction. For him, 'one-flesh union' is basically a biological term. The human mating couple is in an important sense one organism; the individual man and woman really are joined to become biologically one. It is this real unity, demonstrated by the facts of human biology, that will show both that marriage is indissoluble and that sex is legitimate only within a permanent heterosexual marriage. Grisez begins by talking, not about human beings, but about any animal that reproduces sexually. He first draws a distinction between reproduction and other animal functions. He claims that 'every animal, whether male or female, is a complete individual with respect to most functions: growth, nutrition, sensation, emotion, local movement, and so on'. This is not the case, however, where reproduction is concerned. With respect to reproduction,

> each animal is incomplete, for a male or a female individual is only a potential part of the mated pair, which is the complete organism that is capable of reproducing sexually. This is true also of men and women: as mates who engage in sexual intercourse suited to initiate new life, they complete each other and become an organic unit. In doing so, it is literally true that 'they become one flesh'. (*LCL* p. 570)

Becoming one flesh, then, is a matter of engaging in potentially reproductive sexual intercourse. In this activity, male and female animals complete each other; together they form one complete organism, and it is this organism that reproduces sexually.[6] It is immediately clear that there are serious problems with this characterization of animal reproduction. The fundamental difficulty is that, while Grisez speaks of animals and their functions, he fails to distinguish between the activity of an animal and the functioning of its organs and other parts. This makes his list of supposed animal functions difficult to understand. He mentions local movement in this list. Now, if an animal walks, this is an activity of that animal. Animal activity is on the whole voluntary; if a dog walks, it acts, it moves because in some sense it wants to. (This is not to deny that we may have problems in talking about the will of an animal in the same way that we talk about the will of a human being. But we are generally happy to ascribe will to animals in some sense: we speak of a dog wanting to go out, of a cat not wanting to eat, and so on.) Animals are agents. If a dog's heart beats, on the other hand, this is not an activity of that dog; the dog is not doing anything. It is not beating its heart, or making its heart beat. The beating of the dog's heart does not involve the agency of the dog as the dog's walking does. Neither does it involve any agency of the dog's heart. We might be prepared to speak of the heart's beating as an activity of the heart, but it is not a voluntary activity of the heart in the way that the dog's walking is a voluntary activity of the dog. The heart does not beat because it wants to. The heart is not an agent. It does not act; it simply functions, just as a machine or part of a machine functions.

There is thus a clear conceptual distinction between the activity of an animal and the functioning of its parts. Causally, the ability of an animal to act will of course depend on the adequate functioning of its parts: the dog can only walk if the muscles, tendons, nerves, bones, and so on, involved in the activity function sufficiently well. But, conceptually, act and function are not to be confused. The 'local movement' which appears in Grisez's list of animal functions is not a function at all, but an activity. This might seem like a nit-picking distinction, of little consequence; all it appears to do at first sight is to show that Grisez's list is a little confused. But in fact it undermines Grisez's entire argument. The parts of an animal, each of which, we may suppose, has its proper function or set of functions, are combined in such a way as to form the complete animal, capable of acting. In this sense, the parts may be said to be mutually complementary, parts which fit together to form the whole organism. (We might also be happy to say that in this way the different parts complete each other, though this way of speaking must be used with caution; the heart is after all a complete heart, the liver a complete liver, even though the heart does not function as a heart, or the liver as a liver, unless it is, in combination with other necessary organs, part of a living organism.) It is in roughly this way that Grisez describes the potentially reproductive mating of two animals: when it comes to reproduction, 'each animal is incomplete, for a male or a female individual is only a potential part of the mated pair, which is the complete organism that is capable of reproducing sexually'. Grisez treats male and female animals in effect as organs or parts of some other animal or 'organism'. But, while organs are parts of animals or organisms, animals are not parts of animals or organisms. Grisez would have it that the male and female animal are only parts of a mating pair, and that this pair is the complete organism capable of reproducing sexually. This is wrong. Animals, including human beings, may of course form part of a group of animals. Families, peoples, football teams, armies and orchestras are examples of human groups. Many of these groups are based on a joint project, and involve the collaboration of their members. Members of armies collaborate to protect their nation, or to defeat an enemy; members of orchestras collaborate to achieve the performance of a piece of music. When a group works together to achieve a goal, different members of the group often play different roles. In an army there are those who command and those who obey, there are gunners, drivers, radio operators, etc.; in an orchestra one person may play a violin, another a clarinet or a triangle, and so on. In such cases it makes sense to say that each member fulfils a particular function in the group. This means that there is a certain analogy between the people who are members of a group and the organs, limbs, etc. that are part of a living animal. An animal is a body, but we also sometimes speak of a group as a body; people are members of a social body, but we also speak of limbs as members of a physical body. This analogy points to the fact that, just as a living animal acts as one, its limbs and organs working together, so a group like an army or an orchestra may act as one, its members co-operating. But the fact that there is this analogy between an animal and a group should not blind us to the important differences between them. The members of a group are agents, they perform voluntary activities; the organs and members which make up an animal body are not agents and do not perform voluntary activities. The members of a group collaborate by co-ordinating their activities so as to act as a group and achieve a common end, and this co-ordination is itself something they do as agents. The parts of an animal body do not co-ordinate their activities as agents, for they are not agents and have no activities to co-ordinate. They merely have functions as part of the animal. If we speak of a member of a group as fulfilling a particular function within that group, this is shorthand for describing the way the member co-ordinates his or her activities with the rest of the group. There is no such shorthand involved when we speak of the function of the heart or liver of an animal.

A related point is that the living individuals which go to make up a group have an existence as living individuals outside that group. A violinist does not cease to be a living individual when he goes home at night after the evening's performance, separating himself from the rest of the orchestra, nor when he quits the orchestra and gives up playing the violin to become a chemistry teacher or a farmer. The life of an animal (at least a higher animal) is separable from the particular role it plays in the group of which it is part, and separable also from its membership of that group. By contrast, a heart or a liver separated from the animal of which it is part ceases itself to be living. A part of an animal is living only as part of that animal. Grisez's mating couple is not an organism but a group. It is a pair of organisms – a pair of animals – engaged in a joint activity, two agents co-ordinating their acts to achieve a common end. (The end may simply be the joint activity itself.) The real biological unity that Grisez wishes to find, which would make of the two together one complete organism, is simply not there. The couple just are not one flesh in the sense that Grisez wants.[7] Indeed, it would be rather peculiar if Grisez were correct, if it were the case that male and female formed one organism when they mated. For then it would be this single organism that reproduced, as Grisez states. But if a single organism reproduces, this is what we call asexual reproduction. It is characteristic of sexual reproduction, by contrast, that it is carried out by two animals in collaboration. It is as if Grisez cannot conceive of reproduction that is genuinely sexual, and so tries to reduce it, unsuccessfully, to the asexual. Grisez's conception of one-flesh unity, allegedly based on the facts of sexual animal reproduction, is confused and incoherent. All the arguments based on this notion, and which he marshals in favour of the indissolubility of marriage and of the restriction of human sexual activity to the context of marriage, are infected with this confusion, and his conclusions do not follow.

Sexual intercourse as personal communion and self-gift

Grisez's argument would, if correct, apply to all animals which reproduce sexually, not just to human beings. Pairs of ducks, giraffes and cats would also constitute one organism when it comes to reproduction. But for Grisez the idea of one-flesh union goes much further and deeper when applied to human beings. It involves an intimate communion of persons. Here, he appears to trade on the fact that 'one flesh' is used biblically as an expression designating, not simply mating pairs, but married couples, and on the fact that, particularly in modern times, stress has been laid in Christian theology on marriage as a form of deep personal communion based on mutual self-commitment, in which each partner gives himself or herself totally to the other. While Grisez uses 'one-flesh union' to refer to potentially procreative sexual intercourse, it is marriage which is the true one-flesh union in the Christian tradition, not sexual intercourse, even if sexual intercourse is always seen as having its true home within marriage. But it would in fact be unfair to charge Grisez with trading on an ambiguity here. We have already seen that, for other recent Catholic thinkers, one reason why sexual intercourse has its place within the deep personal communion of marriage, and only there, is because for human beings there is an objective meaning to sexual intercourse: it is in itself an act of total self-giving, a physical gift of each partner to the other. Thus sexual intercourse is of itself a kind of physical embodiment and expression of the married state. Grisez takes a similar position. He states:

> A marital act expresses and fosters the couple's marital com-
> munion precisely because, when they willingly and lovingly
> cooperate with each other in an act of itself suited to procreating,
> their mutual self-giving actualizes their one-flesh unity. If one or
> both spouses engage in a sexual act which does not realize one-
> flesh unity in this way, that act is not marital. (*LCL* p. 635)

The couple's sexual intercourse is supposed to be of itself a mutual self-giving, just as their marriage relationship is a mutual self-giving. It is this self-gift that is fundamental to one-flesh union, and which enables the same expression to be used to designate both sexual intercourse and the personal communion of marriage. But there are difficulties here, too. First, even if the same expression can with reason be used both of sexual intercourse and of marriage, that proves no organic connection between them; it does not show that they are in some deep sense the same thing, or that sexual inter-course 'actualizes' or 'realizes' the one-flesh union which is mar-riage. Part of the difficulty is that it is never spelt out what 'actualize' or 'realize' means in this context, and it is not easy to think of a suitable meaning. This language makes it sound as if outside the act of sexual intercourse the unity of the couple were only potential. But if the couple are deeply committed to each other, if in the way they live they give themselves to each other, then their union is already real and actual; it does not need to be actualized or realized. It may be that an act of sexual intercourse can express their personal union, be a physical sign of it, or in some way strengthen it, but that is a different thing. Secondly, if what is now fundamental to one-flesh union is supposed to be mutual self-gift, the concept appears to have shifted. It is no longer the fact that a man and a woman supposedly form part of a complete organism capable of reproduction which makes them one flesh, but their mutual self-gift. Nothing has been done to justify this shift, nor to show that there is in fact any connection between mutual self-gift and being elements of one organism capable of reproduction. Even if it could be demonstrated that there is an objective meaning in sexual intercourse, and that it is objectively a mutual self-donation of the partners, it would still have to be shown that this meaning depended on the procreative potential of sexual intercourse. The shift in the use of 'one-flesh union' makes it appear that this has already been done, or that it does not need to be done. But this is not so; the work needs to be done, and Grisez has not done it. There are also material rather than conceptual difficulties. Grisez here attempts an explanation of why sexual intercourse can express and deepen a married couple's interpersonal communion. Married couples do sometimes find that joint sexual activity is expressive of their mutual love, and that it is capable of strengthening that love. According to Grisez, it does so 'precisely because, when they willingly and lovingly cooperate with each other in an act of itself suited to procreating, their mutual self-giving actualizes their one-flesh unity'. Grisez here offers what appears to be at least in part an empirical hypothesis. There is an observed phenomenon – that married couples' relationships are strengthened by their sexual intercourse – and an explanation is offered for it – that such activity actualizes their one-flesh unity. But Grisez's position here, of course, depends on his idea of one-flesh unity, which is incoherent. Because there is no such thing as one-flesh unity in that, as Grisez understands it, this one-flesh unity is actualized by sexual intercourse, this cannot be the reason why a couple's relationship is expressed and deepened by sex, if it is. Further, Grisez's proffered explanation appears to confuse the psychological and the ontological, in the following sense. Grisez's idea of one-flesh union may be described as ontological, in that it attempts to show the existence of a kind of entity, the single organism capable of reproduction of which a man and woman who mate are allegedly parts. But a couple's personal communion, which might be described as mutual self-gift, is not a matter of their constituting together a single organism capable of reproduction; it is a matter very largely of their attitude towards each other, of their loving each other. It is their taking pleasure in each other's company. It is their wanting to be together and to do things great and small together: to raise children together, to work together for the relief of the needy, to go shopping together, to watch television together, to make love together, to suffer together, to celebrate together. It is their willingness to do things for each other, to carry each other's burdens, to make sacrifices, perhaps great sacrifices, for the sake of the other. It is their thinking of themselves as a couple, rather than as two separate individuals, thinking in terms of 'we' rather than 'I'. And so on. If a couple's sexual activity together strengthens their mutual self-gift, it can only be because it strengthens this attitude. If it expresses their mutual love, this can only be because they do love each other, and because they conceive of what they are doing as a loving activity – as making love. Grisez does not bridge this conceptual gap between the ontological and the psychological, and it is hard to see how he could. The failure to do so further vitiates his entire account of the place of sex in personal relationships. In particular, it substantiates the criticism that Grisez does indeed play on an ambiguity between different uses of the term 'one-flesh union'. While in the Bible and Christian tradition the term denotes a close personal communion, Grisez uses it also to denote his own confused idea of a mating couple as a single complete organism. He never succeeds in demonstrating a link between the two, but merely asserts it. In fact there cannot be a link between the two, for though it does make sense to talk of a close personal communion between two people, it does not make sense to speak of them as forming one complete organism.

In speaking of a gap between the psychological and the ontological, I am not of course relying on any discredited dualistic account of the human person of the kind often associated with the name of Descartes. I am in no sense trying to split off the psychological from the physical aspects of human life. If I speak of love as a series of attitudes and desires, this is not to speak of it as a putative feeling or feelings locked inside people's heads and divorced from their bodily activities in the real physical world. That is not what attitudes and desires are. An attitude, like a desire, expresses itself in what people actually do. My wanting to be with somebody is shown by my taking steps to be with him, if I can. If nothing hinders me from being with him, and if I do not put myself out to be with him, that shows that I do not really want to be with him, unless I want to be with somebody else more, or want to do something else more – and that again will be shown by what I do. Human psychological states are not in general locked away inside people's heads; they are visible in human acts. Grisez says that a married couple's love-making strengthens their personal communion if what they do is 'an act of itself suited to procreating'. Understood in one way this is quite unexceptionable. It is certainly true that if what a couple does together is a potentially reproductive act, this might deepen their relationship, their attitude of self-giving to each other. At least, there is no reason to believe that this is not so. The simple fact of doing things together can strengthen a couple's bonds. This can be doing the washing-up, going to a concert, or one of a multitude of everyday shared activities, including making love. There is no reason to believe that potentially reproductive acts do not also have this capacity to strengthen a relationship. And, of course, if a child results from the love-making this can be a source of great joy and can do much to cement the relationship between the two parents. But Grisez appears to mean something stronger than this. He seems to be saying, not that a sexual act which is potentially reproductive can strengthen the personal communion of the partners, but that its being potentially reproductive is a necessary condition of its ability to strengthen that communion. In other words, he is apparently claiming that love-making can strengthen communion only if that love-making consists in or includes an act which is potentially reproductive. If the couple merely kiss and caress each other, if they only stroke, kiss and lick each other's body, that has no tendency to express or strengthen their mutual love. If they carry out oral or anal intercourse, this cannot deepen their commitment to each other. If they carry out penile-vaginal intercourse which is not potentially reproductive because they use some method of contraception, that cannot actualize their one-flesh unity. What are we to make of this?

Once more, what appears to underlie this assertion – if I interpret Grisez correctly here – is his conception of one-flesh unity as two people forming one organism capable of reproduction. If what counts as actualizing one-flesh unity is coming together in such a way as to form this single reproductive organism is doing something that is potentially reproductive, then of course any activity which is not potentially reproductive will not make the couple into a one-flesh unity, by definition. Kissing and stroking, anal and oral intercourse, are simply not acts by which people reproduce, so they are irrelevant to Grisez's one-flesh unity. So is penile-vaginal intercourse in which use is made of contraception. According to Grisez's conception of one-flesh unity, there is only one kind of act by which it can be actualized, and that is a potentially reproductive sexual act. But Grisez's conception is, as we have seen, confused. The other varieties of sexual activity are made to look somehow defective because they do not fit Grisez's idea of one-flesh unity, but in reality it is Grisez's idea that is defective. This would not matter very much, except that, as we have already seen, Grisez also confuses, or illegitimately identifies, his own idea of one-flesh unity with the traditional Christian idea of marriage as one-flesh unity. This makes it look as if those sexual acts which are not suited to actualize Grisez's putative single reproductive organism are also incapable of expressing and strengthening that mutual commitment and self-giving which are essential to marriage. But he has actually given us no reason to believe that this is the case. As noted above, doing things together in general tends to strengthen bonds between people, including married couples. This is particularly true of pleasant activities performed together, for these are activities which make it pleasant to be together and reinforce each person's delight in the other. Delight can in its turn stimulate goodwill and commitment towards the object of delight. Now the joint sexual activity of two married people can be pleasant, and this can lead each one to delight further in the other and so to be more strongly bound to the other. This is true of any sexual activity which the couple find enjoyable, just because they find it enjoyable. There is therefore good reason to think that *any* sexual activity agreeable to both parties is capable of strengthening the mutual commitment of a married couple, for the same reason that any joint pleasant activity at all can strengthen it. On the other hand, there is no reason to believe that, as Grisez contends on the basis of his conflation of two distinct ideas of one-flesh unity, potentially reproductive sexual activity is the only kind of sexual activity that can strengthen the bonds between two people, their mutual love, their mutual commitment, their mutual self-gift. Sexual activities which are not potentially reproductive may, of course, still be morally objectionable on other grounds, but their being incapable of expressing and strengthening married love is not such a ground. One further point: Grisez speaks here of the sexual activity of a married couple.

This is natural, because it is his chief concern to find an adequate characterization of sex within the marriage relationship. But in the above discussion the marital status of the couple involved plays no part in the argument. If joint activity, including sexual activity which is not potentially reproductive, is capable of expressing and strengthening the mutual commitment of two married people who love each other, it can also express and strengthen the mutual commitment of two unmarried people who love each other. Unmarried people, like married people, can love each other. They can live together and share their lives in all the ways that married people can. They too can and do share together the joys and difficulties of life. They too can co-operate in projects greats and small, such as cleaning the house, having and raising children, working for the relief of the needy. They too can and do make sacrifices for each other. They too can and do delight in each other, and that delight, and the bond of their love, can be expressed and strengthened in their sexual activity together, regardless of whether that activity is potentially reproductive or not. The Christian tradition affirms that sex is legitimate only within marriage, and there may indeed be good reasons why unmarried people should not have sex together. But that their sexual activity cannot express and deepen their mutual love and self-giving is not such a reason.

Homosexuality

After this admittedly long preamble, we are ready to look at Grisez's account of the morality of gay sex. The preamble has been necessary, for Grisez's attitude to homosexual activity is closely linked to his account of sex in general, and depends heavily on it. His basic objection is as follows:

> the coupling of two bodies of the same sex cannot form one complete organism and so cannot contribute to a bodily communion of persons. Hence, the experience of intimacy of the partners in sodomy cannot be the experience of any real unity between them. Rather, each one's experience of intimacy is private and incommunicable, and is no more a common good than is the mere experience of sexual arousal and orgasm. Therefore, the choice to engage in sodomy for the sake of that experience of intimacy in no way contributes to the partners' real common good as committed friends. (p. 653)

We see at once that this objection, like so much else in Grisez's thought on sex, is based on his conception of one-flesh unity: the sexual coupling of two bodies of the same sex 'cannot form one complete organism'. The idea seems to be that, since same-sex coupling is necessarily non-procreative, two men or two women together cannot form a single organism capable of reproduction. But, once again, this idea of one complete organism does not make sense. It is true that two male bodies coupling or two female bodies[8] coupling cannot form one complete organism, but this is not because their sexual activity is of its nature non-reproductive but because no pair of bodies, in whatever sexual combination, could conceivably do so. The idea that they might is confused. Thus Grisez's principal objection against homosexual activity falls to the ground.

Grisez claims that two people of the same sex having sex together cannot contribute to a 'bodily communion of persons'. If this is simply equivalent to saying that they cannot form a complete organism, it gets us no further. But even if Grisez's conception of one-flesh unity were intelligible and correct, so that two men together did not form a complete organism in the way that a married couple could, it would by no means follow that their sexual activity did not contribute to a bodily communion of persons. That would follow only if forming the putative single organism were the only way in which there could be a bodily communion of persons, and Grisez has not attempted to show this. Since in fact this single organism is a confused idea, it follows that either there is no bodily communion of persons at all, not even of married couples, or there must be a different form of bodily communion. If there is none, then that gay sex is not a form of bodily communion is no objection to it; if there is another form, it remains a possibility that it is something available to a same-sex couple. If Grisez did not want to deny that any bodily communion of persons at all is possible, he would have to argue that such bodily communion as exists is not available to two people of the same sex. But this would be a difficult thing to show. It would be natural to say, if we wanted to give a sense to the expression 'bodily communion', that any intimate embrace of two people who loved each other, whatever their sex, constituted a bodily communion.

The experience of intimacy

But Grisez does have an argument here. What he wants to say is that sex should be an intimate bodily communion *of persons*. It is not enough that it should be a coupling of bodies; it should in some way also be a genuine meeting, a joining of the people involved, of which the sexual intimacy is the bodily image and expression. We may well, if we are Christian, have sympathy with this position. But we now have to ask: why should we think that a sexual encounter of two people of the same sex cannot be a genuine meeting of the two men or two women involved, a genuine experience of intimacy between them? why cannot their sexual embrace be the embodiment of personal communion? Grisez has an answer to this: 'the experience of intimacy of the partners ... cannot be the experience of any real unity between them ... [E]ach one's experience of intimacy is private and incommunicable, and is no more a common good than is the mere experience of sexual arousal and orgasm.' There appear to be two separate arguments here, or an argument in two stages. First, Grisez claims that the experience of intimacy that each one has is not an experience of any real unity. Presumably, the reason why this is so is that there is no real unity between them to experience. If there were a real unity between them, it would be difficult to see why the mere fact of their both being of the same sex should debar each one of them from experiencing it. Secondly, he claims that each one's experience of intimacy is 'private and incommunicable' and so is not a common good. This appears to be an argument rather from the nature of experience. Let us look at each of them in turn.

First, the argument that the experience of the partners cannot be the experience of any real unity between them. First of all, we can ask why the experience of each partner *should* be an experience of real unity between them, and if so in what sense. Take the example of two men having sex together. If their experience in doing this cannot be one of real unity between them, why not? I have suggested that this must be because, according to Grisez, there is no real unity between them to experience. But now this raises the question what counts as real unity. What is the unity that two men cannot have, and what makes it legitimate to describe this unity as the only real one that can exist between two people? Suppose they live together, and have done so for thirty years. They have pooled all their wealth and belongings and equally pool all their income. They have helped each other through sufferings of various kinds, physical and spiritual. They share their daily household tasks. They are attentive to each other's needs and preferences, delighting to please each other. They have both on occasion made serious sacrifices for the other. Jointly and individually they are also attentive to the needs of those less fortunate than themselves. They share their joys and sorrows with each other. They like to spend their time as much as possible in each other's company. They delight in each other. In short, they love each other with a real and solid love, a love that shows itself in their day-to-day living. We might say that they live together like a happily married couple. Let us imagine that they have even publicly, before an assembly composed of family and friends, promised to remain faithful to each other and to care for each other until death. They also have a sexual relationship, and throughout the time they have known each other they have kept their relationship sexually exclusive. Now, what kind of unity do these men lack? Biologically, they are incapable, through their sexual activity together, of generating new life. That is an obvious difference – indeed, the only obvious difference – between them and a fertile heterosexual couple; but it is far from obvious why that difference should be thought to constitute a lack of real unity between them. On the other hand, their shared life, their mutual self-giving, their solid mutual love, would most naturally be thought just what constitutes their real unity. They will know that, biologically, they are incapable of generating a child by their love-making, but again it is hard to see why that knowledge should prevent it from being an expression of their mutual love, or from being experienced by them as such.

Grisez appears to admit that real love – and so real unity – can exist between two men who have a sexual relationship. He says: 'it is true that partners in sodomy also could conceivably share in a committed relationship with sincere mutual affection and express their feelings in ways that would be appropriate in any friendship' (*ibid.*). He may also believe – apparently in common with the majority of Christians – that sexual intimacy is not an expression of mutual affection which is appropriate between two men. But even if it is true that it is not, it is as yet hard to see why, if two men do express their mutual affection in this way, they do not experience any real unity; for there is a real unity between them. It is here that Grisez's second argument seems to come into play. The reason why there is no experience of real unity is, apparently, that the experience that each one has while they are making love is 'private and incommunicable'. This, according to Grisez, implies that the experience is not a common good. Grisez does not explain what he means by experiences being private and incommunicable, but the easiest interpretation is that he is alluding to and basing himself on the philosophical theory of the privacy of sensations.[9] According to this theory, the sensations that each person has are private in the sense that nobody else has access to them, nobody else can experience them. You and I can taste the same ice cream, but I cannot have your sensation of taste, and you cannot have mine. Your sensation cannot be transferred to me, nor mine to you. I cannot taste what the ice cream tastes like to you, and you cannot taste what it tastes like to me. My taste sensation is accessible only to me, and is in that sense private. And that means there is something we cannot know. It is possible that the same ice cream tastes quite different to you and to me. We have no way of knowing. We can of course both give descriptions of how it tastes, and if our descriptions agree – say, if we both said 'It tastes like lemon' – we would normally say that it tastes the same to both of us. But, for all we know, the sensation that you call 'the taste of lemon' might be quite different from what I call 'the taste of lemon'. Thus, according to this theory, our sensations are in a real sense private and incommunicable. This theory of sensation is highly controversial and, according to many, discredited. But suppose it were true. What then? Why should it be thought to have any particular consequences for same-sex activity? After all, if the experiences of partners to same-sex activity are private and incommunicable, so are the experiences of partners to mixed-sex activity, including the intercourse of married couples; indeed, so are the experiences of anybody at all doing anything whatsoever. It does not seem, then, that this theory can provide a moral objection against same-sex activity in particular. Whether or not it makes sense to say that, when we share the same ice cream, your sensation and my sensation are private and incommunicable, there remains something in the situation that is perfectly public and communicable: we are both sharing the same ice cream. In that sense, we are both having, indeed both sharing, the same experience, namely, the experience of sharing and tasting the same ice cream. While it might be possible to claim that our experiences, in the sense of our physical sensations, are private and incommunicable (though, it should be said again, this is a very dubious theory in itself), our experience, in the sense of what we are having an experience of, is perfectly public and communicable. In fact, almost all ordinary talk of experience is talk of what is public and accessible. When people recount their experiences, say of a holiday, car crash, or sexual encounter, what they recount is what they have done and what has happened to them, and these are events and situations which are in principle public and accessible, events and situations that might be experienced and shared by others. In the same way, when two people, be they two men, two women or a man and a woman, have sex together, they share a perfectly public and communicable experience, namely their joint sexual activity. What they want is to share this experience; they do not want to have private, incommunicable sensations, if such things exist. They want to do *this* together, just as they might want to play tennis together. And what they enjoy is doing this together, just as they might enjoy playing tennis together.[10] Their sexual activity together is a perfectly good shared experience, which they have and enjoy together.

Grisez seems to want to say that what Christopher and David enjoy about their sexual activity together is their respective orgasms, plus perhaps some other pleasant sensations; and it is these sensations that are supposed to be private and incommunicable; their experience is reducible to their sensations. What is wrong with this account is not only that sensations are not private and incommunicable. More importantly, it will not do also as an account of why they have sex together. If what was important to them were their respective orgasms, they might more easily and with less fuss both masturbate in private. To account for their having sex together we have to suppose at the very least that they both want sexual contact with another person; and it is that contact that forms an essential part of their enjoyment. That enjoyment cannot be reduced to the having of sensations. It has an essentially cognitive element. If Christopher wants and enjoys sexual contact with another person, then his enjoyment depends on his believing that he is in fact having sexual contact with another person. If we suppose that Christopher loves David, and that part of his love is a commitment to sexual fidelity, then an essential part of Christopher's enjoyment of this sexual encounter is that his partner in the activity is David; so that if it should turn out that he is the victim of an elaborate hoax and the man in bed with him is not David, his enjoyment will cease and possibly turn to revulsion. Assuming it really is David, another essential element of Christopher's enjoyment will be the belief that this joint activity which he is enjoying is also enjoyable to David; because he loves him, he wants this to be an enjoyable experience for him, just as he would want a shared meal or game of tennis or visit to the cinema to be an enjoyable experience for him. As well as doing things he enjoys during this encounter, he will do things he hopes David enjoys, and he will enjoy being a source of pleasure for David. If David does things that give pleasure to Christopher, Christopher will hope that David enjoys doing them. If David enjoys certain things that Christopher does not enjoy so much doing, Christopher will do them for the sake of David. If he realizes that David is in fact not enjoying the encounter, his own enjoyment will die. (If he really does not care whether David is enjoying it, and is just intent on his own enjoyment, this is evidence that he does not love David after all.) And the same of course goes for David. If this is an activity of two men who love each other, then their enjoyment is essentially a shared enjoyment. It is thus quite false to claim, as Grisez does, that in any same-sex activity the parties involved are necessarily imprisoned in their own private sensations. It is even more wrong to turn this supposed isolation into an accusation of selfishness, as does Melina, who writes: 'In the homosexual act ... each one of the partners remains locked in himself and experiences his contact with the other's body merely as an opportunity for selfish enjoyment'.[11] This not only compounds Grisez's mistake by confusing epistemology with ethics, but is a calumny against those homosexuals who have sex within a loving relationship. Melina may well think they ought not to be doing this, but he has no justification at all for this accusation of selfishness.

Let us try another tack, and suppose that Grisez's real objection to same-sex activity has nothing to do with experience in the putative sense of private sensations, but rather with experience in the sense of a public object of experience. What he is objecting to is not that the sensations of partners in same-sex activity are private, but that an object of experience which ought to be there is not there: that there is no real unity between them which they might experience when they have sex together. Since there is no real unity between them, no real unity can be experienced, and the attempt to have this experience in sexual activity is doomed to failure. Any experience of unity they might have must be illusory. If this is the sense of Grisez's argument, it is intelligible, but it is also false. For we have already seen that what Grisez thinks is the only real unity available – his version of one-flesh unity – is itself an illusion; and we have also seen that other kinds of genuine unity are available to same-sex couples. If sexual intercourse is properly described as an experience of real unity, that experience can be had by same-sex couples. They are not necessarily suffering from an illusion if they experience their sex in that way, and if they have sex in order to have that experience, the attempt is not doomed to failure. But we might also ask why it should be thought that people, straight or gay, married or single, always have sex together because they are seeking an experience of unity. Grisez has given us no reason why we should believe this, and it appears obviously false. First, people have sex for many different reasons. Secondly, it is not at all clear what an experience of unity, purportedly had in married sexual intercourse, might be, unless it is something like this: that the couple, bound together by a deep mutual commitment which expresses itself in the way they go about their daily lives, perceive their sexual activity as something which expresses the bonds between them. If that is what is meant, then such an experience is not unavailable to same-sex couples, for same-sex couples also can be bound together by a deep mutual commitment, and can perceive their sexual activity as expressing and strengthening the bonds between them.

Grisez believes he knows why same-sex couples engage in sex; sex is not chosen as a means of communicating goodwill and affection, but 'because it provides subjective satisfactions otherwise unavailable' (p. 654). He has, of course, no justification for this belief, and no right to impute motives in a generalizing way to a whole class of people he does not know and has not asked about their motives. Nevertheless, his unwarranted belief that he knows why same-sex couples have sex furnishes him, so he thinks, with another argument against same-sex activity. In their sexual activity they 'choose to use their own and each other's bodies to provide subjective satisfactions, and thus they choose self-disintegrity as masturbators do' (*ibid.*). This objection depends in part on Grisez's concepts of self-integrity and self-disintegrity, but it is not necessary to go into this area in order to understand the basis of his argument. In comparing same-sex couples with those who masturbate, he refers to an argument adduced elsewhere against masturbation. That argument runs as follows:

> In choosing to actuate one's sexual capacity in order to have the conscious experience of the process and its culmination, one chooses to use one's body as an instrument to bring about that experience in the conscious self. Thus, the body becomes an instrument used and the conscious self its user. In most cases, using one's body as an instrument is not problematic. This is done when one works and plays, and also when one commu-

nicates, using the tongue to speak, the finger to point, the genitals to engage in marital intercourse. In such cases the body functions as part of oneself, serving the whole and sharing in the resulting benefits. By contrast, in choosing to masturbate, one does not choose to act for a goal which fulfills oneself as a unified, bodily person. The only immediate goal is satisfaction for the conscious self; and so the body, not being part of the whole for whose sake the act is done, serves only as an extrinsic instrument. Thus, in choosing to masturbate one chooses to alienate one's body from one's conscious subjectivity. (p. 650)

The gist of this argument is that one who masturbates does so for the sake of a 'conscious experience of the process and its culmination'. But this means using the body as an instrument to bring about the experience in the 'conscious self'. This is not a goal of the 'unified, bodily person'. The activity treats the body as an extrinsic instrument, alienating the body from one's conscious subjectivity. This is what masturbation does, and it is also what same-sex activity does, according to Grisez.

Now it is certainly possible to understand the idea of being alienated from one's own body, in the sense of disliking one's own body, having contempt for it, feeling ill at ease with it, or wishing one had a more beautiful body, a stronger body, or no body at all. But that is not the sort of thing Grisez appears to have in mind. He does not appear to be arguing that masturbation leads one to dislike one's body or to have contempt for it or to be ill at ease in it. If he were arguing this, he would be putting forward an empirical hypothesis which could be confirmed or falsified by scientific investigation. It would seem then prima facie to be a false hypothesis, since there is no particular evidence that those who masturbate dislike their own bodies or have contempt for them or feel ill at ease in them more than do those who do not masturbate. Neither does it seem possible to argue that an act of masturbation is in and of itself an act of contempt for the body, or an expression of dislike for the body. Any particular act can only be an act of contempt for anything if the agent in fact has contempt for that thing. If he has, this will express itself in the wider pattern of his behaviour. Suppose Peter has contempt for his body. We can imagine ways in which he may express this contempt. He may speak contemptuously of his body, to himself and/or to others; he may look contemptuously at his body when he examines it; he may take no care over his bodily hygiene, his bodily posture, or how he clothes or adorns his body. He may take no care over his diet, or he may deliberately starve himself to make himself emaciated or gorge himself to make himself fat. Importantly, when asked if he has contempt for his body, he will, if he answers sincerely, reply affirmatively. Having this sort of behaviour pattern, perhaps with accompanying characteristic feelings, is what it is to have contempt for one's body. No doubt masturbation can form part of such a pattern; perhaps, when some people masturbate, that is an expression of contempt for their body. If Peter masturbates, some may suspect that this is an indication that Peter does indeed have contempt for his body. But suppose observation shows that Peter appreciates his body, that he takes care over his appearance, his diet, his health, and so on; suppose that Peter when asked if he has contempt for his body, replies sincerely 'No, of course not', then his masturbation is not an expression of contempt for his body. But it seems to me that Grisez's argument is more philosophical in nature; the alienation of which he writes is not a form of dislike or contempt, but a kind of 'existential dualism between the body and the conscious self, that is, a division between the two insofar as they are coprinciples of oneself considered as an integrated, acting, sexual person' (p. 650). This language is somewhat opaque. In particular, it is not at all clear what an 'existential dualism' is meant to be. Neither is it clear what Grisez means by 'conscious self', unless it is simply the person who is acting, and who is therefore conscious. Grisez himself is clear that one cannot divide up the human agent in this way, between body and conscious self. Nor does he give any clear account of how such 'existential dualism' might be possible, or of why one who masturbates might be guilty of such dualism. He claims that 'in choosing to masturbate, one does not choose to act for a goal which fulfills oneself as a unified, bodily person. The only immediate goal is satisfaction for the conscious self; and so the body, not being part of the whole for whose sake the act is done, serves only as an extrinsic instrument.' But there is no reason to believe any of this.

To begin with, neither Grisez nor anybody else has any right to speak of another's immediate goals in this way. If Peter masturbates, his immediate goal may be to gain a certain temporary fulfilment, it may be to get an orgasm, it may be to amuse an onlooker whom he wishes to amuse, it may be so that a photographer can get a photo of him masturbating, or it may be to procure semen for the purposes of artificial insemination or some other purpose, or it may be to calm himself before gambling, or it may be to express his disagreement with or contempt for those who say he should not masturbate. And so on. Human beings are complicated creatures, and we do the simplest-looking things for very diverse and complicated reasons. We just cannot impute goals without further ado, as Grisez does here. In order to understand why people do things we have to look at the wider pattern of their behaviour; and we can also in many cases find out by asking them why they do what they do. Secondly, there is, as Grisez himself is keen to affirm, no such thing as a conscious self, unless by this is meant simply a person who is not unconscious, or a person who is aware of what he or she is doing. Now it may be the case that Peter masturbates not for any complicated reason, but just because he wants the pleasant complex of feelings that an orgasm gives him and the temporary satisfaction that masturbation will bring.[12] Where is the existential dualism here? He is a conscious agent, and he is aware of what he is doing. The satisfaction he wants is not for any putative conscious self, but simply for himself. He is a bodily being acting bodily on himself in order to satisfy himself. This no more implies a dualism than when an itchy Peter scratches himself in order to procure the satisfaction that comes from that activity. Masturbation might be wrong for other reasons, but not for this one. I have not gone into the question of the appropriateness of the analogy that Grisez draws between same-sex activity and masturbation. Even if that analogy is sustainable, Grisez's argument shows us nothing about the moral status of masturbation; so it shows us nothing about the moral status of same-sex activity, either. Grisez has failed, then, to produce any reason why we should think that one who masturbates goes through a process of self-alienation. Still less has he given us any reason to think that homosexuals having sex together are as such comparable to one who masturbates. In the end, he has produced no reason at all for saying that homosexual acts are morally defective. The principal cause for this, of course, is his reliance on his concept of a 'one-flesh union', which turned out to be simply incoherent. But if Grisez falls, then so do those who imitate and rely upon him, of whom I quoted some examples at the beginning of this chapter.

Meaning

A glance back at those quotations will show that meaning is an important idea in these new approaches to sexuality in general and homosexuality in particular. Sexual acts are deemed to have a certain meaning objectively and inherently, because God created people with a certain sexual nature. Just because this meaning is effectively created by God, it must be respected. Two more quotations will be useful here, both taken from the article of Melina we looked at earlier.

> Human sexuality is included in that primordial and good plan of God the Creator, who called man and woman with their reciprocal complementarity to be an image of his own love and responsible collaborators in the procreation of new individuals. Therefore, objective meanings are inherent in the physical acts related to sexuality and represent as many calls to achieve the person's moral good.

Sometimes, Melina treats this divinely imparted meaning as equivalent to a divinely created symbolism:

> Through the symbolism of the sexual difference which marks their bodily nature, man and woman are called to achieve two closely connected values: 1) the gift of self and the acceptance of the other in an indissoluble union (*una caro*), and 2) openness to the transmission of life. Only in the context of legitimate marriage are these values proper to sexuality adequately respected and achieved.

What are we to make of this claim that sexual intercourse has an objective or inherent meaning? A number of question arise here.

First, what is the kind of objectivity being attributed to this putative meaning? The claim appears to be that this meaning inheres in sexual intercourse simply because God put it there. God, by creating people male and female, or perhaps by some connected creative act, brought it about that this meaning inheres in sexual intercourse. God put the meaning there, and it is up to human beings to recognize and understand that meaning, and to behave in a way that reflects their understanding. If human beings act otherwise, that shows that they misunderstand what sex is really about. Whether the meaning is in fact recognized by all human beings is another question. But its having this meaning is not dependent on all human beings recognizing it; indeed, it is one of the troubles with sexually active homosexuals, among others, that they do not recognize the objective meaning of sexual intercourse.

We may go further and say that since the meaning depends on God, and not on human beings, sexual intercourse would objectively have the meaning it does even if no human beings at all recognized that meaning. This way of putting the matter is heavily theocentric. It puts God at the centre of our understanding of what sexual activity is about. In one way, this is very attractive, for how could any serious Christian not want to have God at the centre of his or her life? In the same way, Christians are dedicated to following the will of God in all things. But there are also grave difficulties in this way of thinking about the objectivity of sexual meanings.

We can see this by asking in what sense meanings in general may be said to be objective. In speaking about sexual intercourse as having a meaning, an analogy is clearly being made with language: as words, phrases and sentences have meaning, so too, it is claimed, do human actions, and particularly sexual intercourse. But now, in what sense can words be said to have a meaning which is objective? The answer seems fairly straightforward: if I am, say, an English-speaker, the meaning of my words does not simply depend on what I want them to mean. In that sense, the meaning of my words is not something subjective. The words together with their meanings are given me, objectively, in the English language. Understanding the meaning of a word comes down to knowing how to the use the word correctly; I show that I understand a word in using it correctly, and if I use it incorrectly, that reveals that I do not understand it properly. In learning that language as a child, I learnt how to use the words correctly. That is to say, there were objective criteria of correct usage – criteria which overruled my personal judgement – and my use of the language was judged – by others – according to those criteria. Now that I have more or less mastered the language, my mastery is shown by the fact that I in general use English words correctly, and that means according to objective criteria, not simply according to my own judgement. In my use of English I am subject to the judgement of others. This must be so, for the point of my speaking English is to communicate in various ways with the English-speaking people around me, and unless I use words in substantially the same way as the linguistic community to which I belong, I will fail to communicate; they will not understand me. Similarly, if I do not use words in the same way as they do, I will not understand them when they speak to me. There must therefore be, in any linguistic community, implicit or even explicit rules governing the use of words by all members of that community, rules which are imparted and assimilated in the teaching and learning of the language. Individuals cannot be free to determine the meaning of the words they use, otherwise the linguistic community will collapse. 'When *I* use a word', Humpty Dumpty says, 'it means just what I choose it to mean – neither more nor less.'[13] But Humpty Dumpty can only assert this at the cost of being unintelligible. If his hearers take him seriously, they will not know what he means by 'word', 'mean', 'use', and so on. Indeed, they cannot take him seriously, for they can only understand him to be saying something if they assume that the sounds he is uttering are words in a rule-governed language.[14] If Humpty Dumpty's words are to *have* meaning, they must also *convey* meaning; they must be intelligible by competent users of the language. A word that does not convey meaning does not have meaning, either; and that means it is not a word. The meaning of a word, though it does not depend on any individual member of a linguistic community, does depend on usage within that community. This means two things. First, that a word has meaning presupposes the existence of a linguistic community in which it has meaning; there can be no meaning without a linguistic community. Secondly, while members of a community who have not sufficiently mastered the language may get the meaning of a particular word in the community's language wrong, it is not possible that *everybody* in that community gets it wrong. It is possible, for instance, that certain English speakers do not know the meaning of the word 'dormitory', and use it wrongly when they try to use it. But it is not possible that *all* speakers of English misuse the word, or do not know what it means. If the sound 'dormitory' were not understood by any English speakers, that would mean that it was not a word in the English language. If all English speakers thought 'dormitory' a meaningless sound, then it would be a meaningless sound (unless it had a use in some other language); it would not be a meaningful word in English. Put simply, a sound has a meaning in a linguistic community if the members of that community say it does, and it has the meaning they say it has. There is no such thing as the 'true' meaning of a word independent of the meaning ascribed to it by the community in whose language the word has a use. A word cannot have an objective meaning in this sense; rather to try to speak of objective meaning in this way is to fail to give the word 'objective' any sense.

Theologians who talk about sex having a meaning want to say that, just as words communicate and have meaning, so too do human acts, particularly human sexual acts. The idea that acts can have a meaning is readily intelligible. We can easily think of examples of human acts which convey a meaning. For example, if a cyclist cycling on public roads raises her right arm sideways, that means she is about to move right – to turn right or to move into a right-hand lane. That this act has a meaning depends, like a word's having meaning, on there being a community that uses this bodily movement as a sign; its having meaning depends on its conveying meaning to other road users. And the meaning that gesture has does not depend on the meaning she wants it to have; its meaning depends on the use it has in the road-using community. In that sense, the meaning of her action is objective, just as are the meanings of the words she uses when she speaks English. The meaning is not intrinsic to the bodily movement itself. Make the same bodily movement outside the context of road travel, and it means anything or nothing. The same person who raises her right arm sideways while sitting on the sofa at home watching television does not mean that she is about to turn right or move into a right-hand lane. She does not mean anything at all by it, unless she has established a convention with other members of her household about what that gesture is to mean in the context of the home.

The meanings of words are, then, not dependent on the will of the individual who uses them, but on the community of whose language the words are part. In this sense, words have objective meanings, objective rules governing their use. And we can understand how actions such as road signals can have objective meaning in a similar way. We could easily imagine how certain sexual activities could have a meaning in a particular society. We could imagine, for instance, that in a certain society, in which women could be considered the property of men, a man's penetrating a woman could signal his asserting possession of that woman, as his wife or as a slave. That is, members of the society would understand a man's penetrating a woman as his asserting possession of her. If the man himself were a member of this society, or familiar with its ways, he would know that it would be so understood; he could, and in normal circumstances would, intend his act to be understood in this way, because in being taught the ways of that society he will have been taught that this is what such an act means. We could imagine a society in which a man's letting himself being anally penetrated by another man was a way of identifying himself as having a particular social status. We could imagine a society in which a man's sucking another man's penis was considered a sign of respect for that man and an expression of the desire to be filled with that man's virtues. We could imagine a society in which for a man and a woman to have vaginal intercourse was a sign of deep mutual love and a commitment to share their life until death. If we can imagine different societies in which sex means different things, we can also imagine a society in which the significance of sex changes. Just as the meanings of words change over time in the same society, as people come to use words in changing ways, so the meanings of human acts can change with changing institutions and habits. We can imagine, too, people in the same society fighting over the meaning of sexual activity, just as they fight over the use of words. Things which have meanings, like words and symbols, have an importance to people; they often don't like it when the words and symbols to which they are accustomed lose their meaning, or when others use them in different ways and therefore attach to them a different meaning. Sometimes, people who find certain words and symbols emblematic of a community they find oppressive or benighted deliberately set out to change the way they are used, or urge that they be abandoned altogether. Sex is no exception to this common phenomenon. People can and do fight over what sex means, and so where and when sex is appropriate; the Christian churches are party to this struggle.

The imaginary society which views PVI as a sign of deep mutual commitment has a view of PVI very close to modern Christian views. If a man and a woman had PVI, members of such a society would understand their action as showing that they loved each other deeply, and would take it as a pledge to live together until death. The man and the woman, if they were members of that society or familiar with its ways, would know that their act would be so understood; they would in normal circumstances intend it to be so understood, by each other and by the wider society, because in being taught that society's ways they will have been taught that this is what such an act means. We can easily imagine such a society. Indeed, it is just such a society that many Christians would want to see. Such a society would be so structured that, unlike in biblical, classical and many modern societies, the act of sexually penetrating another would not signify that the other belonged to one, it would signify that one gave oneself to the other, that one belonged to the other; and allowing oneself to be penetrated by another would signify, not that one became the other's property, but that one entered freely into a relationship of mutual self-donation. And in such a society the way people were taught about sex, the meanings people were taught to invest in sex, would reflect the same values. One could say that, in such a society, sexual activity would have an objective meaning, and one similar to the objective meaning of which people like Melina, Grisez and others talk. But, though the meaning would be similar, the objectivity would not. The kind of objectivity I have been describing depends on a community. This is not the kind of objectivity of meaning ascribed to sexual activity by the thinkers cited above. For them, the putative objective meaning of sexual activity is supposed to be inherent in it, independent of the existence of any community which understands sexual activity to have that meaning. For them, it is just because it really does have this meaning that there is a moral obligation on all societies so to structure themselves and so to teach that their members will think – rightly – that it does have this meaning. It is supposed to have this meaning just because that is the sort of thing sex is, because that is the way God has created it. Indeed, proponents of the theory of the objective meaning of sex need to hold that sex has this meaning even if it bears that meaning in *no* human society, even if *no* human beings recognize its meaning, even if they all think it a meaningless activity or get its meaning wrong. For, according to this theory, the meaning of sex depends *only* on the creative will of God. Sex has this meaning just as a pebble lying at the bottom of the ocean has a certain shape even if nobody knows it; that's just how it is. Even if it is claimed that in fact some human beings do realize the true meaning of sex – these will include Christians who adhere to the theory here being proposed – the meaning of sex cannot depend on this recognition. On the contrary, the claim is that those who know the true meaning of sex recognize a meaning that exists independently of them. In theory, all human beings could get the meaning of sex wrong. All human beings could fail to understand that meaning, but it would still be the true, objective meaning of sex. It would, in those circumstances, have a meaning without actually conveying a meaning to anybody. But that is impossible, for to have a meaning is to convey a meaning. The supposed meaning of sex is just not a meaning at all. Meanings do not inhere in things, independently of communities. Meanings are about human understanding and human communication, and that depends on there being a community. God cannot simply plant a meaning in a human activity, or create an activity which objectively has a certain meaning. This is not a limitation on the power of God; it is because of the sort of thing a meaning is. God cannot endow sex with a meaning just as he cannot create a square circle, not because it is a very difficult task, but because there is no such task. *Pace* Melina, it is not the case that 'objective meanings are inherent in the physical acts related to sexuality' as a result of a 'primordial and good plan of God the Creator'. Melina finds in human sexual activity two principal meanings – gift of self and openness to procreation – and he is certainly not alone in this. But these meanings do not and cannot inhere in human sexual activity because of the creative activity of God. Conceived in the way that Melina wants, these meanings just are not and cannot be there. It is therefore not the case, as he claims, that same-sex activity is an 'intrinsic contradiction to the abovementioned meanings', for there are no such meanings to contradict.

Melina's language is closely related to that of *HP*, which claims that the human body has a 'spousal significance',[15] and relates this putative significance to 'the theology of creation we find in Genesis' (*ibid.*) We have already seen that the theology of creation he says is there is in fact not to be found. But even if it were, that would not justify the idea that there is any intrinsic meaning to be found in the human body or in human acts, for that idea is untenable and unjustifiable. It therefore cannot be true, either, that, as *HP* goes on to assert, 'to choose someone of the same sex for one's sexual activity is to annul the rich symbolism and meaning, not to mention the goals, of the Creator's sexual design' (§7). None of the foregoing argument has the least tendency to show that Melina does not have the right to claim that sexual activity means certain things, that it is a kind of self-gift and signifies openness to procreation. It does not show that *HP* is not entitled to say that the body has a spousal significance. We can understand them as taking one side in a struggle over sexual meanings, over against those who have a different view of sex, in particular against those who approve of same-sex activity. My argument is not that they have no right to take the position they do, but that the alleged theoretical justification for that position – that there are inherent meanings in human sexual activity as a result of God's plan in creation – is no justification at all, but a piece of conceptual confusion. The theory of inherent meanings is muddled and cannot furnish an argument against same-sex activity. Sexual acts are indeed capable of bearing meaning. But meaning is a human affair, a result of human social structures and of human conventions. To try to ground the meaning of sexual activity in the creative activity of God is to make a fundamental mistake.

Conclusion

We have been concerned almost entirely with modern arguments about mostly male homosexuality centred on the Bible and medieval and modern arguments drawn from natural law. In each case arguments current in the Roman Catholic Church have been the centre of attention. Even within these limits, the survey can hardly be said to be complete. I have not tried to examine all the current arguments, but only the most important and the best ones. This sacrifice of breadth has enabled us to see in greater depth into the merits and defects of each particular argument.

If we summarize the results of our investigation, the conclusions are simple to state and substantiate the thesis put forward in the preface: if we look for cogent biblical or natural-law arguments against homosexual relationships and acts in general, we will not find them: there aren't any. There are plenty which look faithful to Scripture and compelling in their logic, but none which actually are. We must be careful in assessing what this conclusion does and does not entail. It does not entail that it is good to be gay and that Christian moral teachers who teach otherwise are wrong. It entails only that there is no good reason for thinking otherwise. Somebody may yet discover a cogent proof for the immorality of homosexuality, but if the application of fine minds has not discovered one after all this time, we are entitled to think that there is no such argument to be found.

But the aim of this book has not been to show that it is very probably good to be gay. Remember that at the end of Chapter 1 we were left with a devout Christian, Christopher, who had reason, from his own experience and observation, to think there was potentially some good to be had in certain kinds of homosexual relationship and the sexual activities these involve. Does Christopher, on the basis of modern Christian teaching on the subject, drawn from Scripture and natural law, have any good reason for rejecting his former belief and embracing what the church says? The answer has be to negative. Christopher has reason to believe that homosexual acts are sometimes morally right. Modern church

281

teaching and theologians who support it have, we have found, produced no sound reason for thinking the contrary. So they furnish Christopher with no sound reason for thinking the contrary either. To change his belief would be to believe contrary to the grounds of his present belief, but also without countervailing grounds; it would be to believe irrationally.

The conclusion of this book is, therefore, not that it is good to be gay, but that it is irrational for serious, reflective Christians in Christopher's position to accept church teaching on homosexuality. This is in itself a serious conclusion, for there are clearly many such Christians; that is why the debate exists within the churches in the first place. The only rational course at the moment for such Christians is to continue to believe in the possible goodness of homosexual relationships. This is not a matter of dissent or materialism; it is simply that the church at the moment produces no good arguments to assent to. Regrettably, in this area, the church teaches badly.

Notes

Preface

1. Henceforth I often refer to this as 'the Catholic church', or even 'the Church'. This is not meant to give offence to members of other churches, including those which think of themselves as Catholic. It is merely for the sake of brevity.

Introduction

1. The 1986 Letter of the Vatican's Congregation for the Doctrine of the Faith *Homosexualitatis Problema* later in this book referred to as *HP*.

Chapter one

1. For example, the document *Homosexualitatis Problema*, issued by the Vatican's Congregation for the Doctrine of the Faith in 1986, and published in English as *Letter ... on the Pastoral Care of Homosexual Persons*, says:

    > It is deplorable that homosexual persons have been and are the object of violent malice in speech or in action. Such treatment deserves condemnation from the Church's pastors wherever it occurs. It reveals a kind of disregard for others which endangers the most fundamental principles of a healthy society. The intrinsic dignity of each person must always be respected in word, in action and in law. (§10)

2. Richard B. Hays, *The Moral Vision of the New Testament: A Contemporary Introduction to New Testament Ethics*, New York, HarperCollins, 1996, p. 402.
3. See, Ephesians 5:25–32
4. The relationship between the two lovers in The Song of Songs has in Christian tradition been seen as symbolizing both the love between Christ and the church and the love between Creator and creature. For a short overview of Christian interpretation of the work, see Marvin H. Pope, *Song of Songs*, New York, Doubleday, 1977, pp. 112–32.
5. Thus *Homosexualitatis Problema* §6 presents the story of Sodom in Genesis 19, which it interprets as a condemnation of homosexual relations, as part of the unfolding of the consequences of the original sin narrated in Genesis 3. Regardless of the question whether the story can in reality be understood as expressing a condemnation of homosexual relations, for which no justification is offered, is problematic. There is no indication at all in the text of Genesis that a link is to be made between chapter 19 and chapter 3. Not only do they lie far apart, but

Notes

while chapter 3 forms part of the universal primeval history of the world (chapters 1–11), chapter 19 belongs to the cycle of Abraham stories and the narrative of the foundation of the people of Israel.

6. This expression is used in the Congregation for the Doctrine of the Faith's document *Persona Humana* (1975) §8, and repeated in *Homosexualitatis Problema* §3, issued by the same Vatican Congregation.

7. Jack A. Bonsor sums up these points thus: 'The heterosexual's impulse toward love and self-giving ranks among humanity's highest potentials. Indeed it can lead couples to become the very sacrament of divine love. But for homosexuals these impulses are taken to be the result of sin and directed toward evil. For the heterosexual the impulse to sexual union is a marvellous gift from God. For the homosexual it is considered the curse of Adam's sin' (Jack A. Bonsor, 'Homosexual Orientation and Anthropology: Reflections on the Category "Objective Disorder"', in *Theological Studies*, p. 59 (1998).

8. *Catechism of the Catholic Church*, London, Geoffrey Chapman, 1994, §2359.

9. Andrew Sullivan, 'Alone Again, Naturally: The Catholic Church and the Homosexual', originally in *New Republic*, 4167, 28 November 1994, reprinted in Gary David Comstock and Susan E. Henking, eds, *Que(e)rying Religion: A Critical Anthology*, New York, Continuum, 1997, pp. 238–50.

10. Congregation for the Doctrine of the Faith, *Homosexualitatis Problema*, 1986, §12.

11. §3. Curiously, the final sentence of this extract is missing from the official Latin version of the document. This is not the only place where the English and Latin versions differ substantially. In the rest of this book I will follow the English version, for three reasons. First, the English version is much more widely available than the Latin. Second, it is much easier to understand, even for those with a smattering of Latin. Third, I have the strong impression – though this is only a guess – that the Latin is a translation of the English rather than vice versa, and that the English represents the true meaning of the authors. I shall nevertheless have occasion to refer to the Latin text when it can be of help in elucidating the meaning of the English version.

12. Examples of those who take this position after what is clearly a good deal of study are John McNeill, first tentatively in *The Church and the Homosexual* (London, Darton, Longman and Todd, 1977) and then in *Taking a Chance on God* (Boston, Massachusetts, Beacon Press, 1988), and Andrew Sullivan, in *Virtually Normal: An Argument About Homosexuality* (London, Picador, 1995).

13. As Bonsor puts it: 'One of the reasons many Catholics, heterosexual and homosexual, reject the Church's teaching on this topic is that their experience of gay relationships contradicts what must follow from the congregation's positions' (*op. cit.*, 81, n. 62). It must be said, though, that there are other – equally critical – ways of explaining this kind of assertion, rather than in terms of ignorance. Mark Jordan, in *The Silence of Sodom* (Chicago, University of Chicago Press, 2000), argues, not entirely unconvincingly, that those responsible for *HP* and other similar documents are only too aware of the facts of homosexual life; that their ignorance is only apparent, and that their assertions are part of a rhetorical strategy designed to prevent sensible discussion of homosexuality in the church.

14. On this, see Wittgenstein, Ludwig, *On Certainty*, Oxford, Blackwell, 1969, especially §§159–66.

15. Germain Grisez, *Living a Christian Life*, (*The Way of the Lord Jesus*, vol. 2), Quincy, Illinois, Franciscan Press, 1993, p. 672.

16. A seminal work in this area, and one which has been much argued over, is

John Boswell, *Christianity, Social Tolerance and Homosexuality: Gay People in Western Europe from the Beginning of the Christian Era to the Fourteenth Century*, Chicago, University of Chicago Press, 1980. See also Mark D. Jordan, *The Invention of Sodomy in Christian Theology*, Chicago, Chicago University Press, 1997. The conceptual question whether the church can even have a tradition, in the sense of a clear and stable teaching, on homosexuality has also been raised a number of times. See for example John J. Markey, 'The "Problem" of Homosexuality', in *New Blackfriars*, October 1994, pp. 476–88.

17.　See particularly, Mark 7:1–15.

18.　*Consuetudo sine veritate vetustas erroris est* (*Epistola ad Pompeium contra epistolam Stephani de haereticis baptizandis*, §IX).

19.　This is not an altogether happy term. 'Command' is a word which sits easily in a military context, but less easily in many others – like churches, schools, orchestras and businesses – where it is the business of some people to tell others what to do. I use the word despite, not because of, its military overtones, and because I cannot find a better one.

20.　Here I am introducing an implicit limitation into the idea of teaching. I am confining the discussion to that kind of teaching which teaches *that* certain things are the case: that history took a certain course, that certain relationships exist between the sides and angles of a triangle, that certain ways of behaving are pleasing to God and others not, and so on. I am not concerned with teaching techniques, teaching *how* to do things: how to ride a bike, how to solve quadratic equations, how to become more spiritual, and so on. There are close connections between these two kinds of teaching, as well as differences. I confine the discussion to teaching *that* in order to simplify matters; I do not believe that this materially affects the argument.

21.　Once again, this is not a felicitous term in this context. We normally speak of commanding in reference to situations where authorities have direct control over subordinates and there are direct sanctions against disobedience. This is not generally the case in the modern church, where most people can disobey their church, if they wish, with impunity. When church authorities tell these what to do, their telling mostly takes the form of urging and exhortation rather than command.

22.　The would-be command to believe that the moon is made of green cheese is of course not the command to say to oneself that the moon is made of green cheese. Saying things to oneself is indeed an activity; one can be commanded to perform it, and one can obey or disobey. But believing something is not the same as saying it to oneself, for one can easily say to oneself things one does not believe.

23.　The principal reason why I insist that this is true only roughly speaking is that in common parlance to say that a proposition *appears* to me to be true is normally to express a certain hesitation, a lack of complete conviction, to give myself room to back off graciously if it should begin to look that it is not true after all. In breach of this usage, I am using 'appear' without any particular implication of hesitation or lack of it. On the other hand, if I believe a proposition strongly, it is normal to express this by saying that I am *convinced* it is true. For the purposes of the present argument I ignore this usage too. I treat the two expressions '*p* appears true to me' and 'I am convinced that *p*' as equivalent. I don't think this unidiomatic but simplifying usage weakens the argument.

24.　The relationship between belief and action, belief and the will, is not without its complications. For a fuller discussion of the problem see Bernard Williams, 'Deciding to Believe' in his *Problems of the Self*, Cambridge, CUP, 1973, pp. 36–51. Various essays in Matthias Steup, ed., *Knowledge, Truth and Duty: Essays on Epistemic Justi-*

Notes

fication, Responsibility and Virtue, New York, OUP, 2001 have relevant things to say; see in particular Robert Audi's 'Doxastic Voluntarism and the Ethics of Belief', pp. 93–111.

25.   Sometimes, when we want to say that somebody has an obligation to do something, we say that they *must* do it. There are circumstances in which it can be said that somebody must believe a particular proposition, and this may make it look as if it is after all possible to be obliged to believe something. But, in these circumstances, the word 'must' functions not as an expression of obligation but as the imposition of a condition. For example, the Flat Earth Society exists as a resource for people who believe the earth is flat. It would be possible for this society to impose belief that the earth is flat as a condition for membership. (I do not know whether in fact it does.) If it did impose such a condition, then it would make sense to say that its members must believe that the earth is flat. But this would not amount to saying that it is a moral obligation to believe such a thing; it would mean only that if somebody did not believe it, then he or she would not be accepted as a member of the society.

26.   For similar reasons, it is unhelpful and potentially misleading to describe Christopher as 'dissenting' from church teaching, for the introduction of this different verb can again create the impression that he is doing something, performing some intellectual activity that puts him at variance with that teaching; it would then constitute disobedience to perform that activity. People can of course dissent, but we go astray if we imagine that the verb somehow names an activity, which one can then be responsible for performing. Dissenting is no more an activity, no more a mental operation, than believing is. Not being any act at all, dissenting is no more an act of disobedience than assenting is an act of obedience.

Chapter Two

1.   Various attempts have been made to define a sexual act. Among these are Alan Goldman, 'Plain Sex', in Alan Soble, ed., *The Philosophy of Sex: Contemporary Readings*, 2nd edition, Savage, Maryland, Rowman and Littlefield, 1991, pp. 73–92; Alan Soble, 'Masturbation and Sexual Philosophy', in Soble, *op. cit.*, pp. 133–58; and Robert Solomon, 'Sexual Paradigms', in Soble, *op. cit.*, pp. 53–62. None of these accounts is satisfactory, but they do illustrate the difficulty of the problem.

2.   This is true given that I am using 'Anne' as the name of a woman and 'Brian' as the name of a man. This is in fact the case. There is no particular philosophical or theological reason why a man should not call himself Anne and a woman Brian; it would merely be unconventional. To facilitate understanding, I follow convention here and throughout, using conventional women's names only for women and conventional men's names only for men. I also avoid names such as 'Evelyn' which are shared between the sexes, except when I wish to exploit the name's ambiguity. I observe this convention merely for ease of exposition.

3.   These simple observations on the centrality of desire to sexuality enable us to avoid a fundamental mistake often made by theologians writing on homosexuality. In a laudable attempt to be as sympathetic as possible to homosexuals, these theologians want to assert that it is not the homosexuals' fault that they are homosexual; and for them this is practically equivalent to saying that they did not choose to be homosexual, for it is with choice that merit and culpability, praise and blame, enter in. There is sometimes an implication that some homosexuals, and perhaps some heterosexuals, may indeed choose their orientation. In this attempt to exculpate at

least some homosexuals, they often seize gladly on the apparent findings of modern science. Thus Coleman writes:

> It is false to conclude that all homosexual persons choose their orientation or could choose to change their orientation. There is a growing body of evidence that definitive homosexuality is biologically determined: i.e., there are some people who may well be born with a fixed orientation toward homosexuality. They do not choose their desire any more than heterosexual people choose theirs. (Gerald D. Coleman, SS, *Homosexuality: Catholic Teaching and Pastoral Practice*, New York, Paulist Press, 1995, p. 5)

But it is not a mistake to suppose, that all homosexuals choose their sexual orientation; it is a mistake to suppose that anybody at all does so. For, as we have seen, to have a particular sexual orientation is, largely, already to have certain desires, to be attracted in certain ways to others. And we do not choose our desires. On the contrary, to make a particular choice is to show that we already have a certain desire. Thus when given a choice of vegetable I may choose mushrooms rather than broccoli because I prefer the one to the other, but I cannot choose to prefer mushrooms to broccoli, since any such choice would already be an expression of my preference. Preference and desire are not the result of choice, but underlie it. It is thus a conceptual error to suppose that one might choose one's sexual orientation. To suppose that one might is to make not a scientific mistake but a logical error.

4. *Persona Humana* does not in fact use this exact expression, though in its brief reference to homosexuals it speaks of 'the condition of such people' (§8).

5. Though it has to be said that neither *HP* nor any other church document of which I am aware produces any evidence for this 'direct impact', or that a claim of equivalence has been made, or any explanation of what such a claim might mean.

6. This is also an instance of the importance of personal experience in the evaluation of theological positions.

7. David M. Halperin, *One Hundred Years of Homosexuality*, New York, Routledge, 1990.

8. Here I exclude cases of mendacity, loss of memory, etc.

9. We can easily imagine a case where it would be true. I might be an eccentric collector who is interested not at all in the content of recordings, but only in the pictures on the case, and I might want to buy a recording if and only if it has a picture of trees on the case.

10. See, for instance, several of the articles in Xavier Lacroix, ed., *L'Amour du semblable: Questions sur l'homosexualité*, Paris, Les éditions du Cerf, 1996. The very title of this book testifies to this understanding of homosexuality.

11. There is another problem with this view which may just be mentioned. If homosexuality is love of the same, why necessarily love of the same sex? Why not of the same skin colour, hair style, height, musical preferences, etc.? If it is sameness, any of these and more ought to count just as much as sameness of sex.

Chapter Three

1. *Summa Theologiae* 1a2ae 107.4c.
2. *Summa Theologiae* 1a2ae 100.11c.
3. See for example the Second Vatican Council's Dogmatic Constitution on Divine Revelation (*Dei Verbum*), 7, and its Decree on the Training of Priests

Notes

(*Optatam Totius*), 16. Both of these passages are quoted approvingly by John Paul II in *Veritatis Splendor*, 28 and 29.

4. Curiously, it omits any reference to Leviticus 18:22 and 20:13.

5. Enzo Cortese, 'Homosexuality in the Old Testament', in L'Osservatore Romano, English edition, 12 March 1997, p. 5.

6. Ronald Lawler, OFM Cap., Joseph Boyle, Jr., and William E. May, *Catholic Sexual Ethics: A Summary, Explanation and Defense*, second edition, Huntington, Indiana, Our Sunday Visitor, 1998, p. 187. In a footnote they give a list of the five references to male homosexual acts and the one reference to female homosexual acts that they identify. This is identical with the list I have given in this section, except that they interestingly omit Genesis 19.

7. Note that this point does not depend upon the truth of the two descriptions of my act. Suppose I do park in a space conveniently near to the shop, but not on a double yellow line, and while I am in the shop somebody takes my car and then returns it, parking it on a double yellow line. The traffic warden will still condemn me for allegedly parking on a double yellow line, not for parking conveniently near to the shop.

8. See, e.g., Anthony Thiselton, 'Can Hermeneutics Ease the Deadlock? Some Biblical Exegesis and Hermeneutical Models', in Timothy Bradshaw, ed., *The Way Forward? Christian Voices on Homosexuality and the Church* (London, Hodder & Stoughton, 1997). See particularly pp. 158–9. His arguments here appear to me weak and confused, but it seems fairly clear that one of the things he is arguing for is that biblical writers had modern concepts, or at least concepts closely related to modern concepts, without having modern vocabulary, using as an example parallels between the biblical concept of the heart and the Freudian concept of the unconscious.

9. §2357, footnote 140.

10. p. 28, §95.

11. Bailey has claimed that what the men of Sodom want when they say they want to know the strangers is to know their identity. (See Derrick Sherwin Bailey, *Homosexuality and the Western Christian Tradition*, London, Longmans, Green & Co., Ltd., 1955, 1–6.) This view is now rightly rejected by the majority of scholars. While the verb *yada'* does normally mean simply 'know', it can have a sexual sense. It clearly does carry a sexual sense in verse 8, which suggests a sexual sense also for verse 5. Further, if all the men want to do is know the identity of the newly arrived strangers, it is hard to see why Lot should consider this such a wicked thing (v. 7).

12. Note too how the text emphasizes that all the men of Sodom partake in inhospitality: 'the men of the city, the men of Sodom, surrounded the house, from youth to old man, all the people to the last man' (v. 4). In this way the concerns of Abraham in his dialogue with God are met: the city was to be spared if even ten good men were found in it, but to a man they participate in this evil deed. So the narrative prepares for the destruction of Sodom that God had envisaged in chapter 18.

13. See, Deut. 22:13–21.

14. Note how the theme of inhospitality is underlined in the crowd's response to Lot's intervention: 'This one came to sojourn, and he would judge us! Now we will treat you worse than them' (v. 9). They recall Lot's status as a non-citizen. In dwelling among them, Lot is himself a recipient of the citizens' hospitality, just like the two men who have just come to lodge in the city. The citizens have a duty of hospitality towards Lot just as they have towards the other two. In saying 'Now we will treat you worse than them' the citizens show their determination to breach violently their obligations towards all three of them. If this story is one of violent inhospitality, the inhospitality goes further than the two angelic visitors.

Incidentally, in saying this the men of Sodom also confirm that their intentions towards the two visitors are hostile; that they do not merely wish to have sex with them but intend to treat them badly.

15. Note that if the anti-homosexual interpretation of this story were correct, the story would be a condemnation of homosexual desire, not of a homosexual act, for no homosexual act is committed here.

16. One may also question the context in which *HP* places the story of Sodom and Gomorrah. It sees it as a consequence of the 'Fall' narrated in Genesis 3, a clouding of a 'spousal significance' attributed to the human body (§6). It then continues: 'Thus, in Genesis 19:1–11, the deterioration due to sin continues in the story of the men of Sodom' (ibid.). The chapters following Genesis 3 do indeed speak of a spread of sin, but this takes the form principally of violence, punished in the Flood. (See Genesis 4:8–16, 23–4; 6:11–13.) Further, if there is a theme of the spread of sin in Genesis it forms part of the primeval history which ends in Genesis 11. The narrative of Sodom and Gomorrah forms part of the cycle of Abraham stories (beginning in chapter 12) which traces Israel's origins, and the theme of the spread of sin has hitherto played no part in it. It therefore appears artificial and unconvincing to connect Genesis 19 with the earlier theme of the spread of sin.

17. That is, the men of the cities of the plain went after flesh that was not their own, not human flesh. Curiously, John F. Harvey (*The Homosexual Person: New Thinking in Pastoral Care*, San Francisco, Ignatius Press, 1987, p. 99) regards this verse as a condemnation of homosexual practice. He does not explain how 'different flesh' can plausibly be regarded as designating the flesh of a human being of the same sex. The normal complaint is that the flesh of one man is too similar to that of another to make sexual relations acceptable.

18. The Revised Standard Version's phrase 'as with a woman' represents the Hebrew noun phrase *mishkeve ishsha*, literally 'the lyings of a woman'. There seems to be no way of keeping the grammatical structure of the Hebrew while producing reasonable English.

19. See Leviticus 18:1, 2.

20. Once again, the Revised Standard Version's rendering of the first part is more elegant: 'When a man lies with a male as with a woman, the two of them have committed an abomination.'

21. For us, the term 'male' normally includes boys as well as adult men. I speak of men for simplicity of exposition. There is no way of telling whether this law implicitly restricts the term 'male' to adult men, or whether it has boys and male adolescents in mind as well. There is certainly no reason to think that the text is particularly concerned with what we would call paedophilia.

22. The 'you' of these laws is normally an adult male householder. Once again, it is not clear whether it is here meant to include sexually mature adolescents. This unclarity is not without importance, for in a number of societies, particularly those with strong segregation of the sexes, it is recognized, either publicly or tacitly, that young unmarried males will take part in sexual activities with other young males. Stephen O. Murray gives a few examples of this in *Homosexualities* (Chicago, University of Chicago Press, 2000), chapter 8. We do not know whether this was so in ancient Israel. To avoid questions of this kind, I will speak as if this law concerns adult men.

23. See, Gal. 3:28.

24. Deuteronomy 24:1–4. It is to this passage that the Pharisees refer in their discussion with Jesus about repudiation in Matt. 19:3–9.

25. See Proverbs 31:10–31.

26. See, Judges 9:52-4.
27. See, particularly, Judith 9:11-14; 13:7.
28. Note how, even in the New Testament, at 1 Timothy 2:11-15, the temporal priority of Adam over Eve is used to justify a sexual hierarchy, to establish the authority of men over women and to ban women from occupying positions of authority over men.
29. Thus a man who takes an unmarried girl and has sex with her is obliged to acknowledge her as his own, to take her as his wife. See Deut. 22:28, 29.
30. So it is that the verb *'innah*, translatable as 'subject', 'humble' or 'humiliate', is used a number of times in the Old Testament to describe what a man does to a woman by having sex with her. See Gen. 34:2; Deut. 21:14; 22:24, 29; 2 Sam. 13:14; Ezek. 22:10, 11. In three of these passages – Gen 34:2, Deut. 22:29 and 2 Sam. 13:14 – the man imposes himself on the woman. From these it may appear that the humiliation or subjection consists in taking somebody by force, in raping her. However, in the other passages there is no suggestion of rape. In Deut. 22:24 it is particularly clear that it is a consensual act. In Deut. 21:14, though the woman in question is a slave, and so taken by force, it is not in her being made a slave that her humiliation consists, but in her being married.
31. We have already seen that Exodus 20:17 lists a wife as one of a man's possessions second to his house and along with his slaves and livestock. As a corollary, Deuteronomy 30:30-1 threatens that one who disobeys the law of God will lose his property to his enemies: he will build a house, but not dwell in it; he will plant a vineyard but not enjoy its fruit; others will take, kill and eat his livestock – and somebody else will lie with his wife.
32. That is, he could not legally offend against her. But of course she could be hurt and offended. This might especially be so if a particular marriage was also a relationship of love. Love could and did exist within marriage, but it was love between unequals.
33. See Lev. 20:10; Deut. 22:23, 24. In these cases, the 'other man' is of course also guilty of a capital offence.
34. See Deut. 22:13-21.
35. 19:19. It is also used in Psalm 139:3, where it simply means lying down, of a man. Clearly, that is not what is involved in the current verse.
36. The same conclusion is reached, on the basis of quite different considerations, by Saul M. Olyan, '"And with a male you shall not lie the lying down of a woman": on the Meaning and Significance of Leviticus 18:22 and 20:13', in Gary David Comstock and Susan E. Henking, eds, *Que(e)rying Religion: A Critical Anthology*, New York, Continuum, 1997, pp. 398-414; reprinted from *Journal of the History of Sexuality*, 5.2 (October 1994), pp. 179-206.
37. This shows that *HP*'s assertion that this verse 'excludes from the People of God those who behave in a homosexual fashion' (§6) is inappropriate because too wide.
38. But it has to be admitted that, as so often when it comes to trying to understand the Bible, things are not quite as simple as that. While the expression of 20:13 'they have both done an abomination' suggests that they are both agents, and so have both agreed to the penetration, a glance at 20:15-16 suggests that the concern of this passage of Leviticus is not with punishing the guilty, those people who have freely entered into illegal acts. Those verses prescribe that if, contrary to 18:23, a man penetrates an animal or a woman lets herself be penetrated by an animal, both the person and the animal involved are to be put to death. There is no suggestion here

that animals are capable of giving consent to sexual acts, as human beings are. The idea seems to be rather that such acts produce, objectively, a breach in the order of things, or a kind of miasma. The execution of the parties to the acts, human and animal, is not conceived of as punishment for a crime, but as a way of expunging the transgression and so restoring the proper order. It is possible that we should understand 20:13 in the same way to this extent; even if both parties are held to have consented to the act, the point of putting them to death is quite possibly not to punish them for a crime, but to dispel the miasma by eliminating those whose action brought it about.

39.   *HP* is not saying in §6 that some biblical texts forbid some homosexual activities and other texts forbid other homosexual activities, so that the relevant texts taken together forbid all homosexual activities. (That would in any case be a thoroughly implausible claim.) Its point is rather that all the relevant texts say roughly the same thing; that they all condemn all homosexual activities.

40.   My taking my annual holiday in September may create problems for my employer. If I demand to take my holiday in September, I do not thereby demand to create problems for my employer.

41.   I want to take my holiday in September because that will please my wife. If my employer opposes my demand to take my holiday in September, he does not thereby oppose my pleasing my wife.

42.   Jesus makes no reference to Leviticus 18:22, but he certainly appears to have understood the Genesis passage in terms of hospitality, for he alludes to it in the context of sending out his disciples to preach and heal. They are not to provide for themselves, but to depend on the hospitality of the villages they enter. Those villages which do not offer them hospitality will fare worse in the judgement than Sodom and Gomorrah. See Matt 10:5–15; Luke 10:1–16. The idea seems to be that the visiting disciples are comparable to the angelic figures who visited those cities; failure to show them hospitality will be as serious a sin as the inhospitality shown to the angels. (Considered as a story of human hospitality and inhospitality to the divine, the story has an interesting parallel in Ovid's story of Philemon and Baucis (*Metamorphoses* VIII, 618–724), an old couple who, alone in their city, offer hospitality to visiting gods and so escape the general destruction, being turned into trees.) This appears to conform to the general scriptural understanding of the Sodom and Gomorrah story. In the Old Testament, the sin of Sodom is never represented as sexual. In Isaiah 1:10–17 Jerusalem is likened to the cities of the plain in being full of injustice and oppression. In Ezekiel 16:49, the sin of Sodom is identified as prosperity side by side with lack of care for the lowly and the poor. In the New Testament, only 2 Peter 2:6–8 and Jude 7 attribute sexual sins to the inhabitants of Sodom and Gomorrah. The 2 Peter passage speaks only vaguely of 'vice' (*aselgeia*) and 'lawless deeds'. Jude says that the citizens went after 'strange flesh' or 'different flesh' (*sarkos heteras*). The meaning here is probably that the visitors the men wanted to rape were in fact not human, but angels. As already remarked, the phrase can hardly be thought to refer to men wanting sex with other men.

Chapter Four

1.   As William Countryman points out in his interesting study of this passage, Paul does not use the vocabulary of sin in connection with this sexual behaviour of the Gentiles; they have rather been given up to uncleanness. See his *Dirt, Greed and*

Notes

Sex: Sexual Ethics in the New Testament and their Implications for Today, London, SCM, 1989, 109–17.

2.   The verbs Paul uses here are aorists, indicating probably not a general present custom of the Gentiles, but a single event in the past. He perhaps has in mind one particular event which led to all subsequent generations of humanity being corrupted, only the Jews being saved from the general corruption by the true God's self-revelation to them. Morna Hooker adduces several reasons for believing that Paul is in fact thinking of the Fall of Adam. See her *From Adam to Christ: Essays on Paul*, Cambridge, CUP, 1990, pp. 73–87.

3.   Eugene F. Rogers, Jr. , *Sexuality and the Christian Body*, Oxford, Blackwell, 1999, p. 53.

4.   This seems to be what Paul is saying. It was not, however, actually the case. Many Gentiles in the Hellenistic world Paul probably has in mind expressed distaste for male, and generally pederastic, same-sex practices, or opposition to them. For examples, see Robin Scroggs, *The New Testament and Homosexuality*, Philadelphia, Fortress Press, 1983, pp. 49–62 and Michel Foucault, *The Use of Pleasure* (The History of Sexuality, vol. 2), London, Penguin Books, 1987, pp. 187–214.

5.   This is well brought out by Countryman, *Dirt, Greed and Sex*, p. 110.

6.   I have tried in the translation to bring out Paul's play on words, which indicates that God's justice here is again poetic, as in the case of his turning all the Gentiles into homosexuals. Just as there the exchange of truth for a lie is met by the exchange of natural sexual use for what is not natural, so here the Gentiles' not seeing fit to acknowledge God is met by his giving them a mind which is not fit.

7.   See also, 16:2, 39; 23:29.

8.   RSV translates well: 'degraded'.

9.   This is obviously a metaphorical passage, and perhaps nakedness and shame are being used as metaphors for sin. But, if that is so, it remains true that the terms in which the metaphor is couched are not in themselves part of the terminology of sin.

10.   Paul also associates these same-sex activities with impurity and dishonour. The latter term is again, like shame, a social one; it has to do with how one is regarded by other people. Impurity is a more complicated notion, and there is no space to go into it here. For a full-length study, see Countryman, *Dirt, Greed & Sex*.

11.   There are, apart from Romans 1, four occurrences:

> 1 Thessalonians 4:5: 'not in the passion of lust like heathen who do not know God'.
> Galatians 5:24: 'And those who belong to Christ Jesus have crucified the flesh with its passions and desires.'
> Romans 7:5: 'While we were living in the flesh, our sinful passions, aroused by the law, were at work in our members to bear fruit for death.'
> Colossians 3:5: 'Put to death therefore what is earthly in you: fornication, impurity, passion, evil desire, and covetousness, which is idolatry.'

The negative tone of these verses in relation to passion is too obvious to need commentary.

12.   Stanley K. Stowers: *A Rereading of Romans*, Yale University Press, New Haven, 1994, pp. 45–6. Throughout this section Stowers reminds us of the central importance of self-mastery to Greek and Roman ethics. For them, what is to be avoided is not so much sin as weakness. To read Romans in this light is helpful, given that Paul is writing as the apostle to the Gentiles, and in particular transforms what are taken to be his references to homosexuality.

13. *The New Testament and Homosexuality, passim.* He surveys the evidence from Classical Greek and Hellenistic sources, and from biblical and Palestinian and Hellenistic Jewish writings.

14. The laws of Leviticus 18:22 and 20:13 also use very general language, talking simply about a male lying with a male the lyings of a woman, without specifying at all the relative ages of the males concerned. However, in reporting Philo's discussion of these laws Scroggs, pp. 88f., makes it quite clear that Philo understands them spontaneously as an attack on Gentile pederasty.

The use of quite general vocabulary to refer to a more specific phenomenon should occasion no surprise. It is standard in cases where the speaker or writer is not aware that there are distinctions to be made. This can be for cultural reasons, as would be the case of Paul and Philo, if the distinctions we make were absent from the culture because only one form of same-sex practice was publicly known. But it can also be through personal ignorance, as when some today speak of 'the homosexual lifestyle' – meaning frequent visits to gay bars and discos, and multiple, obsessive, fleeting sexual encounters – as if all gay men lived like this, and as if there were no lesbians. Sometimes we see the opposite phenomenon, where vocabulary denoting specific people is used in a wider sense, of homosexual people generally. In modern French, the word *pédé*, short for *pédophile*, is frequently used as a label for homosexuals in general.

15. See, *The New Testament and Homosexuality*, pp. 44–65.

16. Murray (*Homosexualities*, pp. 173–8) gives numerous examples of male homosexual relationships in Greece and Rome which cannot be fitted into the pederastic model.

17. *Sexuality and the Christian Body*, p. 64. In this he follows Boswell, *Christianity, Social Tolerance and Homosexuality*, p. 111.

18. *Dirt, Greed and Sex*, p. 112.

19. *Christianity, Social Tolerance and Homosexuality*, p. 109.

20. I continue to use the traditional translation of *para physin*, but it should not be forgotten that this translation is not unproblematic.

21. *The New Testament and Homosexuality*, pp. 140–4.

22. It may be said that it also casts doubt on my argument above that Paul does not see the practices to which he refers as sinful. For him, adultery surely was a sin. So it seems we have to say, in respect to what Paul says in verse 26, that *if* he is referring to adultery, *then* he is talking about sin. But, by the same token, if he is talking about the sin of adultery, he is not talking about lesbianism. No such problem arises in verse 27, where there are no possessive adjectives to hint at adultery.

23. James E. Miller, 'The Practices of Romans 1:26: Homosexual or Heterosexual?', *Novum Testamentum* 37, 1995, p. 1.

24. See, e.g., Martial 3.87; 4.84.

25. Suetonius, *Divus Iulius* 49.

26. The Form of Solemnization of Matrimony, priest's introduction.

27. In the New Testament, see Matthew 11:8.

28. See, Scroggs, *The New Testament and Homosexuality*, pp. 62–5, 106.

29. 'Homosexuality in Ancient Rome', in Ariès and Béjin, eds, *Western Sexuality*, Blackwell, Oxford, 1985, p. 30.

30. Thus early versions of the Revised Standard Version translated the two terms *malakoi* and *arsenokoitai* by the single word 'homosexual', to be replaced in later editions by 'sexual perverts'. The New Revised Standard Version separates the two again as 'male prostitutes' and 'sodomites'.

31.   An example of this 'theology by etymology' approach is to be found in Anthony Thiselton's article 'Can Hermeneutics Ease the Deadlock? Some Biblical Exegesis and Hermeneutical Models', in Timothy Bradshaw, ed., *The Way Forward? Christian Voices on Homosexuality and the Church* (London, Hodder & Stoughton, 1997, pp. 145–96). He says: ' ... no amount of lexicographical manipulation over *malakoi* can avoid the clear meaning of *arsenokoitai* as the activity of males (*arsên*) who have sexual relations with, sleep with (*koitê*) other males' (p. 167). But to give the etymology of a word is not, except *per accidens*, to give its meaning. That is why dictionaries do not and cannot confine themselves to giving the etymologies of words. In any case, Thiselton is going beyond etymology when he claims that part of the clear meaning of *koitê* is having sexual relations. There is no evidence that the Hellenistic world had the concept of sexual relations; that is, that they grouped together roughly the same range of activities as we do when we speak of sexual relations.

32.   The translation is that of F. H. Colson, London, Heinemann, 1937 (Loeb Classical Library, Philo, vol. VII).

33.   See, Scroggs, *The New Testament and Homosexuality*, p. 108.

34.   See below on 1 Timothy 1:10.

35.   That is, Paul does not say that some of the Corinthian Christians were one thing, some another, some yet another. Paul is capable of constructing and treating lists in this way, stressing diversity. See, for example, 1 Corinthians 12:27–30.

36.   I follow the traditional, but much disputed, attribution of this letter simply for ease of exposition. Nothing hangs on it.

37.   *The New Testament and Homosexuality*, p. 120.

38.   In this section, *HP* avoids the language of sin, speaking rather in terms of disharmony. This language is ambiguous: an example of disharmony could be itself an example of sin, which causes disharmony, or it could be merely a phenomenon of disharmony resulting from some sinful activity; disharmony can be a sinful act, or the effect of sin. The ambiguity of *HP*'s language here perhaps reflects an awareness on the part of its authors that Paul is not here presenting homosexual desire and activity as sinful, but as the result of sin. But of course what *HP* wants to show is that Scripture in general presents them as sinful, and it marshals Romans 1 and other texts to that end. The use of the term 'disharmony' enables *HP* to slip imperceptibly, but illegitimately, from the one to the other. I believe I have already presented considerations sufficient to show that Romans 1 cannot be used in this way. If these verses can be said to present homosexual desire and activity as an example of disharmony between Creator and creature (and that itself can be questioned), it is a disharmony consequent on sin, and not a disharmony which is itself sinful. But in order to make its case, *HP* has to present the disharmony – wrongly, in my view – as sinful disharmony.

Chapter Five

1.   Ronald Lawler, OFM Cap., Joseph Boyle, Jr., and William E. May, *Catholic Sexual Ethics: A Summary, Explanation and Defence*, 2nd edition, Huntington, Indiana, Our Sunday Visitor, 1998, p. 34.

2.   Ruth Tiffany Barnhouse makes explicit use of this unfounded idea of a partial image of God. She states that 'the image of God, in which the sacred myth tells us that humanity was created, includes both man and woman'. The use of 'include' here is already somewhat vague, and is wider than the biblical assertion that

male and female are made in the image of God. She then asserts: 'Homosexuality constitutes a rejection, either partial or total, of the possibility of union with the other sex.' This is a claim to which we shall have to return. For the moment, it is enough to note that she concludes: 'Very clearly, the wholeness of the sacred order is neither symbolized nor approximated by sexual practices which are thus grounded in the denial of *half of the image of God.*' (*Homosexuality: A Symbolic Confusion*, New York, Seabury Press, 1977; extract reprinted in Edward Batchelor, ed., *Homosexuality and Ethics*, New York, The Pilgrim Press, 1980, p. 84; my italics.) But the sacred myth does not license Barnhouse to speak of 'half of the image of God' at all in the way she does.

3.   I have chosen the ugly 'it' as a pronoun corresponding to 'humankind' rather than the more natural 'them'. This is to bring out the fact that it is a singular pronoun in Hebrew, as opposed to the plural object pronoun used at the end of the verse: male and female he created *them*. It remains unclear what significance, if any, this shift in the number of the pronoun has. In many versions of the Bible, the word I have translated 'humankind' (*ha'adam*) is translated 'man', which would make 'him' a natural rendering of the current pronoun, but which would also risk giving the false impression that *ha'adam* is in this context a singular rather than a collective noun.

4.   Not exactly 'in his image and likeness', as the text of the *HP* states; while God projects creating people in his image and likeness in verse 26, there is no reference to likeness when he actually creates them in verse 27. But in all probability the difference is not significant; 'image and likeness' is probably a hendiadys and equivalent to 'image'.

5.   Though it is not entirely unambiguous on this point. And Paul, in 1 Corinthians 11:7, appears to imply that it is male human beings who are created in the image of God.

6.   See, e.g., Gen. 6:19; 20:14; Exod. 12:5; Lev. 3:1; 4:28; 23:19.

7.   The sense and appropriateness of this description of sexual intercourse will have to be considered later.

8.   What God does not say to the fish is that they are invited to subdue the watery realm in which they live, whereas he does invite people to subdue the earth. This might be a reason for interpreting the text as implying that it is by occupying this dominant position that people show forth the nature of God: they act effectively as his vicegerents. Some exegetes have in fact interpreted the image of God in this way. For examples, see Claus Westermann, *Genesis 1–11*, London, SPCK, 1984, pp. 151–4.

9.   Ephesians 4:23f.

10.   *De Genesi ad Litteram* 3.20.

11.   *Summa Theologiae* 1.93.2c.

12.   The language Jesus uses is familial. The likeness of the disciples to God is to be like that between father and son; Jesus expects human beings to be like God in the same way that a son may be expected to be like his father. As we say proverbially, 'like father, like son'. A link with the image-language of Genesis may be seen in the way that Adam, already created in the image of God, in turn begets a son Seth 'in his likeness, after his image' (Gen. 5:1–3).

13.   I use this rather ugly translation to bring out the fact that the same word is used here as at the point where Adam names his new companion 'woman'. Hebrew, like many languages, uses the one word where modern English has two. This raises the question whether one might not equally say that Adam names his companion 'wife'. This translation would underline the fact that Eve is not created as a separate individual in her own right, equal to but different from Adam, but is made precisely to belong to him, to be his wife. It would also fit better with the meaning of the story

Notes

as an aetiology of marriage.

14.   For a brief and readable example of this use of this chapter, see Lawler, Boyle and May, *Catholic Sexual Ethics*, 2nd edn, pp. 35–6. A much longer and more difficult exposition of a view of sexual ethics which relies heavily on Genesis 2 is to be found in Germain Grisez, *The Way of the Lord Jesus*, vol. 2, ch. 9, 'Marriage, Sexual Acts and Family Life'.

15.   Thus Lawler, Boyle and May, in the course of their treatment of homosexual activity, clearly allude to Genesis when they say:

> The Bible teaches ... that marriage, rooted in the irrevocable consent of man and woman to be 'one flesh', for life, alone respects the goods of human sexuality. Thus Scripture teaches that marriage provides the normative condition for genital sexual expression; all other expressions of this kind, whether between man and woman or between members of the same sex, are to be evaluated in the light of this norm. (p. 187)

That evaluation, in the case of homosexual acts as of heterosexual activity outside marriage, is of course negative. Grisez similarly gives a negative evaluation of homosexual acts, based on the concept of 'one-flesh communion' which has its origin in Genesis 2. See, Grisez, *op. cit.*, pp. 653–4.

16.   Thus, for example, Pharaoh Neco, having deposed Jehoahaz, installs Eliakim as King of Judah and changes his name to Jehoiakim (2 Kings 23:34). Similarly, a little later, Nebuchadnezzar, King of Babylon, after a successful siege of Jerusalem, installs Mattaniah as King, changing his name to Zedekiah (2 Kings 24:17).

17.   *Catholic Sexual Ethics*, p. 35.

18.   *Ibid.*

19.   *Ibid.*

20.   The exact nuance of the Hebrew word *kenegdo* is notoriously difficult to capture, but the general sense is clear: the helper has to be fit for the man, not for the job of gardening.

21.   We have already noted that Adam here gives a generic name to God's latest production, as he gave generic names to the others; this is a direct continuation of the scene in which Adam names the animals. But here it is significant what kind of name Adam gives her. Because he recognizes in her a partner fit for him he expresses this verbally by giving her a name which is similar to his own: he is a man (*ish*), and he calls her woman (*ishshah*). The close link between their two names mirrors the close link between the two of them.

22.   *Ibid.*

23.   In other words, recognition, in the sense in which I use it here, is intensional. If your car has bad acceleration then, if I recognize that a given car is your car, then the car which I recognize as yours has bad acceleration; but it does not follow that I recognize that the car has bad acceleration.

24.   *Catholic Sexual Ethics*, p. 38.

25.   Jesus's objection to repudiation is therefore closely linked to Malachi's diatribe against repudiation (Mal. 2:14–16).

26.   *The Homosexual Person*, p. 96.

27.   Jesus says, 'What God has joined together, let a man not separate' (Matt. 19:6). In this context, the man of whom he speaks is almost certainly not humankind in general, but the husband who might wish to repudiate his wife. So he is not saying that, for example, a state may not pronounce a marriage at an end, or that a man and wife may not separate by mutual agreement, but that, as the context implies, a

married man may not repudiate his wife. For an argument to this effect, see my *The Body in Context*, p. 147.

28.   *HP* does not claim or imply that it does; unlike Harvey, it makes no reference to Jesus's words in asserting the centrality of the early chapters of Genesis to an understanding of homosexuality.

Chapter Six

1.   See Lev. 11:10–12.

2.   See also Matt. 7:12; Luke 6:27–36; 7:47; John 13:34–5; 15:17; Rom. 13:9–10; 1 Cor. 14:1; 16:14; Gal. 5:6; Eph. 5:2; James 2:8; 1 Peter 4:8; 1 John 3:11, 23. It goes without saying, and hardly needs documenting, that there is a great emphasis on the primacy of love in the postbiblical Christian tradition also.

3.   See, e.g., Deut. 6:1–9; John 14:15.

4.   There is a lovely prayer in the Roman Missal which expresses the same idea: *Deus, qui sacrae legis omnia constituta in tua et proximi dilectione posuisti, da nobis, ut, tua praecepta observantes, ad vitam mereamur pervenire perpetuam.* (God, who has placed all the elements of the divine law in love of yourself and our neighbour, grant us that, observing your precepts, we may deserve to arrive at eternal life.) (Collect for 25th Sunday *per annum*)

5.   Thomas E. Schmidt, in *Straight and Narrow? Compassion and Clarity in the Homosexuality Debate*, (Leicester, Inter-Varsity Press, 1995, p. 108) claims: 'Promiscuity among homosexual men is not a mere stereotype, and it is not merely the majority experience – it is virtually the *only* experience.'

Schmidt does not say how or where he did his research, but his conclusion is certainly wrong. One has to go beyond the superficial world of gay clubs and bars to see how the majority of gays live. There are those who, in increasing numbers, live together in domestic partnership and who are not at all promiscuous.

6.   Evelyn Waugh, *Brideshead Revisited*, London, Penguin, 1962, p. 185.

7.   In these testimonies there was often an air of discovery, as if it came as a surprise to them that gay men should be capable of such love, the same kind of love that a woman might show for her dying husband, or a man for his sick wife. Such surprise is a testimony to the strength of the preconceptions that many people, including Catholic priests and religious, had about gay people, preconceptions that represented them as incapable of the love and devotion one might expect from 'normal' people.

8.   There are indeed conceptual difficulties in the way of such studies. How, for instance, can we measure scientifically how loving somebody is? How can love be quantified? Of course, a system of measures can be devised, but there would remain the question whether and to what extent what they measured corresponded to what we mean, non-scientifically, by 'love'.

9.   The Latin text of *HP* says that engaging in homosexual activity strengthens an interior sexual propensity which 'aims principally at one's own pleasure' [*interiorem sexualem propensionem confirmant a recto ordine alienam, quae suapte natura sui delectationem potissimum intendit*]. But it is surely people who might aim principally at pleasure, not propensities.

10.   The full sentence in §7 runs: 'Homosexual activity is not a complementary union, able to transmit life; and so it thwarts the call to a life of that form of self-giving which the gospel says is the essence of Christian living.' This rather gives the

Notes

impression that the gospel calls us to a specific form – 'that form' – of self-giving, namely a complementary sexual union, in the sense of one able to transmit life; i.e. the gospel calls us to marriage. This must be a slip. The gospel calls us to self-giving, but not to any specific form of self-giving. It certainly does not say that marriage is the essence of Christian living.

11. At best, because a selfish act may be the act of a person who does not fail to live up to the call of the gospel because he or she does not even try to do so.

12. Even if it were legitimate to forget about lesbians, and even if all sexually active gay men were caught up in a self-centred search for sexual pleasure, that would still not legitimate the conclusion that all this was a result of their engaging in homosexual activity. It would have to be shown that this was a more probable explanation than social and cultural factors such as (among others) an increased emphasis on pleasure in modern western societies and the tendency of minorities to group together to form group-specific behaviour patterns.

13. Even the enjoyment of these pleasant sensations must be spoken of with care. The enjoyment of sensations depends much on context, including one's perception of what is happening. For more on this, see my *The Body in Context*, pp. 53–4.

14. If he is inordinately concerned with having these pleasurable sensations, we may expect it to be relatively unimportant to him that he perform these acts with Jane, since he could experience the same bodily sensations by having sex with somebody else. If Andrew is concerned to avoid such infidelity, this in itself indicates that his concern to have pleasurable sexual sensations is not inordinate.

15. I make no reference here to the procreative aspect of Andrew's and Jane's sexual activity, which is so important in modern Catholic approaches to sex. I have no wish to deny the importance of procreation as an aspect of married sexual activity. My aim is only to show that the sexual activity of a married couple undertaken because it is a pleasurable activity is not therefore either self-indulgent or selfish. The fact that I have shown this without reference to procreation, shows in turn that it is not necessary that sexual activity be procreative in order to avoid being self-indulgent or selfish, and therefore contrary to love.

16. As it stands, this is too extreme, for there is another way in which biblical coherence could be maintained. It could be argued that, while the letter of the relevant texts does indeed condemn all homosexual behaviour, we need to understand them in some other way. In a similar way, the letter of Genesis 1 plainly indicates that God made the world in six days, but most Christians would argue that in the light of modern science we have to seek some other message in the text.

Chapter Seven

1. Scroggs, pp. 59–60, gives some examples. See also David E. Fredrickson, 'Natural and Unnatural in Romans 1:24–7: Paul and the Philosophic Critique of Eros', in David L. Balch, ed., *Homosexuality, Science, and the "Plain Sense" of Scripture*, Grand Rapids, Michigan, Eerdmans, 2000, pp. 197–222.

2. Romans 1:26–27

3. 'Now among all others, the rational creature is subject to Divine providence in the most excellent way, in so far as it partakes of a share of providence, by being provident both for itself and for others. Wherefore it has a share of the Eternal Reason, whereby it has a natural inclination to its proper act and end: and this participation of the eternal law in the rational creature is called the natural law ... It

is therefore evident that the natural law is nothing else than the rational creature's participation of the eternal law'. (*Summa Theologiae* 1–2.91.2c)

4. Aquinas uses the Latin adjective *malus*, sometimes in its neuter form as a noun. I translate this simply as 'bad' or 'a bad thing' or 'the bad', according to context. I will sometimes leave it untranslated. In modern anglophone Catholic circles, the Latin adjective *malus* is often translated 'evil', as is the substantive *malum*. I avoid this. It is very misleading to those who do not have the Latin original at the back of their minds, as 'evil' in modern English has roughly the sense 'extremely bad', rather than simply 'bad'; whereas in Latin it is possible for something to be moderately or only slightly *malum*, it cannot be slightly or moderately evil in English. It should be remembered too that the word *malum* is introduced in the present context simply to refer to that which people avoid, and this is much weaker than the English 'evil'. A chess move can be a bad move, a move to be avoided, but we would not think of calling a chess move evil. Further, when 'evil' is applied to acts, it often carries connotations of evil intent and even of the evil nature of the agent; to do something evil is not merely to do something which humans naturally desire to avoid, it is to reveal oneself as evil. In the Latin text of *HP*, the inclination towards homosexual acts is described as *intrinsece mala* (§3), and in the official English version this was given as 'intrinsic ... evil'. This expression gave gratuitous offence to those Christian homosexuals who read the English version. It was also inaccurate as a rendering of the Latin into modern English. If it would be unjust, and a mistake, to call it an evil translation, it is nevertheless a bad one.

5. It is difficult to find a single English word corresponding to *luxuria*, which has, like the English 'luxury', connotations of softness and excess, but has a specific sexual range which the English word does not. I duck the problem by leaving the term untranslated.

6. This difficulty can be put in terms of an ambiguity in Aquinas's language. He speaks of both animals and inanimate objects having a tendency or 'inclination' (*inclinatio*) to self-preservation. This can only mean that both animate and inanimate creatures tend to act in such a way as to preserve themselves. He recognizes that in the case of human beings, inclination is a matter of desire or will, what we want (*ST* 1a.59c). But he appears not to notice that this introduces an important ambiguity into the notion of inclination. Human beings may in fact have two different kinds of inclination or tendency. Andrew can be said to have a tendency to smoke after meals, and also to have a tendency to cough when he smokes. When we say he tends to smoke after meals, we talk about what he habitually wants to do, and we talk about his tendency to act in particular ways. When we say he tends to cough when he smokes, we make no reference to what he actually wants, or to his acts; we may say this even if we presume he does not want to cough, and that coughing is not an act on his part but something he undergoes. It is only this second kind of tendency that human beings may be said to share with animals and with inanimate things, so it must be a reference to this kind of tendency that we understand to underlie Aquinas's argument here. But then, even if the argument turns out to have some merit, it does not touch the first kind of tendency, that which is an expression of human desire. But it is only this first kind of tendency, the tendency to act in certain ways, which is the subject of ethical discourse, and which can be a morally good or bad tendency.

7. Aquinas recognizes this in his treatment of virginity, *ST* 2–2.152.2 *ad* 1.

8. To many Christians, of course, the use of much reproductive technology is repugnant. But that is another matter. I am concerned here only with the purely factual question of the ability of this technology to ensure the survival of the species.

Notes

9.   There is no direct equivalent in Latin to the English 'sex' in its sense of sexual activity. I am using the term to translate *usus venereorum*.

10.   Aquinas has a parallel argument in the *Summa Contra Gentiles* 3.122, this time framed in terms of the necessity not of acts but of semen. Semen, he claims, 'is needed to be emitted for the purpose of generation, to which coitus is ordered. From which it is obvious that every emission of semen in such a way that generation cannot follow is against the good of man.' This argument trades on a similar ambiguity. 'Semen is needed to be emitted for the purpose of generation' can mean either 'All semen is needed to be emitted for the purpose of generation' or 'Some semen is needed to be emitted for the purpose of generation.' On the second interpretation, the assertion is true, but the illegitimacy of non-reproductive sexual activity (including homosexual activity) does not follow from it, for the emission of semen in male homosexual activity does not prevent the emission of some semen, in heterosexual acts, for the purpose of generation. Homosexual activity would only be ruled out by the first interpretation, that all semen is needed to be emitted for the purpose of generation. But on this interpretation, Aquinas's assertion is patently false, for the human race survives very well without the use of all semen for the purpose of generation.

11.   The phrase is not original to Aquinas. He inherits it ultimately from the Roman jurist Ulpian (d. 228).

12.   Elsewhere, Aquinas speaks of natural law in quite different terms. He says: 'The natural law is promulgated by the very fact that God instilled it into man's mind so as to be known by him naturally' (*ST* 1a2ae.90.4 *ad* 1). Here nature does not teach the law, God instills it. But the end result is the same: people know the natural law naturally, without being taught it by other human beings.

13.   See, P. A. Tyler, 'Homosexual Behaviour in Animals', in Kevin Howells ed., *The Psychology of Sexual Diversity*, Basil Blackwell, Oxford, 1984, pp. 42–62.

14.   Though of course Aquinas himself would never argue in this way. As a Christian religious of his time he is committed to arguing for the value of celibacy and of permanent virginity. See, *ST* 2–2.152.2,3,4.

15.   I have raised doubts about it, in discussing the same passage of *De Malo*, in *The Body in Context*, p. 78.

16.   This section contains material taken from my paper 'Nature and Sexual Differences', given at the annual meeting of the English Catholic Theological Association.

17.   See, Veyne, *op. cit.*

18.   *The Use of Pleasure* (*History of Sexuality* II), p. 188.

19.   David F. Greenberg, *The Construction of Homosexuality*, Chicago, University of Chicago Press, 1988, pp. 27f., following Raymond Kelly, *Etoro Social Structure: A Study in Structural Contradiction*, Ann Arbor, University of Michigan Press, 1974.)

20.   Though, as Foucault and others make clear, this case is more problematic, since the free boy will grow up to be the free man's social equal, and nothing must be done to or by the boy to compromise his future status.

21.   For numerous further examples, see Greenberg, *op. cit.*, and Murray, *op. cit.*

22.   Mary Douglas, *Natural Symbols*, London, Penguin, 1973, p. 93.

23.   Ludwig Wittgenstein (trans. G. E. M. Anscombe), *Philosophical Investigations*, Oxford, Blackwell, 2nd edition, 1958, §244.

24.   Many animals, too, learn behaviour from each other. We do not think an animal acts naturally only when it has learned nothing from others.

25.   See, for example, Eric Fuchs, *Sexual Desire and Love: Origins and History of the Christian Ethic of Sexuality and Marriage*, Cambridge, James Clarke & Co., 1983; and Vincent J. Genovesi, S.J., *In Pursuit of Love: Catholic Morality and Human Sexuality*, Dublin, Gill and Macmillan, 1987.

26.   But not, *pace* Freud, polymorphously perverse. Freud famously characterizes unformed infant sexuality in this way, but in doing so appears to miss the point that perversity depends on a norm, and norms are social.

27.   Unless we think that the attitudes of biblical authors necessarily tell us truths about humanity in general. There surely is a temptation here for some people. But why might we be tempted so to value biblical attitudes on sex and not similarly value biblical views on monarchy, war, slavery, usury, race, etc.?

Chapter Eight

1.   This is actually too sweeping. The designer might well make a mistake if he is talking about a machine he designed twenty years ago and whose structure he has since forgotten. But possibilities of this kind do not affect the point being made here.

2.   In the above I have spoken indifferently of reproductive purpose and reproductive function. We might associate the word 'purpose' with the question of what something is for, and the word 'function' with the question of what it does. But we can answer the question of what something is for by giving an account of what it does. An account of the function of a thing – an organ or a machine part – serves as an explanation of its purpose. In this sense, purpose and function are equivalent. Observation that an organ has a purpose and observing what that purpose is amounts simply to observing that it has a function, and observing what that function is.

3.   Though a staunch defender of natural law, Robert P. George recognizes this, saying summarily:

> It is often assumed in treatments of sexual ethics that the central argument from natural law theory against non-marital acts is simply that such acts are unnatural, that is, contrary to the direction inscribed in the reproductive or procreative power. This argument, often described as 'the perverted faculty argument' is easily disposed of.

(Robert P. George, *In Defense of Natural Law*, Oxford, OUP, 2001, p. 161)

4.   I have tried to give an explanation of why this is so in *The Body in Context*, chapter 6, particularly pp. 108–16.

5.   *Humanae Vitae*, 12.

6.   Except in the case of couples who are physically incapable of generating children.

7.   We could imagine Lawrence reacting in a parallel way. He might say that, though he can see that objectively the Brahms has important qualities that the Saint-Saëns lacks, still the Saint-Saëns does something for him, maybe something he cannot explain, while the Brahms does not touch him. This would not be an irrational reaction, but a sensible and even humble recognition of a fact about himself – that he is more susceptible to one piece of music than to another.

8.   But, though we are concentrating here on purposes, we should not forget that an explanation in terms of purpose is not the only kind of explanation of human acts, and sometimes questions like 'What is the purpose of your doing that?' are inappropriate. If

we see a man gulping down water after running for miles under a hot sun, and we ask why they are gulping down water, it would be out of place to ask 'What are you trying to achieve by drinking that water?' He is not drinking the water because he is trying to achieve something, but because he is very thirsty, and this is the sort of thing people do when they are very thirsty. It is perfectly in order to ask 'Why are you drinking like that?' but in this context that question is not a request to know the person's purpose in drinking; it is a request for an explanation of his behaviour, and the kind of explanation that will be given is not in terms of purpose, but in terms rather of the state of the person: 'I'm thirsty'. Equally, the explanation could be in terms of recent events: 'I'm drinking because I've just run miles under a hot sun'. 'I'm thirsty' and 'I've just been running' are perfectly good explanations of why he is drinking, but they are not explanations in terms of purpose. To take a second example, an answer to the question 'Why are you doing that?' might in some circumstances be 'Because the foreman told me to do it.' Once again, there is no reference to the agent's purpose in doing what he does, nor indeed to any purpose of the agent's foreman. But if we know what it is for one person to be subordinate to another, then 'My foreman told me to do it' functions as a perfectly good explanation of why the agent is doing what he is doing. In these circumstances, the question 'What is your purpose in doing that?' may elicit no answer at all, beyond a rejection of the question similar to 'I'm not trying to achieve anything at all. I'm just doing it because I've been told to.'

9.   For the sake of simplicity of exposition I henceforth speak of the function or purpose of an organ in the singular, ignoring the possibility that an organ has several purposes and plays several distinct roles in the functioning of the organism of which it is part. I do not think that this simplification materially affects the argument of this section.

10.   Generally speaking, that is. There are cases where we might find her answer unconvincing, even if sincere. For instance, suppose she has long been on the plump side, and falls in love with Brian in a way that is obvious to everybody but herself. Suppose too that Brian is generally attracted to slim women. If Anne now starts slimming, she may say sincerely that she is doing so for the sake of her health. In these circumstances, we might accept her explanation, but we might instead treat it as evidence of her lack of self-knowledge. But this example confirms, not that the agent's explanation must be the last word, but that it is normative for us in the sense that we need a reason – which, as in this example, might be furnished by the circumstances – not to accept that explanation, whereas we do not in the normal case need a reason to accept it.

11.   For our purposes I am using 'end', 'purpose' and 'finality' as equivalent.

12.   Some people appeal to Genesis 1:28 'Be fruitful and multiply' to support this position. But, apart from the dangerous biblical literalism such an appeal involves, God is at this point in the story not commanding anybody to do anything; he is blessing people, as the text plainly says. When people have children, they are not being obedient to a divine command but responding to a divine invitation, taking advantage of a divine blessing.

Chapter Nine

1.   *L'Osservatore Romano*, English edition, 12 March 1997, p. 5.
2.   *Ibid.*
3.   Harvey, *op. cit.*, pp. 97–8. Italics in the original.
4.   Harvey, *op. cit.*, pp. 100–1.
5.   Harvey, *op. cit.*, p. 102.

Notes

6. Grisez speaks specifically about men and women here, but the beginning of the argument refers to animals in general. If the argument proves the conclusion Grisez draws about people, as he hopes, then it proves it also for animals in general.

7. This is not of course to deny that the expression 'one flesh' may have a perfectly valid use in the context of human marriage. Only, Grisez's use is not a valid one. This has no consequences for the biblical use of the term, which is quite different. The original occurrence is, as noted, in Genesis 2:24; all the other occurrences (Matt. 19:5, 6; Mark 10:8; 1 Cor. 6:16; Eph. 5:31) are references to the Genesis text. In Genesis, the phrase comes immediately after Adam's exclamation: 'This at last is bone of my bones and flesh of my flesh', and is clearly related to it, being a kind of paraphrase of it. This latter locution has, however, nothing to do with any putative organic unity realized in potentially procreative sexual intercourse, as in Grisez's use of 'one flesh'. It refers to being part of the same family or clan. This is clear from a study of Genesis 29:14 and 2 Sam. 19:12–13. When a man and a woman become one flesh by marriage they create a new family unit, a new relationship of blood, or of flesh and bone, where none existed before.

8. Actually, Grisez is concerned in this section of his book almost entirely with male homosexuality. For ease of exposition I will follow him here.

9. One indication that this interpretation of what he says is correct is the following: 'Suppose a device were invented which could create experiences somewhat like motion pictures, but communicated directly to the brain, so as to make the experience a total one in which the individual's awareness of being a spectator was eliminated.' (Grisez, *Christian Moral Principles*, p. 121). Grisez seems here to be using 'experience' as somewhat equivalent to 'sensation', so that, as one might in some sense be said to create a sensation by stimulating a part of the brain with electricity, so one might similarly be said to be creating an experience. But this is hardly the sense of 'experience' that Grisez requires for his argument. The game is given away in the final words 'in which the individual's awareness of being a spectator was eliminated'. This can only mean that the person involved comes to believe that the spectacle presented to him is actually occurring, rather than simply represented on film or some other way.; he is being deceived. Grisez's machine is a machine for deceiving, and can only create illusions. It cannot create, say, the experience of playing tennis, but only the illusion of playing tennis. The only way the experience of playing tennis can be had is by playing tennis. While a machine may give one the sensations one normally has while playing tennis, to have the experience of playing tennis one actually has to do something.

10. It adds nothing to say that they enjoy their *experience* of having sex together, just as it adds nothing to say that they might enjoy their experience of playing tennis together. In fact, in ordinary parlance, an experience is normally an activity or an event: a visit to Egypt can be an interesting experience, an earthquake a devastating experience. When we speak of experiences, we do not speak of putative private incommunicable sensations, but of quite public and communicable events.

11. *Op. cit.*

12. Though we should remark that there is already a degree of complexity here which cannot be ignored. It is inadequate to say that Peter masturbates here and now because he wants nice feelings; it does not explain why he wants *these* pleasant feelings. We all like pleasant feelings, but why is it that Peter wants these particular pleasant feelings just at this time and in this place? In other circumstances he will want rather the enjoyment of listening to Brahms, or of soaking in a bath, or of sipping a gin, or of walking the fells.

Notes

13. Lewis Carroll, *Through the Looking-Glass*, ch. 6.

14. Individuals can of course from time to time declare to other members of their linguistic community that they are using particular words in a special sense, say as technical terms. But their declaration can only be understood if it is expressed in words which have a use in that community, and which are therefore rule-governed.

15. §6. This is the official English translation, representing the Latin '*significationem sponsalem*'. One might equally translate it as 'spousal meaning'. For the purposes of the argument of this chapter, there is no significant difference in meaning between 'meaning' and 'significance'.

Bibliography

Ariès, Philippe and Béjin André, eds, *Western Sexuality: Practice and Precept in Past and Present Times*, Oxford, Basil Blackwell Ltd, 1985.

Bailey, Derrick Sherwin, *Homosexuality and the Western Christian Tradition*, London, Longmans, Green and Co., Ltd, 1955.

Balch, David L., ed., *Homosexuality, Science, and the 'Plain Sense' of Scripture*, Grand Rapids, Michigan, Eerdmans, 2000.

Barnhouse, Ruth Tiffany, *Homosexuality: A Symbolic Confusion*, New York, Seabury Press, 1977; extract reprinted in Batchelor, Edward, ed., *Homosexuality and Ethics*, New York, The Pilgrim Press, 1980.

Batchelor, Edward, ed., *Homosexuality and Ethics*, New York, The Pilgrim Press, 1980.

Bonsor, Jack A., 'Homosexual Orientation and Anthropology: Reflections on the Category "Objective Disorder"', in *Theological Studies*, 59 (1998), p. 81.

Boswell, John, *Christianity, Social Tolerance and Homosexuality: Gay People in Western Europe from the Beginning of the Christian Era to the Fourteenth Century*, Chicago, University of Chicago Press, 1980.

Bradshaw, Timothy, ed., *The Way Forward? Christian Voices on Homosexuality and the Church*, London, Hodder & Stoughton, 1997.

The Catechism of the Catholic Church, London, Geoffrey Chapman, 1994.

Comstock, Gary David and Henking, Susan E., eds, *Que(e)rying Religion: A Critical Anthology*, New York, Continuum, 1997.

Congregation for the Doctrine of the Faith, *Homosexualitatis Problema*, Vatican, 1986.

Congregation for the Doctrine of the Faith, *Persona Humana*, Vatican, 1975.

Cortese, Enzo, 'Homosexuality in the Old Testament', in L'Osservatore Romano, English edition, 12 March 1997, p. 5.

Countryman, L. William, *Dirt, Greed and Sex: Sexual Ethics in the*

Bibliography

New Testament and their Implications for Today, London, SCM, 1989.

Foucault, Michel, *The History of Sexuality vol. 1: An Introduction*, Harmondsworth, Middx., Penguin Books, 1979.

Foucault, Michel, *The History of Sexuality vol. 2: The Use of Pleasure*, Harmondsworth, Middx., Penguin Books, 1987.

Foucault, Michel, *The History of Sexuality vol. 3: The Care of the Self*, New York, Pantheon Books, 1986.

Fredrickson, David E., 'Natural and Unnatural in Romans 1:24–27: Paul and the Philosophic Critique of Eros', in Balch, David L. ed., *Homosexuality, Science, and the 'Plain Sense' of Scripture*, Grand Rapids, Michigan, Eerdmans, 2000, pp. 197–222.

George, Robert P., *In Defense of Natural Law*, Oxford, OUP, 2001.

Goldman, Alan, 'Plain Sex', in Soble, Alan, ed., *The Philosophy of Sex: Contemporary Readings*, 2nd edn, Savage, Maryland, Rowman and Littlefield, 1991, pp. 73–92.

Greenberg, David F., *The Construction of Homosexuality*, Chicago, University of Chicago Press, 1988.

Grisez, Germain, *Christian Moral Principles*, (*The Way of the Lord Jesus, vol. 1*), Chicago, Franciscan Herald Press, 1983.

Grisez, Germain, *Living a Christian Life*, (*The Way of the Lord Jesus, vol. 2*), Quincy, Illinois, Franciscan Press, 1993.

Halperin, David M., *One Hundred Years of Homosexuality*, New York, Routledge, 1990.

Harvey, John F., OSFS, *The Homosexual Person: New Thinking in Pastoral Care*, San Francisco, Ignatius Press, 1987.

Hays, Richard B., *The Moral Vision of the New Testament: A Contemporary Introduction to New Testament Ethics*, New York, HarperCollins, 1996.

Hooker, Morna, *From Adam to Christ: Essays on Paul*, Cambridge, CUP, 1990.

Howells, Kevin, ed., *The Psychology of Sexual Diversity*, Basil Blackwell, Oxford, 1984.

Jordan, Mark D., *The Invention of Sodomy in Christian Theology*, Chicago, Chicago University Press, 1997.

Lacroix, Xavier, ed., *L'Amour du semblable: Questions sur l'homosexualité*, Paris, Les éditions du Cerf, 1996.

Lawler, Ronald, OFM Cap., Boyle, Jr., Joseph, and May, William E., *Catholic Sexual Ethics: A Summary, Explanation and Defence*, 2nd edn, Huntington, Indiana, Our Sunday Visitor, 1998.

Markey, John J., 'The "Problem" of Homosexuality', in *New Blackfriars*, October 1994, pp. 476–88.

McNeill, John, *The Church and the Homosexual*, London, Darton, Longman and Todd, 1977.

McNeill, John, *Taking a Chance on God*, Boston, Massachusetts, Beacon Press, 1988.

Melina, Livio, 'Christian Anthropology and Homosexuality – 13 moral criteria for evaluating homosexuality', in L'Osservatore Romano, English edn, 12 March 1997, p. 5.

Miller, James E., 'The Practices of Romans 1:26: Homosexual or Heterosexual?', in *Novum Testamentum*, 37 (1995), pp. 1–11.

Moore, Gareth, *The Body in Context: Sex and Catholicism*, London, SCM, 1992.

Murray, Stephen O., *Homosexualities*, Chicago, University of Chicago Press, 2000.

Olyan, Saul M., '"And with a male you shall not lie the lying down of a woman": On the Meaning and Significance of Leviticus 18:22 and 20:13', in Comstock, Gary David and Henking, Susan E., eds, *Que(e)rying Religion: A Critical Anthology*, New York, Continuum, 1997, pp. 398–414; reprinted from *Journal of the History of Sexuality*, 5.2 (October 1994), pp. 179–206.

Philo, translated by Colson, F. H., London, Heinemann, 1937 (Loeb Classical Library, Philo, vol. VII).

Pope, Marvin H., *Song of Songs*, New York, Doubleday, 1977.

Rogers, Jr., Eugene F., *Sexuality and the Christian Body*, Oxford, Blackwell, 1999.

Schmidt, Thomas E., *Straight and Narrow? Compassion and Clarity in the Homosexuality Debate*, Leicester, Inter-Varsity Press, 1995.

Scroggs, Robin, *The New Testament and Homosexuality*, Philadelphia, Fortress Press, 1983.

Soble, Alan, 'Masturbation and Sexual Philosophy', in Soble, *The Philosophy of Sex: Contemporary Readings*, 2nd edn, Savage, Maryland, Rowman and Littlefield, 1991, pp. 133–58.

Solomon, Robert, 'Sexual Paradigms', in Soble, *The Philosophy of Sex: Contemporary Readings*, 2nd edn, Savage, Maryland, Rowman and Littlefield, 1991, pp. 53–62.

Stowers, Stanley K., *A Rereading of Romans*, Yale University Press, New Haven, 1994.

Sullivan, Andrew, *Virtually Normal: An Argument About Homosexuality*, London, Picador, 1995.

Sullivan, Andrew, 'Alone Again, Naturally: The Catholic Church and the Homosexual', originally in *New Republic*, 4167, 28 November 1994, reprinted in Comstock, Gary David and

Bibliography

Henking, Susan E., eds, *Que(e)rying Religion: A Critical Anthology*, New York, Continuum, 1997, pp. 238–50.

Thiselton, Anthony, 'Can Hermeneutics Ease the Deadlock? Some Biblical Exegesis and Hermeneutical Models', in Bradshaw, Timothy, ed., *The Way Forward? Christian Voices on Homosexuality and the Church*, London, Hodder & Stoughton, 1997.

Tyler, P. A., 'Homosexual Behaviour in Animals', in Howells, Kevin, ed., *The Psychology of Sexual Diversity*, Basil Blackwell, Oxford, 1984, pp. 42–62.

Veyne, Paul, 'Homosexuality in Ancient Rome', in Ariès, Philippe and Béjin, André, eds, *Western Sexuality*, Blackwell, Oxford, 1985.

Waugh, Evelyn, *Brideshead Revisited*, London, Penguin, 1962.

Weeks, Jeffrey, *Sexuality and its Discontents: Meanings, Myths and Modern Sexualities*, London, Routledge and Kegan Paul, 1985.

Westermann, Claus, *Genesis 1–11*, London, SPCK, 1984.

Wittgenstein, Ludwig, (trans. Anscombe G. E. M.), *Philosophical Investigations*, Oxford, Blackwell, 2nd edn, 1958.